The Taste Culture Reader

Experiencing Food and Drink

Edited by

CAROLYN KORSMEYER

Oxford • New York

English edition
First published in 2005 by
Berg
Editorial offices:
First Floor, Angel Court, 81 St Clements Street, Oxford OX4 1AW, UK
175 Fifth Avenue, New York, NY 10010, USA

Paperback edition reprinted in 2007

Berg is the imprint of Oxford International Publishers Ltd.

Library of Congress Cataloging-in-Publication data

The taste culture reader : experiencing food and drink / edited by Carolyn Korsmeyer.— English ed.
p. cm. — (Sensory formations, ISSN 1741-4725)
Includes bibliographical references and index.
ISBN-13: 978-1-84520-060-2 (cloth)
ISBN-13: 978-1-84520-061-9 (pbk.)
ISBN-10: 1-84520-060-8 (cloth)
ISBN-10: 1-84520-061-6 (pbk.)
1. Cookery. 2. Food. 3. Beverages. I. Title: Experiencing food and drink. II. Korsmeyer, Carolyn. III. Series: Sensory formations series

TX651.T39 2005
641.3—dc22

2005013776

British Library Cataloguing-in-Publication data

A catalogue record for this book is available from the British Library.

ISBN-13 978 1 84520 060 2 (Cloth)
978 1 84520 061 9 (Paper)

ISBN-10 1 84520 060 8 (Cloth)
1 84520 061 6 (Paper)

Typeset by JS Typesetting Ltd, Porthcawl, Mid Glamorgan.
Printed in Great Britain by the MPG Books Group, Bodmin and King's Lynn

www.bergpublishers.com

Contents

Part V: Taste and Aesthetic Discrimination

Part VI: Fine Discernments and the Cultivation of Taste

Part VII: Taste, Emotion, and Memory

Acknowledgments

I am most grateful to David Howes, general editor of Berg's *Sensory Formations* series, for inviting me to edit this volume. His generous advice and quick attention to detail have been of immeasurable assistance in preparing this book. Through his good offices I obtained help from Concordia University with the permissions costs for the volume, and I wish to thank Martin Singer, Provost and Vice President, and Frederick Lowy, President, of Concordia University, Montreal, for their generous financial support of the *Sensory Formations* series, including this volume.

The staff of the Educational Technology Center of the University at Buffalo, State University of New York, came to my aid with their equipment and their advice as this manuscript was being prepared, and I am grateful for their help. Juneko Robinson offered invaluable assistance both at the beginning of this project and with her preparation of the bibliography. Kathryn Hunter averted a last-minute emergency and quickly translated Stoller and Olkes' "Thick Sauce" (Chapter 13) from the original French published text. Several of the authors whose work appears here offered useful editorial suggestions and help with permissions. And finally, the editors and staff at Berg Publishers, including Kathryn Earle, Hannah Shakespeare, and Felicity Howlett, have responded quickly and helpfully to questions and problems. I thank them all.

Notes on the text

Several of the chapters in this volume are reprinted from longer scholarly studies. In certain cases, notes and references have been omitted or abridged, and use of non-English expressions has been reduced and their spellings simplified. Readers who wish to pursue the scholarship presented here in more detail will find full references listed in the Permissions section.

Acknowledgments

Introduction
Perspectives on Taste

Carolyn Korsmeyer

Recorded opinions about the sense of taste are filled with ambivalence and paradox. Some theorists consider it beneath consideration; others recommend its cultivation. Some regard taste as a mere matter of physical sensation, unworthy of extensive attention; others devote a lifetime to its exploration. Some classify taste as a "lower" bodily sense, along with smell and touch; others consider it as complex and informative as vision and hearing. Approaches to taste may be ascetic or sybaritic, dismissive or obsessed—and all attitudes in between.

The functional value of the sense of taste is undeniable, for it is put to use every day. Along with its close companion, smell, taste acts as a scout for foods we eat, selecting things that are nourishing and fresh and rejecting substances that are toxic or foul. Food is necessary to sustain life, but the role that taste plays in bodily sustenance can also suggest that the sense has a certain rudimentary, brute character. In evaluative systems that elevate the "mind" over the "body"—such as one finds in a number of philosophies and religions—the multiple links of taste with physical maintenance frequently lead to neglect or outright derogation of activities associated with tasting and eating.

Taste is pretty hard to ignore, however, for it offers its own rewards. A pleasure–pain valence usually attends taste experiences: the things we eat and drink are either good-tasting (indeed, the term "tasty" is a synonym for "delicious") or bad-tasting. The zone of neutrality is relatively small, possibly reserved for water. This fact adds an inevitable sensuality to the functionality of taste, and the sensual element of eating and drinking is double-edged. Tastes can be intense and enjoyable, and only the strict ascetic would shun them altogether. But its pleasures entice and intoxicate, inviting excess, even gluttony. The widespread—possibly universal—coupling of tasting and eating with sexuality reinforces the picture of taste as rooted in bodily sensation, a sense with a range more or less restricted to the physical.

These are several of the factors that have influenced a strong tendency among theorists, at least of the Western tradition, to downgrade taste (along with touch and smell) as merely "bodily" senses, in contrast to the more intellectually coordinate senses of sight and hearing. Indeed, many have concluded that taste is hardly worth a great deal of attention—any more than, say, digestion; so long as it works, it can be ignored. This derogatory view presumes as well that the objects of taste are relatively inarticulate and meaningless, especially in comparison to objects of vision and hearing, which are senses that are indispensable for communication, empirical investigation, learning, and the creation of works of art.

The foregoing negative assessments of taste, however, are more than counterbalanced by an appreciation for the complexities of taste and gustatory activities. The dour voices derogating taste are all but drowned out by vociferous apologists for its cultivation and refinement. One of the most eloquent of these, the gastronomer Jean-Anthelme Brillat-Savarin, scoffed at the idea that eating is a rudimentary activity: "Animals feed themselves; men eat; but only wise men know the art of eating," he declared.[1] Acknowledgment of such gradations of taste experiences are also to be found mixed within the dominant philosophical approaches that distinguish bodily from intellectual senses. Aristotle, for instance, noted that "brutes" care more about swallowing than tasting; and only humans, he surmised, can reflect upon and savor their food.[2] The presence of diverse opinions within the writings of Western philosophy—or any intellectual tradition—are important to bear in mind, for it is all too easy to obscure complexity and subtlety with sweeping generalizations.

Social scientists have been in the vanguard of research on the importance of eating patterns and their meanings in different cultures, and attention to these matters is gaining ground in other fields, such as philosophy and history, as well. This volume brings together essays from scholars of a range of disciplines, who bring their perspectives to bear on various aspects of food, eating, drinking—and the tastes afforded thereby. Anthropologists, historians, sociologists, philosophers, and psychologists offer their views on these subjects, presenting a sequence of ideas that whet the mind and occasionally the appetite. Just as a full treatment of taste demands approaches from many disciplinary perspectives, it is also enhanced by different genres of writing. Hence this volume also includes contributions from gastronomers and food writers, poets (liberally quoted by several essays), and other literary artists; there is even the occasional recipe, reminding us that any study of taste cannot lose sight of the practice of preparing foods for its assessment.

What is taste? This simple-sounding question may be interpreted in several ways: What is the sense of taste and how does it work? What does it mean to taste something? How does one identify a flavor? When we refer to "the taste of honey," how do we know that the sensations of different tasters are comparable? The latter question arouses a venerable skepticism: all sense experience occurs within a perceiving subject, and we know from experience that not all people see or hear or feel or smell exactly alike (although it is important not to exaggerate differences either; if we did not on the whole share sensory worlds that overlap to some extent, life would be constant blundering). This variability of "subjective" experience—that is, the experience of a perceiving subject—is nowhere more noticeable than with the sense of taste. Here we find variations of sensibility as well as of preference; what is more, these are further multiplied when we take into account the fact that acts of tasting occur within cultural contexts where eating traditions accustom people to a specific range of foods and beverages. Cultures themselves are subject to change as time passes, climate alters, societies undergo migration and colonization, and so forth. What people eat today is not the same as what they ate in the past, and one surmises that their taste worlds also differ.

How do we even begin to address these differences? Can we imagine the tastes described by ancient poets, or are those worlds dead to us? Can we experience an authentic taste of a society half a globe away, or do our own cultural familiarities inevitably impart distortions to our experiences? But as we ask that latter question, another arises: distortions of what, precisely? How one gauges the "genuineness" of taste is a complex issue, and one may even wonder whether there is such a thing as an "authentic" taste left in today's global market, fraught as it is with hybrids, engineered foods, and chemical enhancements.

The contributions to this volume are arranged in eight sections. We begin with a scientific review of the operation of the sense of taste and then turn to various aspects of its exercise in different eating environments and cultures. Part I, "Taste: Physiology and Circumstance," addresses the physical determinants of sensation, for taste experiences at their most basic are the responses of sensitive organs to objects. One of those sensitive organs is the tongue, but of course full experiences of taste require contributions from the olfactory sense and from touch as well. Except where otherwise specified, the word "taste" in this book serves as shorthand for the experience of flavor in all its dimensions, including those supplied by other senses.[3] Brillat-Savarin colorfully describes the collaboration of taste and smell when he says that in the experience of taste, "the mouth is the laboratory and nose the chimney." Although his observations date back to the early nineteenth century, they are cited in the contribution by Linda Bartoshuk and Valerie Duffy, whose research on taste brings us up to date about the scientific understanding of this sense.

It is the "circumstances" in which taste is exercised that occupy Elisabeth Rozin and Paul Rozin in their review of the flavor cultures that have developed in different geographic regions. They investigate how the human organism, equipped as it is with certain senses and an omnivorous capacity to ingest food of many sorts, develops distinct cuisines depending on geography, climate, and available resources. Their work opens the way to understanding taste in terms of culture and identity, subjects of the remainder of the book.

Part II, "Taste Cultures: Gustation in History," presents what is probably the largest field of study for taste, foods, and eating habits. Anthropologists, historians, and sociologists have researched the many ways that eating patterns have developed in relation to historical period, social class, gender, caste, or other social status. The six essays here represent but a tiny sampling of this work, and they have been chosen not only for their emphasis on the social relations manifest in eating habits, but also for their attention to the taste cultures thereby formed. The tastes of history are elusive, and one can only speculate about the eating experiences of times gone by from the written records that remain—and these, as Jean-François Revel rightly observes, represent only the cuisine of the literate upper classes. Replication of actual flavors is near to impossible, even if the raw constituents are still available (many are not; certain plants are no longer grown, for example). All but irretrievable are the flavors of food traditions with which eaters of the past were familiar. What research reveals must be supplemented by the imagination of readers.

Wealth and poverty are considerable forces affecting the foods that are available to people, and consequently taste cultures reflect class and other social relationships. Jack Goody's sweeping survey of the histories of global cuisines summarizes several ways in which complex societies arrange foods (and their tastes) hierarchically, a system that he argues was obtained in such diverse societies as ancient India and China, the empires of the Middle East, and medieval and Renaissance Europe. Sociologist Pierre Bourdieu, with a more focused lens, analyzes the "tastes of necessity and of luxury" that reflect class differences in twentieth-century France. Bourdieu illuminates the fact that tastes are quite literally embodied—foods are consumed, body types developed accordingly, and tastes *of* certain foods induce taste preferences *for* those foods and their flavors.

Different peoples who live in proximity are not always divided in their tastes, for often culinary cultures merge. Such was the case in colonial North America, as Donna Gabaccia observes, when European colonists, African slaves, and Native American peoples blended their cooking traditions. It cannot be said that all such encounters were voluntary, obviously; but once culinary traditions change and become familiar, replacing older foodways, it is the nature of foods to offer sustenance and even pleasure to all who eat them. Another kind of collision between traditional foodways and economic pressures can be seen in the continued changes that indigenous peoples face, as in the Zumbagua region of Peru. Here we see changing food traditions in process; but if the foods change, the meanings assigned to certain tastes persist, as M. J. Weismantel argues in her analysis of flavor clusters in that culture.

As mentioned above, one of the reasons that the sense of taste has traditionally been relegated to the status of a lower sense is the presumption that taste is relatively inarticulate, that foods and flavors do not convey meaning as the objects of sight and hearing do. But this is not the case, as the essays in the previous section indicate, and as structural anthropologists such as Claude Lévi-Strauss and Mary Douglas have shown in their well-known studies.[4] Part III, "Eloquent Flavors," counters any easy dismissal of flavors as merely sensations. Even the so-called "basic" tastes identified by taste researchers—sweet, sour, salt, and bitter—possess a range of meanings and usages. Each of these tastes has a history of meanings ascribed to it, and a few of these are virtually pancultural.

Salt, for instance, is a symbol of hospitality in many societies, as well as a substance of mystery and power, as Margaret Visser points out. Sweetness, a flavor type universally liked (by both human and nonhuman animals), is often assigned meanings of good luck and hope. However, as Sidney Mintz argues, the apparent basic unanimity of meaning fades when we see how one particular sweet substance, sugar, is introduced and diffused through a society. These essays provoke reflection on the parameters of "universal" and "particular" meanings and experiences of tastes.

Not all flavors can be classified according to the four "basic" types, and some of the most sought-after tastes are spices. Now readily available on supermarket shelves, spices such as cinnamon, pepper, cardamom, and clove were originally products of southern Asia, which were lucratively traded to other parts of the world. Expensive and exotic, spices came to symbolize wealth, mystery, and even, as Wolfgang Schivelbusch puts it, the "taste of paradise."

The significance attached to flavors such as salt and sugar is rooted in both biology and history. But tastes can also be deployed deliberately with individual local meanings. The traditional use of spicy sauces, including those with less-than-paradisical flavors, is reported by Paul Stoller and Cheryl Olkes from their researches in West Africa. There they encountered a cook who served them a nasty sauce, inappropriate to the social occasion, to indicate her familial predicament and displeasure—a mute but hardly inarticulate expression of meaning manifest in taste.

One of the most widespread beliefs about eating and drinking concerns overindulgence in taste and the risks associated therewith. Eating is a liminal activity, occurring at the threshold between "inside" and "outside" the body—one of the features it shares with sexual activity. As such it represents both opportunity and danger, and so it stands to reason that it would be freighted with significance that bears upon values and the relative worth of different ways of life. This may be manifest in gender relations and recommendations for health—of the body, the mind, the spirit.

Numerous cultural and religious traditions, despite their other differences, share the belief that pleasures of the body can hinder moral development and obscure spiritual clarity. This is evident in the practices of fasting on particular holy days, and hence an obverse meaning attached to taste appears in its absence. Traditions as different as Buddhism and Christianity both recommend overcoming the needs of the body in order to reach a degree of spiritual enlightenment. In Japanese Zen Buddhism, this belief underlies the formal tea ceremony, whose stark simplicity reduces taste to its subtle minimum. In some of these traditions, body and soul are at odds with each other, and fasting is conceived as a deprivation of sinful flesh, as in some Christian sects. In others, body and soul are more united, and food enters and nourishes both, as R. S. Khare argues with regard to Hindu holy men. Part IV, "Body and Soul," presents a sampling of essays that discuss ideas about the effects of eating on the health of the body, the acuity of the mind, and the purity of the soul. The range here is enormous, from the outright taste deprivation of fasting to the sharing of celebratory foods, whether in worship (as with the Christian Eucharist) or holiday communion with departed loved ones (as with the Mexican Day of the Dead).

Among the paradoxes that surround taste, few loom larger than the fact that taste is supposed to be little more than a bodily sensation, yet at the same time it provides the metaphor for the finest cultivation of perceptual experience. Part V, "Taste and Aesthetic Discrimination," presents just a few of the many theories that have been developed about this subject. While much of this literature completely ignores literal taste in favor of its metaphoric connotation, the selections chosen for inclusion here all compare gustatory taste with aesthetic sensibility. To be sure, not all are sympathetic to the comparison; the influential Immanuel Kant, for instance, retained a separation between gustatory and aesthetic taste that must be taken seriously even by those who disagree with his assessment. Taste in the European, Indian, and Chinese traditions is presented here, indicating the ready availability of this sense for metaphoric extension to aesthetic contexts in many cultures.

This volume does not have the space to explore whether cuisine ought to be considered an art form (a question that is really only problematic in the modern tradition of fine art),[5] but the cultivation of taste sensitivities is relevant in both aesthetic and gustatory contexts. This is the focus of Part VI, "Fine Discernments and the Cultivation of Taste." What accounts for differences of taste preference? Can some people taste "better" than others? The articles of this section investigate the education of taste on two levels: the social movements that encourage the refinement of a populace, and the experiences of individuals assessing their own sensory encounters. Brillat-Savarin's opening piece has already indicated something about the cultivation of taste, as he is one of the early and influential writers on the subject. But there have been many since, and nineteenth-century gastronomy has expanded into twenty-first-century culinary tourism, as Stephen Mennell observes.

Taste is so strongly associated with individual preferences that it has given rise to the old saying, "There is no disputing about taste," meaning that the sensations of the mouth are so relative to the individual that there is no way to adjudicate among them. This relativism, however, is highly suspect, as tastes are also subject to the pressures of social change. As Mennell notes, gastronomic literature both describes and creates taste preferences. More programmatic imposition of refined taste may be found in the unusual case of Stalin's Soviet Union, where, according to Jukka Gronow, the production of luxury goods was mandated as part of the improvement of life for socialist citizens.

Several entries in the previous two sections concern the ability (or inability) to taste fine distinctions. It is this "delicacy" of taste (to use Hume's charming old-fashioned term) that distinguishes the connoisseur from the mere eater. What is more, it can mark certain foods from others because their very localities are imbued in their flavors. As Amy Trubek relates, French culinary discourse has developed the concept of *goût du terroir*, the taste of the soil, a value that has gastronomic, social, and political implications. (For if one can learn to taste the place where foods originate, then the economics of mass production can drastically affect flavor.) While arguing that *terroir* is both actually discoverable in tastes of food and is also a socially created category, Trubek offers evidence for genuine differences to be found by the sophisticated and experienced taster.

If taste were merely subjective and relative (as the old adage suggests), then one would never wonder what one missed from food and drink. But wine expert Emile Peynaud recognizes that there are conditions under which the qualities of wine cannot accurately be discerned, and he also wittily acknowledges that sometimes imagination supplies as much flavor as the wine itself. Even ordinary foods present taste conundrums, as Richard Watson discovered, for during a stay in the Netherlands he found himself virtually blind (as it were) to the variations in cheeses, licorice, cookies, and porridges in the region where he lived. Significantly, his inability to taste these differences did not lead him to doubt their existence; evidently taste is not only in the mouth.

One of the most famous literary reflections on taste is found in Marcel Proust's monumental novel, *The Remembrance of Things Past*. Proust ponders a very well-known yet enigmatic phenomenon associated with tastes—the fact that they are nearly impossible to describe verbally, and yet they may be vividly recalled by the faintest whiff of a familiar smell or flavor. This gives taste (again in the full "intersensorial" sense that includes the participation of smell) a singular and powerful place in memory. It can be a trigger of bodily recollection, a source of both yearning and solace. The essays in Part VII, "Taste, Emotion, and Memory," explore this familiar phenomenon from literary, anecdotal, anthropological, and sociological perspectives.

Emphasis on memory invites a nostalgic recollection of flavors that may seem more vivid and truer than anything present-day life has to offer. In certain cases, that nostalgia may be more than sentimental wishful thinking, for the flavors of contemporary life are highly inflected by artificial enhancements and other alterations devised for the global marketplace. Two essays of the last section, Part VIII, "Artifice and Authenticity." discuss the meanings of "genuine taste" and the complications raised by the manufacture of artificial—or perhaps "artificial"—flavors. Finally, three more essays consider how to assess the authenticity of eating experiences that are delivered by restaurants or by cooks from traditions where local ingredients have been tailored to present a genuine taste experience with a particular ethnic or historical flavor.

But what counts as a "genuine" taste? What in fact *is* a *taste*? We opened with this query, and by the end of this volume it will be clear that there are various ways to pose, explore, and answer the question, none of which can be considered definitive because each takes different sets of problems to the matter at issue. Tastes are subjective but measurable, relative to culture and to individual, yet shared; fleeting sensations that nonetheless endure over many years in memory; transient experiences freighted with the weight of history. And finally, tastes can provide entertainment and intellectual absorption, both when they are experienced in the act of eating and drinking, and when they invite reflection on the ideas presented by the authors who speak in this volume.

Notes

1. See Jean-Anthelme Brillat-Savarin, *The Physiology of Taste* (1825), Aphorism #2. A selection from Brillat-Savarin's work opens this volume; see Chapter 1.

2. Aristotle, *Eudemian Ethics* 1231a 15–16. For a review of the hierarchical ranking of the senses in the Western philosophical tradition, see Carolyn Korsmeyer, *Making Sense of Taste* (1999: Ch. 1).

3. It is important to note that the senses usually work together in interrelation to create sense experience, and rarely function entirely alone. The term that captures this integrative perspective on the senses is "intersensoriality." For an introduction to the notion of intersensoriality, see David Howes, *Empire of the Senses* (2004: Introduction).

4. These two influential anthropologists are not represented in this book, although other writers frequently cite them both approvingly and critically. Some of their best-known works include Claude Lévi-Strauss, *The Raw and the Cooked* (1969); Mary Douglas, *Implicit Meanings* (1975).

5. For a discussion of food as art see Constance Classen, "Crossing Sensory Borders in the Arts" (1998: 131–37 and 156–58), Barbara Kirshenblatt-Gimblett, "Playing to the Senses" (1999), Elizabeth Telfer, *Food for Thought* (1996), and Alan Weiss, *Feast and Folly* (2002). For an argument against considering food as art, see Carolyn Korsmeyer, *Making Sense of Taste* (1999: Ch. 4).

References

Brillat-Savarin, Jean-Anthelme (1825/1949), *The Physiology of Taste*, trans. M. F .K. Fisher, New York: Heritage Press.

Classen, C. (1998), "Crossing Sensory Borders in the Arts," *The Color of Angels: Cosmology, Gender and the Aesthetic Imagination*, London: Routledge.

Douglas, M. (1975), *Implicit Meanings*, London: Routledge and Kegan Paul.

Howes, D. (ed.) (2004), "Introduction: Empire of the Senses." *Empire of the Senses: The Sensual Culture Reader*, Oxford: Berg.

Kirshenblatt-Gimblett, B. (1999), "Playing to the Senses: Food as a Performance Medium," *Performance Research* 4, No. 1: 1–30.

Korsmeyer, C. (1999), *Making Sense of Taste: Food and Philosophy*, Ithaca, NY: Cornell University Press.

Lévi-Strauss, C. (1969), *The Raw and the Cooked*, trans. John and Doreen Weightman, New York: Harper and Row.

Telfer, Elizabeth (1996), *Food for Thought: Philosophy and Food*, London: Routledge.

Weiss, Allan (2002), *Feast and Folly: Cuisine, Intoxication, and the Poetics of the Sublime*, Albany, NY: State University of New York Press.

Part I

Taste: Physiology and Circumstance

Preface

While cuisines differ greatly across the globe, those who eat share the same physical morphology; as a result, our taste worlds are partly determined by the kinds of bodies that human beings have. We begin, therefore, with a discussion of the physical determinants of taste experiences.

It is fitting that the entire volume begins with one of the classic voices on taste, Jean-Anthelme Brillat-Savarin. Brillat-Savarin (1755–1826) was a lawyer who lived much of his life in the town of Belley, France. He lived through the Revolution and spent some prudent time in the US during its worst years. Throughout his long life he was devoted to good eating and its pleasures. As Stephen Mennell points out in Chapter 25, Brillat-Savarin's *Physiology of Taste* (1825) ushered in a tradition of gastronomic writing that continues vigorously today. The author had a scientific approach to eating and its enjoyments, and his eloquent disquisition on the function of the tongue and the olfactory sense opens this section. Brillat-Savarin mixes his empirical investigations with witty and rhapsodic descriptions of the experience of the "gourmand." One of his own recipes concludes his contribution.

Scientists Linda Bartoshuk and Valerie Duffy bring our understanding of the physiology of taste up to date, detailing the taste and smell receptors of the tongue and nose and the neural pathways that eventuate in taste sensations. Their research provides an account of the physical constants and variations in sensations, for while human morphology is basically the same, there are also some dissimilarities in physical makeup that produce different "taste worlds" for different people.

By far the greater source of disparity in taste experiences and preferences, however, stems from geographic and cultural variation. Elisabeth Rozin and Paul Rozin investigate the ambient "circumstances" in which cuisines are developed. They survey the disparities in flavor preferences in a number of culinary cultures, speculating that flavor choices are likely to be the outcome of the "omnivore's dilemma"—that is, the fact that human beings have an enormous range of things that we *can* eat, but a more limited range of things that we can safely include in our culinary range. Familiar flavorings make unfamiliar foods palatable. What is more, they argue, one can classify different cuisines according to the "flavor principles" that dominate cooking practices. Flavor principles so define a food tradition that they are likely to be retained even when eating habits are forced to change through war, migration, and cultural disruption. Several different flavor principles are demonstrated in a selection of Elisabeth Rozin's recipes that follow this essay.

1
On Taste

Jean-Anthelme Brillat-Savarin

The Senses

The senses are the organs by which man places himself in connection with exterior objects. There are at least six:

Sight embraces space and tells us by means of light of the existence and the colors of the objects around us. Hearing, by the motion of the air, informs us of resonant or vibrating bodies. By means of scent we are made aware of the odors bodies possess. Taste enables us to distinguish all that has a flavor or that is merely edible. Touch informs us of the texture and firmness of bodies. And finally, physical love attracts the sexes to each other that they may procreate...

If one were permitted in imagination to travel back in time to the first moments of the existence of the human race, one might surmise that the first sensations were direct; that is to say that all saw but confusedly, heard but dimly, smelled without care, ate without tasting, and copulated brutishly.

However, because the center of sensations is the soul, the special attribute of human beings and the active cause of their perfectibility, sense experience is reflected upon, compared, and judged. Therefore the senses soon came to the assistance of one another for the utility and well-being of the individual.

Thus touch rectifies the errors of sight. Sound, by means of articulate speech, becomes the interpreter of every sentiment. Taste is aided by sight and smell. Hearing compares sounds and appreciates distance; and physical desire takes possession of the organs of all the senses.

The torrent of centuries rolling over the human race has continually brought new perfections, the cause of which, ever active through unseen, is found in the demands made by our senses, which always in their turn demand to be occupied. Sight thus gave birth to painting, to sculpture, and to spectacles of every kind. Sound, to melody, harmony, to the dance, and to music in all its branches. Smell, to the discovery, manufacture, and use of perfumes. Taste, to the production, choice, and preparation of all that is consumed for food. Touch, to all art, trades and occupations…

Definition of Taste

Taste is the sense which puts us in touch with sapid bodies, by means of the sensations which they excite in the organ designed to appreciate them.

The sense of taste, which may be stimulated by appetite, hunger and thirst, is the basis of many operations, the result of which is that the individual grows and develops, preserves himself and repairs the losses occasioned by vital evaporations.

Not all organized bodies are sustained in the same manner. The Author of Creation, varied in his methods and sure in his effects, has assigned to them different modes of preservation.

Vegetables, which are the lowest in the scale of living things, are fed by roots, which, implanted in the native soil, select by the action of their particular mechanisms the different substances that nourish them and make them grow.

As we ascend the scale we find bodies gifted with animal life but deprived of locomotion. They are born into a milieu which favors their existence, and have special and peculiar organs which extract all that is necessary to sustain the portion and duration of life allotted them. They do not seek food, but nourishment comes to seek them.

Another mode has been appointed for animals which are able to move about the world, of which man is doubtless the most perfect. A peculiar instinct warns him of the necessity of food; he seeks; and he seizes the things which he suspects will satisfy his needs; he eats, he restores himself, and throughout his life he pursues this assigned course.

Taste may be considered in three respects.

In physical man it is the apparatus by means of which he appreciates flavors.

In moral man it is the sensation which the organ impressed by any savorous body excites within a common center.

Finally, considered as a material cause, taste is the property which a body has to impress the organ and to arouse a sensation.

Taste seems to have two chief uses:

1. It invites us by pleasure to repair the continual losses brought about by life.
2. It assists us to select, from among the diverse substances that nature presents, those that nourish us best.

In this choice taste is powerfully aided by the sense of smell, as we shall see later, for one can establish as a general principle that nutritious substances are repulsive neither to taste nor to smell.

The Mechanism of Taste

It is not easy to determine exactly what constitutes the faculty of taste. It is more complicated than it first appears.

The tongue certainly plays a prominent part in the mechanism of tasting—for, being endowed with considerable muscular power, it helps to mix, turn, mash, and swallow food.

Also, by means of the more or less numerous papillae that cover it, it becomes impregnated with the sapid and soluble particles of the bodies with which it comes in contact. Yet all this does not suffice, for many adjacent parts unite in completing the sensation—the cheeks, the palate, and especially the nasal passage, to which physiologists have perhaps not paid enough attention.

The cheeks furnish saliva, as necessary to mastication as to the formation of a mass that can be swallowed. They, like the palate, are gifted with a portion of taste appreciation; I do not know whether, in certain cases, even the gums might not participate somewhat. And without the sense of smell that operates at the back of the mouth, the sensation of taste would remain obscure and altogether imperfect.

Persons who have no tongue, or from whom it has been cut out, yet preserve a fairly strong sense of taste. All the books mention the first case; the second was explained to me by an unfortunate devil whose tongue had been cut out by the Algerians to punish him, along with several of his fellow captives, for having formed a plot to escape and flee.

I met this man at Amsterdam, where he made a living by running errands. He was a person of education, and one could easily communicate with him by writing.

After having observed that the entire front of his tongue, to the very attachment, had been cut away, I asked him if he yet preserved any sense of taste when he ate, and if the sense of taste had survived the cruel operation he had undergone.

He told me his greatest annoyance was in swallowing, (which he could only do with difficulty); that he could still taste fairly well; that he appreciated like others what was tasty or agreeable; but that acid and bitter substances caused him intolerable pain...

We have seen above, that the sensation of taste resides chiefly in the papillae of the tongue. But anatomy tells us that not all tongues are equally outfitted, there being three times as many papillae on some tongues as on others. This circumstance explains why, of two guests, sitting at the same banquet, one is delighted, while the other seems to eat out of obligation; the latter has a tongue but slightly furnished with papillae. Thus the empire of taste may also have its blind and deaf subjects.

Sensation of Taste

Five or six opinions have been advanced as to the manner in which the sense of taste operates. Here is my own:

The sensation of taste is a chemical operation, which happens by means of moisture, as we have already noted. That is to say, the savorous particles must be dissolved in some fluid, so as to be subsequently absorbed by the sensitive buds, papillae, or suckers, which cover the interior of the gustatory apparatus...

It would be in vain for the mouth to fill itself with the divided particles of an insoluble body. The tongue would feel by touch the sensation of their presence, but not that of taste.

As for solid and savorous bodies, it is necessary that the teeth divide them, that the saliva and other tasting fluids saturate them, and that the tongue press them against the palate to express a juice, which, when sufficiently sapid, is appreciated by the tasting papillae, which provide the masticated substance the passport it requires for admission into the stomach.

This system, which will receive further developments, easily answers the principal questions that may arise.

If one wonders what is meant by sapid bodies, we reply that it refers to every substance that is soluble and can be registered by the organ of taste.

If asked how a sapid body acts, we reply that it acts when it is reduced to such a state of dissolution that it enters the cavities made to receive and transmit taste.

In a word, nothing is sapid but what is already or nearly dissolved.

Flavors

The number of flavors is infinite, for every soluble body has its own special flavor that does not entirely resemble any other.

Flavors are also modified by their simple, double, or multiple aggregation. It is impossible to describe fully an arrangement of them from the most delectable to the most unpleasant—say, from the raspberry to the bitter apple. All who have tried to do so have failed.

This result should not amaze us, given that there exists an indefinite variety of simple flavors, which can be modified according to the quantity and quality of their mixtures. A new language would he needed to express all their effects, and mountains of folios to describe them, and unknown numerical characters to label them.

Since as yet no flavor has ever been appreciated with rigorous exactness, we have been forced to be satisfied with a limited number of expressions such as *sweet, sugary, acid, bitter,* and similar ones, which, when ultimately analyzed, come down to *agreeable* and *disagreeable,* which suffice to make us understood, and to indicate something close to the flavor of the sapid substance in question.

Those who come after us will know more about this, for doubtless chemistry will reveal the causes or primitive elements of flavors.

Influence of Smell on Taste

The order I set out for myself has gradually led me to the moment when I should grant to smell the rights which belong to it, and to recognize the important services it renders in the appreciation of flavors. Among the authors I have come across, I have found none who seems to me to have done it full justice.

For my own part, I am not only persuaded that without the participation of the sense of smell, there would be no complete taste; I am also inclined to believe that taste and smell form but one sense, of which the mouth is the laboratory and the nose the chimney; or to speak more exactly, that one sense serves to taste tactile substances, and the other to apprehend their vapors.

This view may be vigorously defended; however, as I do not wish to establish a school, I venture on it only to give my readers a subject of thought, and to show that I have carefully considered my subject. Now I continue my demonstration of the importance of the sense of smell, at least as a necessary accessory to taste.

All sapid bodies are necessarily odorous, and therefore belong to the empire of one sense as well as of the other.

We eat nothing without sensing it with more or less awareness. And when food is unfamiliar, the nose always functions as an advance sentinel and cries *Who goes there?*

When the sense of smell is intercepted, taste is paralyzed; this is proved by three experiments anyone can verify with equal success:

First experiment: When the nasal membrane is irritated by a violent cold in the head, taste is entirely obliterated; there is no flavor in anything we swallow, although the tongue is in its normal state.

Second experiment: If when we eat we pinch the nose shut, we are amazed to see how obscure and imperfect the sense of taste is. The most disgusting medicines thus are swallowed almost without taste.

Third experiment: The same effect is observed if, as soon as we have swallowed, instead of restoring the tongue to its usual place, it be kept pressed against the palate. In this case the circulation of the air is intercepted, the organs of smell are not activated, and there is no taste.

These diverse effects proceed from the same cause: the absence of cooperation from the sense of smell. This means that the sapid body is appreciated only for its own juice, and not also for the odorous gas which emanates from it.

Analysis of the Sensation of Taste

Principles being thus presented, I look on it as certain that taste arouses sensations of three different orders, namely: *direct, complete* and *reflective.*

Direct sensation is the first perception brought about by the immediate action of the organs of the mouth, during the time that the sapid body rests on the front of the tongue.

Complete sensation is that composed of this first impression together with the sensation aroused when the food abandons the first position, passes into the back of the mouth, and impresses the entire organ with both its taste and its aroma.

Finally, *reflective* sensation is the judgment which the mind forms of the impressions that have been transmitted to it by the mouth.

Let us put this system into action by observing what takes place when a man either eats or drinks. He who eats a peach, for instance, is first struck agreeably by the odor which emanates from it. He places it in his mouth, and receives sensations of fresh and tart flavors that induce him to continue. But only at the moment he swallows, and the bite passes beneath his nasal passage, does the perfume reveal itself, and the sensation of the peach is completed. Finally, after swallowing and assessing his experience, he says to himself, "That is delicious!"

It is the same when one drinks: While the wine is in the mouth one is pleased but not fully appreciative; it is only at the moment that one has swallowed that one can truly taste, assess, and discover the particular aroma of each variety. And there must pass an interval of time for a gourmet to say, "It is good, passable, or bad. The deuce! It is Chambertin! My God! It is Suresnes!"

It may then be seen that in obedience to principles and well-established practices, true amateurs sip their wine; for, with each mouthful savored slowly, they have the full pleasure with each sip which they would have enjoyed had they swallowed the whole glass at once.

The same thing takes place, although with much more energy, when the taste is disagreeably affected.

Just look at the patient of some doctor who prescribes immense doses of black medicine, such as were given during the reign of Louis XIV.

The sense of smell, like a faithful counselor, warns him of the horrible taste of the nasty liquid. The eyes widen as they do at the approach of danger; disgust is on the lips and the stomach at once rebels. He is however besought to take courage; he gargles with brandy, holds his nose, and drinks...

As long as the odious compound fills the mouth and stuns the organ it is tolerable, but when it has been swallowed the aftertastes develop, nauseous odors arise, and every feature of the patient expresses horror and disgust, which the fear of death alone could induce him to bear.

If the draught be on the contrary merely insipid, as for instance a glass of water, there is neither taste nor aftertaste. Nothing is felt, nothing is experienced, it is swallowed, and that is all there is to it.

Order of the Impressions of Taste

Taste is not so richly endowed as hearing; the latter can appreciate and compare many sounds at once; taste on the contrary is simple in its action; that is to say it cannot be sensible to two flavors at once.

It may though be doubled and multiplied by succession, that is, in the same bite one might experience a second and even a third sensation, each of which gradually grows weaker, and which are designated by the words aftertaste, perfume, or fragrance. In the same manner, when a note is struck, an acute ear distinguishes many series of consonances, the number of which is not as yet perfectly known.

Those who eat quickly and without attention, do not discern impressions of the second level; the latter are the purview only of a small number of the elect, and by the means of these second-level sensations experts can classify and rank the different substances submitted to their examination.

These fugitive nuances resonate for some time in the organ of taste. Connoisseurs automatically assume an appropriate position for assessment, and when they render their verdicts they do so with necks extended and nostrils widened.

The Pleasures of Taste

Let us now look philosophically at the pleasure and pain that taste can occasion.

First of all we come upon the unhappy but well-known truth: that man is constituted so as to be far more sensible of pain than of pleasure.

In fact the imbibing of extremely sour, acid, or bitter substances subjects us to quite painful and unhappy sensations. It is even said that hydrocyanic acid kills so quickly because the pain is too great for the powers of vitality to bear for long.

The scale of agreeable sensations on the other hand is very limited, and if there be an observable difference between something insipid and something that really appeals to taste, the interval is not so great between the good and the excellent. The following example illustrates this: *first,* a dry, hard piece of boiled meat; *second,* a morsel of veal; *third,* a pheasant done to a turn.

Still, of all the senses with which we have been endowed by nature, taste is the one, all things considered, which procures us the most enjoyment.

1. Because the pleasure of eating, when moderately enjoyed, is the only one that is not followed by fatigue.
2. Because it is available to all historical times, all ages, and all circumstances.
3. Because it necessarily occurs at least once a day, and may without inconvenience be twice or thrice repeated in the same day.
4. Because it mingles with all other pleasures, and even consoles us for their absence.
5. Because the impressions it receives are at once more enduring and more voluntary.
6. Finally, because when we eat we experience a certain indefinable and peculiar impression of well-being originating in the instinctive consciousness that when we eat, we also repair our losses and prolong our lives...

The tongue of animals corresponds to their intelligence; in fishes the tongue is but a movable bone, in birds it is usually a membranous cartilage, and in quadrupeds it is often covered with scales and roughness, and it has no rotation.

The tongue of man, on the contrary, from the delicacy of its texture and of the different membranes by which it is surrounded, clearly manifests the sublimity of the operations for which it is destined.

Moreover, I have discovered at least three movements unknown to animals, which I call *spication*, *rotation*, and *verration* (from the Latin verb *verro*, I sweep). The first is when the tongue tip moves beyond the lips which compress it; the second is when the tongue rotates around in the space between the interior of the cheeks and the palate; the third is when the tongue moves up and down and gathers the particles which fall into the semicircular canal formed by the lips and gums.

Animals are limited in their tastes; some live only on vegetables, others on flesh; others feed altogether on grain; none knows anything of composite flavors.

Man is omnivorous. All that is edible is subjected to his vast appetite, a fact that generates gustatory powers proportionate to the use he has to make of them. In other words, the apparatus of taste is a rare perfection of man, and we have only to see him use it to be satisfied with it.

As soon as any edible body is introduced into the mouth it is seized—gas, juice and all.

The lips prevent its escape. The teeth take possession of it and crush it. Saliva soaks it; the tongue turns and mashes it, an aspiration forces it toward the throat; the tongue lifts it up to help it slide by; the sense of smell perceives it en route, and it is precipitated into the stomach to undergo ulterior transformations, without the most minute fragment escaping during the whole of this episode. Every drop, every atom has been appreciated.

In consequence of this perfection, gourmandise is the exclusive privilege of man.

...What more can we desire in a faculty susceptible of such perfection that the gourmands of Rome were able to distinguish the flavors of fish taken between the bridges of that city from those caught lower down? Have we not seen in our own time, that connoisseurs can distinguish the flavor of the thigh on which the partridge sleeps from the other? Are we not surrounded by experts who can tell the latitude in which any wine ripened as surely as one of Biot's or Arago's disciples can foretell an eclipse?

The consequence then is that we must render to Caesar the things which are Caesar's and proclaim man the great *gourmand of nature*.

Brillat-Savarin's *Omelette au Thon*

For six persons, take the roe of two carp and blanch them for several minutes in lightly salted, boiling water. Have ready a small piece of fresh tuna about the size of an egg, to which you must add a minced shallot. Chop together the tuna and the roes so that they are well blended. Put the mixture into a dish with a portion of good butter, and keep on the fire until the butter has melted. This gives the omelette its particular flavor.

Take another lump of butter and mix it with parsley and chives. Place it in a fish-shaped platter that will hold the omelette. (The platter should be deep enough to hold the sauce.) Sprinkle it with lemon juice and place over low heat.

Beat one dozen fresh eggs and add the fish and the roe so that everything is well mixed. (The roe and the fish should be warmed, not boiled; they will thus mingle more easily with the eggs.) Then cook the omelette in the usual way so that it is just firm yet light, shaping it long. Place it gently in the warmed serving platter. Serve at once.

This dish should be reserved for especially good luncheons where the guests are connoisseurs. Washed down with a fine wine, it will create miracles.

2

Chemical Senses

Taste and Smell

Linda M. Bartoshuk and Valerie B. Duffy

Taste and Olfactory Qualities

The universally accepted taste qualities perceived by humans are sweet, salty, sour, and bitter (although a few other terms like metallic, alkaline, and umami have been suggested as potential taste qualities by some authors). A comparison across mammals suggests that taste information falls into these four categories across species. The source of the salty taste is the cation of a salt. The anions of salts contribute other tastes (bitter, sweet, or both, to humans) depending on their structures. The cations also contribute other tastes depending on their size. The smaller cations lithium (Li) and sodium (Na) produce relatively pure saltiness, but larger cations like potassium (K) taste bitter as well as salty. Some species (e.g. rats) have neurons that are sodium specialists (Frank 1985), which may aid in the detection of sodium. Schulkin (1991) has suggested that the salty taste serves a critical function in a variety of mineral deficiencies. In the wild, animals encounter salt licks, which contain sodium but also other minerals. If deficiencies in any of these minerals were to trigger an appetite for saltiness, then as the animal satisfied its desire for saltiness at the salt lick, it would incidentally ingest the other minerals as well.

Bitter and sweet tastes are produced primarily by organic compounds that bind to specific proteins in the taste receptor cell membrane. All mammals have receptors that bind some of the compounds that taste bitter and sweet to humans; however, some species lack certain binding sites available in humans. For example, all mammals taste sugars, but all artificial sweeteners do not taste like sugar to certain species (Glaser, Hellekant, Broower, and van der Wel 1978). Similarly, some species lack the ability to taste some bitter compounds.

The number of molecules that can be sensed by the olfactory system is quite large but has never been determined experimentally despite the frequent citation of the number 10,000 (Engen 1982). Common substances that have odors that we recognize and name (e.g. bacon, Chanel No. 5) usually contain many odorants. Cain has suggested that we process these odor mixtures holistically and form templates to recognize them (Cain 1987). Thus we can recognize a variety of objects by their unique smells even if those objects have some odors in common. Presumably, experience with specific odor mixtures results in the learned ability to recognize and name those combinations that are experienced frequently. The number of unique smells that each individual learns to recognize and name is much smaller than 10,000 (Engen 1982).

Anatomy

The tongue consists of two portions: the anterior, mobile tongue and the posterior tongue. The bumpy appearance of the tongue is produced by four types of papillae. The most numerous type, filiform, does not contain taste buds. The shapes of filiform papillae vary across species from the rasplike structures on the tongues of species like the cat and rat to the more rounded structures on the human tongue. Taste buds are found on the fungiform papillae (named for the button mushrooms they resemble) on the anterior or mobile tongue, foliate papillae at the edges at the base of the mobile tongue, and circumvallate papillae on the back of the tongue just behind the mobile portion. Taste buds are clusters of cells; the apical portion of the cell extends into a long, slender microvillus which projects up into the taste pore (the conduit that connects the taste bud to the tongue surface). The molecular sites that interact with taste stimuli are found on the microvilli. The taste receptors' cells have life spans measured in days and are continually replaced.

Four cranial nerves innervate taste buds: V, VII, IX, and X. Taste information is carried by (1) the chorda tympani branch of VII, the facial nerve, which innervates the taste buds in the fungiform papillae; (2) the greater superficial petrosal branch of VII, which innervates the taste buds on the roof of the mouth; and (3) the glossopharyngeal nerve, IX, which innervates the taste buds in the foliate and circumvallate papillae. The trigeminal nerve, V, carries touch, pain, and thermal sensations from the anterior tongue, and the glossopharyngeal nerve carries these sensations from the rear of the tongue. Individual taste buds on the fungiform papillae are innervated by both VII and V. Neurons from VII enter the taste bud and synapse with taste cells, while neurons from V form a shell around the taste bud (Whitehead, Beeman, and Kinsella 1985). The Xth cranial nerve (vagus) carries taste from the throat.

Taste nerves project to the medulla, then to the thalamus, and finally to the cortex. In some species, there is an additional synapse at the pons (Norgren and Pfaffmann 1975). Of special clinical importance is the chorda tympani nerve, which passes behind the tympanic membrane (and thus receives its name) and through the middle ear on its way to the brain.

A variety of textbooks contain a tongue map that shows sweet on the tip of the tongue, bitter on the back, etc. This tongue map is incorrect. It originated from a misinterpretation (Boring 1942) of an early thesis (Hanig 1901). All four taste qualities are perceived on all tongue loci where there are taste buds (Bartoshuk,1993a, b, Collings 1974)...

Dual Function of Olfaction

The flavors of foods are perceptually localized to the mouth in spite of the fact that flavors are made up of taste sensations, which genuinely originate in the mouth, and olfactory sensations, which do not. To understand the role of olfactory sensations in flavor perception, we must consider the dual functions of the sense of olfaction, which depend on the route by which odorants reach the olfactory receptors. Odorants are pulled into the nasal cavity by sniffing (orthonasal olfaction). The air carrying the odorants passes over the turbinate bones and becomes turbulent, which permits a small sample to reach the olfactory mucosa. Odorants can also reach the mucosa from the mouth (retronasal olfaction). Chewing releases odorants from food, and mouth movements and swallowing pump them behind the palate and up into the nasal cavity. These retronasal olfactory sensations combine with sweet, salty, sour, and bitter to produce flavor.

"Taste" is often used as a synonym for "flavor." This usage of "taste" probably arose because the blend of true taste and retronasal olfaction is perceptually localized to the mouth via touch. The perceptual localization of olfactory sensations appears to depend on the tactile sensations that accompany them. When the odorants pass through the external nares via sniffing, we perceive the odor sensations as coming from the outside. When the odorants are released from foods and beverages that contact the tactile receptors in the mouth, we perceive the odor sensations as arising from the mouth. The use of the same word, *taste,* to refer to flavor and to the true gustatory sensations of salty, sweet, sour, and bitter leads to a variety of confusions. For a clinical example, when patients lose olfaction, they typically report that they cannot taste or smell. However, when questioned, patients acknowledge that they can taste salty, sweet, sour, and bitter, but "nothing else." The "nothing else" is the contribution of retronasal olfaction to flavor.

Genetic Variation in Taste

We do not all live in the same taste worlds. In the 1930s, a minor accident in a laboratory led to the discovery that about 25% of individuals are taste-blind to phenylthiocarbamide (PTC) (Fox 1931); however, the frequency of nontasters varies with sex and race… More recent psychophysical studies showed that some tasters perceive [certain chemicals] to be much more bitter than do other tasters. To these supertasters, certain sweeteners and a variety of bitters taste stronger than they do to medium tasters and nontasters. Anatomical studies of the mobile tongue show that supertasters have the largest number of taste buds and nontasters have the smallest number (Bartoshuk, Duffy and Miller 1994; Miller and Reedy 1990). Possibly because of the presence of trigeminal fibers around taste buds, nontasters perceive less oral burn from substances like capsaicin, the compound responsible for the burn of chili peppers (Karrer and Bartoshuk 1991).

Women are more likely than men to be supertasters. They have, on average, more taste buds and perceive greater sweetness and bitterness from some compounds. It is tempting to speculate that supertasting might help to assure a healthy pregnancy, since poisons are often bitter. Women also perceive, on average, greater oral burn from substances like capsaicin. Since pain is mediated by the same neurons that respond to capsaicin, women presumably experience greater pain from lesions of the tongue (e.g. the mucositic lesions produced as a side effect of chemotherapy and radiation therapy for cancer patients)…

Aberrations of Taste and Smell

When the confusion between taste and flavor is resolved, true taste loss appears to be much less common than olfactory loss (Deems et al. 1991; Goodspeed et al. 1986; Smith 1991). But this poses an interesting puzzle. A variety of etiologies are known to damage taste structures, yet patients often fail to notice any true taste loss. One of the most dramatic examples of this was reported more than a century ago. Brillat-Savarin wrote about a man whose tongue had been cut out (the anterior, mobile part of the tongue that is innervated by VII) but who could still taste (Brillat-Savarin 1825). More recently Carl Pfaffmann, a pioneer in studies of taste and olfaction, documented his own experience with Ramsey-Hunt Syndrome, a reactivation of the virus responsible for chicken pox. The virus damaged both VII and IX so severely that no taste function remained on the left side of Pfaffmann's mouth. In spite of this damage, Pfaffmann experienced no change in everyday taste experience (Pfaffmann and Bartoshuk 1990).

Interactions between two of the cranial nerves subserving taste (VII and IX) provide some insights into the constancy of the taste system in the face of damage. Working with the rat, Halpern and Nelson (1965) anesthetized the chorda tympani (VII) at the point where it crosses the tympanic membrane on its path to the brain and stimulated the area of the mouth innervated by the glossopharyngeal nerve (IX). The neural responses in the medulla that were produced by that stimulation were larger than normal. They hypothesized that input via VII normally inhibits the input via IX, so that when VII was anesthetized, its inhibition of IX was released and responses to the stimulation of IX increased. Studies in humans show similar effects, suggesting that overall taste intensities remain relatively constant because release-of-inhibition compensates for the loss from a damaged area (Lehman et al. 1995). The patient does not detect this compensation because the perceptual localization of taste is controlled by touch (Todrank and Bartoshuk 1991). As long as touch sensations are normal, taste sensations seem to arise from whatever area is touched in the mouth…

The taste worlds of the elderly change little with age (Bartoshuk and Duffy 1995). The small changes that are reported (primarily for sour and bitter substances) must be the combination of age-related losses (if any) and losses associated with pathology, since the probability of suffering a disorder that could impair taste goes up with the number of years lived…

In contrast with the relative robustness of taste with age, olfaction declines steadily after age twenty (Gibbons 1986; Gilbert and Wysocki 1987), but this must reflect losses associated with pathology as well as any age-related losses (Ship and Weiffenbach 1993). It is clinically important to note that a precipitous loss suggests pathology, since the losses associated with normal aging tend to be gradual.

Any damage to the olfactory system will obviously cause losses in both orthonasal and retronasal olfaction. However, retronasal olfaction (and thus flavor perception) can be impaired in individuals who show no losses of orthonasal olfaction. This can result from clinical conditions that change the way volatiles are released and pumped into the nasal cavity by chewing and swallowing during eating…

The Chemical Senses and Nutrition

An examination of the tastes and smells of nutrients provides insight into the roles of taste and smell in nutrition. The macronutrients (sources of calories) consist of proteins, carbohydrates (starch and sugar), and fats. In general, these molecules are too large to stimulate taste or olfactory receptors. The one exception is sugar, which tastes sweet. The flavors of substances like bacon or olive oil can seem to be characteristic of protein or fat, but are due to volatiles mixed with the protein and fat. The micronutrients consist of vitamins and minerals. Vitamins are too dilute to be tasted in foods. Minerals in the form of salts taste salty (e.g. NaCl) and when the cation is larger than sodium (e.g. KCI, $CaC1_2$), they taste bitter as well. Poisons, substances that must be avoided, tend to taste bitter. Note that we cannot identify nutrients by smell, but certain nutrients can be identified by taste. Sodium salts taste salty, sugars taste sweet, and poisons taste bitter. The hedonic properties of these categories are present at birth.

Olfaction is not tuned to nutrients but, rather, serves to label objects. Further, odors take on positive or negative valence based on experience. Positive experiences (e.g. calories, sweet taste, mood elevation, and social reward) paired with an odor make the odor liked (Birch et al. 1990; Zellner et al. 1983), but nausea paired with an odor makes the odor disliked (Pelchat et al. 1983; Pelchat and Rozin 1982).

Genetic variation in the ability to taste PROP has long been associated with food dislikes (Drewnowski 1990). For example, the bitterness of the artificial sweetener saccharin was shown to vary with the ability to taste PROP so that supertasters perceived the greatest bitterness and nontasters the least (Bartoshuk 1979). More recently, the preference for sweetness was shown to depend on both sex and the ability to taste PROP (Duffy, Weingarten, and Bartoshuk 1995; Looy and Weingarten 1992). For men, as PROP bitterness increases, the preference for sweetness increases. Since the sweetness of sugars increases as PROP bitterness increases (Gent and Bartoshuk 1983), this means that for men, "the sweeter the better." However, for women this pattern reverses and the preference for sweetness decreases as PROP bitterness increases. The dislike that female supertasters report for sweetness might be a consequence of the intensity of the sweetness perceived; that is, sweetness may be so strong that it becomes unpleasant. However the sex difference could also result because females in our culture are almost universally concerned with weight and may reject sweetness because of its association with calories.

Conclusions

The senses of taste and smell function in different ways to identify important chemical stimuli. The sense of taste detects specific substances important to nutrition: sodium, sugar, and bitter poisons. The affect these substances evoke is essentially hard-wired and thus universal across species and across individuals within a species; however, variation exists in the receptor mechanisms mediating these basic tastes across species.

Virtually all of the common odors we encounter are actually mixtures of odorous compounds (e.g. bacon, pizza, etc.), yet we are able to perceive these common odors as if they were qualitatively unitary. This occurs because the sense of smell is organized to permit the holistic processing of complex mixtures of odorants. Thus a group of odor mixtures can be perceived as qualitatively distinct from one another even if they contain some of the same components. An individual organism learns to recognize the odor complexes important in its world. Affect associates with these odor complexes based on events associated with the odors (e.g. if an odor is followed by nausea, the odor becomes disliked; if an odor is followed by calories, the odor becomes liked).

Olfaction plays a dual role. The nose samples air from the outside world (orthonasal olfaction) to provide information about the environment. However, the nose also samples air from the mouth (retronasal olfaction) to provide information about what is being consumed. The role of retronasal olfaction is often misunderstood because the tactile stimulation produced by food in the mouth serves to localize the evoked sensations to the mouth. Thus the combination of true taste and retronasal olfaction (which we call "flavor") appears to arise from the mouth.

Genetic variation and pathology affect chemosensory experience. Because taste and smell evoke affect, genetic variation and the pathology of taste and smell have an impact on the pleasure of eating, food choices, and ultimately nutrition.

References

Bartoshuk, L. M. (1979), "Bitter taste of saccharin: Related to the genetic ability to taste the bitter substance 6-*n*-propylthiouracil (PROP)," *Science, 205,* 934–935.

——. (1993a), "The biological basis of food perception and acceptance," *Food Quality and Preference, 4,* 21–32.

——. (ed.) (1993b), *Genetic and pathological taste variation: What can we learn from animal models and human disease?*, New York: John Wiley.

Bartoshuk, L. M., and Duffy, V. B. (1995), "Taste and smell in aging" in E. J. Masoro (ed.), *Handbook of Physiology, Section 11: Aging,* 363–375, New York: Oxford University Press.

Bartoshuk, L. M., Duffy, V. B., and Miller, I. J. (1994), "PTC/PROP tasting: Anatomy, psychophysics, and sex effects," *Physiology and Behavior,* 56, 1165–1171.

Birch, L. L., McPhee, L., Steinberg, L., and Sullivan, S. (1990), "Conditioned flavor preferences in young children," *Physiology and Behavior*, 47, 501–505.

Boring, E. G. (1942), *Sensation and Perception in the History of Experimental Psychology.* New York: Appleton.

Brillat-Savarin, J. A. (1825), *The Physiology of Taste,* trans. M. F. K. Fisher, New York: Alfred A. Knopf.

Cain, W. (1987), "Taste vs. smell in the organization of perceptual experience," in J. Solms, D. A. Booth, R. M. Pangborn, and O. Raunhardt (eds.), *Food Acceptance and Nutrition*, 63–77, New York: Academic Press.

Collings, V. B. (1974), "Human taste response as a function of locus of stimulation on the tongue and soft palate," *Perception and Psychophysics,* 16, 169–174.

Deems, D. A., Doty, R. L., Settle, R. G., Moore-Gillon, V., Shaman, P., Mester, A. F., Kimmelman, C. P., Brightman, V. J., and Snow, J. B. (1991), "Smell and taste disorders: A study of 750 patients from the University of Pennsylvania Smell and Taste Center," *Archives of Otolaryngology-Head and Neck Surgery,* 117, 519–528.

Drewnowski, A. (1990), "Genetics of taste and smell," *World Review of Nutrition and Dietetics*, 63, 194–208.

Duffy, V., Weingarten, H. P., and Bartoshuk, L. M. (1995), "Preference for sweet in young adults associated with PROP (6-n-propylthiouracil) genetic taster status and sex," *Chemical Senses,* 20, 688.

Engen, T. (1982), *The Perception of Odors,* New York: Academic Press.

Fox, A. L. (1931), "Six in ten 'tasteblind' to bitter chemical," *Science News Letter,* 9, 249.

Frank, M. E. (1985), "Sensory physiology of taste and smell discriminations using conditioned food aversion methodology," in *Experimental Assessments and Clinical Applications of Conditioned Food Aversions,* 89–99, New York: New York Academy of Sciences.

Gent, J. F., and Bartoshuk, L. M. (1983), "Sweetness of sucrose, neohesperidin dihyodrochalcone, and saccharin is related to genetic ability to taste the bitter substance 6-*n*-propylthiouracil," *Chemical Senses,* 7, 265–272.

Gibbons, B. (1986), "The intimate sense of smell," *National Geographic,* 170, 324–361.

Gilbert, A. N., and Wysocki, C. J. (1987), "The smell survey results," *National Geographic,* 172, 515–525.

Glaser, D., Hellekant, G., Broower, J. N., and van der Wel, H. (1978), "The taste responses in primates to the proteins thaumatin and monellin and their phylogenetic implications," *Folia Primatologica,* 29, 56–63.

Goodspeed, R. B., Catalanotto, F A., Gent, J. F., Cain, W. S., Bartoshuk, L. M., Leonard, G., and Donaldson, J. O. (1986), "Clinical characteristics of patients with taste and smell disorders," in H. L. Meiselman and R. S. Rivlin (eds.), *Clinical Measurement of Taste and Smell,* 451–466, New York: Macmillan Publishing Co.

Halpern, B. P., and Nelson, L. M. (1965), "Bulbar gustatory responses to anterior and to posterior tongue stimulation in the rat," *American Journal of Physiology,* 209,105–110.

Hanig, D. P. (1901), "Zur Psychophysik des Geschmackssinnes," *Philosophische Studien,* 17, 576–623.

Karrer, T., and Bartoshuk, L. (1991), "Capsaicin desensitization and recovery on the human tongue," *Physiology and Behavior,* 49, 757–764.

Lehman, C. D., Bartoshuk, L. M., Catalanotto, F. C., Kveton, J. F., and Lowlicht, R. A. (1995), "The effect of anesthesia of the chorda tympani nerve on taste perception in humans," *Physiology and Behavior,* 57, 943–951.

Looy, H., and Weingarten, H. P. (1992), "Facial expressions and genetic sensitivity to 6n-propylthiouracil predict hedonic response to sweet," *Physiology and Behavior,* 52, 75–82.

Miller, I. J., and Reedy, F. E. (1990), "Variations in human taste bud density and taste intensity perception," *Physiology and Behavior,* 47, 1213–1219.

Norgren, R., and Pfaffmann, C. (1975), "The pontine taste area in the rat," *Brain Research,* 91, 99–117.

Pelchat, M. L., Grill, H. J., Rozin, P., and Jacobs, J. (1983), "Quality of acquired responses to tastes by *Rattus norvegicus* depends on type of associated discomfort," *Journal of Comparative Psychology,* 97, 140–153.

Pelchat, M. L., and Rozin, P. (1982), "The special role of nausea in the acquisition of food dislikes by humans," *Appetite,* 3, 341–351.

Pfaffmann, C., and Bartoshuk, L. M. (1990), "Taste loss due to herpes zoster oticus: an update after 19 months," *Chemical Senses,* 15, 657–658.

Schulkin, J. (1991), *Sodium Hunger: The Search for a Salty Taste*, New York: Cambridge University Press.

Ship, J., and Weiffenbach, J. (1993), "Age, gender, medical treatment, and medication effects on smell identification," *Journal of Gerontology*, 48, M26–M32.

Smith, D. V. (1991), "Taste and smell dysfunction," in M. M. Paparella, D. A. Shumrick, J. L. Gluckman and W. L. Meyerhoff (eds.) *Otolaryngology: Head and Neck* 1911–1934, Philadelphia: W. B. Saunders.

Todrank, J., and Bartoshuk, L. M. (1991), "A taste illusion: Taste sensation localized by touch," *Physiology and Behavior*, 50, 1027–1031.

Whitehead, M. C., Beeman, C. S., and Kinsella, B. A. (1985), "Distribution of taste and general sensory nerve endings in fungiform papillae of the hamster," *American Journal of Anatomy*, 173, 185–201.

Zellner, D. A., Rozin, P., Aron, M., and Kulish,, C. (1983), Conditioned enhancement of humans' liking for flavor by pairing with sweetness," *Learning and Motivation*, 14, 338–350.

3
Culinary Themes and Variations

Elisabeth Rozin and Paul Rozin

Every morning in a small village in the southern highlands of Mexico one can hear in every home the rhythmic sounds of the grinding stone. Between these stones, or *metates*, are, without fail, chili peppers, and frequently tomatoes, being ground into the *salsa* (sauce) for the day. The salsa will appear at almost every meal; when it is absent, the chili peppers, often combined with tomato or lime, turn up as components of cooked solid foods and soups. A ubiquitous feature of Mexican cuisine, the chili pepper, along with the staples corn and beans, is an essential part of what makes Mexican food "Mexican."

This Mexican village is not unique, for the same processes take place in every other Mexican village although the ingredients may vary slightly from one village to another. So it is in other parts of the world as well. One can observe in the Brahman Tamil cuisine of southern India, for example, the same kind of daily seasoning preparation: the soaking of tamarind, the grinding of chili pepper, the frying of mustard seed, turmeric, and hing powder (asafetida). These and other flavorings, used daily on almost all cooked staple foods, create the identity of this cuisine.

Such flavoring practices are very widespread but seem to occur most frequently in tropical or semitropical areas or, what may be the same thing, in cultures that depend more heavily on plant foods than animal foods. Thus the most distinctive and easily described seasoning traditions occur in China, Southeast Asia, Africa, India, the Mediterranean, and South and Central America. Seasoning practices may range from the use of one specific, pervasive flavoring ingredient (the use of coconut in the islands of Oceania) to much more complex and elaborate bonds or combinations of flavoring ingredients (the spice mixtures of North African or Indian cuisine). Within cultures that characteristically season their foods, the use of combinations of flavoring ingredients is the most common technique: the soy sauce and rice wine and ginger root bond of China; the soy sauce and sesame seed and chili bond of Korea; the "curry" spice mixtures of India; the tomato and garlic and olive oil bond of southern Italy. These distinctive and pervasive flavoring combinations, which we call "flavor principles," seem to impart a clear and characteristic identity to the foods of any group. Cultures that reliably season their cooked foods do not, for the most part, utilize these seasonings in sweets and beverages.

The use of characteristic seasonings, whether singly or in combination, is not universal in human culinary practice; in cuisines that have a high proportion of animal foods (meat or dairy products) in their diet, and in many cuisines of temperate and polar regions, there is typically no strong dependence on flavoring ingredients. This tendency results in culinary products that are relatively less "marked" than the products of cuisines that season heavily. Characteristic seasonings provide a gustatory "theme" that identifies and unites the products of a cuisine so that, for example, having sampled at random several Mexican or Indian dishes, one would have a good chance of identifying new instances of dishes from these cuisines. This would probably not be the case in the relatively less marked cuisines of England or Germany.

Most of the world's people seem to belong to well-marked cuisine groups that create culinary products with distinctive and describable gustatory themes. The traditional seasonings are "loved" by the members of these groups. They find it difficult to imagine food prepared without them. Faced with a hypothetical absence of chili, for instance, members of a Mexican village kept inventing ways of getting some—from neighbors, stores, or markets—rather than face the possibility of eating a meal without it. Chili is craved: food simply doesn' t taste good without it.

This attachment to traditional flavorings seems to be as strong, if not stronger, than the attachment to traditional staple foods. Human beings are remarkably conservative in their food habits and are typically reluctant to try new foods and to abandon old, familiar ones. Although some new foods have been introduced and accepted in both Mexico and China, for example, the ancient flavoring traditions, many of them thousands of years old, persist unchanged to this day. Traditional flavorings are high-priority culinary items and immigrant groups typically go to great lengths and expense to procure them in foreign settings. After many generations in the mixed culture of Israel, the basic flavorings of the original home country (either Eastern European or Mediterranean or indigenous Israeli) still predominate in the individual's daily diet.

The desire to recreate familiar tastes is illustrated nowhere more poignantly than in the behavior of Vietnamese refugees in an American resettlement camp that we visited in the fall of 1975. Vietnamese food is characteristically seasoned with *nuoc mam,* a salty, fermented fish sauce, typically mixed with vinegar and chili. The camp kitchens, staffed by US Army cooks, attempted to accommodate Vietnamese taste by providing some traditional staple foods: chicken, fish, rice, vegetables. But the well-loved *nuoc mam* was not available. When the kitchen staff discovered, by trial and error, that the most popular flavorings were soy sauce and hot pepper sauce, a bottle of each was always placed on every table in the mess hall. The cooks told us, with some incredulity, that the refugees would pour soy sauce and hot pepper sauce on all their foods, mix them together, and then eat them. They went through supplies of these sauces at a most remarkable rate. The refugees were doing the best they could, in a strange environment and with limited ingredients, to duplicate the traditional flavors of their cuisine. (*Nuoc mam* is now widely available in Oriental groceries throughout the United States; the demands of the Vietnamese have produced a steady supply.)

The flavoring of food—that is, the deliberate manipulation of food by adding ingredients that will reliably alter the taste—is a uniquely human behavior. There are no animals that characteristically mix their foods with anything that could be called a flavoring, even including the possibility of marking the food with a bodily secretion. The one possible exception is the troupe of monkeys on Koshima Island in Japan that has developed a tradition, "invented" by an adult female, of dipping sweet potatoes in saltwater before eating them. This one example may be the only reported seasoning behavior from the animal kingdom.

Why do human beings, or at least most human beings, flavor their foods? What is the function of seasoning traditions, handed down from one generation to the next? One can understand how the attachment to the flavors of their native cuisine might develop in individuals as a result of continued exposure from early childhood (and possibly even earlier still from mother's milk). But what is the adaptive value of this generally widespread and ancient practice?

Surely, any particular flavoring ingredients used—chili, cumin, garlic, or whatever—are largely determined by their availability in the environment. But availability alone cannot explain the exclusive, persistent, and prevalent use of certain flavorings in any culture. Frequently, some available flavorings are rejected, while others not easily obtained are widely sought after. The age of exploration in Europe, for example, was largely motivated by a specific lust for seasoning ingredients, particularly pepper.

It is possible that some flavoring ingredients have specific biological value, in terms of either nutritive or physiological effects. Because such seasoning elements are typically eaten in small amounts, they cannot supply a significant amount of macronutrients, like protein and fat, but they might well provide valuable vitamins or minerals. Chili pepper, for example, is a very rich source of vitamins A and C. These vitamins are in short supply in the diets of some cultures that use chili; in these cases chili can provide a significant percentage of vitamin A and C requirements, for example, in some areas of Mexico.

A few flavoring ingredients may have medicinal benefits: one of the better documented examples is the antibacterial effect of garlic. Certain physiological effects of the ingestion of some flavoring ingredients may also have adaptive value: chili pepper causes facial sweating, thereby facilitating heat loss in hot environments. Like some other irritant spices, chili stimulates salivation, gastric secretion, and gut motility, and thus may facilitate the chewing and digestion of high-starch diets. Research and ingenuity could probably provide a possible specific effect for each of the many flavoring ingredients used throughout the world. Although such adaptive explanations might well be valid, they are unsatisfactory because they provide a set of individual and specific explanations for a class of related and general phenomena. And such specific explanations cannot account for the pervasive use of seasonings on almost all staple foods.

There are several other possible general explanations. Traditional flavors may serve the same function as traditional costume or traditional religious practice. They are a means of defining a culture group, of identifying an individual with it, and of separating that group from others. Whatever broad human needs are served by such visible in-group behavior, distinctive culinary practices must surely be a part of it.

Another explanation focuses on the salient sensory properties of flavoring ingredients. These elements, particularly when combined in the bonds of flavor principles, almost always have a strong and distinctive flavor. From a broad cultural–ecological perspective, it is those cultures that rely on a bland starch staple with small amounts of meat that have the most marked cuisines in terms of flavor. Indeed, the common explanation offered by individuals from a marked cuisine that the flavors add "zest" or "taste" to their food has some force.

Flavoring ingredients may also be distinctively colored—for example, chili, turmeric, saffron, soy sauce—and may thus impart a characteristic rich and warm color to the food. Again, with bland or light-colored staples (rice, refined wheat), color can provide visual zest, and through both taste and appearance give a meaty quality to the diet. Given that meat is a highly preferred food in almost all cultures, flavoring traditions might well be a response to an absence or shortage of meat in the diet.

A final explanation, which we shall develop more fully, ascribes the widespread use of flavor principles to a basic feature of human biology: our omnivorous heritage.

Human beings are omnivores, or food "generalists," that is, they consume a wide variety of food substances. Unlike food "specialists," who rely almost completely on one or a few varieties of food, omnivores can select their diet from a theoretically almost limitless range of items, a range defined by availability in the environment and by competition with other species. (For convenience, we will use the term "omnivore" but our comments hold for all generalists, including general herbivores.) The omnivore has much greater flexibility in exploiting the potential nutrient sources of the environment and in exploring and invading new habitats. Furthermore, by consuming a wide variety of foods, the omnivore can minimize the effects of mildly toxic or nutritionally imbalanced substances by utilizing them as only partial nutritional support.

A major cost of omnivorousness is that it makes great demands on behavioral capacities. The food specialist consumes such a small variety of foods that recognition of appropriate food items (specific types of leaves, flying insects, and so on) can be genetically built in. Specifically tuned receptors could never be constructed for the huge number of nutritive or dangerous substances that the omnivore encounters. The omnivore must have another type of system for identifying and evaluating these many substances; this is especially important because of the high incidence of toxic substances in the natural world.

Without an innate food recognition system, how does the generalist manage? Although some mammalian omnivores, including humans, do have minimal preprogrammed guidelines (approach to sweet tastes and avoidance of bitter tastes), individual experience predominates in the evaluation of foods. And of course humans have the mediation of culture, which includes accumulated knowledge about valuable and dangerous substances and methods for treating certain items that, once detoxified, are nutritionally beneficial.

Of all behavior, eating is surely the most intimate because it involves the irrevocable incorporation of things into the body; once past the lips and down the gullet the substance becomes at least cognitively a part of the organism. Such an interaction must be both intensely satisfying and extremely threatening. Strong, positive, affective responses accompany eating, while, when new foods are involved, the possibility of bodily harm promotes fear and hesitation. This approach-avoidance conflict is one aspect of the omnivore's dilemma. Trying new foods is at the core of omnivorousness, but so is being wary of them. A delayed, cautious, and gingerly sampling of new foods is common in a number of omnivorous species.

Within the familiarity of one's culture the fear side of eating is attenuated. But when one leaves the safety of the home environment and travels to far and exotic places, the conflict appears: there is an interest in new foods and a simultaneous fear of eating them, a conflict frequently resolved by restricting eating to the safe haven of the Cairo Hilton or a McDonald's in Bangkok. (Indeed, the uniformity and total predictability of the fast-food chains may be a response to this side of the omnivore's dilemma.) A person may both seek and withdraw from exotic foods, and the balance may shift in different individuals and in different circumstances. Although the preference for a new food increases the more times it is experienced without negative consequences, this may be, at least partially, a result of the dissipation of fear of new things. However, extensive exposure may also lead to boredom and rejection. This encourages the omnivore to continue exploring new food sources and discourages heavy reliance on one food. And so we have a second aspect of the omnivore's dilemma, which can now be seen as twofold: (1) curiosity about new foods versus fear of new foods and (2) the satisfaction with familiar food versus the boredom that overexposure can produce.

It is our belief that the widespread human tendency to season foods with recurrent, predictable combinations of flavoring ingredients can be seen as a cultural response to the omnivore's dilemma. The ambivalence of eating, the pleasure–fear balance, depends on the familiarity of the food. Reliably clothing the food in a distinctive and familiar flavor can tip the balance to the side of pleasure: it provides a taste that has always been safe and enjoyable, that is associated with satiety and the appropriate social context. The flavor furnishes a familiar frame for the food of a culture, passed along from generation to generation.

If the approach-avoidance conflict can be significantly reduced by the use of familiar traditional flavors, it might well be an adaptive means of disseminating a nutritious new food staple within a culture. By labeling a food with the appropriate flavor, it is "certified," as it were, as familiar and safe to eat. Having discovered the safety and nutritional value of a new food through personal experience or through information received from outside, the pioneer "sampler" within a culture could announce its acceptability by treating it as a traditional food, preparing it with familiar flavor principles and cooking techniques. Indeed, Parmentier, the eighteenth-century French agriculturist, did just this in order to persuade the French people to accept the potato, a valuable food staple brought from the New World. The French would have nothing to do with this new food until Parmentier showed them how to prepare it in traditional ways and with familiar seasonings: butter, cheese, herbs. The strategy worked, and the potato has risen in the French culinary repertoire from initial rejection to enormous popularity.

We don't know very much about how, on the individual level, new foods are introduced into a culture. We do have some data, however, indicating the importance of flavor principles in treating new food items. In a Mexican village where we observed food habits closely, a number of women were asked how they would prepare three items they had never eaten before. The three "foods" were sardines (one of the few canned foods available in the village store but rejected by a majority of the residents), alfalfa (an animal food), and a common shrub not considered food. All responses included flavoring the item with chili, the indispensable flavor-principle component. Several of the other responses indicated the use of lime, another traditional flavoring ingredient. In all these cases, the women had no reason to believe these new foods would cause them any harm, although they had no desire to try them. When faced with hypothetical use, however, they treated them like familiar foods. There is something to be said then for the reassuring nature of traditional seasonings; they are the familiar culinary theme, linking together the known and the traditional with the new and the unfamiliar.

But what of the omnivore's second problem, the need for variety and the reduction of boredom? With the rise of agriculture and the growing dependence on a few staple crops, the number of different foods eaten by most cultures dropped; it is probably still the hunter-gatherer who, even in marginal environments, consumes the greatest variety of food items. Elaborate culinary preparation (in terms of techniques, equipment, and novel combinations of ingredients) can produce variety, and this greater complexity of culinary procedure occurs in virtually all cultures that rely primarily on the staple-plant diet. But how can the placing of a recurrent flavor combination on almost all foods at almost all meals, reassuring as it may be, also provide variety and reduce boredom?

The answer may come from a close study of the use of flavor principles in cuisine. What seems a monotonous repetition of flavorings may well be an illusion of the outsider, just as all red burgundies taste alike to the inexperienced wine drinker. A closer look at actual culinary practice reveals a rich and subtle variation of flavoring from dish to dish and from meal to meal. In the Mexican village we studied, for example, chili pepper is used in many ways. It is cooked into soups and stews or sliced and placed upon other foods or ground into a sauce, often with tomatoes and other ingredients. At least ten types of chili peppers are used in this village: some are fresh, some are dried, some are red, others green, some strongly piquant, others less so. They differ somewhat in the type of "burn" they produce in the mouth. And villagers assure us that each type of chili has a different taste. Some kinds of peppers are used interchangeably with others in the making of soups or sauce. A few may be mixed together one day, a different combination on the next, but their use is far from random: some varieties are specified for certain culinary preparations. The chili ancho, for example, a large and relatively mild variety, is used almost exclusively in *moles,* the traditional stewed meat dish of the region. The number of different kinds of chili peppers available in the area is quite large. Nine homes that we surveyed had from three to six different chilis in the house, while in the large regional market of Oaxaca, dozens of varieties can be found. Within the single "theme" of this Mexican chili pepper flavor principle there is a great deal of subtle and controlled variation.

The same kind of theme and variation can be shown to function in other cuisines that consistently utilize recurrent combinations of flavoring ingredients. Indian cookery is characterized by a flavor that naive outsiders call "curry"; curry, in fact, does not refer to the flavor of the food but to dishes that have a sauce. Within the realm of curried, or sauced, preparations, there is no single flavor but, again, a recurrent combination of ingredients that are manipulated with great subtlety and surprising variety. Brahman Tamil cuisine of southern India relies heavily on several core seasoning ingredients; including chili pepper, asafetida, mustard seed, tamarind, fresh coriander, and turmeric. A close inspection of Tamil recipes, however, reveals that this general theme is varied from dish to dish: sometimes all the ingredients appear, sometimes only one or two; the relative proportions differ from preparation to preparation; and the basic flavor is varied with the frequent addition of other seasoning ingredients such as coconut, coriander seed, and cumin. Again, what may look and, indeed, taste, like the very same thing to the outsider is not the same thing at all to the insider. Simple and complex variations are created by the individual cook within the thematic limits set by the traditions of the cuisine.

We suggest, then, that the prevalent human practice of adding characteristic combinations of flavors to most foods may be the result of our omnivorous heritage and an expression of our unique humanity: we have other things to do with food than merely to consume it. To appease our fear of the new and to support our satisfaction with the familiar, we create a label or theme. But at the same time, to avoid monotony and to satisfy our desire for variety, we play with the theme, fashioning as we do so, the elaborate and richly textured composition we call cuisine.

3a
Flavor Principles
Some Applications

Elisabeth Rozin

The "flavor principle" provides a culinary theme that is varied by the addition of other ingredients, by the use of different proportions, and by different cooking techniques. The flavor principle idea is obviously a simplification of sorts, designed to abstract what is absolutely fundamental about a cuisine and, thus, to serve as a guide in cooking. What follows is a list—far from encyclopedic—of some flavor principles and a selection of some recipes that exemplify them.

Flavor Principles

1. Soy sauce—rice wine—gingerroot (China)
   a. + miso and/or garlic and/or sesame (Peking, China)
   b. + sweet—sour—hot (Szechuan, China)
   c. + black bean—garlic (Canton, China)
2. Soy sauce—sake—sugar (Japan)
3. Soy sauce—brown sugar—sesame—chili (Korea)
4. Soy sauce—brown sugar—peanut—chili (Indonesia)
5. Fish sauce—lemon (Vietnam)
6. Fish sauce—coconut (Laos)
7. Fish sauce—curry—chili (Thailand)
8. Onion—gingerroot—garlic—tumeric—chili (Burma)
9. Curry (India)
   a. Cumin—ginger—garlic + variations (Northern India)
   b. Mustard seed—coconut—tamarind—chili + variations (southern India)

10. Cinnamon—fruit—nut (Central Asia)
11. Lemon—parsley (Middle East)
12. Tomato—cinnamon (Middle East)
13. Tomato—peanut—chili (West Africa)
14. Garlic—cumin—mint (Northeast Africa)
15. Cumin—coriander—cinnamon—ginger + onion and/or tomato and/or fruit (Morocco)
16. Tomato—cinnamon (Greece)
17. Olive oil—lemon—oregano (Greece)
18. Olive oil—garlic—parsley and/or anchovy (southern Italy, southern France)
    a. + tomato
19. Olive oil—garlic—basil (Italy, France)
    a. + tomato
20. Olive oil—thyme—rosemary—marjoram—sage (Provence, France)
    a. + tomato
21. Olive oil—garlic—nut (Spain)
22. Olive oil—onion—pepper—tomato (Spain)
23. Onion—lard—paprika (Hungary)
24. Onion—chicken fat (Eastern European Jewish cuisine)
25. Sour cream—dill or paprika or allspice or caraway (Northern and Eastern Europe)
26. Wine—herb (France)
27. Butter and/or cream and/or cheese + wine and/or stock (France)
28. Apple—cider—calvados (Normandy, France)
29. Wine vinegar—garlic (northern Italy)
30. Tomato—chili (Mexico)
31. Lime—chili (Mexico)
32. Sour orange—garlic—achiote (Yucatán, Mexico)
33. Sweet—sour + variations (general)
34. Hot—sour (general)
35. Cultured milk—herb or spice (general)
36. Smoking (general)

Chicken Livers: Four Variations

Japanese Chicken Livers (soy sauce + sake—sugar). In this recipe chicken livers are simmered in a concentrated sauce and then marinated for several hours.

¾–1 lb. chicken livers, cut in half
¼ cup soy sauce
¼ cup sake

½ cup water
1 tablespoon sugar
1 clove garlic, finely minced
½ teaspoon finely minced gingerroot
¼ teaspoon crushed dried red peppers
3–4 scallions, finely chopped
1 × 8oz. can water chestnuts, drained and sliced
Sesame seeds (optional)

In a medium saucepan combine chicken livers with soy sauce, sake, water, sugar, garlic, gingerroot, red peppers, and scallions, and mix well. Bring to boil, then simmer over moderate heat, uncovered, for about 15 minutes. Cool, then cover and refrigerate several hours or overnight. Remove livers from marinade, slice, and serve on wooden picks with sliced water chestnuts. If desired, dip livers into sesame seeds. This dish may also be served hot in its sauce over plain rice.

Charcoal-Broiled Chicken Livers (lemon–oregano). Chicken livers are not ordinarily charcoal broiled, and they are not a common item in Greek cooking. Nonetheless, when marinated according to the Greek lemon–oregano principle, then skewered and charcoal broiled, they make a delicious hot hors d'oeuvre.

Juice of 1 lemon
2 tablespoons olive oil
1 tablespoon crumbled dried oregano
½ teaspoon salt
Dash freshly ground black pepper
10 chicken livers (approximately ½ lb.)

In glass or ceramic bowl combine lemon juice, olive oil, oregano, salt and pepper. Beat well with fork. Cut chicken livers in half and add to marinade, mixing well to insure that they are well coated. Marinate 2–3 hours. Thread chicken livers on skewers and broil over hot charcoal 7–8 minutes, turning once. Do not overcook. Serve hot on wooden picks.

Mousseline of Chicken Livers (wine–herb). Here is a classic example of the French wine–herb flavor principle interacting with the technique of deglazing to give this chicken-liver spread its characteristic taste.

¼ cup butter, plus 2 tablespoons butter, softened
2 scallions or 1 small white onion, minced
1 large clove garlic, finely minced
1 lb. chicken livers, cut in half

1 teaspoon salt
¼ teaspoon freshly ground black pepper
½ teaspoon allspice
1 tablespoon chopped parsley
¼ cup Madeira

In a large frying pan melt ¼ cup butter over moderate heat. Add scallions and garlic and sauté until just wilted. Turn heat up, add chicken livers and sauté, stirring, until chicken livers are just browned on both sides. Add salt, pepper, allspice, and parsley, and stir. Then add the Madeira. Bring to a simmer, scraping up all bits from the bottom of the pan.

Remove chicken livers from pan with slotted spoon, and set aside. Continue to cook sauce rapidly, until liquid is reduced by about half. Remove from heat and allow to cool slightly.

Purée livers and contents of frying pan in blender until smooth, then beat in 2 tablespoons softened butter. Pack into small bowl or crock and cover surface closely with plastic wrap. Chill thoroughly. Serve plain, with tiny sweet gherkins, or spread on crisp crackers or toast.

Chopped Chicken Liver, Jewish Style (chicken fat–onions).

¼ cup rendered chicken fat
2 tablespoons vegetable oil
4 large yellow onions, thinly sliced
1 lb. chicken livers
1 tablespoon salt (preferably coarse kosher salt)
½ teaspoon freshly ground black pepper
½ teaspoon sugar
6 hard-cooked eggs

In a large frying pan heat chicken fat and oil over moderate heat. Add onions and cook slowly, stirring occasionally, until onions are soft and a deep, dark brown (this may take 30–40 minutes). Remove onions from pan with slotted spoon and set aside.

Turn heat to moderately high. Add chicken livers and sauté in remaining fat until quite firm and well browned. Add salt, pepper, and sugar for the last few minutes of cooking. Remove from heat and cool slightly.

Grind onions, livers, and hard-cooked eggs in a meat-grinder, adding all scraped bits and remaining fat from pan. Mix thoroughly and taste for salt. If mixture is crumbly, add 1 tablespoon additional chicken fat and blend well. Chill and serve with crackers or as a sandwich spread with sliced cucumber and Bermuda onion.

Part II

Taste Cultures: Gustation in History

Preface

Tastes are by their very nature transient, and as food historian Jean-François Revel observes, the taste experiences of the past may be all but unimaginable. Who can but wonder what it was like to eat the foods of ancient peoples? Would we enjoy the same flavors that they describe as delectable, or would they be foreign to the point of unpalatable? What is more, traditions of eating tend to be oral and familial and to disappear with the passage of time. There are extant written records that supply a culinary history for some societies, but these tend to describe only the foods of those who occupy high social positions. While literacy and elevated social standing may be critical to development of what we now call an "haute cuisine," this is in fact but one aspect of culinary history. Equally important are the ordinary foods eaten at home, where dishes are developed in households and local communities. The two sources of cuisine should be understood together, Revel asserts, each a counterbalance and corrective to the other.

The difference between "high" and "low" cuisine is the theme of Jack Goody's encyclopedic study of the global history and practice of eating. In this selection, he focuses on cuisines in which sharp distinctions obtain between the food—and hence the taste experiences available—of the rich and of the poor, a distinction that he argues characterizes the classic cultures of antiquity such as those of China and India, and indeed most large-scale societies of the past. His survey describes eating practices from those societies, the Middle East, and pre-modern Europe. Social class is but one aspect of identity that food practices manifest, for we find that eating practices are also intimately linked to gender relations. This is a theme that will appear from time to time throughout this volume, for sexuality and taste are so closely tied that a study of taste and its pleasures is sometimes inseparable from ideas about indulgence (or abstinence) in sexual behavior.

Tastes are thus imbedded in social relations, a theme developed further by Pierre Bourdieu in his social critique of consumption practices in twentieth-century France. Bourdieu uses taste and food as a crucible for understanding preference in general, including tastes in fashion, art, and lifestyle. He relates consumption choices to the material conditions of existence of different social classes. The "taste of necessity" of the working classes emerges as a counterpoint to the "taste of luxury" (or "freedom") of the dominant classes, but the latter is no less conditioned by social pressures than the former. Of particular note is Bourdieu's insistence that tastes in food depend on the ideas people have of the body and the food it requires; this in turn produces a multiplicity of bodies along class lines as "culture" is "turned into nature."

With migration and displacement, eating traditions and taste communities change. Donna Gabaccia reviews the collision of culinary cultures that merged into early American cuisine. Native American, English, French, and Spanish eating traditions were mutually transformative, and in many regions they were further altered by the cooking and flavoring techniques of African slaves who managed the kitchens of large regions of the South of colonial and post-colonial America. Gabaccia's study illuminates another aspect of the links between food and social position, as she argues that, as far as eating is concerned, early American identity was rooted in regional dishes that were blends of the culinary cultures at their roots. Thus regional identities and taste preferences went hand in hand.

A small group of indigenous peoples of the Andes illuminate a specific and local manner in which categories of tastes are imbued with cultural significance. Mary Weismantel's study of a Quichua-speaking people of Zumbagua demonstrates how certain traditionally selected tastes—such as bitter, hot, sweet, strong—and practices of gift-giving related to foods, all possess enduring social meanings that are sustained even in the new contexts necessitated by a changing economy.

All of the entries in this section expand our understanding of how the basic morphology of the gustatory sense is shaped by history, social position, geography, and economy into traditions of preference—that is, into "tastes" in several senses of that term.

4

Retrieving Tastes

Two Sources of Cuisine

Jean-François Revel

Even more than the history of various foods, it is the history of *taste* that is the question here—in the primary meaning of the word or, rather, in both senses of the word. That is to say: What did a meal, a wine *taste like* in the third century before or after Christ? And *what sort of taste* did the guests have? What did they like, what was particularly sought after? What sort of wine was in one of the old bottles that Horace took out of his cellar on any and every occasion? For that matter, what were the Sabine wines like, of which he was not particularly fond? And what about the floods of ordinary wine that flowed into the cups of Agathon's guests at Plato's *Symposium?* To readers of the time, reconstructing the exact taste of these things in their minds presented no problem.

Gastronomical imagination, in fact, precedes experience itself, accompanies it, and in part substitutes for it. To speak today of being served a dozen oysters washed down with a Chablis or a Pouilly immediately evokes a very precise, characteristic marriage of tastes. But in a thousand years it will mean nothing to a reader who will doubtless have no notion as to what Chablis was, just as it will mean nothing to him that around the year 1900, oysters, above all the type known as *belons,* were traditionally served with Sauterne (a fact that is forgotten today, and would strike seafood lovers in the closing years of the twentieth century as monstrous). This future reader may have no way of knowing that Sauternes were sweet white wines and Chablis and Pouilly dry white wines. He would also have to know that "dry" in this context meant "not sweet" rather than "with a high alcohol content." We do not know what taste experience Horace is referring to when he writes, in an invitation to Maecenas, "you will drink bad Sabine wine," adding that he himself put it up and sealed it in "a clay amphora once filled with Greek wine." Why? What Greek wine? The poet then mentions several growths of wine: Cecubo, Cales, wine of Formies, hinting that he is too poor to offer them to his guests (*Odes* Bk I: 20). These names, for us, evoke little or nothing. Habit is everything, and what is habitual is never precisely defined for those to whom it is so familiar as to be self-explanatory, for those who take it completely for granted, so that it is almost impossible to reconstruct it once it is lost. Tourists consider it picturesque and amusing to drink wine with resin in Greece because this preparation is something they know about, but they would be horrified if they were served wine diluted with sea water. Yet this mixture was the general rule in certain regions of ancient Greece, just as wines were later almost universally mixed not only with pure water (a custom that was to persist down to the seventeenth century AD) but also with all sorts of liquids or solids (soluble or not) with a strong scent, a practice that would naturally scandalize a modern oenologist—except, once again, when such a combination resembles one of our own habits, such as the drinking of hot wine with cinnamon in France or sangria in Spain, or champagne with orange juice, and so on. To compound the difficulty of reconstructing what is remote from us, let us add that cuisine travels as badly in space as in time, and the same is true of information about cuisine: the Hungarian goulash to be found in Hungary is not a stew but a soup, the *paella valenciana* that is eaten in Valencia is based not on seafood but on rabbit, and so on...

"This influence of language on sensation," Bergson writes, "is more profound than is generally thought. Language not only makes us believe in the invariability of our sensations; it also sometimes deceives us as to the very nature of the sensation experienced. Thus when I eat a dish reputed to be exquisite, the name that it bears, freighted with the approbation given it, interposes itself between my sensation and my consciousness. I can persuade myself that the taste pleases me, whereas a slight effort of attention would prove the contrary to me" (Bergson 1888: Ch. II).

Bergson has chosen the instance where the "dish reputed to be exquisite" has an indifferent taste or no taste at all. In this case, for lack of anything better, it is the dish's "delicacy" and "lightness" that is praised...

But the difficulty when one explores the past (and even the present) lies in appreciating the difference between silent cuisine and cuisine that talks too much, between the cuisine that exists on the plate and the one that exists only in gastronomical chronicles. Or else, to state the matter in a different way, the difficulty lies in discovering, behind the verbal facade of fancy cuisines, the popular, anonymous, peasant or "bourgeois" cuisine, made up of tricks and little secrets that only evolve very slowly, in silence, and that no individual in particular has invented. It is above all this latter cuisine, the average cuisine, the gastronomical art of the "depths," that is responsible for there being countries where one "eats well" and others where one "eats badly." But by itself, cuisine that is merely practical, traditional family cooking does not suffice either. If it is not stimulated by the innovation, the reflection, and indeed the extravagance of a handful of artists, popular cuisine itself becomes atrophied, dull, and uninteresting. The gastronomical serial written by the centuries has as its "plot" the constant battle between the good amateur cook and the thinking chef, a lover's quarrel that, as in all good adventure novels, ends, after many a stormy scene, with a marriage...

Cuisine stems from two sources: a popular one and an erudite one, this latter necessarily being the appanage of the well-off classes of every era. In the course of history there has been a peasant (or seafarer's) cuisine and a court cuisine; a plebeian cuisine and a family cuisine prepared by the mother (or the humble family cook); and a cuisine of professionals that only chefs fanatically devoted to their art have the time and the knowledge to practice.

The first type of cuisine has the advantage of being linked to the soil, of being able to exploit the products of various regions and different seasons, in close accord with nature, of being based on age-old skills, transmitted unconsciously by way of imitation and habit, of applying methods of cooking patiently tested and associated with certain cooking utensils and recipients prescribed by a long tradition. It is this cuisine that can be said to be unexportable. The second cuisine, the erudite one, is based by contrast on invention, renewal, experimentation. From antiquity to our own day, in Europe and elsewhere, as we shall see, a number of such erudite gastronomic revolutions have taken place, the two most important of which, at least insofar as European cuisine is concerned, occurred at the beginning of the eighteenth century and at the beginning of the nineteenth. As we shall see, certain of these revolutions even represented an unwitting step backward: thus the alliance of sweet and salt, of meat and fruit (duck with peaches for instance), which today is regarded as an eccentric specialty of certain restaurants, was the rule in the Middle Ages and held sway down to the end of the seventeenth century: almost all recipes for meat up to that time contain sugar.[1] But if erudite cuisine for its part innovates, creates, imagines, it also sometimes risks falling into a sort of pointless complication, into a dangerous form of the Baroque, thus impelling amateurs to return periodically to the cuisine whose roots lie in the products of the land. I shall add that a chef who loses all contact with popular cuisine rarely succeeds in putting something really exquisite together. Furthermore, it is a striking fact that truly great erudite cuisine has arisen principally in places where a tasty and varied traditional cuisine already existed, serving it as a sort of basis. Let us point out, finally, that the formation of urban middle classes, in the eighteenth and above all the nineteenth century, brought "marriages" of the two cuisines, the popular and the erudite, the cuisine unconsciously transmitted and the cuisine deliberately created. The result was what is called "bourgeois" cuisine, which was codified in numerous treatises and which retains the heartiness and the savor of peasant cuisine while at the same time introducing into it the subtlety and the "distinction" of *haute gastronomie,* in sauces for instance.

If regional peasant cuisine has sturdy basic qualities that allow it to be compared to the draft horse or the plow horse, if *haute gastronomie* has the elegant virtues and the fragility of the thoroughbred, bourgeois cuisine is what breeders call a half-bred horse: it trots but it does not gallop. It nonetheless trots faster than its peasant mother, from which it has inherited staying power and resistance, and outlasts its galloping father the purebred, from which it has inherited finesse and the ability to sprint. What is more, bourgeois cuisine does not exclude invention, unlike strictly traditional cuisine which is transmitted with the invariability of a genotype. No "cordon bleu" hesitates to incorporate his own personal variations in a recipe, and all of us have seen family recipe books for bourgeois cuisine, stuffed full of yellowed handwritten pages that are precious witnesses to an oral teaching handed down by a forebear or to a little "extra secret" recently discovered.

The history of gastronomy is nothing more nor less than a succession of exchanges, conflicts, quarrels, and reconciliations between everyday cuisine and the high art of cuisine. Art is a personal creation, but this creation is impossible without a base in traditional craftsmanship.

An example will serve to demonstrate what I mean by collaboration between popular cuisine and erudite cuisine. In Tuscany there exists a certain peasant know-how with regard to the preparation of white beans (*fagioli*), which makes them particularly rich and tasty. The process consists of filling a bottle, or better still a flask from which the raffia wrappings have been removed, three-quarters full of beans, of covering the beans with water, and then hanging the flask by a string at a slight angle above a continuous slow fire of charcoal and warm ashes. After eight to ten hours or more of very slow evaporation and cooking, the beans, though still whole, are tender enough to melt in one's mouth and can be eaten either *all'uccelletto,* that is to say with a ragout sauce, or with olive oil and raw onions (which in my opinion sets them off better). A painting by Annibale Carracci, *Il Mangiafagioli (The Bean-Eater),* attests to how far back in time the fondness for this dish goes in Central Italy and in Tuscany.[2] This is a case of genuine popular cuisine, in which intelligence and experience find the best possible preparation for a foodstuff, which costs nothing outside of the basic ingredient. How could *haute cuisine* be grafted onto this gift from peasant tradition? By incorporating beans cooked in a flask within a master chef's recipe (I leave this task to the reader's imagination, since no such recipe exists in Tuscany).

Cuisine is a perfecting of nutrition. Gastronomy is a perfecting of cuisine itself. A chef who does not begin by cooking or seasoning the basic foodstuffs of cuisine, which for him should be the notes of a more complex symphony, at least as well as a peasant, is an impostor, as would be an orchestra leader who would endeavor to improve his art by gathering together a large number of musicians, each of whom played off-key individually. Such cooks ruin cuisine: they are the plague of modern gastronomy. I do not mean to say that culinary art is always the prolongation of popular cuisine, which is a refined way of preparing food but one that never aims at the unexpected and indeed steers clear of it. Often the reformers of gastronomy, on the contrary, must know how to react against family cuisine, which clings to its errors as to its qualities and can both drown in grease and boil to death things that ought to be grilled plain or barely poached. These remarks are intended to demonstrate, however, that great cuisine is not only the cuisine of the privileged. Rich people, the wealthy classes, are not necessarily those that eat the best. Since antiquity, a real connoisseur such as Horace has reacted by deliberately and judiciously embracing rusticity as an antidote to the pretentious mixtures of parvenu gastrophiles who, thanks to their heavy-handed combinations, worshiped their pride rather than their stomachs. It is scarcely my intention to contest the legitimacy of great art, but the sublime marriage of ingredients of an Antonin Carême is no more within the scope of the first kitchen bungler who comes along than the *terribilità* of Michelangelo is a model to assign to the first wielder of a hammer to happen by. There would be something immoral about treating the subject of cuisine as if money were all it takes to consume good food—it is among the poor peoples of the world that this author… has on occasion eaten exquisite dishes: the *barbacoa* of the Indians of Mexico, a young goat cooked slowly beneath warm earth, or *mole poblano* in the same country, or, yet again, *caponata* in Sicily.[3] But it is unfortunately true that even though a high standard of living is not sufficient in and of itself to call forth great culinary art, a gastronomic tradition nonetheless tends to suffer if poverty is too extreme and too prolonged. Sicily is a good example of this: a country where gastronomy flourished in the classic era of Greece (since in Athens itself cookbooks written by Sicilians were used, and Plato, in the *Gorgias,* goes so far as to have Socrates specifically cite a certain "Mithraicos, the author of the treatise on Sicilian cuisine"[4]), Sicily would appear to have had a great deal of difficulty preserving this culinary patrimony in the course of its long dark age. A tradition cannot be perpetuated unless it is applied daily, and it cannot be applied without a modicum of general material well-being. If Mexican *tacos* have a flavor and an aroma alongside which our general run of sandwiches, however numerous the layers, are mere blotting paper embellished with rubber, let us not underestimate the immensity of the cataclysm that engulfed pre-Columbian cuisines once the impoverishment of the Indians in the colonial era set in.

These are the two sources of gastronomic art, which is produced by their subtle and indispensable intermingling. Let us note, however, that the history of gastronomy is above all that of erudite gastronomy, for this is the tradition that has left the greatest number of written traces. The great cookbooks are obviously the fruit of study, of invention, or the reflection of a *change,* rather than the fruit of the everyday run of things. The meals which history has recorded are clearly memorable repasts, princely wedding banquets, the menus served on festive occasions. This is a drawback when one is attempting to trace the history of societies and of their everyday life. It is not a drawback, however, when one is attempting to write the history of gastronomy as art, as it is in exceptional circumstances that the great masters had the freedom and the material means to give full play to their creative imagination.

Notes

1. In Pierre de Lune's *Le Cuisinier* (*The Chef*) (1656) we find recipes mixing oranges with meat, preserved fruits and dates with salted fish; raspberry, melon, muscat grape soups…
2. The recipe obviously does not antedate the sixteenth century, for white beans were imported then from America.
3. *Mole* is turkey served with chocolate sauce. In its natural state chocolate is not sweet; it is pure cocoa flour. This is a pre-Columbian dish par excellence, since both turkey and chocolate originated in the New World and were unknown in Europe before Columbus.
4. *Gorgias* 518B. There is also mention in the *Gorgias* of the existence of another gastronomical author, Archestratus of Gela, some of whose texts have come down to us.

References

Bergson, Henri. (1888), *Essai sur les Données Immédiates de la Conscience (Essay on the Immediate Data of Consciousness)*, Paris.

5

The High and the Low

Culinary Culture in Asia and Europe

Jack Goody

A salient feature of the culinary cultures of the major societies of Europe and Asia is their association with hierarchical man. The extreme form of this differentiation is found in the allocation of specific foods to specific roles, offices or classes, swans to royalty in England, honey wine to the nobility of Ethiopia. But there were more complex, more subtle forms of differentiation than these, and to try and distinguish some of the main features of the hierarchical cuisine we should first turn to the Ancient Middle East, the cradle of Bronze Age 'civilization', where the advent of writing and the elaborateness of graphic and sculptural forms enable us to distinguish the outline of a cooking very different in its social implications from that which existed in Africa. Egypt was not the first culture to acquire writing; that honour appears to belong to another society based on irrigation and the plough, the Sumerians of Mesopotamia. But the evidence for early social life in Egypt is richer because of elaborate graphic testimony associated with the cult of the dead...

The Egyptian tombs demonstrate the arrival of the prerequisites of the *haute cuisine*. But it was in Greece and Rome, when logographic and syllabic forms of writing had given way to the easy art of the alphabet that here, as in so many spheres of human action, cooking was embodied in the written form so as to create a core of practices and recipes that could be subjected to further elaboration in the kitchens and libraries of the rich.[1] The claim to be the first work on cooking is disputed. There is a description of an Athenian banquet by the Scythian visitor Anacharsis in the fourth century BC (Barthélémy 1824). Later on, Petronius provides us with the well-known fictional, indeed satirical, account of Trimalchio's dinner. Here the elaboration of food took a whimsical form characteristic of much conspicuous consumption and included dressing up one meat to look like another, a culinary trick typical of banquet food...

However, the main sources on early cooking are Athenaeus and the much discussed cookbook by Apicius, which some have taken as a medieval forgery (Vehling 1936). The book by Apicius, unmentioned by the former writer, was possibly a trade manual that at first was only for the use of cooks. Or possibly a number of manuals, largely of Greek origin, may have been collected together under the name of a well-known gourmet in the third century AD. Whatever its origin, the book continued to be of great interest right down to Renaissance times. In Italy, the fourteenth and fifteenth centuries produced a dozen manuscripts. The book was no guide to ordinary eating but essentially a book of gastronomy, directed at the 'favoured few'. 'Apicius', Vehling remarks, 'cared nought for time or labor' (24).

The gastronomic pretensions of Rome led to a series of sumptuary laws through which an attempt was made to control the expenditure on food and to limit the extent of conspicuous consumption. While such legislation appears to have had little effect, it shows the constant strand of opposition to the *haute cuisine*, whether in moral or political terms, under the guise of puritanism or egalitarianism. For even if such laws are construed as attempts to preserve the structure of existing inequality, their very introduction implies a threat to the hierarchy. Indeed it is a resentment virtually inherent in the existence of a publicly differentiated cuisine...

This culinary differentiation of culture was not only a phenomenon of the classical world but of all the major societies of the Eurasian continent. For it is linked to a particular kind of hierarchy, with distinct styles of life, a hierarchy that is in turn based upon a certain type of agricultural system. The kind of differentiation we have seen in the Mediterranean world, together with the kind of opposition it engendered both at the conceptual and at the political level, are apparent in perhaps the most complex cuisine of all, the cuisine of China.

Here the differentiation in cooking took both private and public as well as regional and hierarchical forms. Many of the differences in this vast country were geographical. In the thirteenth century, at the Southern Sung capital of Hangchow, known to Marco Polo as Quinsai or Kinsai, the 'City of Heaven', without doubt 'the first and most splendid city in the world' (Polo 1958: 213), or in the twelfth century, at the Northern Sung capital of Kaifeng, restaurants served a variety of regional cooking, catering for refugees as well as for the grand families who had come there from distant parts of the kingdom. It was these regional restaurants at the capital that seem to have formed the basis of the various 'schools' into which the higher cuisine was divided. For this cuisine was not only a distinctive feature of the rich as against the poor. It reached a wider public through the restaurants in which even those of more modest means celebrated family festivals by means of an elaborate banquet.

Chinese cooking is often divided into four main regions, although in Sung times these seem to have been only three (Freeman 1977: 168). In northern cuisine, the dishes tended to be bland and to include much lamb and many preserved foods; some claim them to be 'sour'. Their basis was wheat and millet which were converted into noodles, buns, dumplings and cakes, often with a filling. Southern cooking, as found for example in the Yangtze delta, used pork and fish, and was based on rice; it was more highly seasoned and sometimes included frogs, a dish that the northerners found as incompatible as the English do in France. Szechwanese cooking was also based on rice but was hotter because of the use of chillis; it is often associated with tea and medicinal herbs since Szechwan was the great centre for their production. To these three has now been added Cantonese food, characterized by sweet and sour dishes.

Other authors claim that the traditional division is into five regional cuisines, which they see as an example of the general concern with fives. The northern cuisines are Honan and Shantung, the southern ones, Szechwan, Fukien and Canton. But some see even this categorization as much too limited, even if one uses Wei's criterion for a school, that its restaurants can 'offer... patrons on demand on any night more than one hundred different courses prepared from local products' (Anderson 1977: 354).[2] For Chang also points out (Anderson 1977: 14), while we hear of Ching *ts'ai* (Peking dishes) or Ch'uan (Szechwan) *ts'ai* as major sub-divisions of the Chinese cuisine, these styles are more a classification of restaurants than of local cooking; Peking *ts'ai* for example is the food served in restaurants *outside* Peking and combining many local specialities throughout North China.

However, regional differentiation was clearly not only a matter of restaurant styles. Among other things, it depended upon the staple foods, rice in the south, wheat and millet in the north. As in most cuisines outside Europe, meat played a relatively small part in the diet. But although influenced by Buddhism, the Chinese did not reject meat, as many Indian groups do, for spiritual reasons; there was just not much available.

Leaving aside animal protein, there is a line dividing eastern Asia into two groups, those who depend upon milk products (India, Tibet and the Central Asian nomads) and those who reject these foods, a category that included the Chinese, at least at certain periods. In India the main source of protein comes from pulses and from milk products. In China the absence of milk products was linked to the prevalence of the soya bean which provided the same kind of nutrition but more economically (Anderson 1977: 341).[3] The cultivation of wet rice achieved high yields in the south; but the Chinese also found in the soya bean a much more efficient way of producing protein than by herding livestock. The absence of livestock and the presence of the soya bean permitted high population densities in town and country.

The Chinese themselves have sometimes claimed that the rejection of milk products was a way of differentiating their ways from the border nomads, by which means they could remain independent in terms of food. The two notions are not incompatible. However, today, faced with that key product of early industrial cooking, namely sweetened condensed milk, the attitude is changing rapidly.

As well as regional variation, cooking differed according to the stratum to which a domestic group belonged. An extreme case was that of the exotic luxury of wine, which from the seventh to the tenth centuries was reserved for emperors. But the diversity extended much further. Marco Polo noted that the flesh of the bigger animals 'is eaten by the rich and the upper classes. The others, the lower orders, do not scruple to eat all sorts of unclean flesh.'[4] As Gernet comments: 'There were such extremes of wealth and poverty in the classes forming the population of Hangchow that a distinction must be made between the food eaten by the rich and the food eaten by the poor' (Gernet 1962: 136). Indeed, according to Chang (1977: 15), there was a wider disparity in China between rich and poor than in any other country of the world. Frugality among the peasants is a function of their socio-economic position. Among the rich, frugality is considered to be a virtue, but one that is observed intermittently, as periods of fast alternate with those of feast; at this level a frugal diet is associated more with fasting and voluntary denial than with famine and the ineluctable elements; abstinence was internalized as a way to grace rather than the result of external pressures that heralded starvation.

The importation of Indonesian and other spices during the T'ang period emphasized the differences in the cuisine of the rich and the poor (Schafer, 1977: 110). Rich households were generally addicted to foods from abroad; 'foreign food (to say nothing of foreign clothes, foreign music, and foreign dances) was rigorously required at tastefully prepared banquets and this necessarily included dishes cooked in the Indian style' (127). And it was aristocratic households of the same period that attempted to overcome seasonal deficiencies by the use of ice on a large scale. Nor was this differentiation limited to the secular sphere. Of the Sung period Freeman writes: 'Abbots lived in great luxury; temples gave rich and elaborate maigre feasts on Buddhist holidays' (1977: 164).

The hierarchy of the cuisine was a matter of public as well as private consumption. Publicly, food was provided by a great range of restaurants; these were officially classified into two groups, but in fact eating places and inns offered a variety of facilities appealing to all pockets...

In Hangchow the tea-houses frequented by the rich had a sumptuous decor, with displays of flowers, dwarf evergreens and works by celebrated painters and calligraphers. Others had singing-girls on the top floor and were avoided by the best people. Taverns varied in the drinks and menu they offered. Some served nothing but pies with the drinks, and the more plebeian of them were nothing but rough and ready shelters. 'Others again, where only the lowest class of people were to be met (porters, shop-hands, artisans, servants), did not serve anything along with the drinks except beancurd soup, oysters and mussels' (Gernet 1962: 50). Restaurants catered for the same range of society as the teashops and taverns, all being part of the urban scene that was 'entwined with the world of prostitutes' (Freeman 1977: 159). Every restaurant in the capital had a menu offering a considerable choice of dish. Other shops, such as those selling noodles, catered for a humbler clientele.[5] The range of cooked food was very broad, some even being manufactured in workshops which supplied the vendors and hawkers who flooded the streets of the larger cities.

The other institution providing food to the public was the inn, so widely used by travellers. These inns acted as a social centre for the local population, as in other regions of the world, playing an important part in the exchange of news and gossip, and providing a meeting-place where discussion could take place and even uprisings were planned (Spence 1977: 290).

In Ming China, the Ministry of Rites was responsible for both the feasts for the dead and the great banquets for the living; two characters with the same transliteration were used, even though one referred to 'the ways of the spirits' and the other to 'the ways of men', drawing a parallel between sacrifice and hospitality (Mote 1977: 218); the difference lay in the fact that food for the dead had to be unblemished. Offerings to the gods seem to have consisted of stewed meat, but they also included the flesh of wild animals (134). The animals for both were provided either by levies or from the imperial estates; they were transported to the capital by the fleet of canal barges organized by the eunuch bureaucrats. In such ceremonies, whether religious or secular, the emphasis was placed on traditional foods (Schafer 1977: 133), a mark of ceremonial conservatism.

One of the main reasons for the great banquets, then as now, was the entertainment of foreign visitors (133). As with other major feasts, it was customary for women to be excluded from these banquets. However the Empress ran a parallel dinner at the imperial court for the wives of ambassadors and other guests in the Palace of Female Tranquility.

In contrast, ordinary meals were eaten in the company of one's wife and other family members, in the homes of commoners as well as of the elite.[6] It is recorded that one particular clan did separate husbands and wives at meal times and on other family occasions; but while they were honoured for supposedly following the ways of antiquity, they were not emulated by others (Mote 1977: 254). Essentially similar patterns of familial eating seem to have been practised in medieval Europe, and while the same conjugality did not always exist in Indian homes, these societies still provide a general and valid contrast with Africa where men and women regularly eat in separate places, where there are sexual but few horizontal inhibitions on eating together. The structure of the table is linked to the structure of the marriage, which in turn correlates with the presence of dowry and the system of inheritance. Where women are endowed and ranked, they tend to eat with men of equal status, enjoying the same cuisine.

The differentiation of the cuisine is clearly expressed in the written works on Chinese cooking. During the T'ang period (618–907), and even before, a considerable number of books appeared, known as Food Canons, which constituted definitive texts on food. These were not cookbooks but rather guides to diet whose main intention was to instruct members of the elite about the correct preparation of balanced dishes. Influenced by the recommendations of learned pharmacologists, such as Meng Shen in the seventh century, the dishes were initially prepared for medical purposes, but many of them later came to be regarded as gourmet foods (Schafer 1977: 87)...

Whatever view one takes, it is clear that, by and large, the written expressions of Chinese cuisine represented the culinary culture of the upper classes, whether those expressions were literary or technical. One striking example of the former is the poem written by a poet of the third or second century BC, many centuries before Athenaeus, on the subject of his favourite dishes.

Where thirty cubits high at harvest-time
The corn is stacked;
Where pies are cooked of millet and bearded-maize
Guests watch the steaming bowls
And sniff the pungency of peppered herbs.
The cunning cook adds slices of bird-flesh,
Pigeon and yellow-heron and black-crane.
They taste the badger-stew.
O Soul come back to feed on foods you love!

Next are brought
Fresh turtle, and sweet chicken cooked in cheese
Pressed by the man of Ch'u.
And pickled sucking-pig
And flesh of whelps floating in liver-sauce
With salad of minced radishes in brine;
All served with that hot spice of southernwood
The land of Wu supplies.
O Soul come back to choose the meats you love!

Roasted daw, steamed widgeon and grilled quail –
On every fowl they fare.
Boiled perch and sparrow broth – in each preserved
The separate flavour that is most its own.
O Soul come back to where such dainties wait![7]

In contrast to such rapturous celebration of the rich and rare, here, as in the Ancient World, a parallel theme runs through the literature, one that emphasizes the need to look at cooking from a 'sociological' as well as from a 'cultural' point of view. For expression is also given to the resentment against the sumptuary expenditure of the rich or the reaction to the 'relative deprivation' of the poor, the point of departure depending upon one's social position. The feeling is most clearly expressed by the intellectuals, philosophers and sages whose role was to promote spiritual as against earthly values. One common complaint is that 'while the wine and the meat have spoiled behind the red doors [of rich households], on the road there are skeletons of those who died from exposure' (Tu Fu, AD 715–770, quoted by Chang, 1977: 15). Similar contrasts are drawn by Mencius in the fourth century BC: 'There's fat meat in your kitchen and there are well-fed horses in your stables, yet the people look hungry and in the outskirts of the city men drop dead from starvation' (Mencius 1970: 52). Mencius was certainly not backward in recognizing the value of 'government', rank and respect between the orders. But he was also critical of what he regarded as conspicuous consumption...

The abnegation of rich foods takes on a moral quality. In Mencius resentment of sumptuous living takes the more positive form of valuing asceticism for the good it does to the individual: 'There is nothing better for the nurturing of the heart than to reduce the number of one's desires.' This general attitude, which contrasts with the specific prohibitions an individual acquires through attachment to shrine or clan, because of fast or illness (which constitute the taboos of anthropological discourse), is characteristic of societies where differences in styles of life infuse the social scene. The hierarchy between ranks and classes takes a culinary form; the conflict and tension that this implies and generates are embodied in resentment against luxury that comes out of the writings of scholars of philosophical bent and in one form encourages renunciation of the 'high life' in favour of the 'good life'.

Similar themes are found in the culinary culture of that other great Oriental civilization, India. The link between food and sex is brought out in the whole ideology of caste. In a different way we find it too in Chinese culture, at least as brought out in that sixteenth-century novel, *The Golden Lotus,* which has been characterized as displaying a 'bi-sensual modality' (Mote 1977: 278). Of the Ch'ing period it has been said that 'the vocabularies of food and lust' overlapped and blended into a language of sensuality (Spence 1977: 278). But in India the association of cooking with sex and marriage is at once more intimate and more political, pervading as it does the whole sphere of hierarchy. In a general way... many anthropologists have drawn attention to the link. Lévi-Strauss, for example, has insisted upon the identification of copulation and eating: both involve 'une conjonction par complementarité', when two separate but complementary units unite. Looking at the question from a more concrete point of view, both activities involve a division of labour on a male–female basis, the one physiologically, the other socially, both of which are effectively universal in human societies. Since both activities centre upon the domestic domain, the same individuals are frequently involved, and the cooking of food by the woman is often seen as the reciprocal of the coital acts of the man. The word for 'eat' *(di,* LoDagaa, *dzi,* in Gonja) is frequently used for sex, and covers much of the semantic field of the word 'enjoy' in English. As we have remarked, this reciprocity is especially marked in many African societies; since marriage is polygynous, the woman has to safeguard her share of male attention, and the wife with whom the husband is sleeping is normally the one who provides him with food...

In India, the connection between the two is projected into the domains of politics, religion and indeed economics, being clearly brought out in the prohibitions on intermarriage and interdining, on commensality and *conubium*, that are such central features of the caste system. While we may follow Dumont and see the separation between castes as an aspect of 'interrelations and hierarchy' (1970: 130), as resulting from 'the organization of the whole' (131), the specific features of the relationship centre around prohibitions on interdining and intermarriage, that is, on separation rather than integration. Indeed it has been argued (Stevenson: 1954) that the importance attached to marriage and to food and drink in the separation of castes is linked to the fact that sex and eating represent especially serious forms of contact. Any external and internal pollution that results has to be removed by acts such as bathing. Contact of this kind with members of other groups has to be thoroughly cleansed both for individual and collective reasons. The separation of hierarchy has to be maintained.

India, then, presents the clearest example of the link of hierarchy with food and sex, both topics receiving prolonged attention in life and art. As in China, the earliest records show a widespread concern with the properties of food. There was a firm belief, writes Prakash, that a man is what he eats and that purity of thought depends on purity of food (1961: xx). Works like the *Bhagavadgita, Kamasutra, Smrtis and Puranas*, lay down what is to be eaten, at what time and by whom. Students, widows and ascetics are advised to avoid exciting foodstuffs just as they had to avoid sex. Moreover the caste system itself is partly defined in terms of the type of food a man is allowed to eat. To move upwards meant changing one's diet, usually by becoming more vegetarian.[8] In addition there was a straightforward distinction in economic terms: 'the mass of the people lived on simple and nourishing food. The rich however enjoyed dainty dishes' (Prakash 1961: xxiii)...

The epics show that these differences in distribution were accompanied by the growth of an *haute cuisine,* with its expert cooks, waiter service and the preparation of special dishes. At the same time there is an elaboration of the rules of etiquette and hospitality. According to Manu, a person who cooks for himself is a sinner (Prakash 1961: 100, 120). In towns and villages a man was employed to lay out special food for the gods as well as for the poor. Meals for the rich were very different; the order of courses was formally laid down and it became the practice to listen to music while eating dinner. At this time, according to Prakash, we have a society divided into three broad culinary strata: 'the rich enjoyed many meat preparations and dainties. The food of the middle classes generally consisted of milk and articles cooked in clarified butter while the poor were satisfied with food articles cooked in oil (130–1). The art of cooking was further developed because of the keen interest taken by royal princes, especially in the great feasts produced at marriages and as offerings to the gods.

Since cooking involves contact, which creates pollution depending on the position in the hierarchy, individuals are prohibited from eating food prepared by the lower castes. Hence a banquet had to be prepared by the ritually highest caste of Brahmans whose cooking can pollute no one. But while cooked food enacted hierarchy, raw food was liberated from such constraints and represented the 'food of gifts'.

The concern with food took two other somewhat contradictory directions but similar to those we noted in China. Positively this interest led to the elaboration of cuisine and categories in a body of written works; negatively the rejection of food was seen as a way to health and holiness. The literary works are largely medical compositions which attempted to incorporate edibles into classificatory schemes for remedial purposes; as in medieval England, recipe and prescription were virtually one and the same. In the Sunga period, around the beginning of the Christian era, medical works indicate that Indians used more than forty varieties of rice, sixty varieties of fruits and more than 120 vegetables. 'Treating the subject scientifically', writes Prakash, 'they give a list of food articles which suit people residing in different regions, as also the articles which one should consume in a particular season' (1961: 244). Regional dishes were partly incorporated in a national cuisine. At the same time increased trade brought in foreign foods and new recipes, which, like the national cuisine, was food for the rich rather than the poor.

The other side of the hierarchical cuisine was the extended notion of the fast, the rejection of food for religious, medical or moral reasons. The denial of food to the body, whether some or all foods, was partly associated with the rejection of violence, with avoiding the killing of animals and the culling of plants. But vegetarianism is only one element. Abstinence and prohibition are widely recognized as ways of attaining grace in hierarchical societies such as China and India. The idea is clearly expressed in a verse in the *Manusmrti:* 'There is no harm in eating meat or drinking intoxicating liquors as it is the natural craving of man but abstaining from them is meritorious'. The great Indian religions, Buddhism, Jainism and Brahmanism, all developed this ethical injunction into a way of life, and total abstention from meat was considered meritorious. Blood sacrifices were now seen as an inappropriate means for communicating with the gods. Vegetables and milk replaced meat and liquor, at least in those upper castes with a specifically religious orientation. Indians generally recognized abstemiousness as, in Gandhi's words, 'a great aid to the evolution of the spirit'. Such a philosophy of rejection could develop only within the context of hierarchical society with its stratified cuisine, since abstention only exists in the wider context of indulgence…

The cuisine of the Middle East derives from that of Mesopotamia, of Assyria and later from that of the Persian Empire, dating from 550 BC, the earliest empire to envelop the whole region. Macedonian Greeks, Romans and Parthians struggled for dominance in the area, and during the period of the Sassanid Empire of Persia, from the third to the seventh centuries AD, the culture of food saw major developments. In the latter part of this period, the empire expanded and the extravagance of the court reflected this imperial grandeur. Meat was marinated in yoghurt flavoured with spices, many different kinds of almond pastry were prepared, jams were made with quinces and other fruits, dates stuffed with almonds and walnuts. Regional dishes were gathered from all parts of the empire, and there was a distinct cuisine for the rich. One recipe, for example, was even known as the 'king's dish' and consisted of hot and cold meats, rice jelly, stuffed vine leaves, marinated chicken and a sweet date purée.[9] Such *haute cuisine* contrasted sharply with the food of the rural areas…

This luxury survived… at least until the thirteenth century. At the same time dishes from all over the Muslim world were incorporated in their cuisine. 'All the best dishes were put into the common culinary pool, and trade between the countries of the Arab Empire made it possible for ingredients grown in one country to become available in others' (Roden 1968: 24). Later on, in the seventeenth century, the capital of Islam shifted to Istanbul, the Ottoman capital, which became the home of Middle Eastern cuisine, after a period in medieval times when Egyptian cooking had enjoyed the highest reputation (Ahsan 1979: 155). Meat was a staple mainly of the affluent, especially mutton and chicken, beef being regarded as inferior, while the poor had to be content with fish (78). Foods of the rich were more spiced, their bread more refined, being made of white wheat flour rather than of millet or rice. A great variety of breads were made, some to be eaten with special dishes, for bread was one of the basic foods. Rice was less important than at a later period and milk less important than in earlier Bedouin times. But many species of vegetable and fruit were used, especially by the rich. Some of the fruit was made into the innumerable sweet dishes (*halwa*) of the well-to-do, using honey as well as sugar cane from India. Some was made into the non-alcoholic drinks provided for convivial parties and sold in the market, though the rich avoided those favoured by the poor, especially if they were blackish in colour. Yet more was preserved by drying in the sun or by crystallization in honey or sugar, a technique learned from Rome. Meat, fish and vegetables were preserved not only by drying but also by using salt, vinegar and other condiments. Ice imported from the mountains was extensively used by the rich for preservation as well as for cooling various drinks.

Such a development of the simple repertoire of Arab cooking clearly entailed differentiation into a 'court' and 'peasant' cuisine, the former accompanied by an elaboration of table manners, and the whole crystallized around the formal divisions of rank, giving rise to the kind of distinct sub-cultures illustrated in *Le Livre des Avares* of al Jahiz, who was born in Basra in the eighth century. The relative homogeneity of the nomadic desert Bedouin has been replaced by the sumptuary differentiation of their cousins settled in the cities.

> You chide me with fastening a large basket holding costly fruits and choice dates (to protect them from covetousness), against a gluttonous slave, a greedy child, an abject slave and a stupid wife. But as far as I know, in the rules of politeness, in the organization of command, in the customs of chiefs and in the conduct of lords as far as precious foods, rare drinks, costly clothing and of mounts of noble race, and fine and delicate objects of all kinds are concerned there is no question of treating in the same way the chief and his subordinate, the master and his slave; neither are they placed in the same position in an assembly, they are not addressed in the same way nor are they received with the same marks of politeness.[10]

The contrast was not only with the Bedouin past (and present) of Arab society. The cuisine of the rich contrasted with that of the urban poor and of the peasant farmers. More significantly, from one standpoint it contrasted with the voluntary poverty of the sufis and ascetics for whom fasting was part of the way of life. Some sufis ate no meat; others gave up bread (Ahsan 1979: 135). As in India and in Europe, the absolute rejection of certain foods and the temporary rejection of all, was one of the paths to holiness and grace...

Finally I turn to Western Europe, and specifically to Britain. It has been suggested by Braudel that between 1350 and 1550 the diet of the European peasant may not have been too different from that of the nobility (1973: 128), that the stress on their difference may have been more literary than factual. If so, the period was exceptional and would run counter to the general hypothesis. But in any case one cannot dismiss the court feasts simply as 'the luxury of greed' (127) since it was the ability to indulge this greed at such a luxurious level, in so ostentatious a way, that marked the rich from the poor. It is often true that in the course of this conspicuous consumption 'quantity prevailed over quality', at least as compared with later times. Braudel goes on to make the wider claim that there was 'no sophisticated cooking in Europe before the fifteenth century' (127). Indeed, he sees 'elaborate cooking' as virtually confined to the Chinese from the fifth century, to the Muslims in the eleventh and twelfth, and in the West only to the Italian achievement which was followed from the sixteenth century onwards by France, 'the place where the presentation and the ceremonial of those profane festivals of gourmandising and *bon ton* were perfected' (125). While one can certainly argue, as Freeman does for China, that sophisticated cuisines of a particular type only developed in these few societies, there is surely an important and wider sense in which all the major Eurasian societies developed a sumptuary cuisine, a hierarchical cooking, though it may not have been a 'sophisticated' one. In fourteenth-century England, Geoffrey Chaucer himself describes internal differences in a way that gives 'gastronomic distinction to the moral qualities of the social classes' (Cosman 1976: 105), contrasting the well-provisioned order of the noble banquet with the crude guzzling of the middle class and the simple dignity of farmhouse fare. He presents us too with vivid portraits of the well-mannered Prioress, the careful Physician, the gourmand Franklin – offering a picture of medieval food-ways that is marked by hierarchical distinction and is most unlikely to be purely 'literary'.

Indeed, as Braudel notes, the period following the Black Death which he was discussing is hardly typical as far as the consumption of food is concerned. The underpopulated hectares of Western Europe allowed the rather profligate use of resources that a mass carnivorous diet requires; China and other regions of the Old World fed more people on much less land because they cultivated more intensely. And in Western Europe, which was highly carnivorous compared with other areas of the world, England was especially devoted to the eating of meat (Mead 1931: 79). Despite its relative abundance it was not equally available to all, either before the Black Death or after... From 1600 onwards meat was much more typical of rich than of poor diets... Though there were periods of plenty, there were shortages by season and by year; even during the normal year great feasts were held at the end of harvest, yet periodic famines could cause much hardship on top of a generally deficient diet...

An important element in differentiation, whether of authority or of cooking, is its tendency to breed the opposite. The tension which arises from marked differences of 'degree' and can take the more specific form of 'class conflict', the disorder in the 'society of orders', is related at one level to what Gluckman has analysed as the 'frailty of authority (1955). In one form or other this feature marks societies where a segment has acquired, on a relatively permanent basis, more than is allowed by 'natural justice' or 'reciprocity', concepts used so freely and so vaguely by social scientists but essential to the analysis of human action. Luxury is a focus for discontent, particularly in regimes where the ideology (or one among the ideologies) is egalitarian, where the premise of inequality ... is challenged by other assumptions about the distribution of resources. In the Christian Church, as in others, the divergence between the egalitarian ideology, born of such a challenge, and the hierarchical practices emerging in an established, property-holding corporation (though existing outside the organization as well as within) gave rise to critical attitudes that fuelled the newer movements for reform and reformation. The fact that the original ideological statement, whether in the New Testament or the *Ancren Riwle*, had been embodied in writing meant that it lived on in the present as a persistent reminder of the extent of man's failure to institute God's rule on earth, for such statements constituted a peculiar expression of the way that 'natural justice' was perceived at that time and for that group or organization.

This divergence in attitudes that lay at the heart of stratified societies is sometimes embodied in specific relationships. Certain roles, usually in the religious sphere, are restricted to those who practise abstinence. In one sense such persons as the Hindu sanyasi, the Benedictine monk, the Muslim sufi, the Buddhist priest act for all, or for one side of us all. Another form taken by the ambivalence and contradictions embedded in the value systems of hierarchical societies is when some individuals, philosophers or priests, explicitly condemn the luxury of the *haute cuisine* as the work of the Devil, as a sin against God. In the last analysis the role of the holy man and the acts of the individual reformer can be seen as linked to the open resentment and covert tension that arises between groups in a hierarchical system. Indeed the opposed attitudes may be present not only as external but as internal contradictions; located in the one and the same individual, they give rise to ambivalence.

Notes

1. For an early recipe, see Goody 1977a: 139.
2. Quoting Richard Hughes, 'A toast to monkey head' in *Far Eastern Economic Review*, 29 April 1972: 27–8.
3. The Andersons also note that most Asians cannot digest raw milk except when they are children because the lactose enzyme stops being produced in the gut at about six years of age; hence those dependent upon dairy products treat the milk with bacteria such as *Lactobacillus* to break down the lactose. The technology was too closely identified with northern 'barbarians' for it to spread in China, although similar bacilli are used to make soy sauce and other ferments. Since soya beans are rather indigestible if they are only boiled, they have to be processed into bean curd and other products (Anderson 1977: 341).
4. Marco Polo, *The Travels*, trans. R. Latham (London, 1958: 215). In Arabia too there were 'men of wealth and consequence, who eat foods of better quality' (311). 'They eat all sorts of flesh, including that of dogs and other brute beasts and animals of every kind which Christians would not touch for anything in the world' (220).

5. The Chinese appear to have developed noodles (*mien*) during the Han period but only after the adoption of techniques for large-scale milling of flour from the West; wheat flour seems to have been made in the first century BC (Yü 1977: 81).

6. Eating together seems to be more a town than a village custom. The Hsus report that men and women sat separately although the wife of the most senior male sometimes ate at the men's table. In towns men and women might eat together.

7. Arthur Waley, *More Translations from the Chinese* (New York, 1919: 13–14). I owe this reference to J. Finkel, 'King Mutton, a curious Egyptian tale of the Mamluk period', *Zeitschruft für Semitistik* 8 (1932: 122–48).

8. 'The adoption of vegetarianism, teetotalism, and Sanskritization enables a low caste to rise in status in course of time.' (Srinivas 1952: 226).

9. See Claudia Roden, *A Book of Middle Eastern Food* (London, 1968), and A. Christensen, *L'Iran sous les Sassanides* (Copenhagan, 1936: 447–79), where he gives details of the 'king's dish', the 'Khorassanian dish' and the 'Greek dish', derived from Ta'alibi, *Histoire des Rois de Perse*, trans. H. Kotenberg (Paris, 1900).

10. *Les Livres des Avares de Jahiz*, trans. C. Pellat (Paris, 1951: 15).

References

Ahsan, M. M. (1979), *Social Life under the Abbasids*, London.

Anderson, E. N. and M. L. (1977), 'Modern China, South', in Chang, *Food in Chinese Culture*, New Haven.

Barthélémy, J. J. (1824), *Voyage du Jeune Anacharsis en Grèce vers le Milieu du Quatrième Siècle avant l'Ere Vulgaire*, Paris.

Braudel, F. (1973), *Capitalism and Material Life, 1400–1800*, London.

Chang, K.C. (ed.) (1977), *Food in Chinese Culture: Anthropological and Historical Perspectives*, New Haven.

Cosman, M. P. (1976), *Fabulous Feasts: Medieval Cookery and Ceremony*, New York.

Christensen, A. (1936), *L'Iran sous les Sassanides*, Copenhagen.

Dumont, L. (1970), *Homo Hierarchicus: the Caste System and its Implications*, London.

Freeman, M. (1977), 'Sung' in Chang, *Food in Chinese Culture*, New Haven.

Gernet, J. (1962), *Daily Life in China on the Eve of the Mongol Invasion, 1250–1276*, London.

Gluckman, M. (1955), *Custom and Conflict in Africa*, Oxford.

Goody, J. (1972), *The Myth of the Bagre*, Oxford.

——. (1977), *The Domestication of the Savage Mind*, Cambridge.

al-Jahiz. (1951), *Le Livre des Avares de Jahiz*, trans. C. Pellat, Paris.

Mead, W. E. (1931), *The English Medieval Feast*, London.

Mote, F. W. (1977), 'Yuan and Ming' in Chang, *Food in Chinese Culture*, New Haven.

Polo, Marco (1958), *The Travels*, trans. R. Latham, London.

Prakash, O. (1961), *Food and Drinks in Ancient India*, Delhi.

Roden, C. (1968), *A Book of Middle Eastern Food*, London.

Schafer, E. F. (1977), 'T'ang' in Chang, *Food in Chinese Culture*, New Haven.

Spence, J. (1977), 'Ch'ing' in Chang, *Food in Chinese Culture*, New Haven.

Srivinas, M. N. (1952), *Religion and Society among the Coorgs of South India*, Oxford.

Stevenson, H. N. C. (1954), 'Status elevation in the Hindu caste system,' *Journal of the Royal Anthropological Institute*, 84: 45–64.

Stouff, L. (1970), *Ravitaillement et Alimentation en Provence aux XIVe et XVe Siècles*, Paris.

Vehling, J. D. (trans.) (1936/1970), *Apicius: Cooking and Dining in Imperial Rome*, New York.

Waley, A. (1919), *More Translations from the Chinese*, New York.

Yü, Y. (1977), 'Han', in Chang, *Food in Chinese Culture*, New Haven.

6

Taste of Luxury, Taste of Necessity

Pierre Bourdieu

There is an economy of cultural goods, but it has a specific logic. Sociology endeavours to establish the conditions in which the consumers of cultural goods, and their taste for them, are produced, and at the same time to describe the different ways of appropriating such of these objects as are regarded at a particular moment as works of art, and the social conditions of the constitution of the mode of appropriation that is considered legitimate. But one cannot fully understand cultural practices unless 'culture', in the restricted, normative sense of ordinary usage, is brought back into 'culture' in the anthropological sense, and the elaborated taste for the most refined objects is reconnected with the elementary taste for the flavours of food...

In cultural consumption, the main opposition, by overall capital value, is between the practices designated by their rarity as distinguished, those of the fractions richest in both economic and cultural capital, and the practices socially identified as vulgar because they are both easy and common, those of the fractions poorest in both these respects. In the intermediate position are the practices which are perceived as pretentious, because of the manifest discrepancy between ambition and possibilities. In opposition to the dominated condition, characterized, from the point of view of the dominant, by the combination of forced poverty and unjustified laxity, the dominant aesthetic – of which the work of art and the aesthetic disposition are the most complete embodiments – proposes the combination of ease and asceticism, i.e. self-imposed austerity, restraint, reserve, which are affirmed in that absolute manifestation of excellence, relaxation in tension.

This fundamental opposition is specified according to capital composition. Through the mediation of the means of appropriation available to them, exclusively or principally cultural on the one hand, mainly economic on the other, and the different forms of relation to works of art which result from them, the different fractions of the dominant class are oriented towards cultural practices so different in their style and object and sometimes so antagonistic (those of 'artists' and 'bourgeois')[1] that it is easy to forget that they are variants of the same fundamental relationship to necessity and to those who remain subject to it, and that each pursues the exclusive appropriation of legitimate cultural goods and the associated symbolic profits...

Even the field of primary tastes is organized according to the fundamental opposition, with the antithesis between quantity and quality, belly and palate, matter and manners, substance and form.

The fact that in the realm of food the main opposition broadly corresponds to differences in income has masked the secondary opposition which exists, both within the middle classes and within the dominant class, between the fractions richer in cultural capital and less rich in economic capital and those whose assets are structured in the opposite way. Observers tend to see a simple effect of income in the fact that, as one rises in the social hierarchy, the proportion of income spent on food diminishes, or that, within the food budget, the proportion spent on heavy, fatty, fattening foods, which are also cheap – pasta, potatoes, beans, bacon, pork – declines, as does that spent on wine, whereas an increasing proportion is spent on leaner, lighter (more digestible), non-fattening foods (beef, veal, mutton, lamb, and especially fresh fruit and vegetables). Because the real principle of preferences is taste, a virtue made of necessity, the theory which makes consumption a simple function of income has all the appearances to support it, since income plays an important part in determining distance from necessity. However, it cannot account for cases in which the same income is associated with totally different consumption patterns. Thus, foremen remain attached to 'popular' taste although they earn more than clerical and commercial employees, whose taste differs radically from that of manual workers and is closer to that of teachers.

...The true basis of the differences found in the area of consumption, and far beyond it, is the opposition between the tastes of luxury (or freedom) and the tastes of necessity. The former are the tastes of individuals who are the product of material conditions of existence defined by distance from necessity, by the freedoms or facilities stemming from possession of capital; the latter express, precisely in their adjustment, the necessities of which they are the product. Thus it is possible to deduce popular tastes for the foods that are simultaneously most 'filling' and most economical, from the necessity of reproducing labour power at the lowest cost, which is forced on the proletariat as its very definition. The idea of taste, typically bourgeois, since it presupposes absolute freedom of choice, is so closely associated with the idea of freedom that many people find it hard to grasp the paradoxes of the taste of necessity. Some simply sweep it aside, making practice a direct product of economic necessity (workers eat beans because they cannot afford anything else), failing to realize that necessity can only be fulfilled, most of the time, because the agents are inclined to fulfil it, because they have a taste for what they are anyway condemned to. Others turn it into a taste of freedom, forgetting the conditionings of which it is the product, and so reduce it to pathological or morbid preference for (basic) essentials, a sort of congenital coarseness, the pretext for a class racism which associates the populace with everything heavy, thick and fat. Taste is *amor fati*, the choice of destiny, but a forced choice, produced by conditions of existence which rule out all alternatives as mere daydreams and leave no choice but the taste for the necessary…

Eating habits, especially when represented solely by the produce consumed, cannot of course be considered independently of the whole life-style. The most obvious reason for this is that the taste for particular dishes (of which the statistical shopping-basket gives only the vaguest idea) is associated, through preparation and cooking, with a whole conception of the domestic economy and of the division of labour between the sexes. A taste for elaborate casserole dishes (*pot-au-feu, blanquette, daube*), which demand a big investment of time and interest, is linked to a traditional conception of woman's role. Thus there is a particularly strong opposition in this respect between the working classes and the dominated fractions of the dominant class, in which the women, whose labour has a high market value (and who, perhaps as a result, have a higher sense of their own value) tend to devote their spare time rather to childcare and the transmission of cultural capital, and to contest the traditional division of domestic labour. The aim of saving time and labour in preparation combines with the search for light, low-calorie products, and points towards grilled meat and fish, raw vegetables, frozen foods, yogurt and other milk products, all of which are diametrically opposed to popular dishes, the most typical of which is *pot-au-feu*, made with cheap meat that is boiled (as opposed to grilled or roasted), a method of cooking that chiefly demands time. It is no accident that this form of cooking symbolizes one state of female existence and of the sexual division of labour (a woman entirely devoted to housework is called 'pot-au-feu'), just as the slippers put on before dinner symbolize the complementary male role…

Tastes in food also depend on the idea each class has of the body and of the effects of food on the body, that is, on its strength, health and beauty; and on the categories it uses to evaluate these effects, some of which may be important for one class and ignored by another, and which the different classes may rank in very different ways. Thus, whereas the working classes are more attentive to the strength of the (male) body than its shape, and tend to go for products that are both cheap and nutritious, the professions prefer products that are tasty, health-giving, light and not fattening. Taste, a class culture turned into nature, that is, *embodied*, helps to shape the class body. It is an incorporated principle of classification which governs all forms of incorporation, choosing and modifying everything that the body ingests and digests and assimilates, physiologically and psychologically. It follows that the body is the most indisputable materialization of class taste, which it manifests in several ways. It does this first in the seemingly most natural features of the body, the dimensions (volume, height, weight) and shapes (round or square, stiff or supple, straight or curved) of its visible forms, which express in countless ways a whole relation to the body, i.e. a way of treating it, caring for it, feeding it, maintaining it, which reveals the deepest dispositions of the habitus.[2] It is in fact through preferences with regard to food which may be perpetuated beyond their social conditions of production (as, in other areas, an accent, a walk etc.), and also, of course, through the uses of the body in work and leisure which are bound up with them, that the class distribution of bodily properties is determined...

And the practical philosophy of the male body as a sort of power, big and strong, with enormous, imperative, brutal needs, which is asserted in every male posture, especially when eating, is also the principle of the division of foods between the sexes, a division which both sexes recognize in their practices and their language. It behoves a man to drink and eat more, and to eat and drink stronger things. Thus, men will have two rounds of aperitifs (more on special occasions), big ones in big glasses (the success of Ricard or Pernod is no doubt partly due to its being a drink both strong and copious – not a dainty 'thimbleful'), and they leave the titbits (savoury biscuits, peanuts) to the children and the women, who have a small measure (not enough to 'get tipsy') of homemade aperitif (for which they swap recipes). Similarly, among the hors d'oeuvres, the *charcuterie* is more for the men, and later the cheese, especially if it is strong, whereas the *crudités* (raw vegetables) are more for the women, like the salad; and these affinities are marked by taking a second helping or sharing what is left over. Meat, the nourishing food par excellence, strong and strong-making, giving vigour, blood, and health, is the dish for the men, who take a second helping, whereas the women are satisfied with a small portion. It is not that they are stinting themselves; they really don't want what others might need, especially the men, the natural meat-eaters, and they derive a sort of authority from what they do not see as a privation. Besides, they don't have a taste for men's food, which is reputed to be harmful when eaten to excess (for example, a surfeit of meat can 'turn the blood', overexcite, bring you out in spots etc.) and may even arouse a sort of disgust.

Strictly biological differences are underlined and symbolically accentuated by differences in bearing, differences in gesture, posture and behaviour which express a whole relationship to the social world. To these are added all the deliberate modifications of appearance, especially by use of the set of marks – cosmetic (hairstyle, make-up, beard, moustache, whiskers etc.) or vestimentary – which, because they depend on the economic and cultural means that can be invested in them, function as social markers deriving their meaning and value from their position in the system of distinctive signs which they constitute and which is itself homologous with the system of social positions. The sign-bearing, sign-wearing body is also a producer of signs which are physically marked by the relationship to the body... The signs constituting the perceived body, cultural products which differentiate groups by their degree of culture, that is, their distance from nature, seem grounded in nature. The legitimate use of the body is spontaneously perceived as an index of moral uprightness, so that its opposite, a 'natural' body, is seen as an index of *laissez-aller* ('letting oneself go'), a culpable surrender to facility.

Thus one can begin to map out a universe of class bodies, which (biological accidents apart) tends to reproduce in its specific logic the universe of the social structure. It is no accident that bodily properties are perceived through social systems of classification which are not independent of the distribution of these properties among the social classes. The prevailing taxonomies tend to rank and contrast the properties most frequent among the dominant (i.e. the rarest ones) and those most frequent among the dominated. The social representation of his own body which each agent has to reckon with, from the very beginning, in order to build up his subjective image of his body,... is thus obtained by applying a social system of classification based on the same principle as the social products to which it is applied. Thus, bodies would have every likelihood of receiving a value strictly corresponding to the positions of their owners in the distribution of the other fundamental properties – but for the fact that the logic of social heredity sometimes endows those least endowed in all other respects with the rarest bodily properties, such as beauty (sometimes 'fatally' attractive, because it threatens the other hierarchies) and, conversely, sometimes denies the 'high and mighty' the bodily attributes of their position, such as height or beauty.

It is clear that tastes in food cannot be considered in complete independence of the other dimensions of the relationship to the world, to others and to one's own body, through which the practical philosophy of each class is enacted. To demonstrate this, one would have to make a systematic comparison of the working-class and bourgeois ways of treating food, of serving, presenting and offering it, which are infinitely more revelatory than even the nature of the products involved (especially since most surveys of consumption ignore differences in quality). The analysis is a difficult one, because each lifestyle can only really be constructed in relation to the other, which is its objective and subjective negation, so that the meaning of behaviour is totally reversed depending on which point of view is adopted and on whether the common words which have to be used to name the conduct (e.g. 'manners') are invested with popular or bourgeois connotations...

In opposition to the free-and-easy working-class meal, the bourgeoisie is concerned to eat with all due form. Form is first of all a matter of rhythm, which implies expectations, pauses, restraints; waiting until the last person served has started to eat, taking modest helpings, not appearing over-eager. A strict sequence is observed and all coexistence of dishes which the sequence separates, fish and meat, cheese and dessert, is excluded: for example, before the dessert is served, everything left on the table, even the salt cellar, is removed, and the crumbs are swept up. This extension of rigorous rules into everyday life ... is the expression of a habitus of order, restraint and propriety which may not be abdicated. The relation to food – the primary need and pleasure – is only one dimension of the bourgeois relation to the social world. The opposition between the immediate and the deferred, the easy and the difficult, substance (or function) and form, which is exposed in a particularly striking fashion in bourgeois ways of eating, is the basis of all aestheticization of practice and every aesthetic. Through all the forms and formalisms imposed on the immediate appetite, what is demanded – and inculcated – is not only a disposition to discipline food consumption by a conventional structuring which is also a gentle, indirect, invisible censorship (quite different from enforced privations) and which is an element in an art of living (correct eating, for example, is a way of paying homage to one's hosts and to the mistress of the house, a tribute to her care and effort). It is also a whole relationship to animal nature, to primary needs and the populace who indulge them without restraint; it is a way of denying the meaning and primary function of consumption, which are essentially common, by making the meal a social ceremony, an affirmation of ethical tone and aesthetic refinement. The manner of presenting and consuming the food, the organization of the meal and setting of the places, strictly differentiated according to the sequence of dishes and arranged to please the eye, the presentation of the dishes, considered as much in terms of shape and colour (like works of art) as of their consumable substance, the etiquette governing posture and gesture, ways of serving oneself and others, of using the different utensils, the seating plan, strictly but discreetly hierarchical, the censorship of all bodily manifestations of the act or pleasure of eating (such as noise or haste), the very refinement of the things consumed, with quality more important than quantity – this whole commitment to stylization tends to shift the emphasis from substance and function to form and manner, and so to deny the crudely material reality of the act of eating and of the things consumed, or, which amounts to the same thing, the basely material vulgarity of those who indulge in the immediate satisfactions of food and drink.

Given the basic opposition between form and substance, one could regenerate each of the oppositions between the two antagonistic approaches to the treatment of food and the act of eating. In one case, food is claimed as a material reality, a nourishing substance which sustains the body and gives strength (hence the emphasis on heavy, fatty, strong foods, of which the paradigm is pork – fatty and salty – the antithesis of fish – light, lean and bland); in the other, the priority given to form (the shape of the body, for example) and social form, formality, puts the pursuit of strength and substance in the background and identifies true freedom with the elective asceticism of a self-imposed rule. And it could be shown that two antagonistic world views, two worlds, two representations of human excellence are contained in this matrix. Substance – or matter – is what is substantial, not only 'filling' but also real, as opposed to all appearances, all the fine words and empty gestures that 'butter no parsnips' and are, as the phrase goes, purely symbolic; reality, as against sham, imitation, window-dressing; the little eating-house with its marble-topped tables and paper napkins where you get an honest square meal and aren't 'paying for the wallpaper' as in fancy restaurants; being, as against seeming, nature and the natural, simplicity (pot-luck, 'take it as it comes', 'no standing on ceremony'), as against embarrassment, mincing and posturing, airs and graces, which are always suspected of being a substitute for substance, i.e. for sincerity, for feeling, for what is felt and proved in actions; it is the free-speech and language of the heart which make the true 'nice guy' blunt, straightforward, unbending, honest, genuine, 'straight down the line' and 'straight as a die', as opposed to everything that is pure form, done only for form's sake; it is freedom and the refusal of complications, as opposed to respect for all the forms and formalities spontaneously perceived as instruments of distinction and power. On these moralities, these world views, there is no neutral viewpoint; what for some is shameless and slovenly, for others is straightforward, unpretentious; familiarity is for some the most absolute form of recognition, the abdication of all distance, a trusting openness, a relation of equal to equal; for others, who shun familiarity, it is an unseemly liberty.

Notes

1. 'Bourgeois' is used here as shorthand for 'dominant fractions of the dominant class', and 'intellectual' or 'artist' functions in the same way for 'dominant fractions of the dominant class'.
2. Bourdieu uses 'habitus' to designate the network of practices and social frameworks that structure class position and lifestyle. – *Ed.*

7

Colonial Creoles

The Formation of Tastes in Early America

Donna R. Gabaccia

Beginning with the founding of St. Augustine [Florida], three expanding European empires—centered in France, England, and Spain—pushed their way from opposing directions into the territories already inhabited by approximately four million natives on the continent of North America. A fourth empire, the Dutch, took up temporary residence along the Hudson River. Dutch and English traders in turn transported ten million West Africans to the Americas over the next two hundred years, selling most of them into slavery. All of these groups had developed traditions of eating that marked them as culturally different, one from the other. All, on the other hand, had a recent history of selectively adapting new foods even before they confronted one another on North American soil.

As eaters deeply familiar with their natural environments, Native Americans enjoyed tremendous advantages in the culinary exchanges of the colonial period: centuries of adaptation to a variety of natural environments in North America had already shaped their foodways. If any group involved in the Columbian exchanges might have held firmly to tradition, it was Native Americans, with their vast knowledge of their own land and climate.

In most places in North America, native survival had depended on the successful cultivation of the "three sisters": corn, beans, and squashes. Of these, corn and squashes, including the pumpkin, seemed most distinctively American to newer arrivals, since they were unknown in Europe. Corn is a remarkable grain: it has been called "a machine of marvelous efficiency," so bountifully does the plant produce digestible calories from even small tracts of land, and under a wide range of ecological conditions (Weatherwax 1954: 84). From Mexico's central valley, corn had spread as far as the eastern woodlands but had faltered in the arid highlands of northern New Mexico and southern Colorado. Nor could corn prosper along the Pacific coast, on the dry prairies of the Great Plains, or in the coldest reaches of northern Minnesota or Maine. Instead of cultivating corn, nomadic natives in California gathered nuts and seeds; those on the Great Plains stalked herds of bison for their meat and hides; and tribes in Oregon and Maine made fish and shellfish a major part of their diet.

Still, corn was North America's staple grain, providing two-thirds of Native Americans' calories and influencing every dimension of their cultures. Among the Pueblos in their large New Mexico villages, corn consumption and spirituality were one, for the Pueblo dwellers believed that Mother Earth had literally made humans out of corn, with the help of the male forces of sun and rain. For the Iroquois in the Northeast, as well as the Pueblos, corn cultivation facilitated dense settlement—in large palisaded villages, surrounded by up to 100 acres of cornfields. Settled agriculture, corn cultivation, and dense settlements of related clans established an important precondition for the complex political confederations of the Iroquois, a form of political organization unimaginable among more nomadic hunters and gatherers without a corn diet.

Almost everywhere, it was women's responsibility to cultivate and process the corn. Natives in the East prepared the grain in an astonishing number of ways, from breadlike concoctions and popped corn, through puddings, dumplings, porridges, stews, and thin, gruel-like drinks. Still, nutritional variety was sought by hunting and gathering wild meats, fish, fowl, insects, seeds, berries, nuts, oils, roots, and vegetables. Animal foods, hunted by men—meat and, in some areas, fish—generally enjoyed higher status as foods, but women's gathering of vegetables was more important as a source of dietary variety. A list of the wild greens gathered by Iroquois women would include milkweed stems, immature flower clusters, marigold, waterleaf, yellow dock, pigweed, lambsquarters, mustard, purslane, dandelion, burdock, nettle, skunk cabbage, leek, wild garlic, sensitive fern, and others (Waugh 1991: 117). Adding fungus varieties, roots, and berries would easily expand the list to several hundred items, all eaten over the course of a year. Few modern eaters consume such a wide range of plants, fruits, and animals, even when provisioned by a vast international or multi-ethnic marketplace.

Natives' love of variety fostered definitions of "good taste" that differed somewhat by tribe and even more noticeably by region. In the northern forests, natives flavored their staples with the sap from maples and with animal fats and greases (especially bear grease). In New Mexico and Arizona, by contrast, natives developed a special taste for six colors of corn (yellow, white, blue, black, red, speckled), and four varieties (flint, dent, pop, sweet). Processing their corn in a multitude of ways—adding ash to make hominies, grinding different varieties to different consistencies of meal, eating corn green, fresh, parched, boiled, baked, steamed, and roasted—fundamentally altered the texture and taste of their staple grain.

Women in the Southwest worked with their metate (grinding stone) and comal (flat rock griddle) to produce a wide variety of flat corn crisps and softer breads later called tortillas and piki breads. Beans of various colors, shapes, and sizes supplemented corn as staple ingredients, as did local game—rabbits, boars, snakes, deer, antelope, beaver—and wild vegetables, fruits, and seeds. Fifty different varieties of wild seed grains, along with piñon nuts, sunflower seeds, curly dock, lambsquarters, wild mustard, purslane, wild celery, yucca fruits, prickly pear, juniper, and chokecherries, rounded out their diet. Natives also brewed an alcoholic drink similar to the agave-based pulque of Mexico…

Europeans and Africans faced much larger challenges than natives simply because they had to adapt to a new environment; their survival required it. Europeans were advantaged in many ways by their material and technical culture—guns, ships, animal husbandry, agriculture, salting and preserving, ironware. But the flora, fauna, and native diet of this new land were quite unlike their own. Since they were already accustomed to trading for some part of their food supply, simple common sense would predict that European eating would change more quickly, and more thoroughly, than that of North America's natives during the colonial era.

Still, in most cases Europeans settled in regions not totally unlike their home country, at least in terms of land and climate. The French and English had left behind a land of forests, with changing seasons and a climate that already supported permanent agriculture; the eastern seaboard of the New World was quite similar. The Spanish in the north of Mexico encountered a drier, warmer, treeless environment more familiar to them than it might have been to residents of northern France or southern England. While this rough "match" of settlers and environment was not enough to eliminate all the challenges of settlement, it did ease European adjustments, facilitating the introduction and cultivation of familiar foods.

Today we see sharp contrasts between the plain food of the English and the haute cuisine of the French. In fact, the humble English and French who settled the East Coast of North America brought with them remarkably similar experiences as agriculturalists and eaters from relatively cool, damp climates. Few Englishmen or Frenchmen knew much about hunting or fishing from their homelands—these were aristocratic privileges—but most were quite familiar with a mixed, and somewhat similar, agriculture based on grain, beans and peas, dairying, and animal husbandry. Settlers from the south of England and from France's Atlantic provinces both ate a largely wet diet of potages or soups, porridges of grain and beans, stews of meats and vegetables, and breads and dairy products, mainly butter and cheese (called "white meat" in England). The better-off and urban among them ate more bread, whiter bread, and more meat, cheese, and butter. With a few important exceptions, English and French traditions of mixed agriculture proved quite transplantable to the East Coast of North America, allowing European settlers to continue to eat many of their familiar foods…

The Spanish, too, quickly saw in the New World possible solutions to dietary change at home. Although altered somewhat by years of Arab occupation, the Spanish diet in the late Middle Ages still reflected the grain, oil, and wine culinary complex spread by the Romans throughout their Mediterranean empire centuries before. Wheat bread had been the staff of Spanish life for centuries, supplemented by oil, olives, wine, garbanzos, fish, and fowl. Arab conquest had added a taste for sugar, spices, and dried fruits. In the sixteenth century, as Spain sought land and power in the Americas, the rise of extensive sheep herding to supply Flanders' expanding textile industry sparked a precipitous decline in Spanish acreage devoted to wheat production. One consequence was that poorer Spaniards soon found themselves eating gruels and breads of lesser grains (notably barley) to survive. The Spanish would find the dry climate of their new homes suitable for herding and for the cultivation of grains, including wheat and barley, especially as they ventured northward from Mexico's central valley into what is now southern California and the Southwest of the United States.

Far to the south of these European settlers, the Africans who would be snatched away to work on the plantations of the English colonies had already adapted their eating to New World crops before they left home. By 1700 West Africans regularly ate and cultivated corn, cassava, peppers, sweet potatoes, pineapples, and peanuts from the Americas as well as rice and coconuts from Asia. These relatively new imports supplemented native staples like millet, beans, watermelons, palm oil, and yams. Provisioners of slave ships in Africa often loaded foods of Central and South American origin to feed slaves en route, thus facilitating their transplantation to North America's warm southeastern colonies. Africans rarely enjoyed much control over their destinations in the Americas. But Europeans enslaved them in part because they believed Africans adjusted with greater ease and could perform more work in warm climates. Thus, like the English, French, and Spanish, African traditions of agriculture and their foodways prepared them relatively well for provisioning themselves (and their owners) in the tropical and subtropical regions of the New World…

Africans too left their mark on regional American eating. Indeed, their presence forged a culinary dividing line between the coastal regions of the Carolinas and Georgia (where they settled among English, Caribbean, and French Huguenot planters) and the mountainous regions of these colonies, where native American foodways blended with frontier Scottish–Irish customs. Despite their low social status, Africans were perhaps the main shapers of eating customs in colonial areas where slavery flourished. This was especially clear in the lowland regions of the Carolinas and Georgia, where Africans often outnumbered whites. Not only did they adapt more easily to the semitropical climate, but they also possessed expertise for cultivating and cooking what would become the most important commercial crop of the region, rice. They were without doubt the most important cooks in a society where the wealthiest whites avoided physical labor.

Historians have established through careful research that a significant proportion of the slaves of the Carolina Low Country came from the small but important rice-cultivating districts in western Africa. Some evidence even suggests that planters consciously imported their slaves from this region once rice cultivation became successful. African techniques of sowing, flailing, and storing rice persisted into the nineteenth century. African cooks also developed the "rice kitchen" of the Georgia and Carolina coasts. Here, rice appeared on the planters' table daily, prepared by black hands. Humbler eaters, notably African and African-American slaves, came to enjoy hoppin' john—a blend of cowpeas or beans and rice similar to dishes found elsewhere in the African Caribbean.

English settlers and their descendants liked to believe that Europeans had brought "Carolina gold" rice from Madagascar, and then learned rice cultivation from the Chinese… It is possible that Europeans invented the rice bread popular in the region, which was made two ways: with rice flour, and with whole rice grains incorporated into a wheaten loaf. Cooked by Africans, the Carolina "pilau" and the method of its preparation (which originated in India, not China) more likely first became popular among the French Huguenots of the region. Planters of English descent intermarried with the Huguenots, and… soon enjoyed pilau, daubes, and ragouts.

The eating habits of this colonial elite—like that of Virginia's planters—struck visitors as far more concerned with refinement and hedonistic enjoyment than were New England's prosperous Puritan merchants or the hearty but stolid *bürgerliche* Germans and Dutch of New York and Pennsylvania. Many have attributed this to the French presence in the area. Early visitors rarely mentioned the possibility that African women, who actually did almost all the cooking in elite families, shaped the eating habits of Charleston's and Savannah's wealthy Europeans. This blind spot in descriptions of the elite diet of the Southeast has persisted well into the twentieth century.

Ironically, perhaps, slaves and the European captains and provisioners of the ships that transported them had introduced into the Carolinas and Georgia the central American crops of peppers and peanuts which had been cultivated successfully in western Africa after first being transplanted there. Slave ships brought with them the seeds of benne (sesame) and African yams and watermelons, all of which became well known to eaters, white and black, in the region. Some students of regional cooking do attribute the coastal taste for hot, peppery flavors in local seafood dishes to the hand of generations of African-American cooks—a plausible interpretation, since neither English nor French settlers knew this combination of tomato, onion, and hot red peppers from their homelands…

Comparing the eating habits of Americans in the Northeast, Southeast, and Southwest at the end of the colonial era, we see that in none of these cases did one culture's food habits completely conquer or obliterate another's.

Imperial conquest determined political and economic relationships far more thoroughly than they could shape the cultural dynamics of New World eating. Three centuries of food exchanges occasionally obscured the ethnic origins of some favorites like brown bread or hoppin' john. More often, however, the mixed cultural origins of multi-ethnic blends remained visible—as in the rye 'n' injun bread of New England or the flour tortillas of New Mexico.

With the possible exception of the ubiquitous popularity of corn and beans in all regions and among all groups, the only American eating habits of the colonial era were regional ones. No single American cuisine emerged from these exchanges. At the same time, no group's foodways survived the era completely unchanged. An individual did not have to abandon a connection to a tribal, Spanish, or English past in order to become a Southwesterner or a New Englander, at least not in culinary terms: multi-ethnic blends and regional specialties were synonymous. The only way to become an American, at least as an eater, was to eat creole—the multi-ethnic cuisine of a particular region.

The relationship of region and ethnicity in American eating was thus quite complex. Eating chicken did not transform Cherokees automatically into Englishmen, any more than eating corn made Englishmen into Narragansetts. The Spanish-speaking settlers of New Mexico adopted the corn of the Pueblos without adopting with it native beliefs about the creation of humans from masa dough; they remained Christians even though they ate corn. Similarly, Europeans learned to cultivate corn without—as natives did—either assigning the task to the women of their communities or adopting the communal fields of the Iroquois village. And Cherokees drank European alcohol without opening taverns or aping many other European drinking traditions. Borrowing and commercial exchange alike stripped foods from the myriad associations that tied them in unique fashion to their cultures of origin. Similarly, the adoption of pork, corn, rum, or ash leavening only gradually forged new cultural associations among the people who learned to eat new foods together with their family and friends. Aside from the meal memorialized in Thanksgiving lore, the usual group of people who ate together in the colonial world did not include members of the group from whom corn and pumpkin originated.

It is useful to consider also the new associations that emerged around foods newly adopted from other peoples. The Cherokees did not adopt pork in order to become English, nor drink rum because they wanted closer ties to them. More often, drinking rum or eating corn reflected rather than motivated already-existing connections among groups. Still, the pueblo dwellers continued to eat pork, and the English settlers continued to eat corn because these new foods tasted good and complemented traditional tastes. Food was not so much a common ground on which people declared themselves alike; rather, it provided a visceral record of a shared history of meeting and interaction across cultural and social boundaries. Because the new foods people incorporated into their everyday meals, family rituals, and religious practices were a source of pleasure and variety, neither Europeans, Africans, nor natives seemed inclined to deny or to reject foods of foreign origin once they had adopted them. While we know the colonial era was one of sharp, and often violent, interethnic conflict and warfare, this history did not adhere to the symbolism of food and eating.

I do not mean to suggest that shared foods and everyday exchanges could eliminate the cultural, social, and economic differences between African slave and Charlestonian Huguenot slaveowner, or between Spanish missionary and Pueblo native. Yet all these groups by the end of the colonial era shared eating habits that were characteristic of their home region, and each seemed quite American in having departed substantially from the eating habits of their ancestors. At least in the world of eating and food, region more than ethnicity defined American identities at the end of the colonial era, and pleasure more than pain marked the interactions between the participants in the colonial food exchanges.

As Americans entered their own era of independence and nationalism, they carried with them eating habits and identities that incorporated in pleasurable ways a long history of multi-ethnic interaction and a strong set of ties to American, rather than European or African, home places. The identities, and the eating habits, of Americans in this era little resemble those of the modem world: no colonial-era American of any cultural background, north, south, or west, ate as any American does today. To understand what happened to the regional creoles of the colonial era, and to trace their further evolution, one must understand the expansion and consolidation of the United States as a nation, the gradual formation of a national food marketplace, and the transportation and corporate revolutions of the nineteenth century, as well as the new migrations that changed the demographic face of much of the new nation.

References

Waugh, F.W. (1991), *Iroquois Foods and Food Preparations*, Ohsweken, Ontario: Iroqrafts.

Weatherwax, Paul (1954), *Indian Corn in Old America*, New York: Macmillan.

7a
Hoppin' John

Hoppin' John is the name of a dish of the southern United States that probably originated in West Africa and was spread across the Atlantic with the slave trade. There are many varieties of this rice and bean dish; here is one.

Take equal amounts of black-eyed peas and rice. Soak the dried peas in water overnight. In a deep skillet fry up a 1 lb. of bacon or salt pork and skim off the fat. Chop the meat into bite-sized pieces, add a chopped onion and some herbs and stir. Add the peas and pour in about two quarts of water and boil until the peas are tender. Then add the rice and let it all boil until the rice is done. Season with pepper and salt.

8

Tasty Meals and Bitter Gifts

M. J. Weismantel

The Quichua-speaking inhabitants of Zumbagua, a high rural parish of the Ecuadorian Andes, use a variety of indigenous terms to talk about the foods they cook and eat. Through a close reading of the parish discourses involving three of these terms, *mishqui, jayaj,* and *wanlla,* I argue that while they appear to operate in a sphere of consumption divorced from that of work, the terms contain implicit meanings derived from systems of production and exchange. Further, the deployment of these terms, apparently a symbolic rather than an instrumental action, is in fact a strategy for negotiating crises and hazards that originate in the larger economic system outside the parish. One could interpret the current use of these words in Zumbagua as showing a reluctance to conform to changing economic realities. But according to my interpretation, rather than reflecting a symbolic refusal to adapt to practical circumstances, the Zumbaguans' use of these terms reveals an accurate assessment of their situation and constitutes a realistic response to it.

These three terms are quite different: the opposed pair *jayaj* and *mishqui* (strong/bitter/hot and sweet/tasty) refer to physical taste sensations, while *wanlla* is one of a set of words that categorizes foods as appropriate to specific social contexts. In both cases, however, these terms place foods in a cultural context that shapes how people know them, creating implicit connections between sensory experience, cultural knowledge, and the political and economic structures of social life. The initial referents of the words in turn evoke other, more complex meanings. In the case of *mishqui* and *jayaj,* careful analysis of their uses reveals that for Zumbaguan Quichua-speakers, sensations of sweetness, saltiness, and hotness are subtly related to issues of gender, of the social and productive roles of women and men. Words such as *wanlla,* more explicitly social in their signification, refer to the role foods play in marking and maintaining relationships between individuals and households...

About Zumbagua

Lying in a high valley of the western Cordillera of the Ecuadorian Andes, the parish of Zumbagua is a very high, cold place whose population is poorer and more Indian than are those of much of the Sierra.[1] Seen from outside, Zumbagua appears to be a traditional Indian peasant society, locked into a way of life centuries old. However, the people of Zumbagua are facing changes and conflicts that are both profound and uniquely contemporary...

From the 1600s until the mid-1960s Zumbagua was a hacienda run by a series of white, urban-based owners and managers, ecclesiastic, state, and private. Initially a tremendously lucrative property producing quantities of wool for the Latacunga *obrajes* (textile workshops), as centuries of heavy exploitation with no investment rolled by, the hacienda gradually sank into poverty and obscurity, which its peons inherited when the Agrarian Reform of 1965 made them its owners.

According to De Janvry (1981), in areas where the hacienda was previously the basic institution of agrarian tenure, a new dominant pattern of social relations has emerged, characterized by semiproletarianization. This term aptly describes the situation in which young men and women in Zumbagua find themselves, living suspended between the rural homestead and the urban workplace. Neither economy can fully support the household, and so women, children, and the old eke out a meager living on the farm, with their monetary needs being partially met by the husband' s wages, while he in turn is supported by both his wages and the farm.

The resulting dietary transformations in Zumbagua are unsurprising; trends include increasing poverty and reliance on purchased foods. The importance of manufactured items such as enriched flour and packaged noodles is rising and in some households has come to rival the role played by subsistence foods such as barley, potatoes, and fava beans. Mass-produced sugar and salt are replacing older forms; refined white sugar has become a food of some importance in the diet, and its significance is growing, Inadequate meals are "bolstered" by the addition of white sugar in poor households, while working men who cannot afford staple foods from the city bring home candies instead.

The expanding role of sugar in the diet highlights the fact that for impoverished rural families, the move away from farming is not always a sign of increasing prosperity. In the outlying rural areas of the parish, one finds that many of the families and individuals whose involvement in the cash economy is the heaviest and whose cultural traits are far less "Indian" than their fellows', are in some ways poorer than their neighbors.

Their comparative poverty clearly shows in the nutritional inadequacy of their diet. Orlove (1987: 482) suggests that for the Andean area as a whole, "replacing locally produced native foods with purchased Western-style foods [is] accompanied by a decline in nutritional status," as cheap processed foods are substituted for the grains and vegetables of the agrarian diet.

Within Zumbagua, there are alarming signs that the diet of the parish as a whole is worsening and that the inhabitants are increasingly impoverished. Foods such as maize and vegetables, which cannot be grown in the parish but which parish residents commonly used to acquire through barter or purchase, are out of most people's reach today. In addition, apparently as a result of decreasing soil quality due to erosion, many farmers find themselves unable to grow potatoes, one of the three major subsistence crops in the parish. The lack of potatoes in the diet is keenly felt; families who can afford to buy them do so, using funds they would once have used to buy fruits from the lowlands or maize from the valley lands, foods increasingly defined as exotic or luxury foods.

The primary staple food in the parish today is not potatoes but barley. In some households day follows day with nothing cooked and eaten in the kitchen except barley gruel. In fortunate households sugar or salt or a lump of fat may flavor the potage. However, I have frequently shared meals consisting solely of ground barley and water; as I shall discuss below, such meals are most frequently eaten in households where husbands are absent doing wage labor in the city.

Production and Consumption

These changes in consumption are obviously related to changes in the economy as a whole and especially to changes in the realm of production, as an overdetermined cycle of ecological, economic, and social decline continuously weakens the subsistence economy and as dependence upon wage labor through male temporary migration steadily increases. Although the relationship between these changes and the way people in Zumbagua cook and eat is clear, the actual process by which changes in production transform consumption is not.

Marx emphasized the dialectical relationship between production and consumption: "Production creates the material as outward object of consumption; consumption creates the want as the inward object, the purpose of production" (Marx 1973:93). Consumption is driven not only by material constraints, or what is possible, but also by the immaterial, culturally shaped definition of what is desirable.

What people eat represents the meeting-point between the desirable and the possible; as the latter changes, so must the former. In Zumbagua, for an older man who remembers other times, every month without a maize-based meal to break the monotony of barley is a month of lacking and hardship;

but for his grandchildren the same regimen represents a state of unsurprising normality. For them, dietary variation means occasional indulgences in hard candies and a shared cola, rather than eating meals that contain different kinds of agricultural products.

The cultural concepts ruling the making of meals are far more complex than the simple definition of foods as desirable and undesirable. Scholarly discussions of diet have too often focused simply on quantities and types of food consumed, but this kind of treatment reveals little about how people decide what to eat and what to buy, judgments that are based on a complex structure of categories that define foods as appropriate for specific uses. Analyses of changes in consumption, if they are to reveal the processes by which economy affects culture, must also consider how these categories are altered. What needs to be explored is the process by which new products, perhaps initially perceived as novelties and luxuries, become, to borrow Mintz's succinct formulation, "transformed into the ritual of daily necessity and even into the images of daily decency" (Mintz 1979: 65).

In Zumbagua, potatoes are no longer a necessity but a luxury, while manufactured foods that were once a novelty have become commonplace. The changes are more subtle, however. As the productive structure of the Zumbaguan economy changes, social relations between women and men, as well as relations within and between households, alter accordingly. These shifts in turn produce a transformation of the elaborate rituals of exchange that are intrinsic to Andean economy and society, a transformation that encompasses ongoing dietary shifts and makes them part of a less visible but more profound alteration in the very categories by which foods are defined, understood, and enjoyed. These cultural categories reflect the economy and society in which they arise: both rituals of consumption and the organization of production inform them...

Peasant economies are marked by heterogeneity. By its very nature the modern peasant household is involved in a variety of productive activities, each implying a different type of articulation with the outside world. Subsistence agriculture, wage labor, petty commodity production; buying, selling, trading: no single economic practice characterizes the rural household. Rather, the very multiplicity of their endeavors defines contemporary peasants.

It is not a single peasant but rather the peasant household as a whole that is involved in all these activities; individuals are typically somewhat specialized. The family assigns productive roles to its members according to age and sex or other social criteria. Children may be the primary shepherds, for example, while adults concentrate on agriculture, or women may be the exclusive agents in the petty commodities market while men are engaged in primary production. As a result, of the products that the household receives as the fruits of its collective labor, specific family members contribute certain categories of things.

These productive roles in turn inform the roles assigned to certain foods as consumables. The productive origins of foods affect their categorization in consumption, and, as part of this process, the social roles of the producer become part of the meanings foods carry. These social variables can influence even the sensory experience of eating.

Tasty Insides and Bitter Outsides

Thus in Zumbagua, the taste of certain things is characterized as *jayaj,* bitter or strong. The basic *jaya* product is the hot red pepper or *uchu,* but the symbolic referents of *jayaj* are many, and I can summarize only a few of them here: a *jayaj* food is eaten raw, and it is associated with males, with the hot *yunga* (cloudforest) zone that lies below the parish, and with suprahousehold networks of production and exchange. In its symbolic associations, it is related to other lowland products such as tropical fruits, to rock salt, to cane alcohol, and to tobacco. All of these products share origins outside the parish, involvement in spheres of suprahousehold consumption especially during rituals, and a role in consumption defined by an absence of cooking and by use either as a condiment superfluous to the body of a meal (rock salt in some cases, and *uchu* always) or as a product consumed outside the structure of meals (fruit, tobacco, and alcohol).

These characteristics can be compared with those of *jayaj's* contrasting term, *mishqui.* Modern Ecuadorian Quichua dictionaries (see, for example, Stark and Muysken 1977: 256; Moreno Mora 1955: 295; Guevara 1972: 336) translate *mishqui* as "sweet" or "*dulce,*" with a secondary meaning of "*sabroso,*" "tasty." These brief definitions do not capture the polysemous and seemingly contradictory nature of the word, however. For example, *mishqui* foods may be either sweet or salty: the two items for sale in the markets that Zumbaguan women refer to as *mishqui* are candy ... and the package of instant flavoring for soups, of which the predominant ingredients are salt and monosodium glutamate. However, in Zumbagua *mishqui* is most commonly used in speaking not of things for sale in the market, but of foods cooked at home: starchy, boiled, and (to my palate) typically bland dishes are referred to as *mishqui* when the intent is laudatory.

As with the term "*jayaj,*" epitomized by the hot *yunga* product *uchu,* the best way to grasp the essential meaning of *mishqui* is to begin with its central, most basic usage. Among all the foods adjectivally described as *mishqui,* there is one that is simply named *mishqui* and so may be considered to be the quintessential *mishqui* food. This is the simple gruel made of sweetened ground barley without other ingredients.

The meaning of *mishqui* becomes clearer if we contrast the manner in which this food is produced and used with that of *jayaj* foods. Whereas *jayaj* evokes a masculine realm of exotic foodstuffs acquired beyond the parish, this plain barley gruel is of all the foods eaten in Zumbagua most purely the product of household labor and of subsistence agriculture. Similarly, when many other foods are described as *mishqui,* such as soups, stews, and gruels, the word seems best glossed as "tasty" or "well cooked"; the word then points to the nature of these foods as cooked, nourishing, and made within the home, to be eaten by the members of the household alone. The contrast to *jayaj* foods, with their strong or bitter tastes, their exotic origins, and their role in extrahousehold ritual, is clear. *Mishqui* has a definite sense referent of tastiness, whether sweet or savory, and it thus applies to sugars, salts, and other seasonings used in cooking, and hence to the candies that are as sweet to the taste as raw sugar or *panela.* But the central significance of *mishqui* resides in the warm, comforting, sweet cooked gruel that is perhaps the food most closely associated with family life, with childhood, and with motherhood.

Not only is *mishqui* the first solid food a woman gives her babies and the food she first feeds her family on many days; it is also the food that is most purely the product of women's labor. Cooking is, of course, the fundamentally feminine task, but in Zumbagua the production of a barley-based meal involves women's labor on a much greater scale, from the initial sorting of seeds, to planting, weeding, harvesting, threshing, storing, and grinding, and to the final stages of toasting and boiling. As male labor is increasingly withdrawn from agriculture and becomes wage labor, all of these tasks, not just the final processes, are coming to be defined as feminine (Deere 1976).

The burden of labor placed on women has thus become more onerous, and at the same time, as agricultural yields decline because of the region's degraded ecology, their labor produces progressively smaller portions of the family diet. *Jayaj* and *mishqui,* with their referents of male-raw-outside and female-cooked-inside, may have once referred to an agricultural economy in which both women and men worked in the fields (for the hacienda as well as on their own plots) and in which the task of going outside the parish to acquire exotic products was a male enterprise, while the final processing and cooking of agricultural products were feminine ones. Now, however, the division of labor is changing and so is the composition of the cookpot. Subsistence agriculture is increasingly feminized, but not all of the staple foods used in cooking are the products of that subsistence labor.

Women still cook *mishqui,* but for the most part young men do not go down to the *yunga,* nor are the foods they acquire jungle products. They work in Quito, the capital, and the products they bring home are largely manufactured goods. Like jungle products, some of them are not essential to the meals a household shares; if he meets with a windfall, a man will purchase tropical fruits. And some of the foods men buy, such as breads, crackers, cookies, and candies, play a part in the flow of *fiesta* and special-occasion foods that link households. But many of the processed foods brought home from the city take the form of bags of flour and noodles and Quaker oats, staples that are used in cooking and feeding the family.

Ideally, men would like to return to the parish each weekend bearing all of these foods: a flashy display of candies and cookies, big bags of bread and lush fruits for immediate enjoyment, and beneath it all a substantial amount of foodstuffs for the week ahead. Breads and fruits, however, are expensive; for most men on most weeks, a few bags of the cheapest noodles and flour and a handful of penny candies must suffice. But whatever the actual composition of the groceries brought home, the term that is used to describe them is not *jayaj,* but another, quite different indigenous concept, *wanlla.* And on Saturday morning when he takes his family down to the weekly market, the foods he buys there will also be described as *wanlla.* The use of this term to describe the staple elements of a man's contribution to the household diet, however, seems to contradict the widely accepted meanings of the term.

Wanlla: The Gift

Wanlla is anything that is not part of a meal. In this sense, it can be translated as "snack," "treat," "junk, food," or "dessert food," and *wanlla* can be all of these. There are four types of food that are always *wanlla*: bread, fruit, sweets, and cooked food bought in the market. But just as *uchu* epitomizes the word *jayaj,* or sweet barley gruel *mishqui,* bread is the *wanlla* par excellence. It is the universally appropriate gift, the favorite treat. The distribution of bread is critically important in many social and ceremonial contexts. Large amounts of bread are necessary for certain formal gift-giving exchanges: between bride's and groom's family at weddings, for the dead, on *Finados* (All Saints' Day), when asking a formal favor.

In Zumbaguan minds, bread has none of the qualities of a staple. It is truly a treat, a luxury. Although people express greed for bread, it is not thought of as something to satisfy hunger. Unlike staple foods, the amount of bread a household consumes depends directly on the family's disposable cash income. It is the one special food that everyone would like to have on hand all the time, while at the same time it is agreed that no one ever "needs" bread. Potatoes and barley are necessities; bread, like fruit and sweets, is for enjoyment...

The function of these kinds of treat is obviously more social than dietary. The social uses to which *wanlla* foods are put defines, in fact, the whole category, whether those foods are animal or vegetable, expensive or cheap. *Wanlla* can be defined as treats or snacks, but a more exact translation is "gift." One buys *wanlla* foods primarily in order to redistribute them, but the motive is less altruism than the exercise of power. Giving *wanlla* is a critically important social and political action in Zumbagua; no one can be a successful social actor without understanding how to give and to manipulate others into giving. *Wanlla* is double-edged. When done informally, the giving of *wanlla* expresses a relationship of superiority/inferiority: men give *wanlla* to women, parents to children, rich benefactors to the humble poor. To give *wanlla* to a social equal, such as a sibling, is both to offer them pleasure and to gain a slight advantage in prestige over them; to offer this type of *wanlla* to persons who consider themselves one's social superior is to insult them.

Whereas men spend their Saturdays exchanging toasts of cane alcohol at the *trago* shops, marketday for women is distinguished by gifts of *wanlla, golosinas* as they say in Spanish: little food treats shared among sisters or friends, but especially among persons with blood bonds. It is at the marketplace, among other women and girls, that the giving of *wanlla* becomes a women's affair. A woman gives her *comadre* a two-sucre sweet bread; it is divided in half to be shared with the *comadre's* sister, who breaks it again to split between her two children. Some *wanlla,* once received, can be tucked away to be redistributed later; not the least of the pleasures it gives its recipient is the possibility of using the treat as a gift for someone else.

In other contexts, *wanlla* expresses respect and the acknowledgment of an ongoing relationship. A woman's siblings bring *wanlla* when she bears a new child. Adult children who have established their own household bring *wanlla* when they go to share festive meals with their parents. *Wanlla* of this sort, while it may be embellished with fruit, cookies, or the like, usually takes the form of uncooked staples. Noodles, flour, rice, or other purchased foods are the preferred form.

Intrinsic to the tradition of *wanlla* is the idea that whereas it is a necessary aspect of social interactions and, hence, is necessary for households in their social reproduction, it is not essential to the simple everyday maintenance of the household in an economic sense. *Wanlla* foods are not part of a meal; they play no part in the sustenance of family members; such a role would be antithetical to the concept of *wanlla* itself.

Wanlla is necessary to the household, but only because according to Zumbaguan thinking the household depends upon the goodwill of other households. In the Andean agrarian economy, no household can survive without ties of kin and *compadrazgo* to support it (Alberti and Mayer 1974, Bolton and Mayer 1977). These ties, which primarily provide access to labor and mutual aid, are created and maintained largely through the ritualized exchange of food and drink. The movement of foods between households is also the mark of ongoing exchanges of labor: families that share food share agricultural tasks as well.

Wanlla plays an extremely important role in interactions between members of a household, as well as between households. At the market on Saturday, husbands who work in the city make a point of buying cooked food for their wives, and this is thought of as *wanlla.* So, too, are the little bags of *mote* (hominy) or lupines topped with chopped vegetables, toasted maize, bacon bits, and hot sauce; fried fish; portions of pork; sweet breads; even cooked potatoes with hot sauce are wrapped up in scraps of cloth, paper, or plastic and taken home as *wanlla* for household members who stayed home to care for animals and children. In order to understand why these little food treats that parents bring home from the market, or that husbands and fathers bring back from the city, are defined by the same term as is used to describe formal presentations of food between households, it is necessary to grasp the internal social and economic structure of the household. Unlike the Western family, the indigenous Andean marriage is not based on the principle of the merging of property. Rather, the household is a union of members, each of whom owns certain resources, inalienably theirs, and contributes labor and products to the household in exchange for the labor and products of other household members. The sheep penned behind the house are individually owned but jointly tended; land holdings are similarly individually owned and jointly worked.

When a husband goes to work in the city, the wages he earns are his own; his wife has no right to them. The Western model of the wife as dependent is utterly alien to Zumbaguan minds, although changing circumstances may make it familiar. A man comes home from the city bearing gifts because it is incumbent upon anyone returning from a trip to re-enter the house with *wanlla:* gifts, treats, luxuries, exotic products from distant places.

But while the symbolic role of *wanlla* remains that of snacks and treats, frivolous little elaborations to a diet that depends upon the basic sustenance provided by the family farm, the realities of household economics are quite different. As subsistence farming's ability to support the family erodes, groceries bought with wages are of ever-increasing importance. The *wanlla* a man brings home from the city includes not only the readily consumable items typically referred to by that term—bread, fruits, candies—but also raw ingredients for cooking, such as noodles and Quaker oats, that require a woman's labor to become edible. These items serve as *wanlla,* gifts, like any foodstuff, when the newly arrived family member presents them to his fellow household-members. But they will be transformed into the *mishqui* soups and gruels his wife serves later, although, as Zumbaguans emphasize, only a meal made of ingredients that are homegrown as well as homecooked is truly *mishqui.*

Why do the people of Zumbagua continue to refer to noodles, flour, wheat, and rice destined for the cookpot as *wanlla?* The answer to this question lies not in the realm of culture and symbol, but in the precarious economic situation of the parish. The dietary changes occurring in Zumbagua reveal several related processes: the increasing inability of the land to provide a basic subsistence, so that cash is being used not only to purchase luxury foods but also to provide part of the basic caloric intake; a move on the part of many young males to seek wage-labor jobs instead of remaining in the agrarian economy; and a concomitant interest in abandoning "Indian" ethnic markers of language, dress, and culture in order to compete more successfully for jobs. At the same time, however, there is a great deal of political turmoil and social conflict within the parish over whether to abandon agricultural work and indigenous lifeways. Opposition derives not so much from innate conservatism as from the perception that, to date, few men from Zumbagua have found more than transient employment outside the parish…

The semiproletarianized local economy, coupled with the steadily deteriorating national economy, creates tremendous strain for young adults in Zumbagua. Women and men experience the problem differently, but its roots are the same. For men, the experience of seeking work in the city, which for young boys holds a tremendous glamour and appeal, quickly deteriorates into a grueling battle for scarce, badly paying, temporary jobs… Many women, in the meantime, live a feast-or-famine life. They subsist on barley and water during the week, awaiting the return of a husband…

Under these circumstances the category of *wanlla* comes to have a meaning reciprocal to the full homecooked meal. Wives anxiously prepare the best meal they can on Friday or Saturday, knowing that their husbands have eaten scantily and poorly during the week. And in the days before his arrival, thoughts and conversation turn repeatedly and anxiously to speculation over what *wanlla* he may bring…

Economic Facts and Cultural Fictions

Zumbaguan ideologies continue to emphasize the primacy of the agricultural and domestic world and its ability to maintain the family, and it is men as well as women, the boys who work in the city as well as their elders, who subscribe to these views. For the people of Zumbagua not only the economic primacy of farming, but the social hierarchy within the family that the relations of production in the domestic mode demand, are centrally important to their cultural identity.

Like the Zumbagua valley's isolation from the outside world, the self-sufficiency of the farmstead is a necessary fiction, a self-image contradicted by practice. Describing contributions that come from the urban, cash-based economy and are acquired through wage-labor as *wanlla* allows the household to maintain the image of itself as an agrarian unit, surviving on its own local resources of land, animals, and traditional labor patterns…

Ironically, the demands of the gift-giving relation between households aggravate the need for cash. Increasingly, food produced in the parish is not used in presentations between households. Barley, fava beans, and onions make very poor *wanlla;* the only really acceptable *wanlla* foods are those sold in the cities or in the market. Thus, the demand for cash has permeated even the social and affective ties that bind household and parish together.

Similarly, the bond between husband and wife is increasingly predicated on the gift of manufactured and purchased *wanlla.* Although the women of Zumbagua spend their working lives involved for the most part in the subsistence economy, they fill their hours with reflections on things only money can buy. Sifting ground barley, peeling potatoes, singeing a *cuy,* women frequently turn thoughts and conversation to the deployment of precious Quito-earned sucres.

For men, while the first adventure of going to the big city may have made home seem shabby and unimportant, as years go by these same men are capable of spending almost all their days and nights in the city and yet never faltering in their assertion that they *live* in Zumbagua: Quito is just where they temporarily work. It is very important to them that their home life and the subsistence agriculture on which it is built remain intact, for it is their only security when ill, unemployed, or in their old age. It is the only haven they can offer their children and elderly parents, whom their wages cannot possibly support. And, in fact, although the subsistence economy is weakened, it remains crucial for Zumbagua's survival. Only a tiny percentage of the households in the parish could survive on wages alone; most would starve without the barley gruels and potato soups that make up many meals.

Life in Zumbagua today, then, is based upon a strategy of involvement in two economies in which the distinction between male and female deploys individuals as producers, while the institution of marriage unites them as consumers. The need all household members share for the rural farmstead to remain intact and economically viable keeps alive a strong ideology of agrarian self-sufficiency and indigenous isolationism. Ecological degradation, overpopulation, and the lack of a market for rural products makes the peasant lifeway less and less tenable, yet it remains indispensable for the survival of Zumbagua's residents.

Because of this situation, family members unite in their insistence that the farmstead is the center and home, while urban wage-labor is a temporary and peripheral aspect of modern life. The category of *wanlla,* applied to consumer goods purchased in the city or market, enables Zumbaguan households to maintain this ideology whatever the actual financial and nutritional significance of these contributions. The use of this category reveals a determined insistence on a definition of purchased foods as treats, snacks, luxury foods, and frivolous gifts. By defining starch foods purchased with wages as *wanlla* even when they are destined for simple everyday consumption, Zumbaguan consumption terminology asserts that the subsistence farm, not wage-labor, is the fundamental, dependable locus of household economic activity.

The category of *wanlla* refers to foods only as consumer items; it says nothing about how they are produced or, indeed, about the substances of which they are made. In this it differs from the *mishqui/jayaj* categories, yet, like them, *wanlia* contains implicit meanings about the social and economic structures that make consumption possible. The immediate referents of the term "*wanlla*" and its use as a label for products that originate in the market economy, suggest a commitment to an ideal of agrarian self-sufficiency and indigenous identity. This ideal does not stem from a system of cultural values that ignores economic realities; rather, it relates directly to the household's productive strategy. As long as wage-labor does not offer a permanent and stable alternative to subsistence farming, Zumbaguan households remain wary of endorsing it as central to their survival: men's contributions to the diet from their wages are fundamentally just *wanlla*.

Mishqui and *jayaj* are terms whose immediate meaning is a sensory experience of taste, but they also refer to the relations of production through which foods are made or acquired. Likewise, to call a bag of Quaker oats *wanlla* is to refer to production both directly and indirectly. Directly, the term refers to the male purchaser's role of bringing manufactured goods acquired through wage-labor into the household to complement the subsistence crops produced by his wife; indirectly, the term reflects an ideological insistence on preserving an "Indian-farmer" identity. Far from existing *despite* the household's increasing involvement in urban wage-labor, this ideology is, in fact, maintained *because* of it.

The use of the indigenous categories *jayaj, mishqui,* and *wanlla* to describe foods is not a residual or traditional aspect of Zumbaguan culture, unrelated to current economic transformations. These categories of consumption have a complex relationship to spheres of production and exchange: they not only reflect or react to changes in the latter, but actively speak to them. In describing a food bought with wages as *wanlla,* household members express their experience that wages are inadequate and intermittent. Furthermore, using the word is part of an active strategy, based on this perception, that tries to contain their growing dependence on those wages. Words are not charms: calling manufactured foods *wanlla* will not grow more potatoes from exhausted soils or change the economic crisis of the Andes. But naming foods and, in so doing, naming the crisis and defining a strategy for surviving it, is an act, and such acts are part of the active role Zumbaguan people play in making their own history.

Notes

This paper is based on twenty-four months of research done between 1982 and 1985.

1. Zumbagua is a civil parish located in Cotopaxi Province, Canton Pujilí. It lies just west of the parish of Tigua, with which it shares many cultural traits, and is bisected by the Latecunga–Quevedo highway. The parish encompasses some 10,000 hectares of land, divided more or less evenly between high grasslands used in sheep–llama pastoralism and lower agricultural lands. Elevations range from slightly above 3,200 meters to well above 4,000. Population estimates indicate a figure above 15,000.

References

Alberti, Giorgio, and Mayer, Enrique (eds.) (1974), *Reciprocidad e Intercambio en los Andes Peruanos*, Perú problema 12, Lima: Instituto de Estudios Peruanos.
Bolton, Ralph, and Mayer, Enrique (eds.) (1977), *Andean Kinship and Marriage*, Washington, DC: American Anthropological Association.
Deere, Carmen Diana (1976), "Rural Women's Subsistence Production in the Capitalist Periphery," *Review of Radical Political Economics* 8,1:9–7.
De Janvry, Alain (1981), *The Agrarian Question and Reformism in Latin America*, Baltimore: Johns Hopkins Press.
Guevara, Dario (1972), *El Castellano y el Quichua en el Ecuador*, Quito: Casa de la Cultura Ecuatoriana.
Marx, Karl (1973), *Grundrisse der Kritik der Politischen Ökonomie*, trans. Martin Nicolaus, New York: Random House.
Mintz, Sidney W. (1979), "Time, Sugar and Sweetness," *Marxist Perspectives* 2:56–73.
Moreno Mora, Manuel (1955), *Diccionario Etimológico y Comparado del Kichwa del Ecuador, Vol. 1*, Cuenca: Casa de la Cultura Ecuatoriana, Nucleo del Azuay.
Orlove, Benjamin (1987), "Stability and Change in Highland Andean Dietary Patterns," in *Food and Evolution: Towards a Theory of Human Food Habits*, ed. Marvin Harris and Eric B. Ross, 481–515, Philadelphia: Temple University Press.
Stark, Louisa R., and Muysken, Pieter C. (1977), *Diccionario Español–Quichua/Quichua–Espanol*, Guayaqui: Museo del Banco Central del Ecuador.

Part III

Eloquent Flavors

Preface

Many of the chapters in this volume detail the numerous meanings that come to be assigned to foods through religious, traditional, and social uses. Some of these meanings stem from the visual appearance of food, or its source, or its place in a historical event. Sometimes, however, the very *flavor* of foods possesses meaning, and in certain cases those flavors are so fundamental to diet and patterns of culture that their meanings are recognized by widely disparate societies.

This is the case with salt, as Margaret Visser shows in her review of the paradoxes surrounding the "edible rock." Salt is a substance of mystery which has been sought by human communities since prehistoric times, and it also ties human and animal worlds together in a shared liking for its taste. Visser's chapter dovetails with ideas that the Rozins put forth in Part I regarding the links between salt use and vegetable diets; and she sets the stage for understanding the alchemical meanings of tastes that are discussed by Peterson in Part IV.

Several of the authors in Part I remark upon what appears to be an innate disposition to like the taste of sweet things. Sidney Mintz grants this natural tendency but believes that the assignment of meanings to flavors and foods requires a cultural explanation. He uses the complex case of one particular sweet substance—sugar—in the English diet, arguing that sugar's semantic significance is by no means constant. Rather, changes in the meanings attached to sugar must be charted in relation to the production of sugar in the growing British empire. Consequently the meanings of this particular flavor vary according to the social position of those who produce or consume substances sweetened by sugar.

Salt is an ordinary table item. But as Wolfgang Schivelbusch notes, its twin, pepper, was once far from ordinary. One of the exotic spices that powered the tastes of Europe during the Middle Ages and spurred a vigorous and lucrative trade, pepper was but one flavor that came to mean "paradise" to wealthy Europeans. Schivelbusch argues that the desire for spices powered changes in food preparation and economy, and even may be credited with the refinement of European culture and the transition from "medieval" to "modern" times. Like Mintz, he argues that tastes are historical formations. In the case of spices we see not just a growth of the significance assigned these substances and their exotic flavors, but also a decline as they became both less desired and more ordinary fare. As such, spices remind us of the historicity of "taste" in several senses.

These three chapters all describe the meanings attached to certain flavors on the large scale of entire societies. But individuals may intervene in those meanings and turn them to their own uses. Paul Stoller and Cheryl Olkes discovered both the standard meanings that various sauces have within the culture of the Songhay of Niger, and also the startling ways that those meanings may be violated to make a particular point. One particular incident from their experience opens the chapter and launches their investigation of the deep background of taste meanings in Songhay cookery. This last chapter illustrates how meanings shift not only with social occasions but individual intent.

9

Salt

The Edible Rock

Margaret Visser

In the earliest times, men usually let animals find salt for them. An outcrop of rock salt was called a salt-"lick" because animals went there to lick it. When the Europeans came to North America they did not find it trackless, for buffalo trails had been worn for centuries to the salt-licks, and it was along these smoothed shortcuts through and around natural obstacles that the first explorers began to move across the continent. Amazingly early in human history, men began to dig into the earth to find salt. All over the world, people like the Hallstatt miners have tunneled along salt seams, braving floods, the collapse of roofs and walls, exhaustion, salt-burn, suffocation, and accidents with their light-source, fire.

Modern salt-mining has become, in comparison, almost miraculously safe and productive. In many cases, mining engineers take advantage of what has always been considered one of the eeriest of the attributes of salt: the rock is not only edible but it also dissolves, and can be returned to its solid state again. Water is injected into the salt seams through tunnels bored from the surface; the brine is pumped out and then evaporated to produce salt again…

Another of salt's mysteries is this: if our bodies need so little, why do we crave it so much? Unlike the human "sweet tooth," our salt hunger is shared by animals: cows, for instance, love salt, and will lick a hole in a wall they find pleasantly salty. Our tongues are well supplied with salt-tasting buds, and to compound our frailty, saltiness enhances the taste of sweet things and disguises bitterness. It also helps make stale or spoiled food edible.

But many peoples have simply never known that salt existed and have lived perfectly healthy lives without it. Australian aborigines and American Indians and Inuit often knew no salt. Early human settlements were apparently not built to be near salt-springs. Human beings, it seems, learn about salt (and become addicted to it) at a very precise moment in their history: when they cease being almost exclusively carnivorous and learn to eat vegetables in quantities usually available only when they grow them themselves. When people begin not only to eat a lot of vegetables, but to reduce the salt content in their food by boiling it—a cooking method which presupposes the ability to make metal pots that can be set directly over a fire—then salt becomes more desirable still.

Carnivorous animals and meat-hunting men find enough salt in blood to satisfy them. Certain African tribes who have never been able to assure themselves of a salt supply, prick the necks of their living cattle and drink their blood. There is no immediate need to slaughter a cow for meat since, alive, she is a sort of walking larder, providing protein and salt.

It is herbivorous animals that love salt. One theory about the origin of the domestication of cattle by man is inspired by the "salt tie" which still operates between reindeer herders and their animals. Cattle may originally have been taught when very young that they could get their salt from men. They would then range freely in search of pasture. Their "owners" needed only to visit them occasionally in the field with gifts of salt to remind them that they were no longer wild. Men could then proceed to take advantage of the relationship.

Salt, in myths all over the world, is seen as a "newcomer," an addition whose necessity is not perceived before it arrives, but which is intensely attractive, indeed irresistible, once it is tried. Here, for example, is a North American Indian myth about the presence of a salt-lick near the home of the Indian who told it.

> Salt used to be far away. He was a man and was traveling through the country. The Indians never used salt then. He looked ugly all over, and the people did not like him. He came to a camp and said, "Let me put my hand in there, then the food will taste well."
>
> "No," said the cook, "I want to eat this, you look too ugly."
>
> He went off to another band and said, "Let me put my hand in here, and it will taste well."
>
> "No, your hand is too dirty."
>
> He came to another band and said the same thing, but people declined his offer. At last he came to a single man, and he was a cook. He said, "I want to put my hand into the food, then it will taste better." And the cook allowed him to do so, and he put in his hand.
>
> "Now taste it." The Indian tasted it and it was good. Salt settled there and stayed forever, about ten or twelve miles from St. Thomas.

Notice in this story that people are suspicious about salt. For one thing, eating it is eating earth, and that in itself is peculiar behavior. You add it to your food, it disappears, yet it indescribably alters the taste of everything you eat. Salt is weird, powerful, dangerous, and "extra." In religious symbolism it is always linked with "strong," powerful substances like iron or blood. We feel that a little of it is all we need, that this little has made all the difference, and that we ought not to abuse the privilege of having it. Furthermore, adding salt is being clever, and getting salt has always taxed human intelligence. By the same token we feel that we could easily be tricked by someone who cunningly adds salt without our knowing it, thus imparting a sinister attraction to something we ought not to want. When someone "salts" a mine he wishes to sell, he plants nuggets of gold in his worthless property for dupes to find...

Salt is both "farmed" like wheat, and "searched for" like game or wild berries. Bread (grown, harvested, ground, leavened, and baked) and salt (found, won, collected, and efficiently transported) together cover the field: they represent man as Farmer, patiently and wisely nurturing his crops, but also as Hunter, Scientist, Adventurer, and Organizer. Bread and salt are customarily offered in Russia (where the word for "hospitality" means literally "bread-salt") and in other countries, as a sign of welcome to a guest; bread and salt symbolize the precious stores of the house, the fruits of the host's labor, his patience, his ingenuity, his civilized foresight and preparedness.

Oath-taking, in many cultures, is a ceremony involving salt, just as the act of swearing may employ blood or iron as a sign denoting a person's unbreakable word. Salt is shared at table, in a context of order and contentment. Traditional Bedouin will never fight a man with whom they have once eaten salt. When the Lord God of Israel made a covenant with the Jews, it was a Covenant of Salt, denoting an unalterable bond of friendship. It also meant that the Jews had settled down in the Promised Land, had ceased to be sheep-herding nomads, and would now eat the fruit of their harvests, cooked and seasoned with salt...

Salt is the only rock directly consumed by man. It corrodes but preserves, desiccates but is wrested from the water. It has fascinated man for thousands of years not only as a substance he prized and was willing to labor to obtain, but also as a generator of poetic and of mythic meaning. The contradictions it embodies only intensify its power and its links with experience of the sacred.

Salt brings flavor to life, and people accustomed to salt find their food tasteless, flat, and dull without it. This is the point of the folktale from which Shakespeare derived *King Lear*. In the original story, the younger daughter of the king, unlike her articulate and dishonest sisters, tells her father that her love for him is not like silver or gold, as they had claimed, but "like salt." Enraged, he throws her out of the palace. She eventually is to be married, and invites the king (who does not know who she is or recognize her under her veil) to the wedding feast. She has ordered all the food to be prepared without salt. The king, finding the dinner inedible, weeps for his youngest daughter and finally understands how important a pinch of humble salt is to man's happiness. She identifies herself, the two are reconciled—and presumably the saltcellars are produced with a flourish. The story shows that a daughter's sincere love is unassertive and may be taken for granted, but it is dependable and irreplaceable. In refusing or in losing it, a father is left without the kind of thing that gives zest to life.

When Jesus called his followers "the salt of the earth," he was telling them that they were irreplaceable, and that their mission was to give people what makes life worth living. There were few of them, but they were sufficient to season the whole earth, as a little salt or a tiny bit of leaven is enough. They and their message would persevere and endure, as salt is the great conserver, the image of permanence. Jesus went on immediately, in Matthew's Gospel, to use an image of light. The two metaphors are connected both by opposition (salt is in the earth, light must be raised on high; salt is tasted while light is seen) and by similarity, for salt has always been associated with fire and brightness.

Salt, once isolated, is white and glittering. It is the opposite of wet. You win it by freeing it from water with the help of fire and the sun, and it dries out flesh. Eating salt causes thirst. Dryness, in the pre-Socratic cosmic system which still informs our imagery, is always connected with fire, heat, and light.

For the alchemists, common salt (one of the elements of matter) was neither masculine nor feminine but neuter: the edible rock always has something a little inhuman about it; it disconcertingly sits astride categories. Salt does have to do with sex, however, because it is a dynamic substance which both alters itself and causes change. Like sex, it is exciting and dangerous and gives pleasure. Salt comes out of the sea like the goddess of sex, Aphrodite, whose name the ancient Greeks thought meant "sea-foam-born." In European folk custom, impotence has traditionally been cured by a hilarious, bawdy salting of the disobliging member by a crowd of women.

Often priests or mourners or people who are in a state of crisis—those whom society has marginalized, for whatever reason—must observe a taboo on salt. Eating no salt, which is often accompanied by sexual continence, means a fight to maintain equilibrium at a time of turbulence and difficulty, when one has no need of the dynamic. It also means that one has left society, rejecting the enticements and the comforts of civilization, or that one intends to dramatize a profound discontent with the way society is conducting itself.

Salt represents the civilized: it requires know-how to get it, and a sophisticated combination of cooking and spoilt, jaded appetites to need it. Its sharp taste suggests sharpness of intellect and liveliness of mind. Salt (bright, dry, titillating, and dynamic) is synonymous in several languages with wit and wisdom.

It preserves things from corruption—even as it corrodes other things with its bite. A little of it fertilizes the land; a lot sterilizes it. Because salt stops rot and because it is fiery, salt is intrinsically pure. It is the child of the sun and the sea, two basic symbols of cleanliness and purity. Salt keeps meat safe for the winter and so feeds man; it is, therefore, a blessing. Salt also means barrenness, and it is, therefore, used for cursing. Its imperishable rock-nature, and its purity and wisdom, make it the material of oaths and covenants, which guarantee, if the swearer breaks his oath, that malediction will fall upon him.

Salt as covenant-sealer signifies friendship and hospitality. The silver saltcellar was a central and often highly decorative ornament on the banquet tables of all rich European families: it marked off the close friends of the family from those "below the salt," who were not considered worthy of such intimacy. When someone inadvertently spills salt, it is considered unlucky because it signifies enmity and malediction. Leonardo da Vinci followed this tradition in his fresco of *The Last Supper* when he depicted Judas as upsetting the saltcellar.

Here as before, however, salt is powerfully contradictory: because it is pure and strong, it counteracts malediction. Witches hate salt. They never served it at their Sabbaths, and if you put some under a witch's cushion she could not sit down: this was considered a surefire method of finding out whether someone was a witch or not. Devils also detest it. Therefore, if you are unlucky enough to spill salt, all you have to do is throw some over your left shoulder (where all bad spirits congregate) and the evil will be undone. An owl's cry is a malediction: to neutralize it, one has to sprinkle salt on the bird's tail.

Until recently, salt was part of the Roman Catholic baptismal ceremony (Luther banned it as Popish superstition). A few grains were placed on the baby's tongue to signify purity, endurance, wisdom, power, uniqueness ("You are the salt of the earth"), and protection from evil. It was a sign of God's friendship and his power over Satan.

10
Sweetness and Meaning

Sidney Mintz

Researchers working with infants in the United States have concluded that there is a built-in human liking for sweet tastes, which appears very early in development and is relatively independent of experience (Maller and Desor 1973). Though there are inadequate cross-cultural data to sustain that position, sweetness seems to be so widely favored that it is hard to avoid the inference of some inborn predisposition. The nutrition scholar Norge Jerome has collected information to show how sucrose-rich foods form part of the early acculturational experiences of non-Western peoples in many world areas, and there seems to be little or no resistance to such items. It is perhaps noteworthy that sugar and sugary foods are commonly diffused with stimulants, particularly beverages. There may be some synergy involved in the ingestive learning of new users: to date, there have been no reports on any group with a nonsugar tradition rejecting the introduction of sugar, sweetened condensed milk, sweetened beverages, sweetmeats, pastries, confectionery, or other sweet dietary items into the culture. In fact, a recent study on sucrose intolerance in northern Alaskan Eskimos revealed that sucrose-intolerant individuals continued to consume sucrose despite the discomforts associated with the offending items (Jerome 1977: 243).

Many scholars have promoted the thesis that mammalian responsiveness to sweetness arose because for millions of years a sweet taste served to indicate edibility to the tasting organism (Beidler 1975, Kare 1975, P. Rozin 1976a, b). Hominid evolution from arboreal fruit-eating primate ancestors makes this thesis particularly persuasive, and has encouraged some students of the problem to go to logical extremes:

> ...the least natural environments may sometimes provide the best evidence about human nature... Western peoples consume enormous per capita quantities of refined sugar because, to most people, very sweet foods taste

> very good. The existence of the human sweet tooth can be explained, ultimately, as an adaptation of ancestral populations to favor the ripest—and hence the sweetest—fruit. In other words, the selective pressures of times past are most strikingly revealed by the artificial, supernormal stimulus of refined sugar, despite the evidence that eating refined sugar is maladaptive (Symons 1979: 73)

In fact, it can be argued equally well (and more convincingly, it seems to me) that the widely variant sugar-eating habits of contemporary populations show that no ancestral predisposition within the species can adequately explain what are in fact culturally conventionalized norms, not biological imperatives. That there are links between fruit-eating, the sensation of sweetness, and the evolution of the primates is persuasive. That they "explain" the heavy consumption of refined sugar by some peoples in the modern world is not.

Indeed, all (or at least nearly all) mammals like sweetness (Beauchamp, Maller, and Rogers 1977). That milk, including human milk, is sweet is hardly irrelevant. One scholar, seeking to push the link between human preferences and sweetness just a little further back, has even argued that the fetus experiences sweetness when nourished *in utero* (DeSnoo 1937: 88). The newborn infant usually lives exclusively on milk at first. Jerome notes that the use of sweetened liquids as a substitute for milk for infant feeding occurs across the world. The first nonmilk "food" that a baby is likely to receive in North American hospitals is a 5-percent glucose-and-water solution, used to evaluate its postpartum functioning because "the newborn tolerates glucose better than water" (Jerome 1977: 236). On the one hand, that the human liking for sweetness is not just an acquired disposition is supported by many different kinds of evidence; on the other, the circumstances under which that predisposition is intensified by cultural practice are highly relevant to how strong the "sweet tooth" is.

Sweetness would have been known to our primate ancestors and to early human beings in berries, fruit, and honey—honey being the most intensely sweet, by far. Honey, of course, is an animal product, at least in the sense that its raw material is gathered from flowering plants by bees. "Sugar," particularly sucrose, is a vegetable product extracted by human ingenuity and technical achievement. And whereas honey was known to human beings at all levels of technical achievement the world over from a very early point in the historical record, sugar (sucrose) made from the sugar cane is a late product that spread slowly during the first millennium or so of its existence, and became widespread only during the past five hundred years. Since the nineteenth century, the sugar beet, a temperate crop, has become an almost equally important source of sucrose, and the mastery of sucrose extraction from it has altered the character of the world's sugar industries.[1] In the present century, other caloric sweeteners, particularly those from maize *(Zea mays),* have begun to challenge the primacy of sucrose, and noncaloric sweeteners have also begun to win a place in the human diet.

Sensations of sweetness must be carefully distinguished from the substances that give rise to them; and processed sugars, such as sucrose, dextrose, and fructose, which are manufactured and refined technochemically, must be distinguished from sugars as they occur in nature. For chemists, "sugar" is a generic term for a large, varied class of organic compounds of which sucrose is but one.

I concentrate [here] on sucrose, though there will be occasion to refer to other sugars, and this focus is dictated by the history of sucrose's consumption in recent centuries, which completely outstripped honey (its principal European competitor before the seventeenth century), and made largely irrelevant such other products as maple sugar and palm sugar. The very idea of sweetness came to be associated with sugar in European thought and language, though honey continued to play a privileged minor role, particularly in literary imagery. The lack of clarity or specificity in European conceptions of sweetness as a sensation is noticeable.

I have already remarked that, though there may be certain absolute species-wide features in the human taste apparatus, different peoples eat widely variant substances and have radically different ideas about what tastes good, especially relative to other edible substances. Not only do individuals differ in preferences and the degree of intensity of a particular taste that suits them, but also there is no adequate methodology to bracket or bound the range of tastes typical of persons in any group. To add to the difficulties, the lexicons of taste sensation, even if fully recorded, are immensely difficult to translate for comparative purposes.

Still, there is probably not a people on earth that lacks the lexical means to describe that category of tastes we call "sweet." Though the taste of sweetness is not uniformly liked, either by whole cultures or by all of the members of any one culture, no society rejects sweetness as unpleasant—even though particular sweet things are tabooed or eschewed for various reasons. Sweet tastes have a privileged position in contrast to the more variable attitudes toward sour, salty, and bitter tastes; this, of course, does not rule out the common predilections for certain sour, salty, or bitter substances.

But to say that everyone everywhere likes sweet things says nothing about where such tastes fit into the spectrum of taste possibilities, how important sweetness is, where it occurs in a taste-preference hierarchy, or how it is thought of in relation to other tastes. Moreover, there is much evidence that people's attitudes toward foods, including sweet foods, have varied greatly with time and occasion. In the modern world, one need only contrast the frequency, intensity, and scale of sugar use in the French diet with, say, the English or American, to see how widely attitudes toward sweetness vary. Americans seem to like meals to end with sweetness, in desserts; others also like to start with sweetness. Moreover, sweetness is important in what anthropologists call interval eating, or snacks, in American life. Other peoples seem less inclined to treat sweetness as a "slot taste," suitable in only one or several positions; for them a sweet food might appear at any point in the meal—as one of the middle courses, or as one of several dishes served simultaneously. The propensity to mix sweetness with other tastes is also highly variable.

The widely different ways that sweetness is perceived and employed support my argument that the importance of sweetness in English taste preferences grew over time, and was not characteristic before the eighteenth century. Though in the West sweetness is now generally considered by the culture (and perhaps by most scientists) a quality counterposed to bitterness, sourness, and saltiness, which make up the taste "tetrahedron,"[2] or is contrasted to the piquancy or hotness with which it is sometimes associated in Chinese, Mexican, and West African cuisines, I suspect that this counter-position—in which sweetness becomes the "opposite" of everything—is quite recent. Sweet could only be a countertaste to salt/bitter/sour when there was a plentiful-enough source of sweetness to make this possible. Yet the contrast did not always occur when sugar became plentiful; Britain, Germany, and the Low Countries reacted differently, for instance, from France, Spain, and Italy.

That some built-in predisposition to sweetness is part of the human equipment seems inarguable. But it cannot possibly explain differing food systems, degrees of preference, and taxonomies of taste—any more than the anatomy of the so-called organs of speech can "explain" any particular language. It is the borderline between our human liking for sweetness and the supposed English "sweet tooth" that I hope to illuminate in what follows...

Over the course of less than two centuries, a nation most of whose citizens formerly subsisted almost exclusively on foods produced within its borders, had become a prodigious consumer of imported goods. Usually these foods were new to those who consumed them, supplanting more familiar items, or they were novelties, gradually transformed from exotic treats into ordinary, everyday consumables. As these changes took place, the foods acquired new meanings, but those meanings—what the foods meant to people, and what people signaled by consuming them—were associated with social differences of all sorts, including those of age, gender, class, and occupation. They were also related to the will and intent of the nation's rulers, and to the economic, social, and political destiny of the nation itself.

There are plainly two different senses of the term "meaning" here. One refers to what might be called "inside" kinds of meaning—inside the rituals and schedules of the group, inside the meal or eating event, inside the social group itself—the meanings people indicate when they are demonstrating they know what things are supposed to mean. Thus, for example, hospitality "means" self-respect; self-respect "means" knowing one's place in the class system; and knowing one's place can "mean" offering appropriate forms of hospitality—greeting, inviting in, serving tea and sugar and treacle tarts, or whatever. At births and weddings, funerals and feast days, moments of repose from the day's work following the calendar of hours, days, weeks, months, and the lifetime itself, new forms of consumption might be grafted to older forms with similar or analogous meanings.

I have [suggested that there are] two processes by which inside meanings are acquired and conventionalized. In "intensification," consumption replicates that practiced by others, usually of a higher social status—also imitates, even emulates. The wedding cake and its sculptured decorations, complete with dragées, congratulatory script, hardened sugar figures, was more than just a new "food"; consumption was firmly attached to a special event and ceremonialized as part of it. As the custom of having a wedding cake percolated down through society, one would expect the usages to change, because of great differences in means and circumstances, but since the emulative features of the custom were undoubtedly also important, this process was "intensification" nonetheless.

Much consumption behavior toward sugar and its accompaniments seems to have arisen among the British working classes without any imitation, especially when the contexts were different from those of the more privileged classes. Since sugar products became even more important to the poor than they once had been for the wealthy—as sources of calories even more than of status—and since the occasions for eating them multiplied, new uses and meanings arose at a great remove from the practices of the privileged. To these kinds of innovation the term "extensification" has been applied.

In both instances, new users appropriate the behavior and inside meanings they perceive as their own, and new uses and meanings sometimes appear that are not merely imitative. In "intensification," those in power are responsible both for the presence of the new products and, to a degree, for their meanings; with "extensification," those in power may take charge of the availability of the new products, but the new users inform them with meaning. In the wider historical process that concerns us—the diffusion of sugar to entire national populations—those who controlled the society held a commanding position not only in regard to the availability of sugar, but also in regard to at least some of the meanings that sugar products acquired.

The other sort of meaning can be grasped when one considers what consumption, and its proliferated meanings for the participants, can signify for a society as a whole, and especially for those who rule it; how those who govern or control the society perpetuate their status and profit from the intensified diffusion of inside meanings, and of the consumption which the validations of these meanings entail. One can see here that the kind or level of consumption of social groups is not a God-given constant; and certain beliefs about human character and potentiality are open to amendment. Conversely, the spread of internal meanings can be stimulated and manipulated; the simultaneous control of both the foods themselves and the meanings they are made to connote can be a means to pacific domination.

The substances and acts to which meanings attach—inside kinds of meaning—serve to validate social events. Social learning and practice relate them to one another, and to what they stand for. Rice and rings have meanings in weddings much as lilies and lighted candles do in funerals. These are historically acquired—they arise, grow, change, and die—and they are culture-specific as well as arbitrary, for all are symbols. They have no universal meaning; they "mean" because they occur in specific cultural and historical contexts, where their relevant meanings are already known to the participants. No symbol has a life of its own, and though it lacks any intrinsic connection with any other symbol, it may travel together with other symbols through time, each reinforcing the other by the "signals" its presence creates. Just as the symbols may be traced back to a past when they were not associated (the way tea and sugar were once not associated, for instance), so may there come a time when their substantive associations are dissolved or invalidated by some change or other (the way tea and its meanings dropped out of colonial American drinking habits, and were replaced by coffee).

As for substances like tea, then, events like meals, or ideas and meanings like hospitality and equality, human intelligence puts them together into patterns in the course of social acts in specific times and places, employing certain availabilities and under specific constraints. Birth and death are universal in the sense that they happen to all human beings; our capacity to symbolize, to endow anything with meaning and then to act in terms of that meaning, is similarly universal and intrinsic to our nature—like learning to walk or to speak (or being born, or dying). But which materials we link to events and endow with meaning are unpredictably subject to cultural and historical forces. We make biological events like birth and death into social events because we are human; each human group does it in its own way. Large, complex societies, composed of many overlapping subgroups, usually lack any single assemblage of social practices by which life is endowed with meaning; their members differ widely in the way they can live, and in their historically influenced access to the acts, objects, and persons through which they validate their knowledge of life's meaning.

Seventeenth-century England, like its Continental neighbors, was deeply divided by considerations of birth, wealth, breeding, gender, occupation, and so on. The practices of consumption in such a society were deeply differentiated, and reinforced by rules. Hence the ways that new consumption practices were taken up and by whom, and the ways they spread to members of other groups, with or without their associated meanings, suggest how British society itself was organized, and mark the distribution of power within it.

Before the end of the seventeenth century, while sugar was still a precious and rare substance, it had little meaning for most English people, though if they ever got to taste sugar, they doubtless thought it desirable. The rich and powerful, however, derived an intense pleasure from their access to sugar—the purchase, display, consumption, and waste of sucrose in various forms—which involved social validation, affiliation, and distinction. The blending of sugar with other rare and precious spices in the preparation of food; the use of sugar as a fruit preservative; the combination of sugar with crushed pearls or fine gold in the manufacture of medical "remedies," the magnificent subtleties giving concrete expression to temporal and spiritual power—all confirm what sugar meant, and how sugar use informed meanings, among the privileged.

This multiplicity of meanings was also revealed in language and in literature, and linguistic imagery suggested not only the association of sweet substances with certain sentiments, desires, and moods, but also the historical replacement, in large measure, of honey by sugar. Honey imagery was ancient in British, as in classical Greek and Latin, literature. Both substances were associated with happiness and well-being, with elevation of mood, and often with sexuality. The quality of sweetness, so important in the structure of human taste and preference, was applied to personality, to generous acts, to music, to poetry. The Indo-European root *swad* is the ultimate source of both "sweet" and "persuade"; in contemporary English, "sugared" or "honeyed" speech has been supplemented with "syrupy tones" and "sweet-talking."

Chaucer's references to sugar are scant; they mainly stress its rarity and preciousness. By Shakespeare's time, the references have multiplied, and though they remain concentrated upon rare substances, the imagery flowing from them is highly diversified. "White-handed mistress, one sweet word with thee," says Berowne in *Love' Labour's Lost;* "Honey, and milk, and sugar; there is three," the Princess puns in response. Or Touchstone, the clown, teasing Audrey in *As You Like It,* tells her that "honesty coupled to beauty is to have honey a sauce to sugar." Northumberland to Bolingbroke, in the wolds of Gloucestershire: "Your fair discourse hath been as sugar, / Making the hard way sweet and delectable." Or, finally, Brabantio, before Othello and the Duke of Venice: "These sentences, to sugar, or to gall, / Being strong on both sides, are equivocal." From the seventeenth century onward—and it may be worth noting that Shakespeare died nearly half a century *before* sugar from Barbados, the first English "sugar island," began to reach England—sugar imagery became ever commoner in English literature. Written usage of this sort mattered most to the literate, of course, but sugar imagery became an important part of everyday talk as well, competing with or supplanting honey imagery among the terms of endearment and affection. This imagery bridges the two very different "meanings" we have discussed: the inside meanings as sugar became commoner, and its employment in social settings by even the least privileged and poorest of Britain's citizens; and the significance of sugar for the empire, for the king, and for the classes whose wealth would be made and secured by the growing productivity of British labor at home and British enterprise abroad.

This second meaning is embodied in the writings of political economists like Josiah Child or Dalby Thomas, or physicians like Frederick Slare, whose enthusiasms kept pace with the steady expansion of those portions of the empire within which sugar cane and other plantation crops could be grown. Their encomia were not limited to the medical, preservative, nutritive, and other proclaimed virtues of sugar. In fact, they mostly treated the beneficial character of sugar as self-evident. How trade would follow the flag; why plantation production befitted the nation, the crown, and—of course—the enslaved and coerced workers; the general importance of commerce as a stimulus to manufacturing; the civilizing benefits to the heathen of the British presence—all these themes were pressed into sugar's service. And though sugar was obviously not always and everywhere a moneymaker within the empire—many an investor, as well as many a planter, ended up a bankrupt (and sometimes a jailbird) because of it—its cumulative value to crown and capital alike was enormous.

As far as the British West Indies were concerned, the zenith of sugar's imperial role probably came in the late eighteenth century, during the rule of George III. Lowell Ragatz, historian of the British West Indian planter class, recounts the story, probably apocryphal, of George III's visit to Weymouth in the company of his prime minister. Irritated by the sight of a West Indian planter's opulent equipage, complete with outrider and livery as fine as his own, the king is reported to have exclaimed: "Sugar, sugar, eh?—all *that* sugar! How are the duties, eh, Pitt, how are the duties?" (Ragatz 1928: 50).

The meaning that sugar attained in the imperial economy was a wholly different matter from what it eventually meant in the lives of the English people, but the availability and price of sugar were the direct consequences of imperial policies that took shape partly in terms of what the market was, and more and more in terms of what it might become. As the home market was made to grow, the proportion of sugar that was re-exported dropped sharply, and production itself was levered more securely into the imperial orbit. And as control over production was consolidated, consumption at home continued to rise. Much later, when protectionist policy based on differential duties lost out in Parliament and the West Indian planters lost their protectionist advocates, sugar went on being consumed in ever-increasing quantities, even as African and Asian colonies entered into cane cultivation and sugar-making, and even as beet-sugar production began to overtake cane-sugar production in the world economy at large. By that time—which is to say, by the mid-nineteenth century—the two sorts of meaning suggested here had become united to a certain extent.

The English people came to view sugar as essential; supplying them with it became as much a political as an economic obligation. At the same time, the owners of the immense fortunes created by the labor of millions of slaves stolen from Africa, on millions of acres of the New World stolen from the Indians—wealth in the form of commodities like sugar, molasses, and rum to be sold to Africans, Indians, colonials, and the British working class alike—had become even more solidly attached to the centers of power in English society at large. Many individual merchants, planters, and entrepreneurs lost out, but the long-term economic successes of the new commodity markets at home were never in doubt after the mid-seventeenth century. What sugar meant, from this vantage point, was what all such colonial production, trade, and metropolitan consumption came to mean: the growing strength and solidity of the empire and of the classes that dictated its policies.

But what most anthropologists have in mind when they think about meaning is entirely different. To paraphrase Clifford Geertz, human beings are caught up in webs of signification they themselves have spun. We are able to perceive and interpret the world only in terms of preexisting, culture-specific systems for endowing reality with meaning. This perspective puts the cognitive order between us and the world itself—we must *think* the world to be able to *see* (classify) it, rather than the other way round—and it should be persuasive for anyone who considers culture as the prime defining feature of human uniqueness.

But if humanity gives meaning to the objective world, with different sets of meaning for different human groups, one must still ask how this is done and by whom in any given historical instance. Where does the locus of meaning reside? For most human beings most of the time, the meanings believed to inhere in things and in the relationships among things and acts are not given but, rather, are learned. Most of us, most of the time, act within plays the lines of which were written long ago, the images of which require recognition, not invention. To say this is not to deny individuality or the human capacity to add, transform, and reject meanings, but it is to insist that the webs of signification that we as individuals spin are exceedingly small and fine (and mostly trivial); for the most part they reside within other webs of immense scale, surpassing single lives in time and space.

It is not at all clear that such webs are single-stranded, or that the same webs exist for each of us. In complex modern societies such webs of signification can be imagined more easily than they can be demonstrated to exist. Our ability to explain their meanings is limited, because each generality we offer requires that we believe people in a complex society agree, at least *grosso modo,* that what something means is unmistakable. This is sometimes true, but not always. People's agreeing on what something *is* is not the same as their agreeing on what it *means*. Even on a quite simple level, this difficulty can be real. We need to learn that rice "means" fertility, and though that association may seem commonsensical or "natural" once we learn it, actually it is neither. If there is any explanation, it is historical. When we pass on to our children the meanings of what we do, our explanations consist largely of instructions to do what we learned to do before them. In societies arranged in groups or divisions or layers, the learned meanings will differ from one group to another—just as the learned dialect, say, may differ. The supposed webs of signification ought to be interpretable in terms of such differences, particularly if some meanings diffuse from one group to another. Otherwise, the assumption of a homogeneous web may mask, instead of reveal, how meanings are generated and transmitted. This is perhaps the point where meaning and power touch most clearly…

Still, sugar, tea, and like products represented the growing freedom of ordinary folks, their opportunity to participate in the elevation of their own standards of living. But to assert this is to raise some questions. The proclaimed freedom to choose meant freedom only within a range of possibilities laid down by forces over which those who were, supposedly, freely choosing exercised no control at all. That substances like sugar could be changed from curiosities or adornments in English life into essential ingredients of decent self-respecting hospitality required that people weave them into the fabric of their daily lives, endowing them with meaning and teaching each other to enjoy their consumption.

It was not by processes of symbol-making and meaning investment that sugar was made available to the English people, but because of political, economic, and military undertakings, the organization of which would have been unimaginable to the ordinary citizen. The immense quantities of coerced labor required to produce sucrose and bitter stimulant beverages also had to be arranged for, or the substances in the quantities desired would not have been forthcoming. Only with these arrangements secured could the wonderful and uniquely human capacity to find and bestow meaning be exercised. In short, the creation of a commodity that would permit taste and the symbolic faculty to be exercised was far beyond the reach of both the enslaved Africans who produced the sugar, on the one hand, and of the proletarianized English people who consumed it, on the other. Slave and proletarian together powered the imperial economic system that kept the one supplied with manacles and the other with sugar and rum; but neither had more than minimal influence over it. The growing freedom of the consumer to choose was one kind of freedom, but not another…

With the change in place of such commodities in the English diet, and the growing recognition of the ultimate consequences of mass consumption, the world market gradually set the price of sugar. But even this overstates the case, for probably no single food commodity on the world market has been subjected to so much politicking as sugar. If it earlier was too important to be left to West Indian planters, it later became too important to be left entirely exposed to market forces. Sucrose was a source of bureaucratic, as well as mercantile and industrial, wealth. Once the magnitude of its market and potential market was grasped, maintaining control over it became important. Sugar led all else in dramatizing the tremendous power concealed in mass consumption. Control over it, and responsibility for the eventual outcome, led to a sweeping revision of the philosophy that determined the connections between metropolis and colony. It might not be too much to say that the fate of the British West Indies was sealed, once it became cheaper for the British masses to have their sugar from elsewhere, and more profitable for the British bourgeoisie to sell more sugar at lower prices.

To the extent that we can define things for others under circumstances that make it difficult for them to test the meanings we attribute to those things, we are exercising control over whether those others use these things, consume them or fail to consume them, prize them or disdain them. We affect their self-definition by motivating their consumption, thereby entering intimately into the organization of their very personalities: who and what they think they are. Tobacco, sugar, and tea were the first objects within capitalism that conveyed with their use the complex idea that one could *become* different *by consuming* differently. This idea has little to do with nutrition or primates or sweet tooths, and less than it appears to have with symbols. But it is closely connected to England's fundamental transformation from a hierarchical, status-based, medieval society to a social-democratic, capitalist, and industrial society.

The argument advanced here, that big background alterations in the tempo and nature of work and daily life influenced changes in diet, is difficult or impossible to prove. The further assumption is that the nature of the new foods was important in their eventual acceptance. The substances transformed by British capitalism from upper-class luxuries into working-class necessities are of a certain type. Like alcohol or tobacco, they provide respite from reality, and deaden hunger pangs. Like coffee or chocolate or tea, they provide stimulus to greater effort without providing nutrition. Like sugar they provide calories, while increasing the attractiveness of these other substances when combined with them. There was no conspiracy at work to wreck the nutrition of the British working class, to turn them into addicts, or to ruin their teeth. But the ever-rising consumption of sugar was an artifact of intraclass struggles for profit—struggles that eventuated in a world-market solution for drug foods, as industrial capitalism cut its protectionist losses and expanded a mass market to satisfy proletarian consumers once regarded as sinful or indolent.

In this perspective, sugar was an ideal substance. It served to make a busy life seem less so; in the pause that refreshes, it eased, or seemed to ease, the changes back and forth from work to rest; it provided swifter sensations of fullness or satisfaction than complex carbohydrates did; it combined easily with many other foods, in some of which it was also used (tea and biscuit, coffee and bun, chocolate and jam-smeared bread). And as we have seen, it was symbolically powerful, for its use could be endowed with many subsidiary meanings. No wonder the rich and powerful liked it so much, and no wonder the poor learned to love it.

Notes

1. The improvement of sucrose extraction from the sugar beet, building on studies that were pioneered by Marggraff (1709–1782), was accomplished by his pupil Franz Achard (1753–1821). But it was Benjamin Delessert who manufactured loaves of white sugar in 1812, to Napoleon's delight. The French beet sugar industry received favored treatment until its product was fully competitive with cane sugar coming from French tropical colonies, such as Martinique and Guadeloupe.

2. Henning (1916). A useful discussion can be found in Pfaffman, Bartoshuk, and McBurney (1971). Henning sought to represent the relations among the tastes of bitterness, saltiness, sourness, and sweetness by a diagram having four faces... The implications of a taste system consisting of four scientifically verifiable primary tastes are very substantial, but most authorities treat this position circumspectly.

The use of the term "sweet" to describe water (and not just fresh water as opposed to saltwater or to brackish water, but also to describe the taste of water drunk after something salty, bitter, or sour has been ingested) and to describe certain foods, such as scallops and crabmeat, dramatizes the very wide range of the experience of sweetness as opposed to the relatively narrow range of sugars and of a lexicon of taste. The differences are sufficiently bewildering to lead at least one of the best students of sweetness to write: "As psychologists explore sweetness, and indeed the chemical senses, they are constantly required to emulate Janus—looking one way toward the behavior of model systems in the search for regularities and laws, but also to actual foods, where consumption occurs and where regularities give way to irregularities and laws of behavior to abundant exceptions" (Moskowitz 1974: 62).

References

Beidler, L. M. (1975), "The biological and cultural role of sweeteners," *Sweeteners: Issues and Uncertainties*. Washington, DC: National Academy of Sciences, 11–18.

Beauchamp, G. K., Maller, O. and Rogers, J.G. Jr. (1977), "Flavor preferences in cats," *Journal of Comparative and Physiological Psychology* 91 (5): 1118–27.

DeSnoo, K. (1937), "Das trinkende kind im uterus," *Monatschrift für Geburtshilfe und Gynäkologie*, 105:88.

Henning, H. (1916) *Der Geruch*, Leipzig: Johann Ambrosius Barth.

Jerome, N. W. (1977), "Taste experience and the development of a dietary preference for sweet in humans," *Taste and Development: the Genesis of Sweet Preference*, ed. J. M. Weiffenbach, Bethesda, MD: US Department of Health, Education, and Welfare, 235–48.

Kare, M. (1975), "Monellin," *Sweeteners: Issues and Uncertainties*, Washington, DC: National Academy of Sciences, 196–206.

Maller, O. and Desor, J. A. (1973), "Effect of taste on ingestion by human newborns," *Fourth Symposium on Oral Sensation and Perception*, ed. J. F. Bosma, Washington, DC: Government Printing Office, 279–91.

Moskowitz, H. (1974), "The psychology of sweetness," *Sugars in Nutrition*. ed. H. L. Sipple and K.W. McNutt, New York: Academic Press, 37–64.

Pfaffman, C., Bartoshuk, L. M., and McBurney, D. H. (1971), "Taste psychophysics," *Handbook of Sensory Physiology*, Vol. 4, *Chemical Senses*, ed. L. Beidler, Berlin: Springer, 82–102.

Ragatz, L. J. (1928), *The Fall of the Planter Class in the British Caribbean, 1763–1833*, New York: Century.

Rozin, P. (1976a), "Psychobiological and cultural determinants of food-choice," *Appetite and Food Intake*, ed. T. Silverstone, Berlin: Dahlem Conferenzen, 285–312.

——. (1976b), "The use of characteristic flavorings in human culinary practice," *Flavor: its Chemical, Behavioral and Commercial Aspects*, ed. C. M. Apt, Boulder, CO: Westview, 101–27.

Symons, D. (1979), *The Evolution of Human Sexuality*, New York: Oxford University Press.

11

Spices

Tastes of Paradise

Wolfgang Schivelbusch

Nothing could be more common than the salt and pepper on our tables. In our cuisine these two seasonings are always paired. Their containers are as alike as two eggs, indistinguishable except for the inscription on each. Yet in coupling them this way, two distinct epochs of world history are being conjoined. Salt and pepper represent two fundamentally different phases of human civilization.

Let's start with salt. Undoubtedly its first use dates back to dim prehistory. It is a primordial, sacred substance. The Latin words for "well-being," *salus,* and for "health," *salubritas,* both derive from the Latin *sal*, meaning "salt." The Romans offered salt to their gods, administered it as medication, and used it to preserve and flavor food. Elsewhere it enters the names of cities in areas where salt was obtained: Salzburg, Salzgitter, Salzwedel. In ancient Greece guests were presented with salt and bread as symbols of life and the sanctity of hospitality; and even today we give salt and bread to newlyweds when they set up housekeeping. The biblical expressions "the salt of life" and "salt of the earth" are still used in everyday speech; the more we take those meanings for granted, the less we know of their original sense. For us, salt is one of the cheapest commodities, the most plebeian of condiments; it may well seem strange to us then that the youngest daughter in the fairy tale should compare her love for her father to her love for salt: "Just as the best food is tasteless without salt, so do I love my father as much as I love salt."

Whereas salt has been a part of human civilization since time immemorial, the history of pepper can be dated more precisely. Actually the Romans already seasoned their food with it, but with the Christian Middle Ages a new chapter of universal significance began in its history.

The medieval ruling classes had a peculiar penchant for strongly seasoned dishes. The higher the rank of a household, the greater its use of spices. A cookbook from the fifteenth century gives the following directions for the preparation of meat: rabbit is prepared with ground almonds, saffron, ginger, cypress root, cinnamon, sugar, cloves, and nutmeg; chicken giblets are prepared with pepper, cinnamon, cloves, and nutmeg. Fruit is prepared similarly. Strawberries and cherries are soaked in wine and then boiled; next pepper, cinnamon, and vinegar are added. One recipe reads: "Cook a large piece of pork, not too lean and very tender. Chop it as fine as you wish, add cloves and mace and continue chopping, also chopping in dried currants. Then shape into little round balls, approximately two inches across, and set aside in a bowl; next prepare a good almond milk, mix in some rice and boil well, taking care that it stays very liquid... Sprinkle generously with sugar and mace, and serve."

Although the medieval recipes don't specify any quantities, we can deduce from other sources how much was used. For a banquet with forty guests a late-medieval household account book lists: one pound of colombine powder ... half a pound of ground cinnamon ... two pounds of sugar ... one ounce of saffron ... a quarter-pound of cloves and grains of guinea pepper (grains of paradise) ... an eighth of a pound of pepper ... an eighth of a pound of galingale ... an eighth of a pound of nutmeg ... an eighth of a pound of bay leaves." For festive occasions these quantities were substantially increased. When in 1194 the King of Scotland paid a visit to his fellow monarch Richard I of England, he received, among other tokens of hospitality, daily allotments of two pounds of pepper and four pounds of cinnamon, obviously more than one person could consume. Spices had a ceremonial as well as a culinary function here; in the Middle Ages the two were closely connected. Besides being used in food, spices were presented as gifts, like jewels, and collected like precious objects. Today we would attribute such dishes to an Arabic-Indian cuisine rather than to any Western one. Prepared foods were virtually buried under spices; food was little more than a vehicle for condiments which were used in combinations we nowadays would consider quite bizarre. At especially refined tables spices became emancipated altogether from the prepared food. They were passed around on a gold or silver tray—the spice platter—during the meal or just after it. This platter was divided into various compartments, each of which held a specific spice. Guests helped themselves, adding spices as desired to the already seasoned dish, or they used the tray as a cheese or dessert platter. They consumed pepper, cinnamon, and nutmeg as we nowadays might partake of a delicacy, a glass of sherry, or a cup of coffee. And spices were not only eaten; they were also drunk in beverages. Medieval wines were more solutions or leachates of spices than the juice of fine grapes. They were boiled, like tea, with various ingredients and then decanted.

Historians have tried to explain this powerful medieval appetite for spices by pointing to the prevalence of inadequate food-preserving techniques.

Pepper together with salt, it was said, was the chief means of preservation, of keeping the meat of cattle, slaughtered in the fall, edible throughout the winter. The other spices, according to this explanation, served to make spoiled meat edible again. This is hardly convincing, for spices imported from the Orient were among the most precious substances known in the Middle Ages. That is why they were the prerogative of the upper classes. To limit their function to food preservation and explain their use solely in those terms would be like calling champagne a good thirst quencher. Salt served very well as a meat preservative in the Middle Ages; and there were suitable native herbs which were also used by the poorer people to make spoiled meat palatable. So there must have been a different explanation for the appetite for spices of refined people in the Middle Ages.

The one thing that pepper, cinnamon, cloves, nutmeg, ginger, saffron, and a whole series of other spices had in common was their non-European origin. They all came from the Far East. India and the Moluccas were the chief regions for spices. But that's only a prosaic description of their geographic origin. For the people of the Middle Ages, spices were emissaries from a fabled world. Pepper, they imagined, grew, rather like a bamboo forest, on a plain near Paradise. Ginger and cinnamon were hauled in by Egyptian fishermen casting nets into the floodwaters of the Nile, which in turn had carried them straight from Paradise. The aroma of spices was believed to be a breath wafted from Paradise over the human world. "No medieval writer could envision Paradise without the smell or taste of spices. Whether the poetically described gardens served saints or lovers, the atmosphere was inevitably infused with the rare, intoxicating fragrance of cinnamon, nutmeg, ginger, and cloves. On the basis of such fantasies, it was possible for lovers and friends to exchange certain spices as pledges of their relationship" (Henisch 1976).

Spices as a link to Paradise, and the vision of Paradise as a real place somewhere in the East—their source—fascinated the medieval imagination. The exorbitant price of spices, which reflected the extremely long trade route from India to Europe, further enhanced this fascination. Pepper, cinnamon, and nutmeg were status symbols for the ruling class, emblems of power which were displayed and then consumed. The moderation or excess with which they were served attested to the host's social rank. The more sharply pepper seared the guests' palates, the more respect they felt for their host. This symbolic value appears also in the use of spices beyond meals and banquets. They were presented as gifts of state, and were bequeathed together with other heirlooms; in fact, pepper frequently took the place of gold as a means of payment.

The symbolic meaning and actual physical taste of medieval spices were closely intertwined. Social connections, balance of power, wealth, prestige, and all manner of fantasies were "tasted": what would become matters of social and cultural "taste" or fashion, were first matters of physical tasting. Meanwhile, the ability of people in the Middle Ages to discern social and cultural circumstances through the tasting of food came to be a completely natural, almost unconscious ability. We need only consider the connotations that sweet and dry wines conjure up today, backed by an entire social hierarchy of tastes. In the early Middle Ages, before spices had begun to take on their role, European taste had not yet been sensitized in this way; it was still dull—numb, so to speak. Spices were to give it that first and historically decisive refinement.

The role which oriental spices played in the cultural history of medieval taste is part of a more comprehensive pattern of development—a matter of taste in the broadest sense of the word: taste which the West would begin to cultivate in the high Middle Ages.

In eleventh-century Europe a new way of life was beginning to emerge, a new and unprecedented interest in beautiful objects and elegant manners. Up to that time the feudal society of the West had been more or less a backwoods agrarian civilization. The castles were little more than large fortified farmsteads, just as the life and conduct of a knight were as yet scarcely different from those of a peasant. Lords and vassals wore clothes of similar materials and ate similar foods; in short, the social and therefore cultural separation between them was relatively small. These primitive conditions changed but slowly, in the course of centuries. More and more, feudal lords developed a lifestyle intended to increase the distance between them and their subjects. Everything coarse and plebeian became anathema. The refinement of etiquette and of the objects of everyday life became one of the most effective means of separating the classes.

But let me point out one special aspect of all this refinement: it was *not* essentially an indigenous product, but an import, obtained from the same source that supplied those spices which were themselves a significant, indeed perhaps the most significant, element in this cultural change. Like the spices, all the other trappings of this new upper-class culture came from the Orient.

In the high Middle Ages "Orient" meant Arabic civilization, which Europeans first encountered extensively through the Crusades. Trade with the Orient had existed before; in fact, it had never totally ceased since Graeco-Roman times, though in the early Middle Ages it dropped to a bare minimum. But only through the Crusades did the Orient become a reality for Europe. The Crusades began as a religiously motivated military campaign, their object the liberation of the Holy Sepulcher. The unexpected outcome was the adoption by the Christian West of some of the great achievements of Arabic civilization. This Arabic influence was to have an enormous impact on the further development of Europe, comparable in a sense to the influence of Hellenistic culture on the agrarian republic that was Rome. One can speak of a prelude to, almost an anticipation of, the Renaissance by three centuries. Europe is indebted to Arabic civilization not only for its numerical system, which made possible bookkeeping and, as a consequence, modern forms of capitalist organization; and for the astronomical and nautical knowledge that first made possible the great voyages of discovery in the fifteenth and sixteenth centuries. Its direct and obvious effect upon medieval Europe was in the luxuries that ushered in an entirely new way of life. And many of these new items even brought along their original Arabic names to the West. The carpet, the sofa, and the baldachin, with which previously bare and uncomfortable living quarters were now furnished, were Arabic, as were silk, velvet, damask, and taffeta, in which the upper classes now dressed—in contradistinction to the coarse linen of their subjects. Essentially it can be described as a full-scale refurbishing of the life of the upper classes: they dressed in new materials, refurnished residential quarters in the new style, and even "disguised" the native foods with oriental seasonings.

The historically significant aspect of all this is that all the materials for these new vestments were imported. It would be accurate to speak of a borrowed culture. As a consequence, the Occident became substantially dependent upon the Orient as supplier—a situation comparable to that of twentieth-century European dependence on Arab oil. Just as oil is a vital raw material for the energy supply of industrialized countries, in the Middle Ages oriental luxury goods were indispensable to the lifestyle of the European upper classes. In both instances the Occident depends upon the Orient as its supplier, without whom it cannot function. Modern life cannot maintain itself without oil, any more than medieval civilization could have been what it was without pepper, silk, and velvet. This parallel sounds more far-fetched than it is. History has shown that the hunger for spices was capable of mobilizing forces very much as the present-day need for energy sources has done.

Significant as oriental luxury goods were to European *culture* of the Middle Ages, they were no less important to the medieval *economy*. Foreign trade that provided these luxury items was an economic enterprise on a grand scale. Economic historians agree unanimously that foreign trade was fundamentally spice trade. Spices, with pepper heading the list, were the most highly prized of all luxury goods. They played the same role, historians have noted, as cotton and tea did in English mercantilism of the nineteenth century. One can understand the true significance of pepper and the rest of the spices only when they are viewed in relation to the other luxury items; but it is also true that pepper, as the most important among them, served as a sort of spearhead for the entire Orient trade, and as such can be viewed as representative. Thus if the following discussion centers on pepper and its economic, cultural, and historical significance, keep in mind that it also applies to all the other luxury goods that were reaching Europe. Only on this basis can one speak of the historical role pepper played.

The spice trade was as lucrative an undertaking as it was complex and prone to dislocation. Pepper was first transported from the Molucca Islands and India to Syria and Egypt by Arab middlemen. There it was bought up by

Italian, primarily Venetian, traders who shipped it across the Mediterranean to Italy. Venice became the chief transfer point in Europe. Its heyday closely coincided with the period when Europe consumed the greatest amount of pepper, from the twelfth century to the sixteenth. With the profits from the spice trade the Venetian wholesale merchants built their marble palaces. The splendid architecture of Venice, flamboyantly displaying its oriental influence, became a sort of monument to the spice trade and its accrued profits. Venice marks both the high point and the decline of the medieval spice trade.

Toward the end of the Middle Ages the demand for spices rose once more to unprecedented heights. The circle of consumers expanded as the nouveau-riche urban middle class imitated the nobility in their ostentatious display of luxury. More and more people desired sumptuous, exotic clothes and sharply seasoned dishes, and this change in taste signaled the end of the Middle Ages and the dawn of the modern age. Pepper sauce had become an integral part of middle-class cuisine.

The spice trade reached the limits of its resources, becoming increasingly unable to satisfy this heightened demand. Trade routes that had served for centuries seemed suddenly obsolete. Shipment of goods across the Indian Ocean to Egypt and Syria, transport across the Isthmus of Suez to Alexandria, the reloading and shipping to Venice, and finally the arduous route over the Alps to central and north European markets could no longer satisfy the great demand, to say nothing of the prohibitive prices that resulted. Added to these technical transportation problems were those of a broadly international and political nature. Once the Mamelukes came into power in Egypt and the Turks in Asia Minor, the free trade that had existed up to that point ceased for the most part. Although the caravan route from Suez to Alexandria was not immediately cut off, the new rulers imposed extremely high tariffs.

In the fifteenth century the combination of these three factors—increased demand, stagnant transportation technology, and spiraling customs duties—led to a thirtyfold rise in the price of pepper coming from India to Venice. Rising demand and a limited supply at ever-higher prices resulted in a crisis situation. And crisis engenders a feverish search for a solution. Great innovative forces come into play—whether early capitalism in the fifteenth century or late capitalism in the twentieth, whether the product in short supply happens to be spices or petroleum. The fifteenth-century equivalent of today's quest for alternative fuel sources was a less costly trade route to the lands where spices grew, a route that would at once steer clear of toll restrictions and permit the transport of larger quantities of goods. The answer was a sea route to India, which was perhaps *the* grand obsession of the fifteenth century. A whole generation of entrepreneurs and adventurers went in search of this route. Christopher Columbus and Vasco da Gama were merely the successful heroes who made it into the history books. In any case, all who were caught up in this quest were driven by the prospect of the enormous riches that awaited the man who could put the pepper trade on a new, sounder footing. In the fifteenth century, control of the pepper trade meant having a hold over European taste and the vast sums that would be made available to maintain that taste. Whoever controlled pepper would essentially control the purse-strings of a continent. When the Portuguese, thanks to Vasco da Gama, succeeded in gaining a monopoly over the spice trade, they dictated prices as the Venetians had done before them. "The King of Portugal, Lord of Spices," as the Municipal Council of Nuremberg complains at the beginning of the sixteenth century, "has set ... prices, just as he pleases, for pepper which, at any cost, no matter how dear, will not long go unsold to the Germans."

Thus the great voyages of exploration, the discovery of the New World, the beginning of the modern age, were all closely linked to the European hunger for pepper. This hunger became a driving force in history the moment obstacles arose to interfere with its satisfaction. The taste for pepper showed symptoms of having become an addiction. Once habituated to the spices of India, Europe was ready to do anything to gratify its craving. In the ensuing quest for a sea route to India, land of pepper, the discovery of the New World was, more or less, a by-product.

Though the discovery of America was inadvertent, it proved soon enough to have an impact of the first magnitude on world history. The search for spices which led up to it offers a classic example of the Cunning of Reason. With the help of spices the Middle Ages were, so to speak, outwitted. Spices played a sort of catalytic role in the transition from the Middle Ages to modern times. They straddled the two periods, part of both, not quite belonging to either, yet decisively influencing both. In their cultural significance spices were wholly medieval; this is evident from the fact that they quickly lost that significance in the modern era. At the same time, they existed like foreign bodies in the medieval world, forerunners of the loosened boundaries of modern times. The medieval spice trade had already done away with narrow local borders. Like the money economy, the spice trade had entered the pores of the still-existing old order, already busily contributing to that society's dissolution. The hunger for spices, itself a specific medieval taste, was operating similarly. In its own way, still embedded in the religious conceptions of medieval Christianity, this taste crossed the old boundaries. A peculiarly medieval longing for faraway places—the longing we have seen for the Paradise they thought could be tasted in the spices. Paradise, in a mingling of the Christian and the exotic, was a fantastic world beyond local everyday life, not quite of this world nor of the other, located somewhere in the Orient. Something of this notion survives in the censer-swinging of the Catholic mass.

The modern era starts out in medieval guise with its quest for spices and for Paradise. The New World, discovered in the process, proved too vast, with a dynamic too much its own: "indigestible" for the Middle Ages. Thus spices lured the Old World into the New, where it lost its way. Nor would this historical background fail to leave traces on the New World. From the Spanish conquistadores to the propagandists for the American Way of Life, the New World has been hymned as a potential paradise. The paradise that the Middle Ages had sought became secularized as the land of unlimited possibilities.

The mediating role spices played between medieval and modern times is confirmed when we consider when they were at their peak. Between the eleventh and seventeenth centuries, that is, from the time of the Crusades to the period of the Dutch and English East India companies, spices dominated European taste. They were part of it and stamped it from the first stirrings of interest in lands beyond Europe to the conclusion of the conquest of the colonial world in the seventeenth century. Once there was nothing more worth mentioning to be discovered and conquered, and knowledge of the earth became common, spices apparently lost their tremendous attraction. After the discovery of the sea route to India, consumption once more rose sharply, only to taper off in time. In the seventeenth century, spices lost their supremacy in world trade. The market was saturated, if not glutted. Highly seasoned dishes no longer appealed to the European palate. With the French leading the way, European cuisine had evolved to become very much like the one we know today, more moderate in its use of spices.

This long-term transformation in taste is one factor responsible for the decrease in the importance of spices in international trade. Another, related, reason was the emergence of a new group of flavorings, or rather luxury foods, that would appeal to the Europeans at the beginning of the seventeenth century: coffee, tea, chocolate, and sugar. Economically and culturally they took on the role spices had played, becoming the most important goods in foreign trade and the basis for a new structuring of European taste.

Reference

Henisch, Bridget Ann (1976), *Feast and Fast*, University Park, PA: Pennsylvania State University Press.

12

Thick Sauce

Remarks on the Social Relations of the Songhay

Paul Stoller and Cheryl Olkes

Since Aristotle, sight has been considered the privileged sense in the Western philosophical tradition. But some cultures foreground other senses (taste, hearing, touch) to classify their experience. For the Songhay of Niger, taste plays an important role in social categorization. In this article, we examine the relationship between taste and social relations among the Songhay, demonstrating how the qualities of sauces served during meals measures degrees of social proximity. In Songhay, one should serve thick and spicy sauces to socially distant guests; only close relations should expect thin and tasteless sauces. However, sauce-makers often scramble these expectations (serving thin sauces to guests and thick sauces to relatives) to express socially pertinent themes.

Indeed, it is possible to evaluate ever-changing degrees of social integration by noting the mixtures of meat, vegetables, oil, butter, and of spices in a given sauce. We begin by recounting one incident which dramatizes this phenomenon.[1]

The Dispute

In 1984, we found ourselves in the midst of a dispute in the family of Adamu Jenitongo, wizard and priest of Tillaberi, a town situated in the west of the Republic of Niger. The quarrel reached a boiling point the day before our departure, when we were served what could only be described as a very bad sauce. This meal should have demonstrated the honor of the family, though ironically it conferred on us a new social status: we had become close enough to be singled out as the target of culinary disapproval from a woman of the family.

The source of the incident dates back to 1982. Djebo, the young woman who concocted this terrible sauce, was the mistress of Moru, the youngest son of Adamu Jenitongo; to the great shame of the family, she openly cohabited with him. Even though young Songhay are sexually active, they rarely display their sexual relations flagrantly in this way. When Stoller arrived at the end of 1982, Djebo was visibly pregnant, which increased the public humiliation of Adamu Jenitongo. Moru wanted to marry his mistress, but his father wished that he marry a Songhay; and Ramatu, Djebo's mother, wanted a Fulan for her daughter—a man of her own ethnicity. Thus were sowed the seeds of discord. For both sets of parents, the marriage of Moru, patrilineal descendent of Sonni Ali Ber (Songhay king of the fifteenth century), and of Djebo, a Fulan of noble birth, was unacceptable. Djebo threatened to commit suicide. Moru persisted in his desire to marry her. Finally, the marriage took place, demoralizing the entire family. The birth of their first child, Djamilla, did not alleviate the hostility of Adamu Jenitongo and his family towards Djebo. Before coming to live with them, Djebo had been a rebel adolescent, unpleasant, sullen, and stubborn. How could Moru have married a woman—a worrisome Fulan—who hadn't even learned to cook? Nevertheless, since she was the youngest daughter-in-law of the house, the major part of the housework was her responsibility. She drew the neighbor's well water, cleaned the courtyard, washed the kitchen utensils, crushed the rice and the millet, prepared the meals and served them to the men and women of the house. And while Djebo discharged these menial tasks, Jemma and Hadjo, the wives of Adamu Jenitongo, sat on their thresholds and loudly criticized her work.

In 1984, Djebo was grappling with difficulties from her squabbling "mothers" who, like many mothers-in-law, were of the opinion that she never did anything right: the sauce wasn't cooked enough; the sauce was overcooked; the sauce was too salty; there wasn't enough; the meat was tough; the meat was tasteless; the fire was too strong, she wasted wood; the fire wasn't strong enough to cook the food, and so forth. Djebo also had issues with her husband, Moru, who had the habit of inviting distant friends to dinner, who were more or less freeloaders. When news came that the "Europeans" were here, the crowd of freeloaders multiplied. Djebo had more rice, more spices, more meat, and more wood to buy; she had more water to bring back from the well; she had still more kitchen utensils to clean. To crown it all, Djebo also had issues with the "Europeans," to whom the "good sauces" were due.

Overburdened with work, unappreciated, Djebo had concluded that we should reimburse her for her services. After all, the "Europeans" who live in Niger often hire cooks whom they pay for their services. Earlier on the last afternoon of our visit, Djebo had prepared us a succulent sauce of tomato and meat, with the sweet savor of firewood. When she came to collect our empty bowls, we praised her culinary efforts. Djebo came again to see us an hour later. In Songhay, those who want money often come to the doorstep and wait until they have received what they desire. We knew what Djebo wanted, although she had demanded nothing of us. However, since we were the guests of her father-in-law—who, despite his poverty, made it a point of honor to appear generous—it seemed to us inappropriate to give money directly to Djebo; this would have constituted an infraction of manners. Olkes had already taken Djebo to the market to buy her clothes. Moreover, among the Songhay, money must always be given to the head of the family; it is he who redistributes it. In acting otherwise, we would have showed disrespect, even insult, towards Adamu Jenitongo. But instead of showing her displeasure directly to us, Djebo returned to her kitchen and prepared one of the most inedible sauces that we had ever been given in Africa.

We tasted all kinds of sauce (*hoy* in Songhay) during our stays in that region. We particularly appreciated those that were highly seasoned with a rather acrid pepper, despite their anesthesic effect on the tongue and lips. These are among those classified as "thick sauces," which contain a number of ingredients (meat, poultry, and an assortment of relatively expensive spices). *Mare bi hoy* is one such thick sauce, rather aromatic and highly seasoned, of which the principal ingredient, *mare fumbu*, or "smelly sorrel," emits a sharp odor, rather close to that of the shoe wax that one finds in markets. In contrast, "thin sauces" contain few ingredients and are consumed every day. Djebo's sauce, a *fukko hoy*, was a thin sauce, without meat and only seasoned with salt and fresh *fukko*, which has a vinegary taste. For the Songhay, a thin sauce turns sour in a ceremonial context (which is considered "thick"). Also, in serving us a thin sauce (and moreover a *fukko hoy* of sour taste), Djebo turned a "thick" social situation "sour," since we were the guests of the family. Her sauce demonstrated that the Songhay's sauces are carriers of gustatory messages that can contradict as well as reinforce verbal messages.

For some time, anthropologists have debated the importance of food in culture. Functionalists such as Radcliffe-Brown (1922) stressed the social function of food, investigating how emotions reinforce the membership of an individual in a community. Audrey Richards (1939) examined how exchanges of cooked food provide an index of their social relations. Structuralists such as Lévi-Strauss (1964) insisted on the semiotic function of food, particularly on the transformation of food from "raw" to "cooked," crucial also for the structural analysis of myths. Less preoccupied with knowing what place food has in local social context, Lévi-Strauss, a good rationalist, devoted himself to showing how cooking food—boiling, roasting—reflects certain logical operations (presumed universal). In this way, he slots food into preestablished universalistic and inclusive schemas. Jack Goody (1982) improved upon functionalist and structuralist approaches by focusing on production, social class, and international political economy. In all of these studies, however, food is *visualized*.

Of course, an illustrated recipe book can serve as an intellectual introduction to a given recipe; but only by actually preparing and tasting a dish can we experience its odor, taste, and consistency. In this paper, we want not only "to observe" the sauces of the Songhay, but also to "taste" them, and by means of "thick" descriptions of sensory techniques and contexts of their production, to show how different culinary preparations constitute a range of gustatory messages. At the same time, we distance ourselves from the notions of "thick description" and of "deep play" elaborated by Clifford Geertz in his work, *The Interpretation of Cultures* (1973). One of the most important themes of the interpretive anthropology of Geertz is that a culture is an ensemble of *texts* that anthropologists endeavor *to read* over the shoulder of their informants. This approach is not so much false as limited. The "textualism" which results excludes attention to the senses of social life—taste and smell—which have been devalued in Western speech since the Enlightenment (Howes 1988 and 1990, Stoller 1989b). If, as anthropologists, we are content simply to observe or "to read" social life, our descriptions will only taste of the paper on which they are written. If on the contrary we try to evoke a full range of sensory experience, our descriptions will be full of taste, texture, and scent. Onward, then, into an excursion to Songhay, to discover how Djebo could make her declaration by means of a sauce.

Sauces and Women

The historical (cf. es-Saadi 1900; Kati 1913; Boulnois and Hama 1953; Hama 1968; Kimba 1981; Fugelstad 1985), or ethnographic (cf. Rouch 1953a, 1953b, 1960; Olivier de Sardan 1982, 1984; Stoller and Olkes 1987; Stoller 1989a, 1989b) works on the Songhay give only a partial picture of the society, because they do not reveal a lot about the social life of women. The sociological study of Diarra (1976) is a notable exception, for it analyzes the results of a questionnaire concerning the attitudes of women toward men, marriage, and children. Even this study, however, provides little information about the relationships between men and women in the interior of familial enclosures.

It is not only the women who are forgotten in studies on Niger; no one has written a great deal about the sauces of Songhay either. This comes as no surprise. Sauces have their place in recipe books, not in dissertations. How can one link something as down to earth as sauces with politics, rights, and social relations? But sauces are important for the men and women that we met in their towns and villages. They are deeply interested in the taste of their sauces; they genuinely *taste* them. Certain ones are pungent, others spicy. Certain ones do not contain meat, others are composed of a mix of meat and boiled vegetables. Many mothers affirmed to us that a woman who is not proud of her sauces lacks self-esteem. Others praised the beauty of the fattest members of their family, testifying thereby to their estimate of the culinary talents of the women who cook for them. In 1976–1977, Stoller hired one of the most famous cooks of Songhay, Bankano de Mehanna. His Songhay informants assured him that Bankano, born in Gao, in the Republic of Mali, was still a true Songhay sauce-maker. "When a man sits down to taste Bankano's millet paste (*korba-korba*), covered in okra sauce (*hoy*)," said an old man from Mehanna, "he knew paradise on earth. He will not lift his head before scraping the bottom of the bowl until the last drop, as God is my witness!"

Finally introduced to an expert on all things culinary, Stoller had Bankano cook for him. Delighted, the cook prepared his favorite dishes regularly: the famous millet paste with okra sauce, a fish sauce deliciously aromatized with butter oil and onion flour and served with rice, a mix of rice and meat cooked in a pepper tomato sauce (*surundu*), finally and above all, chicken in a savory sesame sauce. Unlike most of his university colleagues in Niger, Stoller didn't lose weight during his visits. Bankano was very proud of his increasing paunch, which reinforced her own reputation as a cook.

Meals and Sauces

The quality of food in Niger depends on the proximity of the River Niger. In distant villages, the number of sauces that is possible to prepare is limited. Since the river provides both the permanent source of water and a means of transportation, the riverside villages such as Mehanna and Tillaberi are excellent places from which to study the sauces of Songhay. In all Songhay villages, the basic food is millet and sorghum, but in the villages rice, cheaper and more abundant, is rapidly replacing millet. Every afternoon, women prepare millet pulp, called *doonu*. There are two kinds of *doonu*. In order to prepare *ferkusu* pulp, women crush the millet in mortars and add water to make a ball of paste, which they cook in a pot of boiling water for twenty minutes or so. Once the millet is cooked, they shake it up in a bottle filled with water or a mix of water and curdled milk, until they get a thick pulp. A lot of people add to this lightly sour mixture a handful of sugar. Many women drink large quantities of this liquid millet, believed to fatten.

In most residences, evening meals consist of millet paste or *korba-korba* ("stir-stir"). The preparation starts long before the actual cooking, when women pound the millet seeds into very fine flour which they spread on sheets of palm and let dry all afternoon in the sun. Once dry, they sift the flour and boil it in a large pot. The women add small quantities of flour to the boiling water, all the while vigorously stirring the mixture with a stick. When all of the flour has been added, they continue to stir the hot pot, holding the stick with two hands, for fifteen minutes, until the paste holds it upright. Millet is usually served with okra or peanut sauce. In the western regions of Songhay, the wild seed *gensi* is set in flour and prepared the same way as millet. Only plentiful to the next rainy and particularly humid season, *gensi* is a dish reserved only for special occasions...

Sauces

Sauces constitute the distinctive trait of Songhay cuisine. As mentioned above, sauces can be divided in two categories: with or without meat. Sauces with meat may contain pieces of beef, chicken, sheep, goat, camel, fish (*ham isa*, or "meat of the river") or game (*genji ham*, or "meat of the brush"—those wild animals who had their throats cut in order to pass from the prohibited food category into the edible food category). The Songhay delight in meat sauces, because in a number of families, there is only meat once or twice a week: Friday, the day of the Muslim Sabbath, and trading days.

The Songhay call sauces without meat *hoy komo* (literally "without sauce"). These sauces vary according to regional preferences and available spices. In the east of Songhay, the preferred sauce is *gunda hoy*: it begins with onions and garlic in peanut oil, then some water, then at the boiling point, pulverized sheets of *gunda*. The result is a sauce seasoned with salt, a small amount of carob, and a little pepper.

The inhabitants of the riverside regions prefer okra sauce. It is prepared the same way as *gunda hoy*, except that okra powder is added to the boiling mix. This yields a viscous, dull-green sauce with a light, sour taste, which is seasoned with salt, carob, red pepper in varied proportions, and *gebu*, a mix of onion and sesame flour. Another sauce, less appreciated, is made with pulverized leaves from the baobab tree. Prepared in the same way as the other meatless sauces, this lime-green sauce is of a sugary taste, called *ko hoy*, and it is an important source of calcium. Like *gunda hoy*, the meatless sauce of baobab leaves is not highly seasoned.

In the west of Songhay, the inhabitants consume large quantities of okra sauce seasoned with *mare bi*, a black paste with a very pronounced taste, made from seeds of fermented sorrel. For a lot of people in this region, a sauce, even a meatless sauce, is not complete without *mare bi*. A number of inhabitants in the western and riverside regions detest its indescribable flavor. We belong to this group.

Sauces like *fukko hoy* and *gisima hoy*, made with sorrel leaves, only are served during the rainy season (June until September), when these plants can be gathered or bought fresh at the market. Sorrel sauce can be a very refined dish, but a *fukko hoy* seasoned only with salt, just as Djebo served it to us, shrivels up your tongue: it's a sauce that one serves if, and only if, one has nothing else to offer...

When we were with Adamu Jenitongo, we rarely added meat to sauce; it was more common to grill or to spice up meat with onions and garlic and serve it separately from the basic dish and the sauce. This practice is always common in the more isolated regions of Songhay. During our visits to Wanzerbe and Simiri-Sohanci, we were never served meat in sauce. It seemed to us probable that making a meal with meat is rare in these regions because the host emphasizes the event by serving the meat separately. However, one of our hosts in Wanzerbe asserted that meat actually worsens the sauce. In Tillaberi, we ate sauces with meat only if *we* bought the meat for the meal. But if a client of Adamu Jenitongo gave him an animal for sacrifice, we ate it separately, whether a chicken, a sheep, a goat, or a cow. Adamu Jenitongo never gave us an explanation for this, but our own ethnocentric taste buds confirmed to us that which our host had told us: meat negatively affects okra, baobab, or *gunda* sauce…

The merchants of dry and spicy products, who are often Hausa, also reside in Songhay towns. Women go every day to the spice display window, with its black pyramids of *mare bi*, its pepper dunes in orange-colored powder, its salt rocks. The number and the odor of the spice display windows increases tenfold on market days. With the heat, a vague but powerful aroma rises and engulfs the idle onlooker with scents of ginger, garlic, anise, black pepper, pepper, peanut cake, carob, *gurundugu*, which has a nutmeg odor, and onion. It is from these same merchants that the women buy the tomato puree that has become the base for the majority of sauces with meat in these towns. To prepare a typical meat sauce, women put the meat with onions cut in thin slices and some garlic into a large pot. Next they add tomato puree. When the meat has browned nicely, they add an entire half-pot of water and bring it to a boil. During this time, they crush a mixture of carob nuts, pepper, salt, and other desired spices in a mortar. Around five minutes before the sauce is "ripe," as the Songhay say, they incorporate some cassava flour or crushed marrow (according to the season), to make the sauce thicken. A hot, pungent sauce made of beef, sheep, or goat results. These meat sauces are usually served in the afternoon with rice, which is easy to get in the urban and riverside regions.

The Songhay consume chicken and other poultry (guinea-fowl, bustard, quail, duck, goose) less often than sheep, beef, or goat. Chickens, which one never finds at butchers in the market, are killed on two occasions: in honor of a guest, and to offer in sacrifice to the spirits. The majority of the time chickens are roasted in peanut oil and spices. In the riverside towns, however, chicken is sometimes cooked in a tomato sauce. Today, the most popular of these sauces is cooked chicken in a tomato sauce with peanut or marrow. During our stay with Adamu Jenitongo, we consumed an unusual quantity of chicken. In his work as a sorcerer and a spirit-possession priest, Adamu Jenitongo received sacrificial chickens three to four times a week. Certain Songhay affirm that the more one eats meat, the longer one will live. When we asked about the reason for the longevity of the members of Adamu Jenitongo's family—he himself died in 1988 at the age of 106 – the response was invariably that sorcerers eat more meat…

Sauces with fish constitute a category apart from the geographical limits of the fish supply. The River Niger overflows with a number of species of succulent fish, and those who live along the banks enrich their supply of these treasures of the river. Sautéed fish (*soye ye*) seasoned with red pepper constitutes one of the favorites for late afternoon. The fetid odor of fish dried or smoked in the sun and sold at the market is especially strong when a foul fish is left to rot in the sun for three or four days. The rotting fish (*ham isa fumbu*) is a delicate dish for some—but not for us.

The Hierarchy of Sauces

Of course, Songhay cooks are limited to what ingredients they have at their disposal. For example, in the east of Songhay, farmers do not generally use sesame. In the west, *gunda* is not as abundant as in the east. The condiments and the spices are found in greater quantity in the towns than in the villages further out. There are also seasonal fluctuations. During the rainy season (June until September), one gathers or buys fresh ingredients (particularly sorrel and *fukko*). One eats marrow at the end of the dry and cold season (January and February). Finally, the price of ingredients also has an influence on the kinds of sauces that Songhay cooks prepare. It is often the cook who determines if the sauces will be with or without meat. If the cook prepares a meat sauce, it is still the price which determines if they will use filets, chops, or giblets. The region, the size of the community, the season and the price of ingredients constitute therefore four important variables regarding the distribution of Songhay sauces.

In January 1989, Stoller took a trip to Sohanci, a small village situated in the heart of Zermagunda, in eastern Songhay. Its seventy-five inhabitants consider themselves patrilineal descendants of Sonni Ali Ber. Today these descendants are called *Si hamey* or "small children" of Sonni Ali Ber. A small number of *Si hamey* become *sohanci*, sorcerers, and mature to be the guardians of the science of witchcraft of their famous ancestor.

Stoller offered a gift of tobacco and kola and was warmly received. His host killed two chickens in his honor and arranged for his wife to prepare a good meal. Some hours later, Stoller was served a steaming plate of rice covered in okra sauce, a dull green, without tomato and seasoned with *gurundugu*, of which the nutmeg savor offset the lightly sour taste of the sauce. The chicken, roasted, was served separately... For breakfast the next morning, the cooks reheated the leftovers from the night before. Stoller made himself instant coffee. In short, Stoller's hosts underlined his invited status in serving chicken at the first meal, but the following meals were not outstanding. This sequence is explained by the isolation of Sohanci and the relative poverty of his host. He only had five chickens and he killed two of them in Stoller's honor. He had gathered a lot of millet and okra that year, and his wives and his daughters had collected great quantities of *gunda*. Consequently, he offered what he could to his guest, and he made sure that Stoller ate a hot meal at noon. Normally, he and his family drank millet paste at noon and waited until evening to eat millet and sauce.

In these rural regions of eastern Songhay, sauces of *gunda* or of okra, without tomato, are appropriate for guests. These thick sauces must be highly seasoned with salt, strong pepper, and carob. At least one meal must consist of a separate dish of grilled or sautéed meat, or of chicken for preference. The light sauces are not accompanied by meat and are not spiced with carob, ginger, or pepper either. In towns the hierarchy of sauces is more elaborate with the availability of beets, tomato puree, rice, and dozens of spices. Here still, thick sauces—sauces that express consideration, codes of manners, and social distance—will all probably be served with meat and tomato. Tomato sauce with meat, served with rice, is a rare dish far from the banks of the River Niger. But in towns as well as villages, thin, sour sauces without meat, without tomato, and served with millet, are considered low-grade. These sauces express social proximity and are consumed in ordinary circumstances. The lowest rank would include the *gunda hoy* or the *fukko hoy,* with its sour taste and acrid odor.

In western Songhay as well, the inclusion of meat in a meal, such as beef, sheep, goat, or chicken, constitutes a mark of honor for the guest. Since the living conditions were generally good in this region during the time of the visits we made in 1977, 1979–1980 and 1982–1983, Stoller ate a lot of grilled meat and millet paste covered in *mare hoy* (the favorite sauce) while he was there. As in the rural regions of eastern Songhay, Stoller shared his meat with his hosts. When the supply of meat diminished, his hosts served him millet with a sauce of fermented sorrel or an okra sauce.

During our stay in 1984, a famine year, the hospitality of our hosts was limited by the lack of supplies. The climactic conditions and the food shortage had obliged the inhabitants to reduce their consumption of food to one meal a day and even, in certain cases, to one meal every two days. That July, the month of our visit, there was not even any millet. We did not expect great displays of hospitality, and we had brought food to fill the family pantry. In spite of everything, our hosts killed some chickens in our honor. A relatively easygoing woman invited us to eat at her home. She served us three chickens with *gensi*, a very rare dish, and also prepared a dish of tomato sauce with baobab—all in all, a mark of consideration, of respect, and of social distance...

In sum: the sauces prepared for occasions that require observance of social distance (thick sauces) contain meat or tomato puree, onions, garlic, a pinch of peanut flour, and pulverized carob mixed with *gurundugu*, ginger, and black pepper. During the rainy season, when the brushes are covered with buds and the shepherds graze their livestock, a thick sauce can be enriched with butter oil. Fish is also much appreciated in a spicy tomato sauce. Sauces which indicate social proximity (thin sauces) are without meat, without tomato, seasoned simply with salt and black pepper or pimento, and served with rice, sometimes with millet paste. Short on spices, thin sauces are a lot less aromatic than thick sauces.

From these observations, we can establish several links between sauce and social relationships:

The more an event is marked... by the presence of people having an elevated social status (a noble, a European, or an invited stranger); by rituals with sacrifices and with ceremonial meals for the family; *the thicker the sauce is...*

1. It is more likely that cooks will add meat to enhance the quality of the sauce, chicken conferring the highest social status to the invited guests from his hosts.
2. It is more likely that cooks will prepare a spicy tomato sauce with an assortment of aromatic condiments and not sour ones (*gurundugu*, white and black pepper, anise, carob).
3. It is more likely that cooks will add marrow or cassava flakes to thicken the sauce.
4. It is more likely that cooks will prepare food out of the ordinary (eastern or western Songhay rice, *gensi* from western Songhay, expensive fish, such as perch from the Nile, in riverside Songhay).

How to Play with Sauces

Until this point, we have described a very widespread social phenomenon in Songhay. It is hardly original to suggest that sauces and special dishes are prepared to mark ritualistic events or to make homage to important guests. But this only mentions the basic ingredients of our "analytical recipe." How do Songhay cooks play with their sauces? How do they handle the ingredients, the tastes, the consistencies, in order to send socially significant messages? In most cases, they use "correct" ingredients, so that the taste and the texture of food are appropriate to the social situation. But during our stay in Niger, we observed or participated in unseemly meals where cooks deliberately prepared a thin sauce for a thick social occasion, to the great disgust and shame of the host.

It is an incident of this sort that took place the night before our departure from Tillaberi in 1984, when Djebo served us her infamous *fukko hoy*—without meat, without tomato, and without spices. This sauce was a declaration of protest. Her political situation in Adamu Jenitongo's family was a completely helpless one. Since she was of a different ethnic group and the youngest adult of the family, her verbal complaints were ignored. By serving us a thin sauce in a thick situation, she succeeded in attracting the attention of everyone. Djebo's bad sauce emitted emphatic messages: (1) she was displeased with her position in the family; and (2) she was displeased with our presence, which had transformed a thin social situation into a thick social situation, where the rules and the etiquette obliged her to spend a great deal of her time preparing thick sauces. She discharged her task with submission, despite the criticism of her in-laws, according to whom she always failed to make good sauces. At the conclusion of our stay, Djebo had reached the end of her rope, and she prepared her *fukko hoy*: thin, repulsive—so bad that we have described it elsewhere as a sociocultural equivalent of vomit (Stoller and Olkes 1986).

It goes without saying that Djebo acted with full knowledge of the meaning of her actions. At the beginning, she protested against her situation in playing with "correct" ingredients to concoct thick but deficient sauces. These drew mutterings of discontent from the family, but no one wanted to reprimand her because her sauces were correct: they were thick, they were aromatic, they contained meat. When finally she prepared a thin and deficient sauce, her action ignited arguments, reprimands, insults, and apologies, because the family was shamed to have so insulted their guests. The older son of Adamu Jenitongo, Moussa, stated: "She treats you like she treats us: now you are part of the family." In other words, Djebo's sauce had changed our social category from marked to non-marked. Actually, the quality of sauces did not show any sign of improvement during Stoller's subsequent visits. In 1987, they were so bad that Moussa had nearly every meal in town and, during Stoller's visit, he made an agreement that the daughter of the sister of his father, Ramatu, prepare the meals in the afternoon. Moussa did not forget to bring a portion of the sauce to his father. For Moussa, who still had not married, the only solution to the meal problem was marriage. His new wife would replace Djebo as the principal cook of the family.

Note

1. This chapter is based on extensive stays with the Songhay, in the Republic of Niger, in 1976–1977, 1979–1980, 1981, 1982–1983, 1984, 1985–1986, 1988–1989.

References

Boulnois, J. and Hama, B. (1953), *L'Empire de Gao. Magie, Coutume et Religion*, Paris: Maisonneuve.

Diarra, A. (1976), *Femmes Songhay-Zerma*, Paris: Éditions Anthropos.

Es-Saadi, M. (1900), *Tarikh al-Soudan*, Paris: Maisonneuve.

Fugelstad, F. (1985), *The Colonial History of Niger*, London: Cambridge University Press.

Geertz, C. (1973), *The Interpretation of Cultures*, New York: Basic Books.
Goody J. (1982), *Cooking, Cuisine and Class*, Cambridge: Cambridge University Press.
Hama, B. (1968), *L'Histoire Songhaï*, Paris: Présence Africaine.
Howes, D. (1988), "On the odor of the soul: spatial representation and olfactory classification in Eastern Indonesia and Western Melanesia," *Bijdragen tot de Taal Landen Volkenkunde*, 124: 84–113.
——. (1990), "Controlling textuality: a call for a return to the senses," *Anthropologica*, 32.
Kati, M. (1913), *Tarick al Fattach*, Paris: Maisonneuve.
Kimba, I. (1981), *Guerres et Sociétés*, Niamey: Université de Niamey.
Lévi-Strauss C. (1964), *Le Cru et le Cuit*, Paris: Plon.
Olivier de Sardan, J. P. (1982), *Concepts et Conceptions Sonay-Serma*, Paris: Nubia.
——. (1984), *Société Sonay-Serma*, Paris: Karthala.
Radcliffe-Brown, A. R. (1922), *The Andaman Islanders*, Cambridge: Cambridge University Press.
Richards, A. (1939), *Land, Labour and Diet in Northern Rhodesia: An Economic Study of the Bemba Tribe*, Oxford: Oxford University Press.
Rouch, J. (1953a), *Les Songhay*, Paris: Presses Universitaires de France.
——. (1953b), *Essai sur l'Histoire Songhay*, Dakar: Institut Français d'Afrique Noire.
——. (1960), *La Religion et la Magie Songhay*, Paris: Presses Universitaires de France.
Stoller, P. (1989a), *Fusion of the Worlds: An Ethnography of Possession Among the Songhay of Niger*, Chicago: University of Chicago Press.
——. (1989b), *The Taste of Ethnographic Things: The Senses in Anthropology*, Philadelphia: University of Pennsylvania Press.
Stoller, P. and Olkes, C. (1986) "Bad Sauce, Good Ethnography," *Cultural Anthropology*, 1, 3: 336–352.
——. (1987), *In Sorcery's Shadow: A Memoir of Apprenticeship Among the Songhay of Niger*, Chicago: University of Chicago Press.

Part IV

Body and Soul

Preface

Tasting and eating are frequently categorized as purely physical activities, the chief function of which is to fuel the body. Any such reduction, however, ignores the myriad ways that specific foods, drinks, and tastes have been conceived to nourish not only the body but the soul. Concepts of foods as spiritual nourishment abound in numerous cultural and religious traditions, and this section presents perspectives on a number of them.

Use of food and drink in ceremonies and rituals is probably one of the most common ways that foods and their flavors achieve meaning and social significance. But the ways that this occurs vary profoundly. Sometimes revelry accompanies eating, and tastes are offered for their pleasures as well as their meanings. Weddings and birthdays may be the most common instances of this. Other times the consumption is so formalized that it hardly counts as "eating" in the ordinary sense of the term, as with the Christian Eucharist, where the body and blood of Christ are ritually consumed. Although this sacrament echoes the Passover meal of the Last Supper, it can no longer be called a "meal" in any ordinary sense at all. Still other times the meanings of foods are represented by their absence, as with the many traditions in which fasting—the deprivation of taste altogether—plays a role in meditation and purification.

Although the differences among the practices here reviewed are profound, there are some general themes that unite many religious uses of foods. In traditions as diverse as Buddhist, Hindu, Christian, and Muslim, indulgence in the pleasures of the flesh is considered on the whole both unhealthy and spiritually corrupting. Thus we see that restrictions on consumption are often advised, from complete abstinence to ritual limitations on what may be eaten during special holy days. Secondly, foods and their peculiar tastes are imbued with special meanings that are invoked both for the health of the body (as with the alchemical medicines described by T. Sarah Peterson in her account of ancient medicinal traditions) and for the cleansing of the mind (as R. S. Khare describes in his analysis of Hindu holy men). D. T. Suzuki's presentation of the Japanese ceremony of tea links the very taste of tea to Zen philosophy and its devotion to simplicity and spiritual clarity.

Particular proscriptions on eating and drinking are apparent in cyclic holidays such as Ramadan and Passover, when special foods and prohibitions call religious obligations to attention. In traditions such as these, the community of observers is even more tightly knit than usual, for (ideally) all and only members of the religious community observe the ritual eating patterns together.

The first of the entries in this section is historical, as Peterson details the extraordinary practices of classical and medieval medicine, when even the planets which were thought to govern human fate were assigned special tastes and smells. The three succeeding entries concern religious and cultural traditions—Hindu, Buddhist, Muslim—where abstinence or food prohibitions play at least some role in the meanings assigned to gustatory experience. A brief selection from the Haggadah, the service that attends the celebration of Passover, illustrates meanings of particular tastes in the Jewish tradition, which have been observed for millennia. Finally, the Mexican Day of the Dead extends the pleasures of the table to the souls of the dead, a practice that Carmichael and Sayer analyze in their study of the eating that attends this unique Mexican holiday.

13

Food as Divine Medicine

T. Sarah Peterson

Arabic food developed in a culture that associated medical concepts with the divine. The author of the tenth-century history of the world known as *Meadows of Gold* revels in the voluptuous meal that is part of the sensual paradise brought down to earth. Images connect this food to cordial, alchemical, and astral medicine. The tinting of food in hues of rose and gold, the jewel-like quality of the preparations, the emphasis on light coming out of darkness and subtle odors offered to the soul—all point to a cuisine at once sensual and luxurious, medicinal and divine.

The bowls for the meal are scarlet and yellow, and eggs have been dyed red (*Baghdad Cookery Book* 21, 24).

> Here capers grace a sauce vermilion
> Whose fragrant odours to the soul are blown
> Like powder'd musk in druggist's fingers strewn.
> Here, too, sweet marjoram's delicious scent
> With breath of choicest doves is richly blent;
> While cinnamon, of condiments the king,
> Unblemished hue, unrivalled seasoning,
> Like musk in subtle odour rises there,
> Tempting the palate, sweetening the air. [p. 22]
> . . .
> With sugar of Ahwaz complete
> In taste 'tis sweeter than the sweet.
> Its trembling mass in butter drowned
> With scent the eater wraps around;
> As smooth and soft as dotted cream,
> Its breath like ambergris dothe seem;
> And when within the bowl 'tis seen,

> A star in darkness shines serene,
> Or as cornelian's gold is strung
> Upon the throat of virgin young;
> It is more sweet than sudden peace
> That brings the quaking heart release... [p. 28]

Sugar, spice, and saffron made for more than a sensuous experience at table. Their properties were vital to a system of medicine that offered relief from melancholia and sundry bodily ills and the means to stave off old age. By the fifteenth century, streams of cordial, alchemical, and astral medicine ran together into a broad river of divine medicine. In this system the medicinal properties of fragrance and color did not work directly upon the body, as sweetness did; they worked on the *spiritus*, or the breath—the entity that connected body and soul.

Avicenna and Cordials

This divine medicine had Arabic sources. A prominent advocate, known to medieval and Renaissance Europe as the "prince of physicians," was born in 980 near Bukhara, on the eastern edge of the Islamic empire. Avicenna traveled widely, treated the politically powerful, and through his voluminous writings on philosophy and medicine influenced the whole of his society. His *Canon of Medicine* included ideas derived from Galen and from the writings that went under the name of Hippocrates, ideas of Avicenna's predecessors and contemporaries in the Arabic world, and Avicenna's own thoughts. One of his shorter treatises (*Powers of the Heart*), known in Europe as *De Viribus Cordis,* described a manner of curing melancholia through treatment of the *spiritus.* To this end he prescribed cordials, so called because they were supposed to work upon the heart. The heart in turn was thought to generate food for the *spiritus* (Avicenna, *Treatise*: 548)...

The aromatic cordial was intended to rarefy the *spiritus*—to make it finer and less matter-like; to make it, that is, into subtle matter. In treating the melancholic with fragrant cordial prescriptions, the physician attempted to attentuate the *spiritus* by forcing it up a ladder of rarefaction. The more rarefied the *spiritus,* the nobler. "The nobler the character possessed by it and the nobler its substance, the more luminous does it become, and the more like celestial substance will it be." In fact, the *spiritus* glows more and more as it "approaches toward the likeness of celestial beings. It is a ray of light." Cordials that "supply the breath with brilliance and luminosity" are pearl and silk. The shinier and more abundant the *spiritus,* the more invigorated the "natural faculties" and the less the darkness of melancholia shadows the mind (*Treatise*: 123, 535, 538, 547, 549).

Alchemy: Matter Made Celestial

A second stream, alchemical medicine, flowed together with cordial medicine to constitute divine medicine in Europe. Early Greco-Middle Eastern alchemy, a marriage of mysticism and technology, at first aimed to create not actual gold but a catalyst. This catalyst, a stone later known in Europe as the philosopher's stone, or *lapis,* was said to be purplish or reddish-gold, of sweet taste, and fragrant (Multhauf 1967: 106–7). The alchemist claimed that with the stone he could transform matter into a celestial-like or incorruptible substance; he could, for example, turn base metal into gold. The alchemist's aim was to spiritualize the world by restoring it to its former purity. Because the human body was part of the material world, alchemists turned to the magic of the metallic ritual to free themselves of their own corporeal bounds.

The Greco-Middle Eastern alchemist was a dyer. In his attempt to spiritualize base metals and make them into gold, he used tinctures. The tincture might be the color desired to begin with, say yellow, or a substance that, though not itself yellow, would in the chemical process impart the color yellow. The spirit or essence of gold was carried in its tincture. Our earliest clearly alchemical text outside of China, a work from the Hellenistic period, notes that "anything which can yellow is the same as anything which can produce gold or the color of gold." A later European alchemical text based on an Arabic source said that the philosopher's stone was like crushed saffron (Multhauf: 125; Taylor 1962: 32–3, Hopkins 1934: 65). Saffron is red, but it dyes other substances a golden yellow.

By the seventh century, technical alchemy seems to have dropped away in Alexandria. The language of the texts is distant from anything that could be followed as a laboratory procedure. The alchemists seem to have ceased their efforts to restore the world, including themselves, to primal purity by chemical means. Their now strictly meditative alchemy aimed, like the procedures of Neoplatonists, Christians, and Gnostics, at ushering them into divine light. The works of these late Alexandrian alchemists present a terrible vision of a constant night-like, stinking world. Their wails against the dross of darkness and putrescence resemble the cry of melancholics as they flee their shadowy existence. An eighth-century alchemical text mourns the present state and strains toward a future bathed in radiant light: "When the spirit of darkness and of foul odour is rejected, so that no stench and no shadow of darkness appear, then the body is clothed with light and the soul and spirit rejoice, because darkness has fled from the body" (Holmyard 1957: 29–30).

This mystical side of alchemy was all that remained of the Greco-Middle Eastern "art" until the Arabs revitalized its laboratory aspect in about the eighth century. Arabic alchemy, however, was not simply a resuscitation of Alexandrian alchemical visionaries. The Arabic alchemist sought an elixir of miraculous medical powers, including the key to longevity. The Chinese had practiced alchemical elixir medicine for centuries before the Arabs took it up, and the Arabs most likely derived the idea of elixir medicine from them, either directly during journeys to China or indirectly through learned communities in Persia, which also traded in East Asia. Whether Chinese and Greco-Middle Eastern alchemy stemmed from a common system we do not know. Alchemy in East Asia and the Hellenistic world did arise at roughly the same time—the first few centuries before the Common Era.

Chinese texts show the alchemist as a person of benevolence, a physician on a holy mission to free the frail human body from the ravages of sickness and melancholy through elixirs, or panaceas. Chinese practitioners prescribed fragrances, gold, and liquid pearl (for its luminous quality) among the materials in their alchemically prepared mixtures to be ingested. Greek pharmacy included no gold or pearl at all to be taken internally; yet both were among Avicenna's cordials. Avicenna is, strictly speaking, not an alchemist in the Greco-Middle Eastern sense (he denied that his peers could transform base metal into gold), but his use of gold and pearl to work upon the *spiritus* does show his connection with Chinese alchemy (Sivin 1968: 25–6, 169–214).

Astral Magic: Drawing on the Planets

The third principal kind of divine medicine is derived from astral magic. Astrology simply foretold events on the basis of the configuration of the heavenly bodies, but astral magic attempted to interfere with fate by manipulating the environment to ward off evil influences.

The art of controlling planetary influences had been developing since antiquity and perhaps reached its zenith, at least so far as details are concerned, in an Arabic book of magic, the *Picatrix,* in twelfth-century Spain. The theory it embodied was that each planet is associated with certain terrestrial substances, and that a person who wishes benefits from a heavenly body must assemble and use the terrestrial substances that are correlated with that planet. In rites for Saturn, evil-smelling incenses such as castor and asafetida were to be used, for Mars, pepper, long pepper, and ginger; for the Sun, musk and amber; for Venus, rose, violet, and green myrtle; for Mercury, a blend of perfumes; for the Moon, camphor and rose. General incense fumigations for the planets are said to contain cinnamon, cardamom, and nutmeg. Taste, too, is correlated with the planets. Bad tastes attract Saturn; sweet and mellow ones, Jupiter; the hot, dry, and bitter, Mars; sweet and rich, the Sun; all good-tasting sweet things, Venus; all sour things, Mercury; all insipid things, the Moon. The planets are also linked with colors, jewels, languages, religion, the arts and crafts, organs of the body, plants, animals, and signs (Yates 1979: 50–1, Majriti 1962: 157–63, 167–8, 228–9). A prescription for living offered by an astral physician would read something like this: Place yourself in a certain kind of landscape; surround yourself with specific plants and animals; exhibit particular jewels and create gem-like things; eat special foods; and smell certain odors. Do whatever is feasible to adjust to particular configurations of heavenly bodies...

By the end of the thirteenth century the kind of cordial medical theory that Avicenna's *De Viribus Cordis* represents had borne fruit in Italian pharmaceutical collections. A prescription concocted by Taddeo Alderotti, who spent his academic career at Bologna, includes as basic components precious stones, pearls, coral, gold, silver, silk, saffron, aromatics, and sugar. The ingredients, which he spelled out in detailed measure, are taken with wine:

> The heart is soothed from the inside and from the outside. To comfort the heart internally take one half drachma each of beryl, emerald, saffire, red jacinth. Also two drachmas each of gold and silver. Also one drachma and a half of both kinds of pearls. Also four drachmas each of bugloss, *doronicum*, and zedoary, white and red ben, cinnamon, clove, aloewood. One drachma each of ground silk, saffron, cubebs, cardamom, amber, camphor, and musk. Also two and a half drachmas of coral, sandal, rose, dross of metals (spodium), *terra sigillata*, coriander. Pulverize everything which must be pulverized. To one ounce of the spices put one pound of sugar. Musk, however, [is not ground] but dissolved with bugloss water. One drachma of this electuary is taken with fragrant wine.
>
> (Aldarotti: 132)

The kind of recipe found in Aldarotti appears also in many variations of the cordials in Marsilio Ficino's celebrated late fifteenth-century *De Vita Libri Tres*. This book exhausted nearly thirty editions as Europeans soaked up its theories and recipes, before it basically dropped out of sight after its 1647 edition. Ficino began his studies in medicine at the University of Florence, but turned more and more to philosophy and especially to Plato. He was in the process of translating Plato's *Dialogues* for his patron, Cosimo de' Medici, when Cosimo put into his hands the *Corpus Hermeticum,* which Cosimo had just acquired from a Byzantine source, and asked him to translate it. This mystical and magical collection, thought to be the work of an ancient Egyptian sage known as Hermes Trismegistus, was to influence Ficino's own future work. In the course of his career as head of the Platonic Academy in Florence, Ficino became increasingly involved with the concept of a *prisca theologica,* an ancient theology of divine wisdom said to have passed in succession from the Persian Zoroaster to the Egyptian Hermes Trismegistus, then to Moses, to Plato, and finally to the Christian fathers, including Pseudo-Dionysius (Yates: 12–13).

Ficino's fifteenth-century society was in the grip of astrology, which, with the arrival of the new Arabic ideas, had again become a potent force... Saturn, believed to bode evil, was central to these early Renaissance astrological concerns. Saturn was thought to cause melancholy, its principal manifestation an excess of black bile. It was the Arabs who had firmly linked Saturn to this pathological disorder of darkness, but even they conceded that Saturn was not wholly malevolent; melancholy brought benefits along with its disadvantages. Ficino observed that though it was true that Jupiter smiled on those who led ordinary lives, Saturn, "the most powerful of all" to "the Arabic writers," took in the sequestered and intellectual. To them he was "friendly as to his kinfolk." Simply to be born under Saturn got you only bad effects. You were a mere ordinary melancholic. But if you were doubly Saturnian—that is, if you were born under Saturn and were intellectual, as Ficino was—or if you engaged in lofty mental pursuits even though you had been born under another planet, you were a special kind of melancholic and a marvelous path to wisdom was open to you. Not everyone chose this option, for it required an intrepid traveler, an intellectual who did not fear to move by means of contemplative exercises deep into Saturn's shadow. Thus Ficino claimed that gifts awaited persons "who give themselves over with their whole mind to the divine contemplation signified by Saturn himself" (Klibansky, Panofsky, and Saxl 1964: 188, 198; Ficino 365–7, Bk. III Ch. 22)...

Besides courting Saturn through contemplation, one could draw down beneficial effects from that and other planets by using specific substances keyed to them—that is, by employing astral magic in a Neoplatonist universe where all things are connected. Ficino's fullest model showing these chains of materials pulling down astral (planetary) influences was actually from the *Picatrix*. He avoided crediting this Arab work directly, as it was an illicit book of magic. Ficino would also have seen some reference to such chains in Proclus, the fifth-century Neoplatonist. In the following recipe, cordial and astral medical systems overlap. Sweet-smelling spices and saffron are prominent in efforts to avail oneself of solar power.

> If you want your body and spirit to receive power from some member of the cosmos, say from the Sun, seek the things which above all are most Solar among metal and gems, still more among plants, and more yet among animals, especially human beings; for surely things which are more similar to you confer more of it. These must both be brought to bear externally and, so far as possible, taken internally, especially in the day and the hour of the Sun and while the Sun is dominant in a theme of the heavens. Solar things are: all those gems and flowers which are called heliotrope because they turn toward the Sun, likewise gold, orpiment and golden colors, chrysolite, carbuncle, myrrh, frankincense, musk, amber, balsam, yellow honey, sweet calamus, saffron, spikenard, cinnamon, aloe-wood, and the rest of the spices... (247, 249).

All of these solar-related substances "can be adapted partly to foods, partly to ointments and fumigations, partly to usages and habits" (249).

"Wonderful" consequences can be expected if any individual substance has an "elemental" power of its own that "subserves the occult property." Consider saffron: "When saffron seeks the heart, dilates the spirit, and provokes laughter, it is not only the occult power of the Sun which is doing this in a wondrous way; but the very nature of saffron—subtle, diffusible, aromatic, and clear—also conduces to the same end" (303)...

Cookery to Fend Off Harm and Evil

For people who believed in cordial, alchemical, or astral medicines, the experience of eating colored and sweetly fragrant food at table was congruent with taking the tonic-elixirs. Similar ingredients appeared in both. Further, explicit reference in the cookery works to the power of spices to ward off malevolence and their recipes' emphasis on golden preparations and cordial gelatins (seen as jewel-like) reinforce the inference that the philosophical underpinnings of the cooking style and those of divine medicine were one and the same.

The author of the Hispanic-Moorish cookery text (*La Cocina Hispano-Magribi*) refers to the demonifuge properties of aroma; in spices are "benefit and avoidance of harm and evil." A dish is said to appear like gold because of the saffron in it. Diego Granado's *Libro del Arte de Cocina* (1599) echoes the words of that thirteenth-century text: use saffron specifically "because it has the color of gold." Alchemical texts say that if one colors a base material gold, the properties of gold are imparted to it. By coloring food yellow, one makes the food noble like gold. The diner, then, absorbs food that, like gold, prevents decay. Although saffron dyes food golden more effectively than the other spices, they also were thought of as food dyes. A recipe in the 1420 English cookery manuscript instructs the reader to mix together and then boil wine, almond milk, powdered cinnamon, ginger, and saffron; but if two different colors are desired, make part yellow by using spices and the other white by omitting them. A dish of fish is "colored" with saffron or cinnamon. Two fifteenth-century English texts recommend sandalwood as a red tint. The alchemical texts speak of gold as either yellowish, purplish, or reddish (*Traducción espanola* 1966: 85, 40; Granado 1599: 42; *Two Fifteenth-Century Cookery Books* 1988: 30, 33, 35).

Black food, because of its Saturnian connections, is as suspect as golden food is beneficial. Although the *Picatrix* uses the hotness and smell of pepper to court Mars, the harmful blackness of this spice overshadowed Mars's benefits in a Europe stricken with fear of Saturn. The Arabic astrologer Alcabitius, in his list of items linked to the potentially threatening planet, listed black pepper and "everything whatsoever that is black." Ficino also advised the melancholic against anything black. Ginger, by far the most widely used spice in fourteenth-century Italy, France, and England, totally overshadowed pepper in the recipes. When pepper was used, it was mitigated usually by use of a golden spice and presumably by yellowed foods served with the peppered dish. Cooks also avoided pepper by making "yellow pepper" from ginger and saffron.

Golden color was derived from other substances and processes as well. The Hispanic-Moorish text emphasizes decorations of hard-cooked egg yolks. (Recall that the egg yolk was also a cordial for Avicenna.) Dishes were often toasted or roasted, and the Hispanic-Moorish cookbook notes that if a food is toasted and thus takes on color, saffron will not be needed. The process was included in the cookery texts that followed in the West. Cooks made food "golden" by painting it with egg yolk, as the Hispanic-Moorish text prescribed. The fourteenth-century *Libro di Cucina* advised the reader to make the dish yellow by adding orange or lemon juice (23).

Gelatin recipes called for a base of fish or meat stock, not Avicenna's cordial derived from the *jus* of meat but a broth obtained by the boiling of meat or poaching of fish. Some of Avicenna's contemporaries did call such a broth a cordial. For the gelatins cooks usually added saffron to the stock for color, and occasionally other tints to produce red, green, blue, and pink. Recall that colors were connected to all the planets, not just to the Sun and Saturn. Spices were always added to the gelatins, and sugar sometimes. Cooks might clarify the broth by pouring it through doubled linen or adding beaten egg white. But one sixteenth-century Italian cookbook avoids the clarifying process, labeling the result a cloudy gelatin for its translucent, not transparent, appearance. The liquids, clarified or not, were put to cool, and thus to set, to be served simply as a gelatin or as a covering poured over meat or fish to create the equivalent of today's chicken or fish in aspic (Messisbugo 203–4).

The contrast between the solid fish or meat and its translucent or transparent jewel coating of gelatin was seen as a symbol of the contrast between the body and the spirit of the meat. In the light of candles, oil, or sunshine these colored cordials appeared like luminescent jewels. If the sweet cherry is made into a jelly and is looked at "in the brightness of the Sun or by the lamp, you will find it is beautiful as a ruby." So observed the physician Michel de Nostredame in 1556. The color of quince jelly is so diaphanous that it resembles "an oriental ruby" (Nostredame: 151, 165–6). To swallow these jewel-like jellies in which the essence or juice had been extracted from the flesh of the fruit was akin to swallowing *jus,* an extract of meat or fish.

This jewel-like food was linked to drugs endowed with divine power. When the Plotinian world fell from favor in the seventeenth century, the idea of a heavenly connected pharmacy fell with it. Food, in consequence, changed dramatically. The French led the way, drawing on the motifs the Italians had culled from the texts of Greek and Roman antiquity. It was France, not Italy, that first jettisoned fragrant golden food with its magical implications. All Europe came to recognize the new French cooking as the required taste.

References

Aldarotti, Taddeo (1937), *I 'Consilia,'* ed. Giuseppe Nardi, Turin: Minerva Medica.

Avicenna (Abu 'Ali al-Husain Ibn Sina) (1930), *A Treatise on the Canon of Medicine of Avicenna,* trans. O. Cameron, Gruner. London: Luzac.

Baghdad Cookery Book (1939), trans. Arthur J. Arberry, *Islamic Culture* 13, 21–47 (Pt. I), 189–214 (Pt. II).

Ficino, Marsilio (1989), *Three Books on Life: A Critical Edition,* ed. John R. Clark, trans. Carol V. Kaske, Binghamton, NY: Medieval and Renaissance Texts and Studies.

Garin, Eugenio (1983) *Astrology in the Renaissance: The Zodiac of Life,* trans. Carol Jackson and June Allen, London: Routledge and Kegan Paul.

Granado, Diego (1971), *Libro del Arte de Cocina* [1599], Madrid: Sociedad de Bibliófilos Espanoles.

Holmyard, Eric John (1957), *Alchemy,* Harmondsworth: Penguin.

Hopkins, Arthur John (1934), *Alchemy, Child of Greek Philosophy,* New York: Columbia University Press.

Klibansky, Raymond, Panofsky, Erwin and Saxl, Fritz (1964), *Saturn and Melancholy: Studies in the History of Natural Philosophy, Religion, and Art,* London: Nelson.

Libro di Cucina del Secolo XIV (1899), ed. Ludovico Frati, Bologna: Forni.

Majriti, Maslamah ibn Ahmad al- [Pseudo] (1962), *'Picatrix': Das Ziel des Weisen von Pseudo-Majriti,* trans. Hellmut Ritter and Martin Plessner, London: Warburg Institute, University of London.

Messisbugo, Cristoforo di Banchetti (1960), *Composizioni di Vivande e Apparecchio Generale* [1549], ed. F. Bandini, Venice: Pozza.

Multhauf, Robert P. (1967), *The Origins of Chemistry,* New York: Franklin Watts.

Nostredame, Michel de. (1556), *Excellent et Moult Utile Opuscule à Touts Nécessaire,* Paris: Oliver de Harsy.

Seznec, Jean (1972), *The Survival of the Pagan Gods,* trans. Barbara F. Sessions, Princeton: Princeton University Press.

Sivin, Nathan (1968), *Chinese Alchemy: Preliminary Studies,* Cambridge, MA: Harvard University Press.

Taylor, Frank Sherwood (1962), *The Alchemists,* New York: Collier.

Traducción Espanola de un Manuscrito Anónimo del Siglo XIII Sobre la Cocina Hispano-Magribi (1966), trans. Ambrosio Huici Miranda, Madrid: Ayuntamiento de Valencia.

Two Fifteenth-Century Cookery Books (1888), ed. and trans. Arthur Edward Waite, London: Trübner.

Yates, Frances Amelia (1979), *Giordano Bruno and the Hermetic Tradition,* Chicago: University of Chicago Press.

14
Food with Saints

R. S. Khare

The Cultural Language of Food

India provides us with virtually an inexhaustible repository of instances where food loads itself with mundane and profound meanings. The subject is so central to the culture that we have called it gastrosemantics, to refer to its unusual powers of multiple symbolization and communication via food.[1] Embedded within his quest for self-identity and ultimate reality, the Hindu's food "loads" and "unloads" meanings and messages as it passes through diverse domains of existence—physical, human, and divine. We will consider in this paper how food conveys a range of meanings and experiences that conjoin the worldly to the otherworldly, and the microcosmic to the macrocosmic. The Hindu world rather demands that its food "speak" a language that conjoins the gross and the subtle, body and spirit, the seen and the unseen, outside and inside, and the particular and the general.

The Hindu food meets this goal by representing extensive interrelationships between the three corners of the gastrosemantic triangle—"self," food, and body (including the societal; for the Hindu's "self" see Bharati 1985), and by becoming a principle of the eternal moral order (dharma) and cycles of creation. Food becomes a reflexive medium for conceiving and experiencing interpenetrations of food, mind, and breath, most often by the yogic control of one's body and what one eats. In anthropological terms, food becomes a powerful, polyvocal interlocutor between matter and spirit, and body and self. Such a "language" transforms according to one's life-stage and the path of spiritual pursuit. But whether it is a householder, a saint, or a renouncer, food, body, self, and personhood remain guided by some universal principles, and these hold key to a proper understanding of food to the issues of ontology and ultimate reality. In the following discussion, I shall emphasize the food of the Hindu holy person, always a yogi (i.e. a conjoiner) of some sort. He most often influences the gastrosemantics of the rest of the society in a distinct way. Householders routinely look up to him for guidance. In sickness they go to him for cures and healing; in everyday life, they approach him as a guru…

We focus on Hindu interrelationships between food, self, and the ultimate reality by two crucial cultural formulations: First, "You eat what you are," and second, "You are what you eat." These are integral to the Hindu's authoritative tradition. The first is well grounded in the *Gita* (XVII, 7–10), where foods are classified according to the three "strands" or dispositions that humans betray.[2] The second formulation bases itself on the Upanishadic instruction—pure nourishment leads to pure mind or nature (see Hume 1985: 262). As a corollary, therefore, a healthy body is considered to be a byproduct of discriminating and controlled nourishment. Diseases follow from flaws—moral, mental, and physical. Holy persons rigorously control these and produce examples for the householders to follow…

"Speaking Food" of the Holy: Three Contexts and Expressions

The Hindu holy person handles food to serve clearly designated moral and spiritual purposes, including efforts to alleviate human sorrow and suffering and to bring one nearer to liberation. Renouncers and sadhus do not view food as a commodity. They do not trade in foods to earn profit, and they neither hoard nor covet. They similarly should not cultivate their palate. Put another way, a holy person must regulate and control food only to cultivate his or her spiritual power. He masters his desires and senses by fasting and minimal eating. With increasing self-control and austerities, his sight and touch make food express special powers and messages. Detached from food, as we will see below, he makes food "speak" and "act" on his behalf. His food conveys his blessings and curses. As blessing, his food heals, uplifts, and brings good fortune to the faithful. As leftovers, his food guides disciples toward spiritual experiences and divine imminence (Babb 1987).

Food for Sustaining Life

Within the Hindu world, food is necessary to remain healthy and stay alive. Food is viewed as the source of all strength in the Upanishads:

> [Sanatkumara said:] Food is, verily, greater than strength. Therefore if a man abstains from food for ten days, even though he might live, yet he would not be able to see, hear, reflect, become convinced, act, and enjoy the result. But when he obtains food, he is able to see, hear, reflect, become convinced, act, and enjoy the result.
>
> (*Chandogya Upanishad* VII, ix, 1; see Nikhilananda 1963, 341)

One is enjoined to stay alive, in extremity, by eating forbidden or abominable foods. Today's Hindu knows that the sages have done so under *apaddharma* (dharma under distress). Applicable to householders and holy persons alike, such lifesaving pragmatic strategies render food procurement necessary for all—even the staunchest yogi or recluse. There is no provision for death by starvation (in contrast to the Jains). Under normal conditions, all dharma-upholding persons, householders, and renouncers must regulate their eating (*Gita* VI, 17). They must fast, control their senses, and view food as a cosmic sacrificial process and product (e.g. *Gita*, III, 14).

Though all holy persons must eat, not all "handle food" (as does a householder by storing and cooking), nor must all beg. Yet all Hindus, whether saints or householders, extract special messages and portents from food. But saints especially encode foods with special messages as they go about eating, producing leftovers, and creating "blessed foods" (with sight, touch, giving by hand, or by verbal command; see Babb 1987). They convey equally well by fasting, maintaining silence, or favoring specific fruits and flowers, for granting boons to devotees. Still, not all holy persons may engage in such transactions. Some may "rise above" such a necessity and bless simply by "willing" (literally "flashing on the mind").

Within the Hindu world, one should eat only enough to live. Fasting therefore is a necessary moral underside of eating, and it intensifies one's food–self dialogue. Fasting also emphasizes the dominance of soul over body. Non-eating, like eating, thoroughly affects one's physical, social, psychological, and spiritual states...

Saint's Healing Foods

Hindu holy persons in everyday life freely recommend special diets, herbs, and fasts for treating diseases, undesirable psychological dispositions, and mental tardiness. The enormous banyan tree of the Ayurveda provides them with congenial therapeutic ground, while their learning of healing from gurus and saints equips them with actual skills. As comprehensive healers, they freely dispense healing foods and herbs. Over time, they acquire the dual therapeutic-spiritual authority which even *vaidyas* (or "doctors") cannot dispute.

In principle, the holy person can heal with or without intention. He himself may not fully know the powers he possesses. His spiritual presence and contact are automatically considered beneficial to the body as well as the soul. Such qualities make gurus, sadhus, and saints the "ultimate healers." They cure all the three "fevers" (i.e. of the body, ill-fortune, and evil circumstance). If they are known to cure incurable bodily diseases, they also treat the "disease" of transmigration—*samsara*.

These holy healers respond according to a person's physical condition, age, sex, life-phase, spiritual path, and psychological dispositions. Though some sadhus in Lucknow were adept even in the "science of pulse and humors" most depended on their "spiritual" powers. The general principles governing their healing were that (a) only disciplined daily eating and living ensured health and longevity; (b) healing foods required firm resolve and faith; and (c) such foods should adjust with a patient's age, gender, and karmic condition (for food, disease, and karma, see Khare 1976).

However, for the Hindu, a holy person's healing foods or prescriptions can seldom be equated to that of a doctor's. Only the first one infuses (intentionally or unintentionally) his spiritual powers into whatever he prescribes. Devoid of any motive of economic profit or fame, and impelled by service to the needy and suffering, the holy person is the ideal healer. He ideally practices desireless action (*niskama karma*). But one only rarely comes across such a healer. He appears only by the divine will. He heals both the body and the soul of a person. Whatever he gives, whether flowers, herbs, roots, fruits, or elaborately cooked foods, it heals as no other medicine can. Even the dying are brought back to life (i.e. when the physicians have given up).

No wonder therefore that major Ayurvedic doctors in India are also found practicing selfless austerities and devotion. Prabhu Datta Brahmachari (1977: 19–20) mentions cases of *vaidyas* who treated not only free of charge but also refused to eat or drink water at the patient's house during such visits (even if they were of the appropriate caste status). In popular thought, rigorous self-discipline in diet and austere lifestyle considerably enhances the efficacy of an Ayurvedic doctor.

Thus a holy person acts like a "doctor," and a doctor like a holy person. To paraphrase Brahmachari (18), a sadhu writing as a "doctor," Ayurveda's responsibility does not end with curing the body. Its goal is actually liberation (*moksa*). Its attention is not on the body but on one's soul (*atman*). Body is after all ephemeral; it is destructible. One desires "diseaselessness" or health (*arogyata*) because it enables one to progress toward liberation.

The issue is mentioned thus by a doctor in the same book: "Ayurveda came about because of this sage tradition [of compassion toward those suffering]. So many times ancient sages have promoted Ayurveda... Whenever sages, seeing human misery, have been overcome with compassion, then, they have organized a significant new phase for augmenting and completing the [science of] Ayurveda" (Brahamachari 1977: 8; my interpolations).

Super-Foods with Sadhus, Yogis and Devotees

Since a genuine sadhu or renouncer views food in the context of faith, austerity, and devotion, he sees what eludes the ordinary. To him food is what self is—in the "seen" (gross) as well as "unseen" (subtle) dimensions. His austerities (*tapas*) empower self, and his self, the food. He blesses his devotees by accepting devotees' offerings and by returning them as his leftovers. Though milk preparations, sweets, and flowers are most often so exchanged, special offerings attract specific meaning and messages. For instance, rice pudding may represent auspiciousness, fertility, and spiritual grace for many. Fruits received from a saint are "read" for hidden messages because foods readily acquire the intrinsic properties (*guna, dosa,* and *rasa*) of the transactors and their intentions. Some fruits represent maleness (banana), and others femaleness (orange); some represent astrological planets by color and shape, while others speak about the saint's equalitarianism. Blessed sweets widely connote divine agreeableness, desirable ritual consequences, convergent social goals and concerns, and auspiciousness (Toomey 1986). "Fruits, leaves, and flowers" constitute a devottee's normal food offerings to the divine, within homes and in temples (on different properties of *prasad,* see Khare 1976: 92–110).

Some saints become widely known by the food they eat most, or bless with (e.g. a saint was known as *Payahari* because he drank only milk to subsist; see *Bhaktamala* 1969: 302). A famous *mauni* sadhu (i.e. a saint with vow of silence) in Lucknow was known to bless with sweets and flowers. Known as the flower-bearing saint, he was never seen without these accompaniments. Devotees believed that these appeared miraculously before him during his night worship and contained supernatural powers. His devotees had developed a whole language of interpretation for the sweets and flowers received from him. For example, red flowers meant auspiciousness and progeny, white stood for true knowledge, and yellow for prosperity, family happiness, and personal fame. Flowers and foods were the saint's ubiquitous language of communication, though he complemented it with suitable eye contacts and bodily gestures.

Deities, in turn, essentially authenticate such a gastrosemantic paradigm of communication shared between the divine, saints, and their devotees. Popular devotional literature in different parts of India underscores how deities routinely "speak" through foods (e.g. see such hagiographies as *Bhaktamala* 1969). Major saints often establish the models of (and for) such a total communication. Invariably, within such stories, a deity sides with his devotees when challenged by orthodox Brahmans, priests, or other ritualists. For example, the deity refused the food offerings of the Brahmans to receive the same from the Untouchable saint, Ravidas. He "came in his lap" to eat from him. This model underscores the superiority of love over social status or wealth, and it derives from Krishna's acceptance of leftovers from his devotee (Vidura) over the elaborate feast from a vain king (e.g. Duryodhana).

The deity even sustains a true devotee when the devotee does not (or cannot) feed or protect himself (since he is usually lost in devotion). The deity even cleans and tends him when sick (and then cures the sickness). The divine grace is known to come to those who feed other devotees and who offer them hospitality even at a great personal cost. (Illustrating these properties is the story of Madhava Das Jagannath in *Bhaktamala* 1969: 540–551). With Mira Bai, the famous woman saint of northern India, the deity neutralized poison to prove his commitment to devotees.

Faith, devotion, otherworldly aestheticism, and saintly compassion thus charge the saint's food with special powers and messages. The contemporary religious culture widely recognizes this devotion-induced transformation of food. For example:

> One time he [Raghunath Gosain, a Caitanyaite saint] became indisposed and worshiped his deity [Lord Jagan Nath] mentally, feeding him with rice and milk. He ate the same afterward as offering. Its essence *(rasa)* pervaded his mortal body [just as the actual preparation would]. When a Vaidya practitioner felt his pulse [to treat his disease], he declared that the saint had just eaten rice and milk. O! gentlemen [says the commentator], how much more could I emphasize that you understand it all yourself.
>
> (*Bhaktamala* 1969: 553; my translation and interpolation)

The devotional literature abounds with such examples... Since the deity remains at the beck and call of a genuine devotee to this extent, the devotees rigorously control their desire for food.

Simultaneously, once he has become spiritually accomplished (a *siddha*), a saint's speech is instantaneously realized. Whatever such a saint says or desires, occurs, especially for others' welfare. For such saints, speech and action, and thought and food become coextensive. It is a good example of Hindu's idea of gastrosemanticity. Thus, "As a devotee was mentally offering buttermilk to the deity, a disciple touched the saint's feet and startled him, and in the lap of the devotee spilled the actual buttermilk [for everybody to see]." (This case was related to me by an informant-Bhakta in Lucknow during 1986.)

A climax of such deity and devotee intimacies occurs when the two share their saliva via food. For instance,

> [Once Vallabhacarya] had the milk *prasad* given to [saint] Paramanandadasa in order to find out whether or not Krishna [the deity] found the milk-offering well prepared and rich in flavor. Since [the deity] is passionately fond of milk, giving milk as *prasad* to a Vaisnava [devotee], who had received [the deity's] favor, is just like giving him the ecstasy *(rasa)* of union with the [deity] in the [divine sport]. If the [devotee] praises the taste of the milk *prasad,* then it may be taken as certain that [the deity] is indicating, through that [devotee], that he enjoyed the milk.
>
> The interpretive account of the episode continues:
>
> Since Paramanandadasa drank some of the saliva from [the deity's] lips along with the milk, he plunged into experience of the *rasa* [love-permeated, selfless devotion] of all of the nocturnal [divine] sports.
>
> (From the *Vartas,* on Paramanandadasa; see Barz 1976:156–7)

For the devotional and popular Hindu culture, these are examples of gastrosemanticity par excellence. The divine-tasted milk *prasad* in the above example transports the devotee into a direct and powerful spiritual experience. For Paramandadasa, such an experience is beyond all the conceivable materiality or symbology of foods; it represents the most exalted divine intimacy. At this level, food, deity and self become coextensive, collapsing our two opening formulations—"you are what you eat" and "you eat what you are"—into one supreme divine essence and experience.

Experience and Expressions

Not only do such examples produce a commentary on the dichotomous "opposites" (i.e. the *dvanda* as represented by matter and spirit, food and mind, and self and the other), but they also illustrate some general properties of the Hindu cultural logic. The Hindu's food pursues a nondichotomous logic and language suitable to convey the unity of expression and experience. Food to him is one of the most versatile interlocutors, and his saints and the divine elaborate, enrich, magnify, and empower it to transcend normal channels of signification and communication. Relying on more than ordinary logic, such Hindu food, like other crucial principles (dharma, karma, *atman,* etc.), expresses itself most where faith, practice, suggestion, experience, and intuition converge.

Let us now return to our opening allusion to the Hindu's gastrosemantic triangle (food-self-body). With "self" (referring to *jiva* and its "I-ness" but culminating in the realization of Atman) at the apex, food and body must cater to self's purposes and priorities. Given this Hindu view, the basic source of all gastrosemantics must also come from self and its journey within the creation. But such a triangle, by definition, is *multiform* (i.e. it is capable of transformation, and it produces varying signification by cultural context and purpose). It is manipulable. Thus, once we juxtapose this triangle to our general analytic triangle (i.e. food-language-self or food-discourse-self), we may see how the two interrelate, especially since the Hindu system treats language and discourse as a function of self (and its *manas*), while this "mind" depends on food and breath. The food thus also becomes the basis for breath and mind, underscoring an interplay between gross and subtle constitutive elements. Similarly applicable to food is the triangle of the three basic "qualities" or constituents of nature (*sattva, rajas,* and *tamas*). In life, such triangular "qualities" swirl within oneself and outside, attracting an interplay of food with innate strands, flaws, moods, aesthetics, and attachments. Whether one is a renouncer, a householder, or a woman, these triangles remain the generating source for food's multiple meanings and "voices" within the Hindu universe.

We may decode the food-breath-mind triangle a little further to emphasize the point that the Hindu cosmological constituents stand squarely behind the food. For example, breath (*prana*) via food yields the *buddhi* (intellect), which, in turn, works in terms of five sensory organs, five organs of action, five subtle elements, and five gross elements (for a summary discussion and schematic representation of such cosmological constituents, see Satprakashananda 1965: 314). However, all of this conceptual and semantic complexity translates into a simple, direct, and forceful principle: One should practice self-control via austerities to control the swirl of preceding triangular constituents of the world (*trigunatmaka samsara*). And only a genuine relationship between the divine and devotee, guru and disciple, and learned texts and practice ensures such a goal, where food becomes a crucial link between finite (body) and the infinite (soul). Food and body become soul's sheaths, and not the other way round. Yogis, sadhus, renouncers, and gurus (even sagely householders) in India continuously try to "realize" this truth. They remind themselves that only their bodies are perishable; they are not. Since the *atman* alone is real, it is considered capable of creating bodies (and the foods it needs). As Ramakrishna Paramahamsa said, even food cooking conveys them a message: "As potato and brijnal when *siddha*, i.e. when boiled properly, become soft and pulpy; so a man when he becomes *siddha*, i.e. reaches perfection, is seen to be all humility and tenderness" (see Abhedananda 1946: 74).

But the devotional movement, where the deity takes over the devotee's life and his senses, complicates the above austere picture. Both food and body are divinized, and they return center stage with a divine-inspired substantivity and aesthetics. As our devout saints illustrated, they employ creative expressions to convey how a devotee "tastes" the divine name, and "eats" and "drinks" the divine praise by his ears. All senses thus immerse themselves in the divine's presence, making the double entendre a standard fare of devotional expressions... The following, again the master stroke of a saint, employs a battery of such switches which lights up the relationship between self (a part) and the divine (the whole), morality and aesthetics, and expression and experience.

> For the milk-made delicacy of Rama's Name, the sugar is Krishna's Name, and the Name of the Lord Vitthala, the ghee; mix, put it into your mouth and see the taste! Take the wheat of Ego, put it into the milk of dispassion and pound it into soft flour and prepare it into fine vermicelli, boil it, and put it into the vessel of your heart, fill it with water of feeling and cook it with your intellect; take it on a plate and eat; and when you get a belching, think of the Lord Purandara Vitthala, who is of the form of joy.
>
> (Purandaradasa (1480–1564) quoted in V. Raghavan 1966: 128–129)

With such expressions, joyous and blissful relationships between food and self, food and deity, and self and deity redraw the nondualist ideal with a definite purpose. Here emotion, intimacy, experience, and insight become the lifeblood of the Hindu's being and becoming (compare "ethnosociological" accounts; see Marriott 1976, 1989). We also experience a corresponding metamorphosis in the "substance" of body and self, self and food, and self and cosmos...

Foods with Saints

Now we can make some general comments on the gastrosemantics of the holy food. The pervasive unifying logic of the Hindu food derives from the nature of the Hindu's cosmology. The Creator of the Hindu universe is a yogi, a conjoiner. Like him, food's cosmic place and meanings are therefore held self-evident and indisputable; they are found one with the rest of the cosmic moral order (for basic pronouncements in the Upanishads, see Hume 1985: 153, 284, 290). In practice, the food-body-self and self-dharma-cosmos paradigms work together to reveal the vast meaningful range within which the holy person places foods. The ascetic, orthodox or not, constantly approaches foods and food exchanges to proclaim and maintain his self-identity and to conjoin by yoga one's various bodily and spiritual states. To holy persons more than householders, foods constitute a comprehensive yet delicate and subtle language, marked with a wide array of cosmic, social, emotional, karmic, and spiritual messages. Foods ... produce indirect (as in meditation or dreams) as well as direct (as by health or sickness) consequences for the *yogi*...

A yogi's food rests with the classical Upanishadic notion of food as one of the soul's "five sheaths" (food, breath, mind, intellect, and bliss). Though constituting the outermost sheath, food successively transforms itself into the innermost (and the subtlest) experience—spiritual bliss. Each succeeding subtler sheath represents to the yogi a transformation and transcendence of the one before. He "experiences" how the moral food substance changes into the rarefied breath, the breath into mind, the mind into (still rarer) intellect, and the last into bliss (*ananda*).

[Many Hindi and Sanskrit expressions have been omitted from this abridged text.]

Notes

1. Gastrosemantics may be generally defined as a culture's distinct capacity to signify, experience, systematize, philosophize, and communicate with food and food practices by pressing appropriate linguistic and cultural devices to render food as a central subject of attention. To refer to the cultural depth and density of meanings foods invoke, I will employ "gastrosemanticity."

2. All references to the *Gita* in the chapter are to R. C. Zaehner's 1969 translation and annotation of this classical text. However, sometimes in my text, I have purposely retained some popularly conveyed senses and interpretations from my field discussions, conveying to the reader an idea of how today's Hindus widely regard the *Gita* a living—life-guiding—text.

References

Abhedananda, Swami (1946), *The Sayings of Ramakrishna*, Calcutta: Ramakrishna Vedanta Math.

Babb, Lawrence (1987), *Redemptive Encounters: Three Modern Styles in the Hindu Tradition*, Delhi: Oxford University Press.

Barz, Richard (1976), *The Bhakti Sect of Vallabhacarya*, Faridabad: Thomson Press (India).

Bhaktamala [Hindi] (1969), Nabhadasa (Fifth edition, with commentaries in poetry and prose by Priyadasa Sri Bhagwan Prasad Rapakala), Lucknow: Teja Kumar Press.

Bharati, Agehananda (1985), "The self in Hindu thought and action," in *Culture and Self: Asian and Western Perspectives* (eds.), A. J. Marsella and George DeVos London: Tavistock Publications.

Brahmachari, Prabhu Datta (1977), *Motapan Kam Karne Ka Upaya* [Hindi] (A Way to Reduce Fatness), Calcutta: Sri Baidyanath Ayurveda Bhavan Limited.

Hume, Robert Ernest (1985/1921), *The Thirteen Principal Upanishads*, Delhi: Oxford University Press.

Khare, R. S. (1976), *Culture and Reality: Essays on the Hindu System of Managing Foods*, Shimla: Indian Institute of Advanced Study.

Marriott, McKim (1976), "Hindu transactions: diversity without dualism," in *Transaction and Meaning*, (ed.), Bruce Kapferer, Philadelphia: Institute for the Study of Human Issues.

——. (1989), "Constructing an Indian ethnosociology," *Contributions to Indian Sociology*, 23:1–39.

Nikhilananda, Swami (1963), *The Upanishads*, New York: Harper Torchbooks.

Raghavan, V. (1966), *The Great Integrators: The Saint-Singers of India*, Delhi: Ministry of Information and Broadcasting.

Satprakashananda, Swami (1965), *Methods of Knowledge*, London: George Allen and Unwin Ltd.

Toomey, Paul (1986), "Food from the mouth of Krishna: socio-religious aspects of sacred food in two Krishnaite sects," in *Food, Society and Culture* (eds.), R. S. Khare and M. S. A. Rao, Durham: Carolina Academic Press.

Zaehner, R. C. (1969), *The Bhagavad-Gita*, Oxford: Oxford University Press.

15

Zen and the Art of Tea

D. T. Suzuki

What is common to Zen and the art of tea is the constant attempt both make at simplification. The elimination of the unnecessary is achieved by Zen in its intuitive grasp of final reality; by the art of tea, in the way of living typified by serving tea in the tearoom. The art of tea is the aestheticism of primitive simplicity. Its ideal, to come closer to Nature, is realized by sheltering oneself under a thatched roof in a room which is hardly ten feet square but which must be artistically constructed and furnished. Zen also aims at stripping off all the artificial wrappings humanity has devised, supposedly for its own solemnization. Zen first of all combats the intellect; for, in spite of its practical usefulness, the intellect goes against our effort to delve into the depths of being. Philosophy may propose all kinds of questions for intellectual solution, but it never claims to give us the spiritual satisfaction which must be accessible to every one of us, however intellectually undeveloped he may be. Philosophy is accessible only to those who are intellectually equipped, and thus it cannot be a discipline of universal appreciation. Zen—or, more broadly speaking, religion—is to cast off all one thinks he possesses, even life, and to get back to the ultimate state of being, the "Original Abode," one's own father or mother. This can be done by every one of us, for we are what we are because of it or him or her, and without it or him or her we are nothing. This is to be called the last stage of simplification, since things cannot be reduced to any simpler terms. The art of tea symbolizes simplification, first of all, by an inconspicuous, solitary thatched hut erected, perhaps, under an old pine tree, as if the hut were part of Nature and not specially constructed by human hands. When form is thus once for all symbolized it allows itself to be artistically treated. It goes without saying that the principle of treatment is to be in perfect conformity with the original idea which prompted it, that is, the elimination of unnecessaries.

Tea was known in Japan even before the Kamakura era (1185–1338), but its first wider propagation is generally ascribed to Eisai (1141–1215), the Zen teacher, who brought tea seeds from China and had them cultivated in his friend's monastery grounds. It is said that his book on tea, together with some tea prepared from his plants, was presented to Minamoto Sanetomo (1192–1219), the shogun of the time, who happened to be ill. Eisai thus came to be known as the father of tea cultivation in Japan. He thought that tea had some medicinal qualities and was good for a variety of diseases. Apparently he did not teach how one conducts the tea ceremony, which he must have observed while at the Zen monasteries in China. The tea ceremony is a way of entertaining visitors to the monastery, or sometimes a way of entertaining its own occupants among themselves. The Zen monk who brought the ritual to Japan was Dai-o the National Teacher (1236–1308), about half a century later than Eisai. After Dai-o came several monks who became masters of the art, and finally Ikkyu (1394–1481), the noted abbot of Daitokuji, taught the technique to one of his disciples, Shuko (1422–1502), whose artistic genius developed it and succeeded in adapting it to Japanese taste. Shuko thus became the originator of the art of tea and taught it to Ashikaga Yoshimasa (1435–90), shogun of the time, who was a great patron of the arts. Later, Jo-o (1504–55) and especially Rikyu further improved it and gave a finishing touch to what is now known as *cha-no-yu*, generally translated "tea ceremony" or "tea cult." The original tea ceremony as practiced at Zen monasteries is carried on independently of the art now in vogue among the general public.

I have often thought of the art of tea in connection with Buddhist life, which seems to partake so much of the characteristics of the art. Tea keeps the mind fresh and vigilant, but it does not intoxicate. It has qualities naturally to be appreciated by scholars and monks. It is in the nature of things that tea came to be extensively used in Buddhist monasteries and that its first introduction to Japan came through the monks. If tea symbolizes Buddhism, can we not say that wine stands for Christianity? Wine is used extensively by the Christians. It is used in the church as the symbol of Christ's blood, which, according to the Christian tradition, was shed for sinful humanity. Probably for this reason the medieval monks kept wine cellars in their monasteries. They look jovial and happy, surrounding the cask and holding up the wine cups. Wine first excites and then inebriates. In many ways it contrasts with tea, and this contrast is also that between Buddhism and Christianity.

We can see now that the art of tea is most intimately connected with Zen not only in its practical development but principally in the observance of the spirit that runs through the ceremony itself. The spirit in terms of feeling consists of "harmony" (*wa*), "reverence" (*kei*), "purity" (*sei*), and "tranquillity" (*jaku*). These four elements are needed to bring the art to a successful end; they are all the essential constituents of a brotherly and orderly life, which is no other than the life of the Zen monastery. That the monks behaved in perfect orderliness can be inferred from the remark made by Tei Meido, a Confucian scholar of the Sung dynasty, who once visited a monastery called Jorinji: "Here, indeed, we witness the classical form of ritualism as it was practiced in the ancient three dynasties." The ancient three dynasties are the ideal days dreamed of by every Chinese scholar-statesman, when a most desirable state of things prevailed and people enjoyed all the happiness that could be expected of a good government. Even now, the Zen monks are well trained individually and collectively in conducting ceremonies. The Ogasawara school of etiquette is thought to have its origin in the "Monastery Regulations" compiled by Hyakujo and known as *Hyakujo Shingi*. While Zen teaching consists in grasping the spirit by transcending form, it unfailingly reminds us of the fact that the world in which we live is a world of particular forms and that the spirit expresses itself only by means of form. Zen is, therefore, at once antimonian and disciplinarian.

The character for "harmony" also reads "gentleness of spirit" (*yawaragi*), and to my mind "gentleness of spirit" seems to describe better the spirit governing the whole procedure of the art of tea. Harmony refers more to form, while gentleness is suggestive of an inward feeling. The general atmosphere of the tearoom tends to create this kind of gentleness all around—gentleness of touch, gentleness of odor, gentleness of light, and gentleness of sound. You take up a teacup, handmade and irregularly shaped, the glaze probably not uniformly overlaid, but in spite of this primitiveness the little utensil has a peculiar charm of gentleness, quietness, and unobtrusiveness. The incense burning is never strong and stimulating, but gentle and pervading. The windows and screens are another source of a gentle prevailing charm, for the light admitted into the room is always soft and restful and conducive to a meditative mood. The breeze passing through the needles of the old pine tree harmoniously blends with the sizzling of the iron kettle over the fire. The entire environment thus reflects the personality of the one who has created it.

"What is most valuable is gentleness of spirit; what is most essential is not to contradict others"—these are the first words of the so-called "Constitution of Seventeen Articles" compiled by Prince Shotoku in 604. It is a kind of moral and spiritual admonition given by the Prince Regent to his subjects. But it is significant that such an admonition, whatever its political bearings, should begin by placing unusual emphasis on gentleness of spirit... When Dogen (1200–55) came back from China after some years of study of Zen there, he was asked what he had learned. He said, "Not much except soft-heartednness (*nyunan-shin*)." "Soft-heartedness" is "tender-mindedness" and in this case means "gentleness of spirit." Generally we are too egotistic, too full of hard, resisting spirit. We are individualistic, unable to accept things as they are or as they come to us. Resistance means friction, friction is the source of all trouble. When there is no self, the heart is soft and offers no resistance to outside influences. This does not necessarily mean the absence of all sensitivities or emotionalities. They are controlled in the totality of a spiritual outlook on life. And in this aspect I am sure that Christians and Buddhists alike know how to follow Dogen in the appreciation of the significance of selflessness or "soft-heartedness." In the art of tea the "gentleness of spirit" is spoken of in the same spirit enjoined by Prince Shotoku. Indeed, "gentleness of spirit" or "soft-heartedness" is the foundation of our life on earth. If the art of tea purports to establish a Buddha-land in its small group, it has to start with gentleness of spirit. To illustrate this point further, let us quote the Zen Master Takuan (1573–1645).

Takuan on the Art of Tea (Cha-No-Yu)

> The principle of *cha-no-yu* is the spirit of harmonious blending of Heaven and Earth and provides the means for establishing universal peace. People of the present time have turned it into a mere occasion for meeting friends, talking of worldly affairs, and indulging in palatable food and drink; besides, they are proud of their elegantly furnished tearooms, where, surrounded by rare objects of art, they would serve tea in a most accomplished manner, and deride those who are not so skillful as themselves. This is, however, far from being the original intention of *cha-no-yu*.
>
> Let us then construct a small room in a bamboo grove or under trees, arrange streams and rocks and plant trees and bushes, while [inside the room] let us pile up charcoal, set a kettle, arrange flowers, and arrange in order the necessary tea utensils. And let all this be carried out in accordance with the idea that in this room we can enjoy the streams and rocks as we do the rivers and mountains in Nature, and appreciate the various moods and sentiments suggested by the snow, the moon, and the trees and flowers, as they go through the transformation of seasons, appearing and disappearing, blooming and withering. As visitors are greeted here with due reverence, we listen quietly to the boiling water in the kettle, which sounds like a breeze passing through the pine needles, and become oblivious of all worldly woes and worries; we then pour out a dipperful of water from the kettle, reminding us of the mountain stream, and thereby our mental dust is wiped off. This is truly a world of recluses, saints on earth.
>
> The principle of propriety is reverence, which in practical life functions as harmonious relationship. This is the statement made by Confucius when he defines the use of propriety, and is also the mental attitude one should cultivate in *cha-no-yu*. For instance, when a man is associated with persons of high social rank his conduct is simple and natural, and there is no cringing self-deprecation on his part. When he sits in the company of people socially below him he retains a respectful attitude toward them, being entirely free from the feeling of self-importance. This is due to the presence of something pervading the entire tearoom, which results in the harmonious relationship of all who come here. However long the association, there is always the persisting sense of reverence. The spirit of the smiling Kasyapa and the nodding Soshi must be said to be moving here; this spirit, in words is the mysterious Suchness that is beyond all comprehension.

> For this reason, the principle animating the tearoom, from its first construction down to the choice of tea utensils, the technique of service, the cooking of food, wearing apparel, etc., is to be sought in the avoidance of complicated ritual and mere ostentation. The implements may be old, but the mind can be invigorated therewith so that it is ever fresh and ready to respond to the changing seasons and the varying views resulting therefrom; it never curries favor, it is never covetous, never inclined to extravagance, but always watchful and considerate for others. The owner of such a mind is naturally gentle-mannered and always sincere—this is *cha-no-yu.*
>
> The way of *cha-no-yu,* therefore, is to appreciate the spirit of a naturally harmonious blending of Heaven and Earth, to see the pervading presence of the five elements by one's fireside, where the mountains, rivers, rocks, and trees are found as they are in Nature, to draw the refreshing water from the well of Nature, to taste with one's own mouth the flavor supplied by Nature. How grand this enjoyment of the harmonious blending of Heaven and Earth!...

Toyotomi Hideyoshi was the great patron of the art of tea in his day and an admirer of Sen no Rikyu (1521–91), who was virtually the founder of the art. Although he was always after something sensational, grandiose, and ostentatious, he seems to have understood finally something of the spirit of the art as advocated by Rikyu and his followers, when he gave this verse to Rikyu at one of the latter's "tea parties":

> When tea is made with water drawn from the well of Mind
> Whose bottom is beyond measure,
> We really have what is called *cha-no-yu.*

Hideyoshi was a crude and cruel despot in many ways, but in his liking for the art of tea we are inclined to find something genuine beyond just "using" the art for his political purposes. His verse touches the spirit of reverence when he can refer to the water deeply drawn from the well of the mind.

Rikyu teaches that "the art of *cha-no-yu* consists in nothing else but in boiling water, making tea, and sipping it." This is simple enough as far as it goes. Human life, we can say, consists in being born, eating and drinking, working and sleeping, marrying and giving birth to children, and finally in passing away—whither, no one knows. Nothing seems to be simpler than living this life, when it is so stated. But how many of us are there who can live this kind of matter-of-fact or rather God-intoxicated life, cherishing no desires, leaving no regrets, but absolutely trustful of God? While living we think of death; while dying we long for life; while one thing is being accomplished, so many other things, not necessarily cognate and usually irrelevant, crowd into our brains and divert and dissipate the energy which is to be concentrated on the matter in hand. When water is poured into the bowl, it is not the water alone that is poured into it—a variety of things go into it, good and bad, pure and impure, things about which one has to blush, things which can never be poured out anywhere except into one's own deep unconscious. The tea water when analyzed contains all the filth disturbing and contaminating the stream of our consciousness. An art is perfected only when it ceases to be art: when there is the perfection of artlessness, when the innermost sincerity of our being asserts itself, and this is the meaning of reverence in the art of tea. Reverence is, therefore, sincerity or simplicity of heart.

"Purity," estimated as constituting the spirit of the art of tea, may be said to be the contribution of Japanese mentality. Purity is cleanliness or sometimes orderliness, which is observable in everything everywhere concerned with the art. Fresh water is liberally used in the garden, called *roji* (courtyard); in case natural running water is not available, there is a stone basin filled with water as one approaches the tearoom, which is naturally kept clean and free from dust and dirt.

Purity in the art of tea may remind us of the Taoistic teaching of Purity. There is something common to both, for the object of discipline in both is to free one's mind from the defilements of the senses.

A tea master says: "The spirit of *cha-no-yu* is to cleanse the six senses from contamination. By seeing the *kakemono* in the *tokonoma* (alcove) and the flower in the vase, one's sense of smell is cleansed; by listening to the boiling of water in the iron kettle and to the dripping of water from the bamboo pipe, one's ears are cleansed; by tasting tea one's mouth is cleansed; and by handling the tea utensils one's sense of touch is cleansed. When thus all the sense organs are cleansed, the mind itself is cleansed of defilements. The art of tea is after all a spiritual discipline, and my aspiration for every hour of the day is not to depart from the spirit of the tea, which is by no means a matter of mere entertainment."[1]

In one of Rikyu's poems we have this:

While the *roji* is meant to be a passageway
Altogether outside this earthly life,
How is it that people only contrive
To besprinkle it with dust of mind?

Here as in the following poems he refers to his own state of mind while looking out quietly from his tearoom:

The court is left covered
With the fallen leaves
Of the pine tree;
No dust is stirred,
And calm is my mind!

The moonlight
Far up in the sky,
Looking through the eaves,
Shines on a mind
Undisturbed with remorse.

It is, indeed, a mind pure, serene, and free from disturbing emotions that can enjoy the aloneness of the Absolute:

> The snow-covered mountain path
> Winding through the rocks
> Has come to its end;
> Here stands a hut,
> The master is all alone;
> No visitors he has,
> Nor are any expected.

In a book called *Nambo-roku,* which is one of the most important, almost sacred, textbooks of the art of tea, we have the following passage, showing that the ideal of the art is to realize a Buddha-land of Purity on earth, however small in scale, and to see an ideal community gathered here, however temporary the gathering and however few its members:

> The spirit of *wabi* is to give an expression to the Buddha-land of Purity altogether free from defilements, and, therefore, in this *roji* (courtyard) and in this thatched hut there ought not to be a speck of dust of any kind; both master and visitors are expected to be on terms of absolute sincerity; no ordinary measures of proportion or etiquette or conventionalism are to be followed. A fire is made, water is boiled, and tea is served: this is all that is needed here, no other worldly considerations are to intrude. For what we want here is to give full expression to the Buddha-mind. When ceremony, etiquette, and other such things are insisted on, worldly considerations of various kinds creep in, and master and visitors alike feel inclined to find fault with each other. It becomes thus more and more difficult to find such ones as fully comprehend the meaning of the art. If we were to have Joshu for master and Bodhidharma, the first Zen patriarch, for a guest, and Rikyu and myself picked up the dust in the *roji,* would not such a gathering be a happy one indeed?

We see how thoroughly imbued with the spirit of Zen is this statement of one of the chief disciples of Rikyu.

The next section will be devoted to the elucidation of *sabi* or *wabi,* the concept constituting the fourth principle of the art of tea, "tranquillity." In fact, this is the most essential factor in the tea art, and without it there can be no *cha-no-yu* whatever. It is in this connection, indeed, that Zen enters deeply into the art of tea.

I have used the term "tranquillity" for the fourth element making up the spirit of the art of tea, but it may not be a good term for all that is implied in the Chinese character *chi,* or *jaku* in Japanese. *Jaku* is *sabi,* but *sabi* contains much more than "tranquillity." Its Sanskrit equivalent, *santa* or *santi,* it is true, means "tranquillity," "peace," "serenity," and *jaku* has been frequently used in Buddhist literature to denote "death" or "nirvana." But as the term is used in the tea, its implication is "poverty," "simplification," "aloneness," and here *sabi* becomes synonymous with *wabi*. To appreciate poverty, to accept whatever is given, a tranquil, passive mind is needed, but in both *sabi* and *wabi* there is a suggestion of objectivity. Just to be tranquil or passive is not *sabi* nor is it *wabi*. There is always something objective that evokes in one a mood to be called *wabi*. And *wabi* is not merely a psychological reaction to a certain pattern of environment. There is an active principle of aestheticism in it; when this is lacking poverty becomes indigence, aloneness becomes ostracism or misanthropy or inhuman unsociability. *Wabi* or *sabi*, therefore, may be defined as an active, aesthetical appreciation of poverty; when it is used as a constituent of the tea, it is the creating or remodeling of an environment in such a way as to awaken the feeling of *wabi* or *sabi*. Nowadays, as, these terms are used, we may say that *sabi* applies more to the individual objects and environment generally, and *wabi* to the living of a life ordinarily associated with poverty or insufficiency or imperfection. *Sabi* is thus more objective, whereas *wabi* is more subjective and personal. We speak of a *wabi-zumai*, "the wabi way of living," but when a vessel such as a tea caddy or a bowl or a flower vase comes in for appraisal, it is often characterized as having a "*sabi* taste," or *kanmi*. *Kan* and *sabi* are synonymous, while *mi* is "taste." The tea utensils are, as far as I know, never qualified as being of "*wabi* taste."

Of the following two verses the first is considered expressive of the idea of *wabi*, while the second gives the idea of *sabi*:

> Among the weeds growing along the wall
> The crickets are hiding, as if forsaken,
> From the garden we with autumnal showers.
> The yomogi herbs in the garden
> Are beginning to wither from below;
> Autumn is deepening,
> Its colors are fading;
> Not knowing why, my heart is filled with melancholy.

The idea of *sabi is* said to come primarily from *renga* masters, who show great aesthetic appreciation for things suggestive of age, desiccation, numbness, chilliness, obscurity—all of which are negative feelings opposed to warmth, the spring, expansiveness, transparency, etc. They are, in fact, feelings growing out of poverty and deficiency; but they have also a certain quality lending themselves to highly cultivated aesthetic ecstasy. The teamen will say that this is "objectively negated but subjectively affirmed," whereby external emptiness is filled with inner richness. In some ways, *wabi* is *sabi* and *sabi* is *wabi;* they are interchangeable terms.

Shuko, a disciple of Ikkyu (1394–1481) and tea master to Ashikaga Yoshimasa (1435–90) used to teach his pupils about the spirit of the tea with this story. A Chinese poet happened to compose this couplet:

> In the woods over there deeply buried in snow,
> Last night a few branches of the plum tree burst out in bloom.

He showed it to his friend, who suggested that he alter "a few branches" into "one branch." The author followed the friend's advice, praising him as his "teacher of one character." A solitary branch of the plum tree in bloom among the snow-covered woods—here is the idea of *wabi*.

On another occasion, Shuko is reported to have said: "It is good to see a fine steed tied in the straw-roofed shed. This being so, it also is specially fine to find a rare object of art in an ordinarily furnished room." This reminds one of the Zen phrase, "To fill a monk's tattered robe with a cool refreshing breeze." Outwardly there is not a sign of distinction, appearances all go against the contents, which are in every way priceless. A life of *wabi* can then be defined: an inexpressible quiet joy deeply hidden beneath sheer poverty; and it is the art of tea that tries to express this idea artistically.

But if there is anything betraying a trace of insincerity, the whole thing is utterly ruined. The priceless contents must be there most genuinely, they must be there as if they were never there, they must be rather accidentally discovered. In the beginning there is no suspicion of the presence of anything extraordinary, yet something attracts—a closer approach, a tentative examination, and, behold, a mine of solid gold glitters from among the unexpected. But the gold itself remains ever the same, discovered or not. It retains its reality, that is, its sincerity to itself, regardless of accidents. *Wabi* means to be true to itself. A master lives quietly in his unpretentious hut, a friend comes in unexpectedly, tea is served, a fresh spray of flowers is arranged, and the visitor enjoys a peaceful afternoon charmed with his conversation and entertainment. Is this not the tea rite in its reality?...

In *wabi,* aestheticism is fused with morality or spirituality, and it is for this reason that the tea masters declare the tea to be life itself and not merely a thing for pleasure, however refined this may be. Zen is thus directly connected with the tea; indeed, most ancient tea masters studied Zen in real earnest and applied their attainment in Zen to the art of their profession.

Note

1. By Nakano Kazuma in the *Hagakure*... The book is also known as the "Nabeshima Rongo" in imitation of the Confucian *Analects* (*Rongo*).

16

Living Ramadan

Fasting and Feasting in Morocco

Marjo Buitelaar

Fasting during Ramadan is one of the 'five pillars' or religious duties which Muslims must perform. For an entire month, fasting people abstain from food, drink and sexual relations between dawn and dusk. Towards the evening, the call for the sunset prayer from the muezzin, the crier in the minaret who calls people to prayer, is anxiously awaited, since it announces the moment to break the fast. The self-control exerted during the daytime then makes way for self-indulgence. People gather around the table and eat lavish meals. Afterwards, some townspeople stay at home to watch television, while others go out to attend the special Ramadan prayers in the mosque or to stroll along illuminated shopping avenues, buying sweets from one of the many street vendors. Unlike the other months of the year, during Ramadan towns are bustling with activities until late in the evening, and most people do not go to bed until after midnight.

For Moroccans, and probably for many Muslims elsewhere as well, Ramadan is the most important religious ritual of the year. Although most people agree that, especially in summer, fasting may be an ordeal, the fasting month is much looked forward to...

Cleaning the house is one of the ways people, and women in particular, prepare themselves for the coming fasting month. In fact, the whole month preceding Ramadan, named Shaban, is dedicated to these preparations. About a week before the advent of Ramadan, the changing streets in the medina of Marrakech make one realize that the fasting month is approaching. Many of the vendors, who sit along the side of the road behind a piece of cloth with a few displayed articles, have replaced their usual merchandise, such as washcloths and scrubstones for the public bath, with the bowls and wooden spoons that are used to eat *hrîra*, the special Ramadan soup. Other peddlers have substituted copies of the Koran for second-hand books and magazines. Small restaurants are decorated with glittering festoons and paper stars, like those used in Europe as Christmas decorations, and switch from serving quick lunches to selling *sebbakîyas*, the special Ramadan cookies. On Jemaa al-Fna, the central square in the medina of Marrakech, rows of stalls selling the same kind of cookies, which can also be found in all confectionery shops this time of the year, are set up. One confectionary, which is famous for the excellent quality of its *sebbakîyas* and other pastries that are eaten almost exclusively during Ramadan, rents a second shop for the months of Shaban and Ramadan in the middle of Semmarine, the *sûq* or bazaar of Marrakech and traditional shopping centre of the town. The smell of the *sebbakîyas* penetrates the whole medina.

Olives and dates are also much desired delicacies during Ramadan. Some days before the fasting month begins, small shopkeepers who usually sell anything from kitchenware to tools, suddenly have devoted plenty of room in their shops to crates of dates and jars or even washtubs full of olives and other preserves…

[During Ramadan] the quality of the food is better than usual, the amount of food is larger, and many women restore traditional cooking methods. Although during Ramadan the number of meals is reduced, both quantity and quality are increased. People may even have saved money in order to eat more sumptuously during Ramadan. Rich people, for instance, who are used to eating meat every day, improve the quality of their *tajins*, stews prepared in earthenware cone-shaped pots, by adding extra olives or dried prunes and almonds. On their tables one can also find a large variety of Ramadan pastries. Poorer families, who normally eat little meat or can afford to do so only on Fridays, try to have meat, if not every day, then at least a few times a week during Ramadan. Equally, nearly all families I visited served at least some crumbs of the special Ramadan cookies.

In most cases, the amount of food prepared exceeds the quantity needed to fill the stomach. There should always be enough food to serve unexpected visitors their share of the lavish Ramadan meal. While this is also done in other months, during Ramadan being prepared to serve unexpected guests is of greater importance, since the chances that somebody will visit the house unexpectedly are greater. Another reason for preparing extra food is that during the fasting month, it is customary to send a share of one's own delicacies to neighbours, relatives or close friends every now and then.

Sharing lavish meals is a major preoccupation of Moroccans during Ramadan and women have the responsibility of making sure that the family can indulge in excessive consumption after sunset. In preparing food they often employ traditional cooking methods. A few days before the beginning of Ramadan, one of my informants began to collect wood to burn under an old stove she almost exclusively uses during Ramadan. She usually cooks on a gas burner, but in her view, the *hrîra*, the special Ramadan soup, never tastes as good as when prepared on the old stove. Another example is the stew which during Ramadan is eaten for the meal that is consumed a few hours after 'breakfast'. Usually this stew is prepared in pressure cookers on gas burners. During Ramadan, however, many women use charcoal burners and cook in a *tajin*. This takes much more time, but the better taste is considered ample compensation.

Tasting food is generally believed to be forbidden while fasting, so women have to rely on habit in measuring how much salt and spices must be added to the food. It is Important for the *hrîra* to taste right the first day of Ramadan. If this is the case, women know that the soup will be tasty the whole month. Should, however, the *hrîra* be too salty or not spicy enough, then no matter how you try, the soup will not taste good the rest of the month.

Breaking the Fast

The last half hour before sunset is rush hour. Conflicts occur easily when hundreds of people, whose hunger by this time has made them irritated, try to push their way through the narrow alleys in the medina to get home, despite the fact that quarrelling during the fast is reprehensible.

Among those who elbow their way through the crowd are many young men who have been jogging during the last hour before sunset. Their faces show gratification and pride. They obviously enjoy demonstrating their excellent condition by accomplishing such performances on an empty stomach. People respond to these young sportsmen with respect for their strength. For the same reason, soccer games just before sunset are very popular. Almost every neighbourhood of the medina has its own soccer team and during Ramadan a competition is held between them, which attracts many male supporters. Special Ramadan soccer competition is also organized nationally between different towns.

At home, mothers or wives by this time have set the table for breakfast. In most families, this consists of at least a plate with boiled eggs and one with *sebbakîyas*. In richer families, additional pastries such as pancakes sprinkled with olive oil or honey, or *slílu*, ground nuts mixed with roasted flour and spices, may be featured on the breakfast menu, together with different kinds of salads and drinks such as fresh orange juice or buttermilk. In the middle of the table of any family in Marrakech, Berkane and probably everywhere in Morocco, one finds the indispensable soup tureen with *hrîra*. The soup tureen is surrounded by bowls which each have a wooden spoon over them. This is another example of a tradition being restored during Ramadan. The restoration of old Moroccan traditions and, more particularly, the fact that everywhere in Morocco people break the fast by eating the same soup affirms the notion that Moroccans are one people.

This sense of communion is concretely experienced when all family members gather around the table at sunset to share 'breakfast'. The family ethos is strongly emphasized during Ramadan. Ideally, close relatives share breakfast at least twice a week. In my host family, one sister moved in with us for the duration of Ramadan and almost every day we were joined by one or two relatives for breakfast. Ramadan is also the time to invite friends over for breakfast. Such invitations render the host *ajr* [having religious merit]. To a lesser extent the guests also achieve *ajr* for paying a visit...

The Moroccan Nation

Eating *hrîra* is so closely associated with breaking the fast in Morocco, that this soup has become a national symbol for Ramadan. Cartoons in the newspapers depict people jumping into a bowl of *hrîra* or showering themselves with the soup, all to show the gratification this favourite Moroccan dish offers after a long day of fasting.

What makes *hrîra so* suitable as the national dish for breaking the fast is that the ingredients can easily be adjusted to meet any budget and family size. Rich families use chopped meat and kilos of fresh tomatoes, whereas poorer and very large families replace fresh tomatoes with tomato paste, meat with extra chickpeas and lentils and add more flour and water to make the volume of the soup meet the size of the family. Although each household has its own recipe, these are all variations on the famous Moroccan *hrîra*. The fact that nearly all people eat the same soup directly after sunset enhances a sense of communion; it stimulates the notion of establishing one Moroccan people of fasting Muslims. Restoring Moroccan traditions such as cooking in earthenware *tajins* on charcoal burners and wearing *jellabas* also expresses the 'typical Moroccan way' of fasting...

I have described Ramadan in Morocco by addressing two issues: first, what it is that makes fasting a meaningful act for Moroccans, and second, in what ways the practice of the fast is embedded in the Moroccan world-view. To this end, I have analysed three notions through which Moroccans construct the practice of fasting. Performance of the fast distinguishes Muslims from non-Muslims. Simultaneously going through the extraordinary, repetitive routine of fasting at daytime and feasting at night-time connects Muslims over the entire world, marking off the *umma* or community of believers who express their loyalty to God by following his Prophet Muhammed. This unification of the Islamic community is emphasized not only at the level of the Greater Umma encompassing all Muslims. Notions of *al-watan*, the (Moroccan) nation, and *qarâba*, 'closeness', are likewise stressed, the former through restoration of Moroccan traditions...

More than any other act of worship, fasting during Ramadan permeates all spheres of life, public and private. Women's participation is more manifest in the fast than in other collective rites, in which men appear to be the leading actors. Expressing membership of the *umma* through fasting is, therefore, of special significance to women. Consistent with the distribution of responsibilities between the genders, women are most active in exchanging Ramadan delicacies and visits among the *qurâb* or 'close ones'.

Another key notion in performance of the fast is *tahâra*, purity. Not only must fasters be in a pure condition for their fast to be valid, but performance of the fast itself is seen as a physical and moral purification process with beneficial effects on health. The notion of *tahâra* is linked to the notion of health. Fasting is believed to 'clean' the stomach and to allow vital organs to come to a rest. Fasting involves both the body and the mind: people who fast ideally focus on God and avoid arguments. As a reward, past sins are forgiven by God at the end of Ramadan. This moral purification not only affects fasting individuals, but also brings about a regeneration of society at large.

In the case of women, the purification process is hampered by menstruation. Their compulsory breaking of the fast during the days that they are in this impure state is interpreted as a sign of weakness and their compensatory fasting later in the year is not valued as highly as fasting during Ramadan. Women have developed several strategies to make up for these restrictions, one of which is working harder for *ajr*, religious merit, than men.

Ajr is the third notion which shapes people's fasting activities and their interpretation thereof. The *ajr* that is earned by performing religious deeds will be credited on the Day of Judgement, thus facilitating one's entrance into Paradise. Ramadan is the pre-eminent month to undertake acts for *ajr*, since it is believed to be an effect of the sacredness of the fasting month that good deeds are rewarded twice as much as during the other months of the year.

Praying the special Ramadan prayers and spending the night of the 27th of Ramadan in the mosque reciting the Koran are ways to earn *ajr* that are specific to men, while women tend to perform good deeds for *ajr* by distributing alms, usually in kind. They also emphasize that *ajr* is earned by demonstrating patience, which they conceive of as a specific female quality.

On an analytical level, the three notions of Islamic community, purity and religious merit are part of a complex configuration. Not only does each of the terms refer to a set of related notions, but they are also interrelated: purity is only attainable by members of the Islamic community, while religious merit can only be collected by those who are in a pure state. On a more abstract level, they have in common the characteristic of realizing, in one way or another, unification. The native term for unification, *tawhîd*, was mentioned by informants in relation to the quality of the fast of approaching the ideal of *umma*. As a doctrinal concept, *tawhîd* refers to the oneness of God and the unification that believers seek with Him by total submission and service. I would argue that the entire practice of fasting can be interpreted as an exercise in unification. Linking Muslims everywhere in the world in a joint action of alternately fasting and feasting, the fast unifies the Islamic Community. The conscious effort to abstain not only from eating, drinking and sexual contacts but also from quarrelling and sinful thoughts is an example of the unification of the body and the mind. Since it brings one's possible place in Paradise closer within reach, *ajr* can be interpreted as a kind of unification of life on earth and the afterlife in Paradise.

17

Bitter Herbs and Unleavened Bread

(from the Passover Haggadah)

Passover, the Jewish holiday celebrated every spring, recalls the liberation of the Jews from bondage in Egypt as told in the Book of Exodus. The holiday enjoins special kosher regulations, including prohibition on leavened or risen breads, commemorating the fact that the Jews had to leave Egypt too quickly to allow the dough in preparation to rise. (Passover is also sometimes referred to as the "Festival of Unleavened Bread".)

While many Jewish communities celebrate Passover with traditional foods at the evening meal or seder, there are also ritual foods present that have symbolic roles in the service that accompanies the meal. At the center of the table there is a plate of matzoh, which is unleavened bread; a bowl of salt water, by some accounts symbolizing tears shed in captivity; a plate holding a lamb shankbone (standing in for the sacrifice that the Jews offered up before God "passed over" their households, sparing their firstborn sons from the death meted out to Egyptians); bitter herbs (horseradish or sharp green herbs, representing the bitterness of bondage); parsley or other spring herb representing renewal of life; a roasted egg, representing new life or another version of the sacrifice (accounts differ); and *charoseth*, a mixture of apples, ground nuts, and honey, representing the mortar that the Jews used to build the temples of the pharaoh. Four cups of wine are consumed during the seder service.

The following is excerpted from the Haggadah, the ceremonial text that is read during the meal.

Editor

Seder leader, gesturing toward the matzoh: This is the bread of affliction which our forefathers ate in the land of Egypt. Let all who are hungry enter and eat; let all who are in distress join us in feasting. This year we are here; next year may we be in the land of Israel. This year we are slaves; next year may we be free.

The four questions (asked by children): Why is this night different from all other nights? On all other nights we may eat either leavened or unleavened bread, but tonight why do we eat only unleavened bread?

On all other nights we eat all kinds of herbs; but why on this night do we eat only bitter herbs?

On all other nights we do not dip our herbs; why on this night do we dip them twice?

On all other nights we eat sitting up or reclined; why on this night do we recline during the meal?

Because we were Pharaoh's slaves in the land of Egypt, and the Eternal our God brought us forth from there with a mighty hand and an outstretched arm. And if the Most Holy One, blessed be He, had not brought our ancestors forth from Egypt, then we, our children, and our children's children would still be Pharaoh's slaves in Egypt.

So, even if all of us were wise and full of understanding, all of us learned in the Torah, we would still be commanded tell the story of the departure from Egypt. And all who tell the story are to be praised.

. . .

The Paschal lamb which our fathers used to eat at the time when the Temple stood—what was the reason for it? Because the Holy One, blessed be he, passed over the houses of our fathers in Egypt.

As it is said: "It is the sacrifice of the Lord's Passover, for He passed over the houses of the people of Israel in Egypt, when He smote the Egyptians, and spared our houses." And the people bowed their heads and worshiped. (Exodus 12:27)

The unleavened bread which we now eat, what is the reason for it? Because the dough our ancestors had prepared had not yet leavened when the Holy One, blessed be he, revealed himself to them and redeemed them.

And it is said: "And they baked unleavened cakes of the dough which they brought out of Egypt, for it was not leavened, because they were thrust out of Egypt, and could not tarry, neither had they prepared for themselves any provisions." (Exodus 12:39)

These bitter herbs we eat, what is their meaning? Because the Egyptians made the lives of our forebears bitter in Egypt.

As it is said: "And they made their lives bitter with hard service, in mortar and in brick, and in all kinds of work in the field; in all their work they made them serve with rigor." (Exodus 1: 14)

. . .

Blessed art thou, O Lord, our God, king of the universe, who redeemed us and brought forth our forefathers from Egypt, and has brought us to this night, to eat unleavened bread and bitter herbs. O Lord our God and God of our fathers, bring us to other festivals and holy days, that we may rejoice in the building of thy city and be joyous in thy service. And there may we eat of the sacrifices and the paschal offerings, whose blood will mark the walls of thy altar for acceptance. Then shall we give thanks to thee with a new song, for our redemption and the liberation of our souls. Blessed art thou, O Lord our Redeemer.

Blessed art thou, O Lord, king of the universe, creator of the fruit of the vine.

Blessed art thou, O Lord, king of the universe, who commanded us in the washing of the hands.

Blessed art thou, O Lord our God, king of the universe, who brings forth bread from the earth.

Blessed art thou, O Lord our God, king of the universe, who sanctified us with thy commandments, and commanded us to eat unleavened bread.

Blessed art thou, O Lord our God, king of the universe, who sanctified us with thy commandments and commanded us to eat bitter herbs.

In the custom of Hillel when the Temple yet stood, who combined unleavened bread and bitter herbs and ate them together, to perform that which is commanded: "They shall eat it with unleavened bread and bitter herbs." (Numbers 9:11)

. . .

Blessed art thou, O Lord our God, ruler of the world, who feeds the whole world in goodness, with grace, kindness, and beneficence. He gives food to all creatures for his mercy is forever. And through his great goodness, food has never failed us, and may it never fail us, for his Name's sake. For he feeds and sustains all, and does good unto all, and nourishes all his creatures which he did create.

Blessed art thou, O Lord the Eternal, who feeds all.

18
Feasting with Dead Souls

Elizabeth Carmichael and Chloë Sayer

> Death revenges us against life, stripping it of all its vanities and pretensions and showing it for what it is: some bare bones and a dreadful grimace... Skulls made of sugar or tissue paper, painted skeletons hung with fireworks, our popular representations of death always mock at life; they are the affirmation of the nothingness and insignificance of human existence. We decorate our houses with skulls and on the Day of the Dead we eat bread in the form of bones and enjoy the songs and jokes in which bald death has the laughs; but all this swaggering familiarity does nothing to rid us of the question we all have to ask: 'What is death?'
>
> (Paz:1959)

For the first two days of November a sweet-smelling cloud of copal incense hangs over most of Mexico. The Day of the Dead is being celebrated. Nominally this is the Christian feast of All Saints' Day and All Souls' Day, but it is celebrated in Mexico as nowhere else in the Catholic world. The Mexican festival of *Todos Santos* (All Saints), also called *Día* or *Días de Muertos* (Day, or Days of the Dead), is the most important celebration in the yearly cycle. This is especially so in rural areas, where the preparations in anticipation of the event are a major preoccupation for much of the year.

Celebrations at Christmas and Eastertide are also of note but less distinctive in form. Only the festivals celebrated in honour of local patron saints display some of the same intensity and devotion evident on the Day of the Dead, perhaps because the saints themselves are regarded rather as lesser deities who intercede with God. The dead too ultimately achieve this semi-divine status in the folk-Catholicism of Mexico. As intermediaries they can intervene on behalf of the living, either with the Christian God or, as among some

Indian groups, with divinities that have their origin in pre-Hispanic religion (Herrasti and Vargas 1985).

The Day of the Dead in Mexico is essentially a private or family feast. It has a public aspect at community level, but the core of the celebration takes place within the family home. It is a time of family reunion not only for the living but also the dead who, for a few brief hours each year, return to be with their relatives in this world.

As a time of reunion, there is nothing sombre or macabre about the event: the returning souls do not bring the odour of death and the grave with them, but come as spirits who have returned from another world, which for many Mexican Indians is very like this one (Madsen 1960). These worlds of the living and the dead exist in a state of permanent interaction.

As celebrated today, *Todos Santos* incorporates elements of pre-Hispanic religious belief and practice, which differentiate it from the orthodox Catholic feast of All Saints' and All Souls'. The origin of the Catholic feasts is obscure. All Saints' (All-Hallows' or Hallowmas), 1 November, is the commemorative festival of all Christian saints and martyrs known or unknown. Some sources indicate that it was introduced into the festival cycle by Pope Boniface IV in the seventh century in substitution for a pagan festival of the dead. Originally observed in May, it was moved to November by Gregory III in the eighth century...

By the end of the thirteenth century, All Souls' was almost universally accepted in Western Christendom as a liturgical day commemorating all the faithful departed, despite the reluctance of the church to establish a specific day for propitiating and honouring the dead. 'The reason for this reluctance was apparently the desire to dissociate the church from the persistent and tenacious pre-Christian rites and ceremonies of the cult of the dead and ancestor worship ... which from the beginning the church regarded as "superstitious"' (Nutini 1988).

It was, however, found expedient to incorporate the practice of feasting, often associated with the commemoration of the dead in pagan custom, into Christian ritual. Peter Brown, in his excellent account of the way in which the family-centred feasts of the ancient world were transmuted in early Christianity into the 'Cult of the Saints', writes that:

> For one generation, a lively debate on 'superstition' within the Christian church flickered around the cemeteries of the Mediterranean. In the 380s, Ambrose at Milan and in the 390s, Augustine at Hippo, attempted to restrict among their Christian congregations certain funerary customs, most notably the habit of feasting at the graves of the dead, either at the family tombs or in the memoriae of the martyrs. In Augustine's explicit opinion, these practices were a contaminating legacy of the pagan beliefs: `When peace came to the church, a mass of pagans who wished to come to Christianity were held back because their feast days with their idols used to be spent in an abundance of eating and drinking.'
>
> (Brown 1981)

The Christian church sought to refocus the pagan feasting for the dead and establish celebrations for the saints. But family-centred practices associated with the dead showed great strength and persistence and survived for many centuries. When the Spaniards conquered the New World, they brought with them not only the official Catholic religion, but also some of the more popular or folk-religious practices of early sixteenth-century Spain (Nutini 1988, Foster 1960, Hoyos Saínz and Hoyos Sancho 1947). The European customs of making food-offerings and feasting with the dead found fertile ground in Mexico where superficially similar ceremonies were an important aspect of pre-Hispanic religious ritual.

Because of this and other apparent similarities between the two religions, it is often extremely difficult to determine the origins of particular aspects of celebrations such as the Day of the Dead. It is nonetheless quite clear that in Mexico, the observation of this feast is a deeply rooted and complex event that continues to be of great significance for many people.

The Celebration of *Todos Santos*

Everywhere in Mexico, the days between the evenings of 31 October and 2 November are central to the celebration of *Todos Santos*. These are the days upon which the household offerings of foods and drinks are made to the dead. Other dates which may be included vary from region to region. Among the Totonac of Veracruz State for example, the period for the commemoration of the dead begins on the Day of San Lucas (18 October) and continues until the Day of San Andrés (30 November). In many places there are further celebrations including household offerings, or feasting in the cemeteries (or both), at the *octava*, on 9 November. The Totonac also celebrate an *octava* for the souls of dead children on 8 November.

Days are set aside for the remembrance of particular categories of the dead. Quite commonly, those who have died in accidents (*los accidentados*) are remembered on 28 November but there is considerable variation concerning these special categories which seem to be largely a matter of local custom. Galinier, writing of the Otomi of the Sierra Madre, suggests that the dates are hierarchical, with the ancient and therefore 'deified' dead and prominent forbears having their cult celebrated in October. Victims of violent death are remembered on the Day of San Lucas in a ritual performed outside the house (because such souls are feared), and the family dead on 1 and 2 November (Galinier 1987).

The cleaning and dressing of graves in the cemeteries is most typically carried out within the days of *Todos Santos*. Decoration of tombs takes many forms and the nature of the activities in the cemetery again varies a great deal regionally and locally. At Chilac, in the State of Puebla, it is on 2 November that the community goes in procession to the cemetery, carrying armfuls of flowers, candles, incense and new or refurbished crosses to place upon the tombs. There is much music-making of all kinds, but no conspicuous feasting.

In Tancoco, Veracruz, the decoration, offering and feasting in the cemetery takes place upon the *octava*. *Rezanderos* (professional prayer-makers) chant at the gravesides, there is music and masked dancing, and the singing of improvised songs which poke fun at local figures. Both here and in Chilac these are daytime celebrations. In other areas, the visits to the cemetery take the form of a night-long candlelit vigil, as for example at many places in the State of Michoacán such as on the island of Janitzio on Lake Pátzcuaro and in the nearby town of Tzintzuntzan (Brandes 1988)...

The organized religious content of the fiesta is variable. Where a priest is available special masses will be said and he may, as at San Pablito, lead the activities which take place in the cemeteries but his presence is not essential. It is often among the Mestizo population that the Catholic rites are of greatest importance, while the Indian population may carry out their own observances. Among the Cora Indians of western Mexico, Herrasti and Vargas (1985) describe the curate as being 'a few metres away [from the Indians making their offerings in the church], kneeling before the central altar, trying to recite the rosary but failing to attract much attention for his orations.'

The Offering or 'Ofrenda'

Many preparations for the Day of the Dead take place much earlier in the year. In areas where pottery is made, the production of large cooking vessels (*ollas*), incense burners and other necessary items starts in September or even earlier. Traditionally, everything should be new for the offering, even down to the clothes the family wear; in practice, this cannot always be adhered to. But when needed, this is the time to consider replacing household items such as the enormous round-bellied cooking pots used in rural areas to prepare *tamales* and other festival dishes that are consumed in large quantities.

Goods for the offering to the dead may be gradually acquired throughout the year, but the period of intense preparation begins in the period immediately preceding *Todos Santos*. The rural markets in the week or so before the critical date are the finest of the year, humming with colour and excitement. Everything essential for the offering is on sale: the flowers, breads, fruits and vegetables, candles, sugar sweets, pottery dishes and toys and many grades of incense. Traders come from afar to the larger markets, bringing goods not available locally – pottery from other centres, factory-made ceramics, baskets, wooden cooking utensils, tissue papers with punched or cut-out decorative designs, paper puppets, and so on. While many of these things are quite common in urban markets, they are exotic in many rural areas, as are the plastic toys and masks representing the pumpkins and witches of Halloween, although even these make an occasional appearance. The sense of anticipation and exhilaration is infectious, and excited family groups stand before the stalls debating their choice of plastic sheeting for the offering table or a new vase or pottery candlestick.

The flowers form brilliant mounds of colour. Predominant is the vivid orange and yellow of the *cempasúchil*, the 'flower of the dead', which has been associated with festivals for the dead since pre-Hispanic times. Both its colour and aromatic scent are important for they are thought to attract the souls towards the offering. 'Paths' of marigold petals are strewn from the *ofrenda* to the door of the house to guide the souls to their feast. Sometimes the flower-path also leads from the door of the house out into the roadway in the direction of the cemetery. This is to ensure that the souls will not only find their way to the offering, but also back to the cemetery; should they lose their way, they might remain in this world to trouble the living.

The other most common flower is the brilliant magenta cockscomb, or *mano de leon* (lion's paw). Although this and, above all, the *cempasúchil* are the most important flowers for the decoration of offerings, many others are used including a gypsophila-like white flower, *nube*, gladioli and carnations. All purchases are ideally completed before 28 October and the final preparations in the houses will by then be well underway.

When a family has a bread oven, the baking of the bread for the dead will begin before 30 October; it is a duty always carried out by men, either the head of the family or a close relative. Otherwise, a wide variety of breads in many different forms[1] will be purchased from bakeries or the market. The cooking of the special dishes for the offering, and the making of such items as chocolate figures in many forms, is also begun well in advance.

On 30 or 31 October, according to local custom, if not begun before, the *ofrenda* itself will be constructed. The whole family will probably play some part in this. A table is set up (or, as with the Totonac, a platform suspended from the roof-beams of the house), covered with a white or embroidered cloth or perhaps decorative plastic sheeting. It is usually set close to the permanent household altar for the saints.

Above the table, framing the front of the offering, an arch is constructed using supple canes which is then decorated with palm or other green leaves and sometimes sugar canes. This is then embellished with an arrangement of flowers, fruits and other ornaments. Additional ornaments may be added which will vary from region to region. A cloth or plastic sheet can be draped above the arch to form a 'sky' *(cielo)* over the offering. There may be tissue paper tied into decorative forms adorning the arch and table, or *papeles picados* (sheets of multicoloured tissue paper with punched or cut-out designs) or *papeles recortados* (layered sheets of coloured paper with cut designs of saints, virgins, churches, birds and flowers). These are hung in front of and behind the offering table.

On the table are placed pictures or figures of particular saints, a Virgin or a Christ, of importance to the family. Candles of various types and candlesticks are placed both on and before the offering; the candles are sometimes set into a section of the stem of a banana plant set up on wooden trestles. Before the table will be a new *petate*, a rush or palm-leaf mat upon which the incense burners are placed ready for use.

If the family have portraits or photographs of the deceased, these will be given a central position on the offering, although this is not common in Indian households. More vases of flowers will complete the decorations, leaving only space for the food offerings which will follow.

The Return of the Souls

The most widely held belief is that the souls of children return first, and food and gifts appropriate to their age and tastes will be set out for them. When the children withdraw, the souls of the adult dead are in turn offered the foods and drinks that they preferred in life. The child souls are sometimes divided into two categories, those who die before baptism, *los ninos limbos* (infants in limbo) who return on 30 October (Nutini 1988), and the souls of other children who return on 31 October. The foods for children will on the whole be simpler and less highly seasoned than for adults. Breads and water are always included, sweets of various kinds, fruits and perhaps milk or soft drinks. It is sometimes the custom to set out an offering table especially for children alongside that for the adults, with everything in miniature: cups, plates, and miniature breads and sugar animals.

The adult dead return on 1 November and are, in their turn, given the most splendid offering of foods and drinks the family can afford. In addition to the breads there may be biscuits of various types, sugar figures, fresh and candied fruits, especially *dulce de calabaza* (candied pumpkin) and fruit pastes. Cooked dishes might include chicken or turkey in *mole*, and certainly various forms of *tamales*, the maize dough 'cakes', with various fillings both savoury and sweet, which are wrapped in maize husks and steamed. These and other dishes such as *enchiladas* (*tortillas* with red chilli sauce) and *chalupas* (fried *tortillas* with meat or cheese) are made ready in abundance, and brought in succession to be placed steaming upon the offering table. The beverages offered in addition to water range from coffee, chocolate and *atole* (a drink of maize meal with various flavourings) to whatever form of alcohol the deceased favoured when alive: beer, tequila, mescal, or *aguardiente* (cane spirit).

When the offering table is fully decorated and provisioned it can be a magnificent sight. Everything is very carefully arranged; boxes and packing cases covered with paper or cloth will perhaps have been arranged to form several 'tiers' above the surface of the table for the better display of the goods offered. Some dishes will be covered with brightly embroidered cloths, or piled into painted wooden dishes.

Clothing and personal goods, either favourite possessions of the deceased when alive, or new items specially made or purchased for the occasion, are added to some offerings. These will be placed to the side of the table. For a man, these might include a sombrero, carrying bag (*moral*), *machete*, or *sarape* (blanket); for a woman, possibly a woven belt (*faja*), embroidered blouse or cloth. As with the food offering, these items will eventually be used by the living.

The souls are not usually seen but their presence is sensed. They do not physically consume the foods and drinks, but rather absorb their essence. When the souls have had their fill, it will be the turn of the living members of the family to take their share of the *ofrenda*. Some part of the offering will also be distributed among relatives, godparents, friends and neighbours and some part will be taken to the cemetery to be placed upon the graves of the deceased. The community-wide sharing of the offerings is an important social occasion during which relationships of all kinds are reaffirmed. When all is over, the community settles back into its normal routines; the members of the family who have come from afar leave to take up their lives elsewhere; the dead have already returned to the other world.

In rural communities with a generally more wealthy Mestizo population, the style of offerings may closely resemble the local Indian *ofrendas*, but will include a higher proportion of 'exotic' goods. There may be some commercially produced chocolate instead of the home-made variety, or packets of biscuits, tinned foods, or other expensive goods. One offering for a child seen in the town of Huaquechula consisted entirely of 'junk' foods. The principle is the same: whatever pleased the dead in life they are to have again. There is also an element in this of impressing one's neighbours – the ability to make an elaborate and expensive offering confers status upon the family…

In truly urban contexts, the offerings may also resemble those of the surrounding villages but occasionally vestiges of older urban customs are found. This is the case in Puebla where a few people still continue the almost obsolete custom of setting the family dining room table with a place for each dead relative. On the chairs, or nearby are placed some favourite possessions or clothing of the deceased.

Mexico City

In Mexico City there are no limits. People often build an offering in the regional style of the place they originally come from. In quite wealthy middle-class homes there may well be an *ofrenda*, perhaps traditional in form, perhaps consisting merely of a few photographs, flowers and candles. There are *ofrendas* that are highly idiosyncratic in style, with perhaps coloured neon lights bathing the assemblage of objects, or indeed whatever the ingenuity of the individual suggests in the way of unusual decoration. Food, apart perhaps from some token gesture – an *hojaldra* (bread of the dead) and some fruit – may not feature at all.

And here the skulls and skeletons which only rarely make their appearance in rural areas hold sway. They belong in the urban context: not only in Mexico City but at other major centres (notably Oaxaca City, famous for its craftsmen) every material is pressed into skeleton form, and the grinning skulls, who bear no malice or trace of malevolence, cheerily rattle their bones in the markets and ape the antics of the living...

It is traditional for bread-shop windows to be painted with scenes of skeletons hugging, munching and savouring *hojaldras*. Beyond this the window displays of many other shops now sport skulls, skeletons and grotesque masks whatever the goods on sale inside. It is a strange notion to us perhaps that skulls and grotesqueries might be a help in selling the latest in menswear, ladies' underwear or electrical goods, but at this time of year it is part of the general exhilaration in the city air. And that exhilaration is one of the unifying factors that draws together all the manifest expressions of the Day of the Dead. Whether in rural villages or in towns, there is excitement abroad, and everywhere activity devoted to the preparations and ultimately the celebration of the fiesta...

All this diversity is part of the present-day celebration of the Day of the Dead, and the examples cited do not begin to encompass the variety of forms. If in the cities the impulse that prompts the desire to make an offering to the dead is becoming customary rather than obligatory, and is often far divorced from any religious significance the event still holds, in rural areas, especially among Indian peoples, the sense of obligation is still very deeply felt. In substantiation of this, there are the stories told almost everywhere, although with many variations upon the theme, of the dire consequences of not fulfilling the necessary rites in honour of the dead. In most versions the outcome of failure to conform is sickness or death. In every story someone, who has either through disbelief or sheer neglectfulness failed to prepare a suitable offering, sees the dead returning to their graves (usually only people with special powers can see the dead), delightedly bearing the goods from the *ofrendas*. His or her own dead kin come last, weeping and in distress. Even remorse, in the form of a hasty rush home to make an offering, fails to save the recalcitrant. The making of the offering is then an obligation, a vital part of maintaining good relations with the dead.

Note

1. The breads of Mexico are of such astonishing variety that there are monographs on the subject. For the Day of the Dead in rural areas, they are often shaped into animal and human figures ('souls'). Some of the anthropomorphic forms have small

heads of pottery or paste inserted into them. Many are sprinkled with vivid pink sugar or painted with pink dye. Some have very elaborate geometric and floral patterns marked out in paler dough. The typical city form is the *hojaldra*, a round bread with stylized 'bones' on the upper surface. As well as breads, many forms of biscuits and small cakes will be added to the *ofrenda*.

References

Brandes, Stanley (1988), *Power and Persuasion: Fiestas and Social Control in Rural Mexico*, Philadelphia.

Brown, Peter (1981), *The Cult of the Saints*, London.

Foster, George M. (1960), *Culture and Conquest: America's Spanish Heritage*, New York.

Galinier, Jacques (1987), *Pueblos de la Sierra Madre: Etnografía de la Comunidad Otomí*, Spanish trans. M. Sánchez Ventura and P. Chéron, Mexico.

Herrasti, Lourdes and Vargas, Enrique (1985), 'Día de Muertos entre los Coras', *México Indígena* 7.

Hoyos, Sáinz, Luis de and Hoyos Sancho, Nieves de (1947), *Manual de Folklore: la Vida Popular Tradicional*, Madrid.

Madsen, William (1960), 'Christo-paganism: A study of Mexican religious syncretism', *Nativism and Syncretism*, New Orleans: Middle American Research Institute.

Nutini, Hugo G. (1988), *Todos Santos in Rural Tlaxcala: A Syncretic, Expressive, and Symbolic Analysis of the Cult of the Dead*, Princeton.

Paz, Octavio (1959), *The Labyrinth of Solitude*, London.

Part V

Taste and Aesthetic Discrimination

Preface

While the term "taste" refers originally to gustatory taste and the sensations of the mouth, it also has a wide use as a metaphor for aesthetic sensibility. During the time that this usage became a subject of extensive theorizing in eighteenth-century European philosophy, dominant opinion considered the eyes and ears the "aesthetic" senses, whereas smell, taste, and touch were excluded from this designation. The latter senses, it was argued, direct attention to the body rather than to the world around. The pleasures they afford are sensual rather than aesthetic; and their objects are unlikely candidates to become works of art.

Despite the low esteem that the bodily senses often were accorded in the Western philosophical tradition, "taste" was also widely recognized as an apt metaphor for the ability to discern the subtle qualities of objects through firsthand, intimate acquaintance. Two perspectives from philosophers of this period are included in this section. The first is from David Hume (1711–76), whose influential essay "Of the Standard of Taste" presents a view of taste that has considerable sympathy for the comparability between gustatory taste and (what in English would later be called) "aesthetic" taste. His famous story (taken from Cervantes) of the two wine-tasters whose delicate sensibilities can detect the qualities of wine that others cannot perceive serves as an example of sensitivity to qualities of food and drink, as well as art, that may be developed into full-blown aesthetic capacities.

In comparison, Immanuel Kant (1724–1804) retained a rigorous separation of gustatory and aesthetic taste. In his influential *Critique of Judgment* (1790), for example, he used the example of food preferences to illustrate judgments about taste preference that are merely relative and do not demand philosophical investigation of their foundation, in contrast to genuine aesthetic judgments, which he argued are "universal" and "necessary." The excerpt here is from his *Anthropology from a Pragmatic Point of View* (1798), in which he compares the senses according to the direction of attention that they encourage. While Kant is not much of an apologist for literal taste and gustatory pleasure, his analysis of the operation of this sense provides a thought-provoking view of the possibilities and limits of different sense experiences.

The metaphor of taste has an even longer and considerably more complicated heritage in classical Indian aesthetics, in which it has been a key term of description and analysis for the perception of artistic qualities since at least the third century AD. The essay here by B. N. Goswamy presents some of the meanings of *rasa*, the multivalent term—usually rendered as "taste" in English, although that translation oversimplifies this complicated concept—that is employed in Indian aesthetic theory in ways that conjoin aesthetic, emotional, and sensuous appreciation.

The section concludes with a piece by Yi-Fu Tuan, who offers a view of the importance of literal taste in Chinese aesthetics, along with a sensitive reflection on its history in Western philosophy. His essay, along with Goswamy's, reestablishes the link between aesthetic and literal taste and returns us to gustatory experience and its refinements. The essays in this section highlight the fact that literal taste, perhaps the most denigrated of the senses (with some competition from smell), is capable of some of the finest discriminations. What is more, it can be cultivated to a high degree of discernment, a topic that will be pursued further in the following section.

19

Of the Standard of Taste

David Hume

The great variety of taste, as well as of opinion, which prevails in the world, is too obvious not to have fallen under everyone's observation. Men of the most confined knowledge are able to remark a difference of taste in the narrow circle of their acquaintance, even where the persons have been educated under the same government, and have early imbibed the same prejudices. But those who can enlarge their view to contemplate distant nations and remote ages are still more surprised at the great inconsistence and contrariety. We are apt to call barbarous whatever departs widely from our own taste and apprehension; but soon find the epithet of reproach retorted on us. And the highest arrogance and self-conceit is at last startled, on observing an equal assurance on all sides, and scruples, amidst such a contest of sentiment, to pronounce positively in its own favour.

As this variety of taste is obvious to the most careless enquirer, so will it be found, on examination, to be still greater in reality than in appearance. The sentiments of men often differ with regard to beauty and deformity of all kinds, even while their general discourse is the same. There are certain terms in every language which import blame, and others praise; and all men who use the same tongue must agree in their application of them. Every voice is united in applauding elegance, propriety, simplicity, spirit in writing; and in blaming fustian, affectation, coldness and a false brilliancy: but when critics come to particulars, this seeming unanimity vanishes; and it is found that they had affixed a very different meaning to their expressions. In all matters of opinion and science, the case is opposite: The difference among men is there oftener found to lie in generals than in particulars, and to be less in reality than in appearance. An explanation of the terms commonly ends the controversy, and the disputants are surprised to find that they had been quarrelling, while at bottom they agreed in their judgement.

Those who found morality on sentiment, more than on reason, are inclined to comprehend ethics under the former observation, and to maintain that in all questions which regard conduct and manners, the difference among men is really greater than at first sight it appears. It is indeed obvious that writers of all nations and all ages concur in applauding justice, humanity, magnanimity, prudence, veracity; and in blaming the opposite qualities. Even poets and other authors, whose compositions are chiefly calculated to please the imagination, are yet found, from Homer down to Fenelon, to inculcate the same moral precepts and to bestow their applause and blame on the same virtues and vices. This great unanimity is usually ascribed to the influence of plain reason, which in all these cases maintains similar sentiments in all men and prevents those controversies to which the abstract sciences are so much exposed. So far as the unanimity is real, this account may be admitted as satisfactory. But we must also allow that some part of the seeming harmony in morals may be accounted for from the very nature of language. The word *virtue*, with its equivalent in every tongue, implies praise, as that of *vice* does blame. And no one, without the most obvious and grossest impropriety, could affix reproach to a term, which in general acceptation is understood in a good sense; or bestow applause, where the idiom requires disapprobation. Homer's general precepts, where he delivers any such, will never be controverted; but it is obvious that, when he draws particular pictures of manners and represents heroism in Achilles and prudence in Ulysses, he intermixes a much greater degree of ferocity in the former and of cunning and fraud in the latter, than Fenelon would admit of. The sage Ulysses in the Greek poet seems to delight in lies and fictions and often employs them without any necessity or even advantage. But his more scrupulous son, in the French epic writer, exposes himself to the most imminent perils, rather than depart from the most exact line of truth and veracity…

The merit of delivering true general precepts in ethics is indeed very small. Whoever recommends any moral virtues, really does no more than is implied in the terms themselves. That people who invented the word *charity*, and use it in a good sense, inculcated more clearly and much more efficaciously, the precept, *be charitable*, than any pretended legislator or prophet, who should insert such a *maxim* in his writings. Of all expressions, those which, together with their other meaning, imply a degree either of blame or approbation, are the least liable to be perverted or mistaken.

It is natural for us to seek a Standard of Taste; a rule, by which the various sentiments of men may be reconciled; at least, a decision, afforded, confirming one sentiment, and condemning another.

There is a species of philosophy, which cuts off all hopes of success in such an attempt, and represents the impossibility of ever attaining any standard of taste. The difference, it is said, is very wide between judgement and sentiment. All sentiment is right, because sentiment has a reference to nothing beyond itself, and is always real, wherever a man is conscious of it. But all determinations of the understanding are not right, because they have a reference to something beyond themselves, to wit, real matter of fact, and are not always conformable to that standard. Among a thousand different opinions which different men may entertain of the same subject, there is one and but one, that is just and true; and the only difficulty is to fix and ascertain it. On the contrary, a thousand different sentiments, excited by the same object, are all right; because no sentiment represents what is really in the object. It only marks a certain conformity or relation between the object and the organs or faculties of the mind; and if that conformity did not really exist, the sentiment could never possibly have being. Beauty is no quality in things themselves: it exists merely in the mind which contemplates them; and each mind perceives a different beauty. One person may even perceive deformity, where another is sensible of beauty; and every individual ought to acquiesce in his own sentiment, without pretending to regulate those of others. To seek in the real beauty, or real deformity, is as fruitless an enquiry, as to pretend to ascertain the real sweet or real bitter. According to the disposition of the organs, the same object may be both sweet and bitter; and the proverb has justly determined it to be fruitless to dispute concerning tastes. It is very natural, and even quite necessary to extend this axiom to mental, as well as bodily taste; and thus common sense, which is so often at variance with philosophy, especially with the sceptical kind, is found, in one instance at least, to agree in pronouncing the same decision.

But though this axiom, by passing into a proverb, seems to have attained the sanction of common sense, there is certainly a species of common sense which opposes it, at least serves to modify and restrain it. Whoever would assert an equality of genius and elegance between Ogilby and Milton, or Bunyan and Addison, would be thought to defend no less an extravagance, than if he had maintained a molehill to be as high as Tenerife, or a pond as extensive as the ocean. Though there may be found persons who give the preference to the former authors, no one pays attention to such a taste; and we pronounce without scruple the sentiment of these pretended critics to be absurd and ridiculous. The principle of the natural equality of tastes is then totally forgot, and while we admit it on some occasions where the objects seem near an equality, it appears an extravagant paradox, or rather a palpable absurdity, where objects so disproportioned are compared together.

It is evident that none of the rules of composition are fixed by reasonings a priori, or can be esteemed abstract conclusions of the understanding, from comparing those habitudes and relations of ideas, which are eternal and immutable. Their foundation is the same with that of all the practical sciences, experience; nor are they any thing but general observations, concerning what has been universally found to please in all countries and in all ages. Many of the beauties of poetry and even of eloquence are founded on falsehood and fiction, on hyperboles, metaphors, and an abuse or perversion of terms from their natural meaning. To check the sallies of the imagination, and to reduce every expression to geometrical truth and exactness, would be the most contrary to the laws of criticism; because it would produce a work, which, by universal experience, has been found the most insipid and disagreeable. But though poetry can never submit to exact truth, it must be confined by rules of art, discovered to the author either by genius or observation. If some negligent or irregular writers have pleased, they have not pleased by their transgressions of rule or order, but in spite of these transgressions: They have possessed other beauties, which were conformable to just criticism; and the force of these beauties has been able to overpower censure and give the mind a satisfaction superior to the disgust arising from the blemishes. Ariosto pleases; but not by his monstrous and improbable fictions, by his bizarre mixture of the serious and comic styles, by the want of coherence in his stories, or by the continual interruptions of his narration. He charms by the force and clearness of his expression, by the readiness and variety of his inventions, and by his natural pictures of the passions, especially those of the gay and amorous kind. And however his faults may diminish our satisfaction, they are not able entirely to destroy it. Did our pleasure really arise from those parts of his poem which we denominate faults, this would be no objection to criticism in general; it would only be an objection to those particular rules of criticism which would establish such circumstances to be faults, and would represent them as universally blamable. If they are found to please, they cannot be faults, let the pleasure which they produce be ever so unexpected and unaccountable.

But though all the general rules of art are founded only on experience and on the observation of the common sentiments of human nature, we must not imagine that on every occasion the feelings of men will be conformable to these rules. Those finer emotions of the mind are of a very tender and delicate nature, and require the concurrence of many favourable circumstances to make them play with facility and exactness, according to their general and established principles. The least exterior hindrance to such small springs, or the least internal disorder, disturbs their motion and confounds the operation of the whole machine. When we would make an experiment of this nature and would try the force of any beauty or deformity, we must choose with care a proper time and place, and bring the fancy to a suitable situation and disposition. A perfect serenity of mind, a recollection of thought, a due attention to the object; if any of these circumstances be wanting, our experiment will be fallacious, and we shall be unable to judge of the catholic and universal beauty. The relation which nature has placed between the form and the sentiment will at least be more obscure, and it will require greater accuracy to trace and discern it. We shall be able to ascertain its influence not so much from the operation of each particular beauty as from the durable admiration which attends those works that have survived all the caprices of mode and fashion, all the mistakes of ignorance and envy.

The same Homer, who pleased at Athens and Rome two thousand years ago, is still admired at Paris and at London. All the changes of climate, government, religion, and language, have not been able to obscure his glory. Authority or prejudice may give a temporary vogue to a bad poet or orator, but his reputation will never be durable or general. When his compositions are examined by posterity or by foreigners, the enchantment is dissipated, and his faults appear in their true colours. On the contrary, a real genius, the longer his works endure, and the more wide they are spread, the more sincere is the admiration which he meets with. Envy and jealousy have too much place in a narrow circle; and even familiar acquaintance with his person may diminish the applause due to his performances. But when these obstructions are removed, the beauties, which are naturally fitted to excite agreeable sentiments, immediately display their energy and while the world endures, they maintain their authority over the minds of men.

It appears then, that, amidst all the variety and caprice of taste, there are certain general principles of approbation or blame, whose influence a careful eye may trace in all operations of the mind. Some particular forms or qualities, from the original structure of the internal fabric, are calculated to please, and others to displease; and if they fail of their effect in any particular instance, it is from some apparent defect or imperfection in the organ. A man in a fever would not insist on his palate as able to decide concerning flavours; nor would one affected with the jaundice pretend to give a verdict with regard to colours. In each creature, there is a sound and a defective state; and the former alone can be supposed to afford us a true standard of a taste and sentiment. If in the sound state of the organ there be an entire or considerable uniformity of sentiment among men, we may thence derive an idea of the perfect beauty; in like manner as the appearance of objects in daylight, to the eye of a man in health, is denominated their true and real colour, even while colour is allowed to be merely a phantasm of the senses.

Many and frequent are the defects in the internal organs, which prevent or weaken the influence of those general principles, on which depends our sentiment of beauty or deformity. Though some objects, by the structure of the mind, be naturally calculated to give pleasure, it is not to be expected that in every individual the pleasure will be equally felt. Particular incidents and situations occur which either throw a false light on the objects, or hinder the true from conveying to the imagination the proper sentiment and perception.

One obvious cause why many feel not the proper sentiment of beauty, is the want of that *delicacy* of imagination which is requisite to convey a sensibility of those finer emotions. This delicacy everyone pretends to; everyone talks of it and would reduce every kind of taste or sentiment to its standard. But as our intention in this essay is to mingle some light of the understanding with the feelings of sentiment, it will be proper to give a more accurate definition of delicacy than has hitherto been attempted. And not to draw our philosophy from too profound a source, we shall have recourse to a noted story in Don Quixote.

It is with good reason, says Sancho to the squire with the great nose, that I pretend to have a judgement in wine: this is a quality hereditary in our family. Two of my kinsmen were once called to give their opinion of a hogshead, which was supposed to be excellent, being old and of a good vintage. One of them tastes it; considers it; and after mature reflection pronounces the wine to be good, were it not for a small taste of leather which he perceived in it. The other, after using the same precautions, gives also his verdict in favour of the wine; but with the reserve of a taste of iron, which he could easily distinguish. You cannot imagine how much they were both ridiculed for their judgement. But who laughed in the end? On emptying the hogshead, there was found at the bottom an old key with a leathern thong tied to it.

The great resemblance between mental and bodily taste will easily teach us to apply this story. Though it be certain, that beauty and deformity, more than sweet and bitter, are not qualities in objects, but belong entirely to the sentiment, internal or external; it must be allowed, that there are certain qualities in objects, which are fitted by nature to produce those particular feelings. Now as these qualities may be found in a smaller degree, or may be mixed and confounded with each other, it often happens that the taste is not affected with such minute qualities, or is not able to distinguish all the particular flavours, amidst the disorder in which they are presented. Where the organs are so fine, as to allow nothing to escape them, and at the same time so exact as to perceive every ingredient in the composition: This we call delicacy of taste, whether we employ these terms in the literal or metaphorical sense. Here then the general rules of beauty are of use, being drawn from established models and from the observation of what pleases or displeases, when presented singly and in a high degree: And if the same qualities in a continued composition and in a small degree affect not the organs with a sensible delight or uneasiness, we exclude the person from all pretensions to this delicacy. To produce these general rules or avowed patterns of composition is like finding the key with the leathern thong, which justified the verdict of Sancho's kinsmen and confounded those pretended judges who had condemned them. Though the hogshead had never been emptied, the taste of the one was still equally delicate, and that of the other equally dull and languid. But it would have been more difficult to have proved the superiority of the former to the conviction of every by-stander. In like manner, though the beauties of writing had never been methodized, or reduced to general principles, though no excellent models had ever been acknowledged, the different degrees of taste would still have subsisted, and the judgement of one man had been preferable to that of another; but it would not have been so easy to silence the bad critic, who might always insist upon his particular sentiment, and refuse to submit to his antagonist. But when we show him an avowed principle of art, when we illustrate this principle by examples, whose operation from his own particular taste he acknowledges to be conformable to the principle; when we prove, that the same principle may be applied to the present case, where he did not perceive or feel its influence: He must conclude, upon the whole, that the fault lies in himself, and that he wants the delicacy, which is requisite to make him sensible of every beauty and every blemish, in any composition or discourse.

It is acknowledged to be the perfection of every sense or faculty, to perceive with exactness its most minute objects, and allow nothing to escape its notice and observation. The smaller the objects are which become sensible to the eye, the finer is that organ, and the more elaborate its make and composition. A good palate is not tried by strong flavours, but by a mixture of small ingredients, where we are still sensible of each part, notwithstanding its minuteness and its confusion with the rest. In like manner, a quick and acute perception of beauty and deformity must be the perfection of our mental taste; nor can a man be satisfied with himself while he suspects that any excellence or blemish in a discourse has passed him unobserved. In this case, the perfection of the man and the perfection of the sense or feeling, are found to be united. A very delicate palate, on many occasions, may be a great inconvenience both to a man himself and to his friends: But a delicate taste of wit or beauty must always be a desirable quality, because it is the source of all the finest and most innocent enjoyments of which human nature is susceptible. In this decision the sentiments of all mankind are agreed. Wherever you can ascertain a delicacy of taste, it is sure to meet with approbation; and the best way of ascertaining it is to appeal to those models and principles, which have been established by the uniform consent and experience of nations and ages.

But though there be naturally a wide difference in point of delicacy between one person and another, nothing tends further to increase and improve this talent, than practice in a particular art, and the frequent survey or contemplation of a particular species of beauty. When objects of any kind are first presented to the eye or imagination, the sentiment which attends them is obscure and confused, and the mind is, in a great measure, incapable of pronouncing concerning their merits or defects. The taste cannot perceive the several excellences of the performance, much less distinguish the particular character of each excellency, and ascertain its quality and degree. If it pronounce the whole in general to be beautiful or deformed, it is the utmost that can be expected; and even this judgement, a person, so unpractised, will be apt to deliver with great hesitation and reserve. But allow him to acquire experience in those objects, his feeling becomes more exact and nice. He not only perceives the beauties and defects of each part, but marks the distinguishing species of each quality and assigns it suitable praise or blame. A clear and distinct sentiment attends him through the whole survey of the objects, and he discerns that very degree and kind of approbation or displeasure which each part is naturally fitted to produce. The mist dissipates which seemed formerly to hang over the object; the organ acquires greater perfection in its operations and can pronounce, without danger of mistake, concerning the merits of every performance. In a word, the same address and dexterity which practice gives to the execution of any work is also acquired by the same means in the judging of it.

So advantageous is practice to the discernment of beauty, that, before we can give judgement of any work of importance, it will even be requisite, that that very individual performance be more than once perused by us, and be surveyed in different lights with attention and deliberation. There is a flutter or hurry of thought which attends the first perusal of any piece, and which confounds the genuine sentiment of beauty. The relation of the parts is not discerned; the true characters of style are little distinguished. The several perfections and defects seem wrapped up in a species of confusion, and present themselves indistinctly to the imagination. Not to mention that there is a species of beauty which, as it is florid and superficial, pleases at first; but being found incompatible with a just expression either of reason or passion, soon palls upon the taste, and is then rejected with disdain, at least rated at a much lower value.

It is impossible to continue in the practice of contemplating any order of beauty, without being frequently obliged to form *comparisons* between the several species and degrees of excellence, and estimating their proportion to each other. A man, who has had no opportunity of comparing the different kinds of beauty, is indeed totally unqualified to pronounce an opinion with regard to any object presented to him. By comparison alone we fix the epithets of praise or blame, and learn how to assign the due degree of each. The coarsest daubing contains a certain lustre of colours and exactness of imitation, which are so far beauties, and would affect the mind of a peasant or Indian with the highest admiration. The most vulgar ballads are not entirely destitute of harmony or nature; and none but a person, familiarized to superior beauties, would pronounce their numbers harsh, or narration uninteresting. A great inferiority of beauty gives pain to a person conversant in the highest excellence of the kind, and is for that reason pronounced a deformity; as the most finished object with which we are acquainted is naturally supposed to have reached the pinnacle of perfection, and to be entitled to the highest applause. One accustomed to see, and examine, and weigh the several performances, admired in different ages and nations, can only rate the merits of a work exhibited to his view, and assign its proper rank among the productions of genius.

But to enable a critic the more fully to execute this undertaking, he must preserve his mind free from all prejudice, and allow nothing to enter into his consideration but the very object which is submitted to his examination. We may observe, that every work of art, in order to produce its due effect on the mind, must be surveyed in a certain point of view, and not be fully relished by persons whose situation, real or imaginary, is not conformable to that which is required by the performance. An orator addresses himself to a particular audience and must have a regard to their particular genius, interests, opinions, passions, and prejudices; otherwise he hopes in vain to govern their resolutions and inflame their affections. Should they even have entertained some prepossessions against him, however unreasonable, he must not overlook this disadvantage; but, before he enters upon the subject, must endeavour to conciliate their affection, and acquire their good graces. A critic of a different age or nation, who should peruse this discourse, must have all these circumstances in his eye, and must place himself in the same situation as the audience in order to form a true judgement of the oration. In like manner, when any work is addressed to the public, though I should have a friendship or enmity with the author, I must depart from this situation, and considering myself as a man in general, forget, if possible, my individual being and my peculiar circumstances. A person influenced by prejudice, complies not with this condition, but obstinately maintains his natural position, without placing himself in that point of view, which the performance supposes. If the work be addressed to persons of a different age or nation, he makes no allowance for their peculiar views and prejudices; but, full of the manners of his own age and country, rashly condemns what seemed admirable in the eyes of those for whom alone the discourse was calculated. If the work be executed for the public, he never sufficiently enlarges his comprehension, or forgets his interest as a friend or enemy, as a rival or commentator. By this means, his sentiments are perverted; nor have the same beauties and blemishes the same influence upon him, as if he had imposed a proper violence on his imagination, and had forgotten himself for a moment. So far his taste evidently departs from the true standard; and of consequence loses all credit and authority.

It is well known, that in all questions, submitted to the understanding, prejudice is destructive of sound judgement, and perverts all operations of the intellectual faculties: It is no less contrary to good taste; nor has it less influence to corrupt our sentiment of beauty. It belongs to *good sense* to check its influence in both cases; and in this respect, as well as in many others, reason, if not an essential part of taste, is at least requisite to the operations of this latter faculty. In all the nobler productions of genius, there is a mutual relation and correspondence of parts, nor can either the beauties or blemishes be perceived by him whose thought is not capacious enough to comprehend all those parts and compare them with each other, in order to perceive the consistence and uniformity of the whole. Every work of art has also a certain end or purpose for which it is calculated, and is to be deemed more or less perfect as it is more or less fitted to attain this end. The object of eloquence is to persuade, of history to instruct, of poetry to please by means of the passions and the imagination. These ends we must carry constantly in our view when we peruse any performance, and we must be able to judge how far the means employed are adapted to their respective purposes. Besides, every kind of composition, even the most poetical, is nothing but a chain of propositions and reasonings; not always, indeed, the justest and most exact, but still plausible and specious, however disguised by the colouring of the imagination. The persons introduced in tragedy and epic poetry, must be represented as reasoning, and thinking, and concluding, and acting, suitably to their character and circumstances; and without judgement, as well as taste and invention, a poet can never hope to succeed in so delicate an undertaking. Not to mention, that the same excellence of faculties which contributes to the improvement of reason, the same clearness of conception, the same exactness of distinction, the same vivacity of apprehension, are essential to the operations of true taste, and are its infallible concomitants. It seldom, or never happens that a man of sense who has experience in any art, cannot judge of its beauty; and it is no less rare to meet with a man who has a just taste without a sound understanding.

Thus, though the principles of taste be universal, and nearly if not entirely the same in all men, yet few are qualified to give judgement on any work of art, or establish their own sentiment as the standard of beauty. The organs of internal sensation are seldom so perfect as to allow the general principles their full play, and produce a feeling correspondent to those principles. They either labour under some defect or are vitiated by some disorder, and by that means excite a sentiment which may be pronounced erroneous. When the critic has no delicacy, he judges without any distinction, and is only affected by the grosser and more palpable qualities of the object: The finer touches pass unnoticed and disregarded. Where he is not aided by practice, his verdict is attended with confusion and hesitation. Where no comparison has been employed, the most frivolous beauties, such as rather merit the name of defects, are the object of his admiration. Where he lies under the influence of prejudice, all his natural sentiments are perverted. Where good sense is wanting, he is not qualified to discern the beauties of design and reasoning, which are the highest and most excellent. Under some or other of these imperfections, the generality of men labour; and hence a true judge in the finer arts is observed, even during the most polished ages, to be so rare a character. Strong sense, united to delicate sentiment, improved by practice, perfected by comparison, and cleared of all prejudice, can alone entitle critics to this valuable character; and the joint verdict of such, wherever they are to be found, is the true standard of taste and beauty.

But where are such critics to be found? By what marks are they to be known? How distinguish them from pretenders? These questions are embarrassing; and seem to throw us back into the same uncertainty, from which, during the course of this essay, we have endeavoured to extricate ourselves.

But if we consider the matter aright, these are questions of fact, not of sentiment. Whether any particular person be endowed with good sense and a delicate imagination, free from prejudice, may often be the subject of dispute, and be liable to great discussion and enquiry; but that such a character is valuable and estimable will be agreed on by all mankind. Where these doubts occur, men can do no more than in other disputable questions which are submitted to the understanding: They must produce the best arguments that their invention suggests to them; they must acknowledge a true and decisive standard to exist somewhere, to wit, real existence and matter of fact; and they must have indulgence to such as differ from them in their appeals to this standard. It is sufficient for our present purpose, if we have proved that the taste of all individuals is not upon an equal footing, and that some men in general, however difficult to be particularly pitched upon, will be acknowledged by universal sentiment to have a preference above others...

Though men of delicate taste be rare, they are easily to be distinguished in society by the soundness of their understanding and the superiority of their faculties above the rest of mankind. The ascendant which they acquire gives a prevalence to that lively approbation with which they receive any productions of genius, and renders it generally predominant. Many men, when left to themselves, have but a faint and dubious perception of beauty, who yet are capable of relishing any fine stroke, which is pointed out to them. Every convert to the admiration of the real poet or orator is the cause of some new conversion. And though prejudices may prevail for a time, they never unite in celebrating any rival to the true genius, but yield at last to the force of nature and just sentiment. Thus, though a civilized nation may easily be mistaken in the choice of their admired philosopher, they never have been found long to err, in their affection for a favourite epic or tragic author.

But notwithstanding all our endeavours to fix a standard of taste, and reconcile the discordant apprehensions of men, there still remain two sources of variation, which are not sufficient indeed to confound all the boundaries of beauty and deformity, but will often serve to produce a difference in the degrees of our approbation or blame. The one is the different humours of particular men, the other, the particular manners and opinions of our age and country. The general principles of taste are uniform in human nature. Where men vary in their judgements, some defect or perversion in the faculties may commonly be remarked, proceeding either from prejudice, from want of practice, or want of delicacy; and there is just reason for approving one taste, and condemning another. But where there is such a diversity in the internal frame or external situation as is entirely blameless on both sides, and leaves no room to give one the preference above the other, in that case a certain degree of diversity in judgement is unavoidable, and we seek in vain for a standard, by which we can reconcile the contrary sentiments.

A young man, whose passions are warm, will be more sensibly touched with amorous and tender images, than a man more advanced in years, who takes pleasure in wise, philosophical reflections concerning the conduct of life and moderation of the passions. At twenty, Ovid may be the favourite author; Horace at forty; and perhaps Tacitus at fifty. Vainly would we in such cases endeavour to enter into the sentiments of others and divest ourselves of those propensities which are natural to us. We choose our favourite author as we do our friend, from a conformity of humour and disposition. Mirth or passion, sentiment or reflection: whichever of these most predominates in our temper, it gives us a peculiar sympathy with the writer who resembles us.

One person is more pleased with the sublime; another with the tender; a third with raillery. One has a strong sensibility to blemishes, and is extremely studious of correctness: Another has a more lively feeling of beauties, and pardons twenty absurdities and defects for one elevated or pathetic stroke. The ear of this man is entirely turned towards conciseness and energy; that man is delighted with a copious, rich, and harmonious expression. Simplicity is affected by one; ornament by another. Comedy, tragedy, satire, odes, have each its partisans, who prefer that particular species of writing to all others. It is plainly an error in a critic, to confine his approbation to one species or style of writing, and condemn all the rest. But it is almost impossible not to feel a predilection for that which suits our particular turn and disposition. Such preferences are innocent and unavoidable, and can never reasonably be the object of dispute, because there is no standard, by which they can be decided…

20

Objective and Subjective Senses

The Sense of Taste

Immanuel Kant

Sensibility in the cognitive faculty (the faculty of intuitive ideas) is twofold: sense and imagination. Sense is the faculty of intuition in the presence of an object. Imagination is intuition without the presence of the object. The senses, however, are in turn divided into outer and inner (*sensus internus*). The outer sense is where the human body is affected by physical things. The inner sense is where the human body is affected by the mind. It should be noticed that this inner sense, as a bare faculty perception (of the empirical intuition), must be regarded as differing from the feeling of pleasure and pain, that is, from the susceptibility of the subject to be determined through certain ideas for the conservation or rejection of the condition of these ideas, which might be called the interior sense (*sensus interior*). An idea that comes through the senses, and of which one is conscious as it arises, is specifically called sensation, when at the same time the perception centers our attention on the state of the subject.

To begin with, we can divide the senses of physical sensation into those of the sensation of vitality (*sensus vagus*), and those of organic sensation (*sensus fixus*), and, since they are met with only where there are nerves, into those which affect the whole system of nerves, and those which affect only those nerves which belong to a certain member of the body. The sensations of warmth and cold, even those which are aroused by the mind (for example, through quickly rising hope or fear), belong to the vital sense. The shudder which seizes men even at the idea of something sublime, and the terror, with which nurses' tales drive children to bed late at night, belong to the latter type. They penetrate the body to the center of life.

The organic senses, however, so far as they relate to external sensation, we can conveniently reckon as five, no more and no less.

Three of them are more objective than subjective, that is, they contribute, as empirical intuition, more to the cognition of the exterior object, than they arouse the consciousness of the affected organ. Two, however, are more subjective than objective, that is, the idea obtained from them is more an idea of enjoyment, rather than the cognition of the external object. Consequently, we can easily agree with others in respect to the three objective senses. But with respect to the other two, the manner in which the subject responds can be quite different from whatever the external empirical perception and designation of the object might have been.

The senses of the first class are (1) touch (*tactus*), (2) sight (*visus*), (3) hearing (*auditus*). Of the latter class are (A) taste (*gustus*), (B) smell (*olfactus*). All together they are senses of organic sensation which correspond in number to the inlets from the outside, provided by nature so that the creature is able to distinguish between objects...

On the Senses of Taste and Smell

The senses of taste and smell are both more subjective than objective. The sense of taste is activated when the organ of the tongue, the gullet, and the palate come into touch with an external object. The sense of smell is activated by drawing in air which is mixed with alien vapors; the body itself from which the vapors emanate may be distant from the sensory organ. Both senses are closely related, and he who is deficient in the sense of smell is likewise weak in taste. Neither of the two senses can lead by itself to the cognition of the object without the help of one of the other senses; for example, one can say that both are affected by salts (stable and volatile) of which one must be broken up by liquefaction in the mouth, the other by air which has to penetrate the organ, in order to allow its specific sensation to reach it.

General Remarks Concerning the External Senses

We may divide the sensations of the external senses into those of mechanical and those of chemical operation. To the mechanical belong the three higher senses, to the chemical the two lower senses. The first three senses are those of perception (of the surface), while the other two are senses of pleasure (of innermost sensation). Therefore it happens that nausea, a stimulus to rid oneself of food the quickest way through the gullet by vomiting, is given to man as such a strong vital sensation, since such an internal feeling can be dangerous to the animal.

However, there is also a pleasure of the intellect, consisting in the communication of thought. But when it is forced upon us, the mind finds it repugnant and it ceases to be nutritive as food for the intellect. (A good example of this is the constant repetition of amusing or witty quips, which can become indigestible through sameness.) Thus the natural instinct to be free of it is by analogy called nausea, although it belongs to the inner sense.

Smell is, so to speak, taste at a distance, and other people are forced to share a scent whether they want to or not. Hence, by interfering with individual freedom, smell is less sociable than taste; when confronted with many dishes and bottles, one can choose that which suits his pleasure without forcing others to participate in that pleasure. Filth seems to awaken nausea less through what is repulsive to eye and tongue than through the stench associated with it. Internal penetration (into the lungs) through smell is even more intimate than through the absorptive vessels of mouth or gullet.

The more strongly the senses themselves feel affected by the intensity of the inflow which comes to them, the less information they provide. On the other hand, if they are expected to yield a great deal of information, they must be affected moderately. In the strongest light we see (distinguish) nothing; and a stentorian, forced voice stupefies (suppresses thought).

The more susceptible to impressions the vital sense (that is, the more delicate and sensitive), the more unfortunate is the man. The more susceptible man is toward the organic sense (the more sensitive), and, on the other hand, the more callous he is toward the vital sense, the more fortunate he is. I say more fortunate, certainly not morally better, for he has the feeling of his own well-being more under control. The capacity for sensation derived from the subject's own power (*sensibilitas sthenica*) may be called delicate sensitivity; that coming from the subject's weakness which cannot adequately withstand the penetration of sense impressions into consciousness, that is, attending to sense impressions against one's will, can be called tender-hearted submission (*sensibilitas asthenica*).

Questions

To which organic sense do we owe the least and which seems to be the most dispensable? The sense of smell. It does not pay us to cultivate it or to refine it in order to gain enjoyment; this sense can pick up more objects of aversion than of pleasure (especially in crowded places) and, besides, the pleasure coming from the sense of smell cannot be other than fleeting and transitory. Yet as a negative condition of well-being, this sense is not unimportant, as, for example, when it warns us not to breathe noxious air (such as vapor from a stove, or the stench from a swamp or from dead animals), or keeps us from eating rotten food. The second pleasure-sense, the sense of taste, is of similar importance; it has, however, the specific advantage of furthering companionship in eating, something the sense of smell does not do; moreover, taste is superior because by anticipation it judges the benefit of food beforehand, at the very gate of entrance to the alimentary canal. The benefit of food is closely linked with a rather certain prediction of pleasure as long as luxury and indulgence have not overrefined the sense. In the case of people who are ill, the appetite, which is usually of benefit to them and something of a medicine, fails in its function. Smell of food is, so to speak, a foretaste, and to the hungry man it is an invitation to enjoy his favorite food, while the satisfied man is repelled by the same smell...

On the Feeling for the Beautiful, i.e. On the Partly Sensuous, Partly Intellectual Pleasure in the Reflective Perception, or On Taste

Taste, in the proper sense of the word, is, as has already been stated above, the property of an organ (the tongue, the palate, and the gullet) to be specifically affected by certain dissolved matter in food or drink. According to its use it is to be understood either as a differentiating taste alone or, at the same time, as a pleasant taste (for example, whether something is sweet or bitter, or whether what is tasted [sweet or bitter] is pleasant). Distinguishing taste can provide universal agreement as to how certain things are to be labeled, but pleasant taste can never yield a universally valid judgment: namely, that something (for example, something bitter) which is pleasant to me will also be pleasant to everybody. The reason for this is clear because neither pleasure nor displeasure belong to the cognitive faculty concerning objects; they are rather determinations of the subject which, therefore, cannot be attributed to external objects. Pleasant taste also contains the concept of a distinction between satisfaction and dissatisfaction, which I relate to the idea of the object in the perception or imagination.

The word "taste" is, however, also used for a sensory faculty of judgment, which is not merely to choose for myself, according to my own sense perception, but also according to a certain rule believed to be valid for everybody. This rule may be empirical, in which case, however, it can neither lay any claim to true universality, nor, consequently, to necessity (because the judgment of everyone else about pleasant taste would have to agree with my own). This kind of rule is illustrated by the habits of taste which apply to meals. The Germans begin with a soup, whereas the English begin with solid food, because a custom, gradually extended by imitation, has turned into a rule as to the sequence of courses.

There is also a pleasant taste whose rule must be established a priori, because it indicates with necessity, hence it is valid for everybody, how the idea of an object is to be judged in relation to the feeling of pleasure or displeasure (where, consequently, reason is secretly at play, although one cannot derive its judgment from principles of reason, and demonstrate it accordingly). One could classify this taste as a rationalizing taste in distinction to the empirical as the sensuous taste, (the former being the *gustus reflectens*, the other *gustus reflexus*).

Every tasteful reference to oneself or one's own skills presupposes a social intention (to express oneself), which is not always sociable (sharing in the pleasure of others), but initially usually barbaric, unsociable, and merely competitive. No one in complete solitude will dress up and sweep out his house; he will not even do it for his own wife and children, but only for a guest, in order to present himself in a favorable light. In taste (discrimination), however, that is, in aesthetic judgment, it is not directly the sensation (the material of the idea of an object), but rather how the free (productive) imagination combines it through its creativity, that is, the form, which produces satisfaction in an object. Only the form is capable of stating a general rule for the feeling of pleasure. One need not expect such a general rule from sense perception which may vary greatly according to the different sense-capacity of subjects. One may therefore explain taste as follows: "Taste is the faculty of aesthetic judgment which makes universally valid discriminations."

Taste is, therefore, a faculty of the social judgment of external objects within the imagination. Here the mind feels its freedom in the play of images (therefore of sensibility), since sociability with other people presupposes freedom; and this feeling is pleasure. But the universal validity of this pleasure for everyone, whereby discrimination (of the beautiful) with taste is distinguished from discrimination through mere sense perception (of what is only subjectively pleasing), that is, of what is agreeable, contains the concept of a law within itself, because only in accordance with this law can the validity of satisfaction be universal for the person who makes the judgment. The faculty of perceiving the universal, however, is the understanding. Thus, the judgment of taste is just as much an aesthetic judgment as it is a judgment of the understanding; but they are both in combination, (and therefore the latter is not considered to be pure). The judging of an object through taste is a judgment about the harmony or discord concerning the freedom of play between imagination and the law-abiding character of the understanding, and, therefore, applies only to the form of judging aesthetically (the compatibility of the sense perceptions), and not to the generation of products in which the form is perceived. It would otherwise apply to the genius whose passionate vitality often needs to be moderated and limited by the propriety of taste.

The beautiful alone is that which appertains to taste; the sublime, however, appertains also to the aesthetic judgment, but not to taste. But the idea of the sublime can and should be beautiful in itself; otherwise it would be crude, barbaric, and contrary to taste. Even the portrayal of the evil or ugly (for example, in the figure of the personified Death in Milton) can and must be beautiful whenever an object is to be aesthetically imagined, even if a Thersites were to be portrayed. Otherwise the portrayal would arouse either distaste or disgust which both involve an endeavor to reject an idea that has been offered for enjoyment; whereas the beautiful contains in itself the concept of the invitation to the most intimate union with the object, that is, to immediate enjoyment. With the expression of a "beautiful soul" one says all that can be said about the purpose of the innermost union with the beautiful. Greatness of soul and strength of soul relate to the matter (the tools for certain purposes); but goodness of soul, the pure form under which all purposes must be united, is therefore, wherever it is encountered, similar to Eros in the world of myth, archetypically creative and also supernatural. Such goodness of soul is still the focal point around which the judgment of taste assembles all its judgments of sensuous pleasure as long as they are compatible with the freedom of the understanding.

NOTE. How might it have happened that the modern languages particularly have chosen to name the aesthetic faculty of judgment with an expression (*gustus, sapor*) which merely refers to a certain sense-organ (the inside of the mouth), and that the discrimination as well as the choice of palatable things is determined by it? There is no situation in which sensibility and understanding, united in enjoyment, can be as long continued and as often repeated with satisfaction as a good meal in good company. The sensibility, however, is regarded in this case only as a vehicle of conversation for the understanding. The aesthetic taste of the host manifests itself in his ability to make a universally acceptable selection, something which he cannot accomplish completely with his own sense of taste, because his guests might perhaps wish to choose other foods or drinks, each according to his own private sense. Consequently, the host makes his decisions with the tastes of his guests in mind, so that everyone finds something to his own liking; such a procedure yields a comparatively universal validity. His skill in choosing guests who can engage themselves in mutual and general conversation (which is indeed also called taste, but in reality it is reason applied to taste, and yet is distinct from taste), cannot enter into the present question. And so the feeling of an organ through a particular sense has been able to yield the name for an ideal feeling, a feeling for a sensory, universally valid choice in general. It is even more strange that the skill to test by sense whether something is an object of enjoyment for one and the same subject (not whether the choice of it is universally valid) (*sapor*) has even been exaggerated to designate wisdom (*sapientia*). Perhaps the reason for this is that an unconditional, necessary purpose requires neither deliberation nor experiment, but comes to mind immediately by, so to speak, the tasting of what is wholesome.

21

Rasa: Delight of the Reason

B. N. Goswamy

If one were not so much immersed in it oneself, it could be quite an experience to attend a recital in India of classical Indian music simply to observe the responses of the listeners. We can think of a great Indian vocalist presenting, interpreting, a *raga,* the audience sitting on the floor, not far from him, not far even physically, but quite close, almost within touching distance, accompanists in place, instruments tuned. As the singer opens with the slow, ruminative passage of pure voice movement with no words used, the *alaap,* something that—depending upon which tradition, or *gharana,* he comes from—he can elaborate upon and embellish very considerably (being in no hurry at all, in a deliberate, leisurely fashion), one would notice several persons in the audience closing their eyes, inclining their heads slightly, and slowly, very slowly swaying with a gentle, lyrical movement. An occasional nodding or shaking of the head becomes visible. The listeners open their eyes ever so briefly from time to time to look at the singer when he provides a surprising twist or adds a new flourish or grace, but generally they appear as if they were hearing the note patterns twice over: once physically, through the ears, as being performed at that moment and in that space; but also inwardly at the same time, in the mind's ear, as it were. It is as if they know the pattern well and are seeking some kind of confirmation, a correspondence between what is in their minds and what they are hearing at this moment. The cadenced, almost involuntary motions of the singer' s hands vary greatly from performance to performance. As he gets into the body of the *raga,* eyes often closed, his gestures lend emphasis, complete a statement, suggest other possibilities, open different kinds of windows. While he does this, a certain number of listeners can also be seen picking up these movements imperceptibly, not matching each gesture of the singer with their own but catching the essence of the motions, for these go with the unheard music within them...

Then, in a faster tempo, when the theme or the burden of the composition is picked up again, a new energy seems to be released among the listeners. Now two different kinds of exchanges take place, those between the singer and audience, and those between him and his accompanists, the player of a stringed instrument such as the *sarangi,* or the percussionist using a pair of *tabla* drums. The singer suddenly springs surprises of all kinds, uses crossrhythms, while the percussionists try to keep pace, even anticipate him on occasions, as if a game of great sophistication were being played among them, all within the approved, strictly laid-down ambit of a *raga*.

At the same time, between singer and listeners, sometimes even between the instrumental accompanists and the listeners, a new rapport is established. Eyes close and then open again in surprise or admiration; heads sway, and whole bodily movements become accentuated. Since the singer is using poetry that is by this point familiar to the audience (if it were not known to it previously), and the burden of the song is fully understood and identified with, one can hear the last words of a verse sung by the performer being picked up and softly whispered by the more alert listeners...

At this point, regardless of the theme of the song incorporated in the *raga*—it could be love-in-union, or love-in-separation, or even a song about death or the final realities of life; this is immaterial—a certain lifting of the spirits among the listeners becomes noticeable. No depression descends, even if the burden of the music is sad; on the other hand, there is an elevation of the mind, a rushing forward. It is as if a spark had jumped from singer to listeners. A particularly graceful or difficult movement of notes, an uncommon elegance improvised and inducted into the structure of the *raga,* a verse that has suddenly assumed the character of a revelation because so ably and creatively interpreted by the singer, send a tingle down the spine of many a listener. The word frequently used in India to describe this sensation is "horripilation," hair standing on end. The audience is having an experience of delight: it is tasting *rasa*...

The single most important term that figures in the formal theory of art developed in India from very early times is undoubtedly *rasa*. To understand the term outwardly is not difficult, and its several meanings are within easy reach. In its most obvious sense, the sense in which it is still employed most widely in daily parlance in India, it means the sap or juice of plants, extract, fluid. In this physical sense, it is easy to identify: when one speaks thus of the *rasa* of orange or sugarcane, for instance, one is certain that the word means the same thing to everyone. In its secondary sense, *rasa* signifies the nonmaterial essence of a thing, the best or finest part of it, like perfume, which comes from matter but is not so easy to describe or comprehend. In its tertiary sense, *rasa* denotes taste, flavor, relish related to consuming or handling either the physical object or taking in its nonphysical properties, often yielding pleasure.

In its final and subtlest sense, however—and this is close to the tertiary sense in which the word is applied to art and aesthetic experience—*rasa* comes to signify a state of heightened delight, in the sense of *ananda,* the kind of bliss that can be experienced only by the spirit. As later writers such as Vishwanatha, fourteenth-century author of the *Sahitya Darpana,* a celebrated work on poetics, say: *rasa* is an experience akin to ultimate reality, "twin brother to the tasting of Brahma." In Vishwanatha, the very definition of poetry involves invoking the word *rasa.* His dictum is often quoted: "Poetry is a sentence the soul of which is *rasa.*"

The theory of art that centers around the idea of *rasa* was enunciated for the first time, in the form that it has come down to us, by Bharata in the *Natyashastra,* that extraordinary work on the arts of the theater, which is generally placed close to the beginning of the Christian era. But its roots go back still farther, for even as he sets it forth in outline, Bharata acknowledges his debt to older masters. Bharata enunciates and applies the *rasa* theory to the arts of the stage, incorporating dance and music (*natya*), but, as Coomaraswamy says, the theory is immediately applicable to art of all kinds, much of its terminology specifically employing the concept of color...

So pervasive and widespread is the use of the term *rasa* in the context of the arts in India, so often is it evoked by critics and common viewers or readers, that it forms a central part of the vocabulary of art. A performance of dance or music or of a play often might be criticized as being devoid of *rasa* (*nirasa*), or praised for yielding *rasa* in great measure. The voice of a singer would be acclaimed for being charged with *rasa* (*rasili*), the eyes of the beloved would be described as filled with *rasa,* and so on. Whatever philosophers and theoreticians might have to say of the term and the many complexities that attend its proper understanding when applied to art, the simple appreciator of art knows his mind quite well and uses the term frequently, often with remarkable accuracy. Great and considered works on rhetoric might insist that the justification of art lies in its service of the fourfold purposes of life, its aims (*purusharthas*) as generally understood in India: right action (*dharma*), pleasure (*karma*), wealth (*artha*), and spiritual freedom (*moksha*). At the ordinary level, it is understood that art must result in an experience of *rasa,* must yield delight. Of the four ends of life, as Coomaraswamy says, "the first three represent the proximate and last the ultimate. The work of art is determined in the same way ... proximately with regard to immediate use, and ultimately with regard to aesthetic experience." Referring to Vishwanatha, he maintains:

> ...Mere narration, bare utility, are not art, or are only art in a rudimentary sense. Nor has art as such a merely informative value confined to its explicit

> meaning: only the man of little wit can fail to recognize that art is by nature a well-spring of delight, whatever may have been the occasion of its appearance.
>
> (Coomaraswamy 1934)

That *rasa* is what art is all about may not be specifically stated in so many words by everyone, but in a very real sense it is what a viewer is looking for in a work of art. I remember quite sharply an occasion when I took some keen doubt of mine, a small inquiry regarding the date or style of a painting, to that great connoisseur of the arts of India, the late Rai Krishna Dasa in Benaras. Rai Sahib, as he was almost universally called, heard my questions with his usual grace and patience, then leaned back on the comfortable round bolster on his simple divan and said softly: "These questions I will now leave to you eager historians of art. All that I want to do, at this stage of my life—he was past seventy years of age then and in frail health—"is to taste *rasa*." Nobody knew more than Rai Sahib about the kinds of questions that I had taken to him at that time, but somehow he had moved on to, or back toward, what the real meaning or purpose of art was, in his eyes...

An impressive amount of literature has been written in India on rhetoric in which ideas on *rasa* figure most prominently. A lively debate seems to have gone on for nearly fifteen hundred years with regard to the true nature of *rasa:* some things are clear, but others remain obscure or elusive. For any understanding of *rasa,* however, a prerequisite is to gain familiarity with some basic terms. The terms had to be expounded at some length by Bharata and some later writers, for the whole understanding of the ideas contained in this theory of art would depend on a precise comprehension of these forms. It needs to be remembered that many of them are not employed in common parlance, certainly not as commonly or easily as *rasa* is, and some writers have been quick to point out that some of these terms were coined or bent toward specific usage by Bharata, so that they are not easily confused with ordinarily employed terms and are seen as possessing special meanings. To this generally difficult situation, we have to add the difficulty of translating them from Sanskrit into Western languages. The difficulty is compounded because different translators of Sanskrit texts in which these terms occur have used different English equivalents for Sanskrit originals. One cannot speak of any standard renderings of these terms: it would serve the interests of clarity, therefore, if the Sanskrit originals are used with some frequency along with their translations.

As we have observed, the word *rasa is* variously rendered. At one point, Coomaraswamy uses for it the term "ideal beauty." While "tincture" or "essence" are not employed in the context of aesthetic experience, the word commonly favored is "flavor." Manmohan Ghosh, in his translation of the text of Bharata's *Natyashastra,* preferred the term "sentiment"; other writers have used the word "relish" for *rasa.* Aesthetic experience is described as the "tasting of flavor" (*rasasvadana*); the taster, in other words the viewer or reader, more specifically a scholar or connoisseur, is referred to as a *rasika*. A work of art possessing *rasa* is often described as being *rasavat,* or *rasavant.* Other terms, a little more difficult to understand because they are used in a very special sense, are: *bhava* (rendered as mood or emotional state), *vibhavas* (determinants), *anubhavas* (consequents), and *vyabhicharibhavas* (complementary emotional states). A *sthayibhava* is an enduring or durable emotional state; *sattvika bhavas* are involuntary bodily responses in states of emotion. Each of these terms needs to be clearly understood, but to this we can return later.

Some idea of the controversies that obtain in the domain of the *rasa* theory can be gained from the fact that there is no clear agreement even about how many *rasas* there are. Bharata speaks of eight sentiments (to which a widely accepted ninth has been added by later writers): Shringara (the erotic), Hasya (the comic), Karuna (the pathetic), Raudra (the furious), Vira (the heroic), Bhayanaka (the terrible), Bibhatsa (the odious), and Adbhuta (the marvelous). The ninth *rasa* spoken of is Shanta (the quiescent). These are separately listed because even though *rasa is* defined as one and undivided it is one or the other of these nine *rasas* through which an aesthetic experience takes place, in the language employed by Bharata and later rhetoricians. Because out of these nine, one sentiment or flavor dominates, a work of art propels a spectator toward, or becomes the occasion for, a *rasa* experience.

Aesthetic experience as defined in this context is the act of tasting a rasa, "of immersing oneself in it to the exclusion of all else." In essence, Bharata seems to say, with reference to theatrical performance, the focus of his work, "*rasa is* born from the union of the play with the performance of the actors." A great deal of later discussion verges on the interpretation of a terse statement of Bharata's, a *sutra* or aphorism, which reads: "*Rasa is* born out of the union of the determinants, the consequents and the complementary emotional states." In explanation, Bharata says rather little—later writers were to debate the point with heat and acrimony—but it is appropriate that his exact words be taken in first. After making this brief pronouncement, he asks a rhetorical question: "Is there any instance [parallel to it]?" and proceeds to answer:

> [Yes], it is said that as taste [*rasa*] results from a combination of various spices, vegetables and other articles, and as six tastes are produced by articles, such as raw sugar or spices or vegetables, so the durable emotional states, when they come together with various other psychological states, attain the quality of a sentiment [i.e. become sentiment]. Now one inquires, "What is the meaning of the word *rasa*?" It is said in reply [that *rasa* is so called] because it is capable of being tasted. How is *rasa* tasted? [In reply] it is said that just as well-disposed persons while eating food cooked with many kinds of spices enjoy its taste, and attain pleasure and satisfaction, so the cultured people taste the durable emotional states while they see them represented by an expression

> of the various emotional states with words, gestures, and derive pleasure and satisfaction. Just as a connoisseur of cooked food while eating food which has been prepared from various spices and other articles tastes it, so the learned people taste in their heart the durable emotional states [such as love, sorrow etc.] when they are represented by an expression of the emotional states with gestures. Hence, these durable emotional states in a drama are called sentiments.
>
> (Ghosh 1967)

Much else follows and several issues arise, but it might be useful first to try to gain a rudimentary understanding of how all this operates. If *rasa* is born of or arises from a combination of determinants, consequents, and complementary emotional states, we begin with these. Determinants are essentially "the physical stimulants to aesthetic reproduction, particularly the theme and its parts, the indications of time and place and other apparatus of representation—the whole *factible.*" Of these, too, two different categories are spoken of: *alambana vibhavas* and *uddipana vibhavas* meaning, respectively, the substantial determinants and the excitant determinants. Taking help from later writers, and taking the example of a specific *rasa* like Shringara, the erotic, its determinants would be of two kinds. The substantial determinants would be a lover and beloved, hero or heroine, or in Sanskrit, a *nayaka* and *nayika*. Without these, the erotic sentiment or mood of love would be difficult to imagine. The excitants would be, among other things, the moon, sandalwood ointment and other unguents, the humming of bees, attractive clothing and jewelry, an empty house or a secluded grove in a garden appropriate as a trysting place. Consequents are "the specific and conventional means of registering emotional states, in particular gestures and glances etc.," something to which the *Natyashastra* pays such wonderfully elaborate attention. Continuing with Shringara, in this case the appropriate consequents could be raising of the eyebrows, sidelong glances, embracing, kissing, holding hands. The range of gestures and movements appropriate to the theme is remarkably rich in both dance and drama, and the performer can draw upon his whole repertoire.

Then there are the complementary (or transitory) emotional states, of which Bharata lists as many as thirty-three. These range from agitation, depression, weariness, distraction, and stupor to fright, shame, joy, envy, anxiety, and indecision. They are referred to as complementary or transitory because while they arise in the course, say, of a play, and actors interpreting characters go through them, they do not last long and serve eventually only to feed into the dominant mood of a performance. They complement the principal mood or emotional state and do not in themselves leave a lasting impression. Finally, there are listed eight involuntary bodily responses (*sattvika bhavas*) in states of emotions, including perspiration, paralysis, trembling, fainting, change of voice, change of color, and horripilation.

Continuing with Shringara, it is stated that any complementary emotional state could be brought into a work except cruelty, death, indolence, or disgust, because they are opposed to the rise of the principal sentiment, the erotic. In the course of a performance in which the appropriate determinants and consequents and complementary emotional states have been selected, developed, and used, the viewer's heart is constantly and subtly being worked on by these properties, conditions, or representations of states. A "churning of the heart" takes place, at the end of which a dominant emotional state emerges, a *bhava* that is called *sthayi,* or durable. Any one of the nine *bhavas* of this durable kind could come floating to the surface of the mind of the viewer. These nine emotional states are *rati* (love), *hasa* (mirth, playfulness), *shoka* (sorrow), *krodha* (anger), *utsaha* (energy), *bhaya* (fear), *jugupsa* (disgust), *vismaya* (astonishment) and *shama* (equanimity). It would be seen that these durable emotional states (*sthayibhavas*) correspond to the nine *rasas* or sentiments listed earlier. Thus, the emotional state of love has its correspondence in the erotic sentiment, that of laughter or mirth its correspondence in the comic sentiment, and so on.

At this point an elusive, inscrutable element is introduced in the *rasa* theory. It is stated that when, as a result of this churning of the heart, this mixing of the elements, a durable emotional state has emerged, this very state transmutes itself into a *rasa* in a competent person. If the circumstances have been right, if the performance is of the proper order, and if the viewer is cultured and sensitive enough (a *rasika*) a spark would leap from the performance to the viewer, resulting in an experience that would suffuse the entire being of the *rasika*. The experience might possess the suddenness of a flash of lightning, leaving the viewer unprepared for the moment and unaware of the swiftness with which it comes, deeply moved by it. This is the moment when, as a later writer put it, "magical flowers would blossom" in his awareness: *rasa* would be tasted. The experience is genuine and definable, but, it is stated, there are so many variables in the situation that it cannot be predicted or even worked toward. The same viewer may have a *rasa* experience of one level at one time from a performance, and not have it at another; the intensity of one viewer's experience may be different from another's. Many factors intervene, but this at least seems to be the essence of the *rasa* experience.

Aesthetic experience (*rasasvadana*) has been defined by different writers, each in his own terms and according to his own understanding. Bharata's chapter on *rasa* has been commented and elaborated upon by generations of scholars and theoreticians, the most important among them being Abhinavagupta, that great Kashmiri scholar of the eleventh century. After Bharata, an authoritative definition comes from Vishwanatha, author of the celebrated *Sahitya Darpana* (Mirror of Composition). Coomaraswamy regards Vishwanatha's passage defining the nature of aesthetic experience "of such authority and value as to demand translation *in extenso*":

> Flavor [*rasa*] is tasted by men having an innate knowledge of absolute values in exaltation of the pure consciousness as self-luminous, in the mode at once of ecstasy and intellect, void of contact with things knowable, twin brother to the tasting of Brahma, whereof the life is a superworldly lightning flash, an intrinsic aspect in indivisibility... Pure aesthetic experience is theirs in whom the knowledge of ideal beauty is innate; it is known intuitively in intellectual ecstasy without accompaniment of ideation, at the highest level of conscious being; born of one mother with the vision of God, its life is as it were a flash of blinding light of transmundane origin, impossible to analyze, and yet in the image of our very being.
>
> (Coomaraswamy 1934)

Appropriately, Coomaraswamy reminds us that there are two senses in which the word *rasa* is commonly used: first, "relatively, in the plural with reference to the various, usually eight or nine, emotional conditions which may constitute the burden of a given work," and second, "absolutely, in the singular, with reference to the interior act of tasting flavor unparticularized. In the latter sense, the idea of an aesthetic beauty to be tasted, and knowable only in the activity of tasting, is to be clearly distinguished from the relative beauties or loveliness of the separate parts of the work or of the work itself considered merely as a surface."

Aesthetic experience, it has been stated, is "just as a flower born of magic" which has "as its essence, solely the present, it is co-related neither with what came before nor with what comes after." Between the spectator and the experience of *rasa* lie many obstacles, much the same way in which obstacles lie between a meditator and his realization of that supreme bliss that comes from perfect knowledge. These need to be removed, not the easiest of tasks. In fact, long discussions center around this question of the nature of obstacles, and the possibilities of their removal in different kinds and categories of viewers. But once removed, the dust wiped clean from the mirror of the heart, what is experienced is that sense of exalted delight "different from the forms of bliss of practical life, and just because it is devoid of obstacles, it is called Tasting, Delibation, Lysis, Perception, Rest, in the nature of the knowing subject." Aesthetic experience is thus a transformation not merely of feeling, but equally of understanding, "a condensed understanding in the mode of ecstasy." As Gnoli, paraphrasing Abhinavagupta, puts it:

> The so-called supreme bliss, the lysis, the wonder is ... nothing but a tasting, that is, a cognitation in all its compact density, of our own liberty. This liberty is *realissima* [that is to say, not metaphorical] and inseparable from the very nature of consciousness. We must not, however, forget that in the tasting of a juice or sweet flavor, etc., there is, between this bliss and us, the separating screen, so to say, of the exterior reality. In poetry, in drama, and so on, this screen is actually missing, but it remains in a latent state. Also in these forms of limited bliss, however, those people whose hearts are carefully devoted

to canceling the part which performs the functions of a screen succeed in reaching the supreme bliss.

(Gnoli 1971)

As would be noticed, there is a marked emphasis in this entire enunciation on the spectator. The words used to denote him are carefully chosen, because the clear assumption behind this entire theory of art is that it is not given to everyone to attain that state, that lightning flash of understanding and delight which is the *rasa* experience. We have to remind ourselves once again that the theory is worked out in the context of drama, and that only the spectator who is a *rasika* will have this experience. For it is he who knows what *rasa* is, and whose mind is prepared to receive the experience. It is clear through several assertions in the *Natyashastra,* and by later writers, that the experience of *rasa* depends a great deal on the energy (*utsaha*) that the spectator brings with him to the experience of a work of art. As is stated, it is his own energy "that is the cause of tasting, just as when children play with clay elephants." The durable emotional state that is subtly brought into being by or through a work of art is one thing: its transmutation into a *rasa* is dependent upon the energy, the inner ability, the singleness of heart of the *rasika*. The faculty of imagination and wonder is greatly emphasized.

It is asserted by several authorities that the *rasa* experience belongs not to the poet or to the actor but exclusively to the viewer. The whole question of where *rasa* lies has been the subject of much debate. Abhinavagupta examines various ideas on the subject and states quite emphatically:

> *Rasa* does not lie in the actor. But where then? You have all forgotten and I remind you again [of what I have already said]. Indeed I have said that *rasa* is not limited by any difference of space, times, and knowing subjects. Your doubt is then devoid of sense. But what is the actor? The actor, I say, is the means of the tasting, and hence he is called by the name "vessel." The taste of wine, indeed, does not stay in the vessel, which is only a means necessary to the tasting of it. The actor then is necessary and useful only in the beginning.
>
> (Gnoli 1971)

To the natural question whether the actor or the artist also experiences *rasa,* several writers including Vishwanatha maintain that he "may obtain aesthetic experience from the spectacle of his own performance." The actor is understood quite naturally not to be unmoved by "the passions he depicts." Likewise the musician, the dancer, the maker of an image would be involved in the emotion that he brings to his performance or work, but the experiencing of emotion before or during the act of making or performing, it is stated, is of an order different from the *rasa* experience, which has that illuminating, suffusing character, is that lightning flash of delight, and can be experienced by the maker or the performer only when and if he puts himself in the position of a viewer of himself and his work.

There is more cerebration about the *rasa* experience. Is it in the nature of a revelation, an unveiling, of entering a state of manifestness? Or, does it imply the coming into being of a state that did not exist before and is therefore something new and fresh? According to Vishwanatha, when it is said that *rasa* is something brought out into manifestness, what is meant is that it is made manifest "in a different character to which it is changed." Examples from the area of food and tasting—appropriate to the whole question of *asvadana*—illustrate this. It is stated thus that milk and curd are of the same substance, curd being milk presented under a change of character; it is not something previously completed and previously so extant; it is certainly not something only revealed. A change is involved between what one sees and what one experiences, the perception, the act of gustation, identifying the nature of the change. It is along these lines that much of the discussion proceeds, but for our purposes it is not necessary to go at any length into these discussions, except to remind ourselves of an oft-cited aphorism that "*bhava,* the durable emotional state, is the flower, and *rasa* is the fruit thereof." The second is evidently not possible to think of without the first, but this does not mean that the first will, in all cases, result in the second. Flower and fruit are clearly related, being parts of the same plant, but they are different in character and, of course, each flower does not necessarily yield or lead to fruit.

A predictable measure of attention in these discussions is claimed by the question: how does aesthetic experience differ from experience of the kinds of emotions which are part of our real, everyday life? The issue is brought to a head through a relatively simple example. If, as is maintained, the *rasa* experience is one of delight, how is it, it might well be asked, that things that are painful in reality become, in art, the sources of pleasure? The states of sorrow, fear, or disgust obviously do not yield pleasure in real life, and yet one speaks of them as leading to an aesthetic experience. As Vishwanatha puts it: "No one possessed of understanding engages—knowingly, and without some ulterior view—in paining himself; and yet we see that everyone enters with engrossing interest into the 'Pathetic' [sentiment] . . ." He answers himself by stating that the *rasa* experience is not experience at an everyday, mundane level. The nature of *rasa* experience is transcendental, hyperphysical, literally *lokottara,* beyond ordinary experience. If this were not so, who would read the *Ramayana,* that great epic, the leading sentiment of which is *Karuna,* the pathetic? As it is, we hold it as being one of the most heart-delighting compositions of Indian literature. The distancing from the mundane experience of emotions made possible by a fine work or performance is what makes the difference.

The notion here is different from catharsis. The heart is not lightened through a performance; the *rasa* that it yields is a kind of "delight of the reason," as Coomaraswamy puts it, "an ecstasy in itself inscrutable." Another illuminating instance is that of the *Mahabharata,* that other great epic, in which the unutterably sad adventures of a just and truthful king, Harishchandra, are told at great length, involving the grief of deprivation and tear-shedding. To this it is said that the audience sheds tears not because of the pain that it actually experiences, but because through witnessing the performance of Harishchandra's tale, the heart is melted. This melting of the heart is a matter of moment, and it is from this that further discussion proceeds about why everyone cannot "receive" from a work of art. It is here that the role of imagination, of cultivated intellectual sensibility, is emphasized. This imagination, this capacity for conceiving whatever passion is intended to be depicted, is what characterizes a *rasika.*

Another point made is that *rasa* is, essentially, considered unique, indivisible. Its division into eight or nine varieties possesses only limited value and is adopted for the sake of convenience. Were it not so, its universality would come into doubt. The various divisions that we characterize as sentiments are like rays of different colors that we perceive when light is passed through a prism. Another image often employed by writers is of the various *rasas* being like different-colored precious stones all strung on the same necklace. *Rasa* is one, we are told; it is only approached or colored differently...

Whether the Indian theory is *sui generis* in origins or formulation is a matter of some interest. Coomaraswamy did not see it as being far removed from other points of view in the East (and in the West, up to a point of time), and emphasized only that it differed essentially "from the modern nonintellectual interpretations of art as sensation." In his view "merely because of the specific idiomatic and mythical form in which it finds expression, it need not be thought of as otherwise than universal." He held that it does not differ, at least in its essentials, from "what is implicit in the Far Eastern view of art, or on the other hand from the scholastic Christian point of view, or what is asserted in the aphorisms of Blake." Other writers do see it as being so strongly rooted in Indian ideas that it is difficult to conceive of it as belonging, even in its essentials, to another culture. In any event its flavor is so Indian, and its presence in the Indian modes of seeing and thinking so pervasive, that one would do well to think of it as one of the keys to the code that is Indian culture.

References

Coomaraswamy, Ananda K. (1934), *The Transformation of Nature in Art,* Cambridge, MA: Harvard University Press.

Ghosh, Manomohan (1967), *The Natyashastra, A Treatise on Ancient Indian Dramaturgy and Histrionics, Ascribed to Bharata-Muni,* rev. 2nd Ed. Vol. VI, Calcutta.

Gnoli, Raniero (1971), *Aesthetic Experience According to Abhinavagupta,* Varanasi.

Vishwanatha (1923), *Sahityadarpana,* Bombay. (Or *The Mirror of Composition,* trans. J. R. Ballantyne and Pramadesa Mitra, Calcutta: 1875).

22

Pleasures of the Proximate Senses

Eating, Taste, and Culture

Yi-Fu Tuan

The senses, under the aegis and direction of the mind, give us a world. Some are "proximate," others "distant." The proximate senses yield the world closest to us, including our own bodies. The position and movements of our bodies produce proprioception or kinesthesia, somatic awareness of the basic dimensions of space. The other proximate senses are touch, sensitivity to changes in temperature, taste, and smell. Hearing and sight are considered the senses that make the world "out there" truly accessible. Since that distancing, momentary removal of self from object or event is essential to the aesthetic experience, it is not surprising that the aesthetic potential of the proximate senses has been undervalued by Kant, among others. Yet the proximate senses, separately and together, add immensely to the vitality and beauty of the world, and distancing can and does occur in our experience of them...

Eating, Taste, and Culture

Eating is a mode of touch. "Eating is touch carried to the bitter end," says Samuel Butler. It forcefully reminds us of our animal nature. Culture masks human animality; when the mask slips, the fact that we live by devouring other organisms rises to haunt us.

Watching people eat and noting what they eat, especially if they are of a different culture, is seldom an elevating experience. For the Chinese, eating has close ties to health, medicine, and a cosmological world view. Food preparation and consumption are considered an art. Yet these elevated cultural concepts are not always evident, at least not everywhere in China, and not to an outsider. Colin Thubron, for one, finds the Chinese national obsession with food, ascending to "a guzzling crescendo," repellent. He describes an eating quarter in the nontourist part of Canton around 1980. Feasters, mostly men, gather around the tables. "Every course drops into a gloating circumference of famished stares and rapt cries. Diners burp and smack their lips in hoggish celebration." The concept of taboo, Thubron notes, seems wholly absent. "In Cantonese cooking, nothing edible is sacred. It reflects an old Chinese mercilessness toward their surroundings. Every part of every animal—pig stomach, lynx breast, whole bamboo rats and salamanders—is consumed." Thubron, searching for something he can eat, enters a rowdy restaurant, where the waitress relentlessly plies him with "shredded cat thick soup and braised python with mushrooms" (Thubron 1987: 182–84).

This account, blind though it is to different tastes and values, should make any thinking person uneasy about food preparation and eating. In these activities, biological imperatives are worrisomely joined to sensual delight, the killing and evisceration of living things to art, animality to the claims of culture, taste (a process in the mouth's cavern) to that refined achievement known as "good taste." As people become more and more conscious of their status as dignified cultural beings, eating/tasting tends to be done in public only when it is accompanied by some other, more obviously respectable activity, such as social conversation and music. And if one has to eat alone in a restaurant, one pretends to be engaged simultaneously in the higher occupation of reading a magazine.

Nevertheless, eating/tasting is a cultural activity in its own right, with a long history. Let us consider the aesthetics of food preparation and eating in two parts of the world—Europe and China.

Food and Manners in Europe

From the Middle Ages to modern times, Europe underwent progressive refinement in all things concerning food—its preparation, the dishes offered, table manners, utensils, and the larger setting of hall or room. It experienced the development of taste—good taste. The progression was by no means linear. There have been several swings between an ideal of simplicity and an ideal of luxuriance, between foods commended for their natural and exquisite flavor and foods commended for their symphonic richness—the effect of using artfully simple ingredients.

In the late Middle Ages, food still tended to be messy, prepared pell-mell. Expensive spices and viands might find themselves bedded in the same dish with meats that were none too fresh and were very probably contaminated by the filth in the kitchen. The range and quantity of food would have bewildered and repelled a modern gourmet. Plantagenet kings of the fourteenth and fifteenth centuries ate everything that had wings, from bustards to sparrows, herons, egrets, and bitterns; and everything that swam, from minnows to porpoises. Medieval cooks used vegetables and herbs profusely and indiscriminately. Many dishes were created by combining every scrap of greenstuff that came to hand. In a hare stew one might find cabbage, beets, borage, mallows, parsley, betony, the white part of leeks, the tops of young nettles, and violets. Roses, hawthorn, and primroses might also find their way into a dish (Henisch 1976: 110–11).

For the wealthy, a medieval dinner consisted of two or three courses, but each course could contain more than a dozen different kinds of food heaped high on large platters. Guests were confronted by such rich fare as shields of boiled and pickled boar, hulled wheat boiled in milk and venison, oily stews, salted hart, pheasant, swan, capons, lampreys, perch, rabbit, mutton, baked custard, and tart fruit. The second course was again made up of a large array of rich meat and fish hardly distinguishable from the first (Burton 1976: 129). The concept of an orderly sequence—soup, fish, meat, and dessert—did not appear until the end of the seventeenth century. Copiousness, rather than discrimination, was the key concept in premodern culinary art. Cooks were indifferent to the unique textures and flavors of the materials that went into a cauldron. The French critic and poet Nicolas Boileau-Despréaux mentions an enormous mixed grill consisting of a hare, six chickens, three rabbits, and six pigeons, all served on the same plate. These hodgepodges were relentlessly overcooked, probably because the game was usually "high." One of the recipes for ragout, which Louis XIV and his courtiers were fond of, called for putting a number of different kinds of flesh and fowl in a cauldron, adding a large quantity of spice, and stewing the mixture for twelve hours. It is unlikely, in W. H. Lewis's view, that this dish "would be saved at the twelfth hour by a lavish top dressing of musk, amber, and assorted perfumes (Lewis 1978: 208–9).

Before the seventeenth century, the preparation of most dishes, even of the pâtés, meats, and side dishes of ostentatious feasts, required little imaginative forethought. Thereafter, carefully prepared meals for discerning people began to emerge. The French words *gourmand* and *gourmet*, both initially used to express unqualified approval, won general acceptance in urbane Europe. A further sign of refinement in taste lay in the serving of foods on several small dishes rather than on a few large platters. Incompatible flavors were thus kept apart. After 1700, more and more diners accepted the notion that the distinctive flavor and texture of a dish rather than the quantity and expense of its ingredients should be the primary criteria of excellence. The care that went into cooking by the middle of the eighteenth century is suggested by the menu for a reception in honor of the Archbishop of Besançon. Among the dishes listed were "Bisque d'écrevisse, potage à la reine, grenouilles à la poulette, truites grillées, anguilles en serpentin, filets de brochet, carpes du Doubs avec coulis d'écrevisse, tourte de laitances de carpes" (Mandrou 1977: 25).

After the French Revolution, France led Europe in transforming cooking into an art in the grand style and an honored profession, with its own literature and roster of famous names. The most distinguished chef of this time was Antonin Carême. In the creation of dishes he strove, paradoxically, for both ostentation and simplicity. Trained in *patisserie,* an art that encouraged creative leanings, he extended the architectural style to cooking generally. For a grand dinner, he might erect picturesque ruins made of lard and Greek temples in sugar and marzipan so that the gastronome's mind, and not just his palate, could be pleasurably stimulated. Carême's creations were also architectural in that they had a "built" character: they were made of purees, essences, and sauces that were themselves complex creations and yet were listed simply as ingredients along with a piece of celery or a chopped onion. A dish, in other words, was the culmination of a long and elaborate process (Mennell 1985: 146–7).

Carême achieved simplification by eliminating medieval survivals such as trimmings of cockscombs and sweetbreads. More important, he established the principle of garnishing meat with meat, fish with fish. His culinary aesthetic is caught in Lady Sydney Morgan's description of a dinner at the Baron de Rothschild's: "no dark-brown gravies, no flavor of cayenne and allspice, no tincture of catsup and walnut pickle, no visible agency of those vulgar elements of cooking of the good old times, fire and water. Distillations of the most delicate viands, extracted in silver dews, with chemical precision... formed the *fond* of all. Every meat presented its own natural aroma—every vegetable its own shade of verdure" (quoted in Mennell: 147). Even in Carême's elaborate achievements, his aim was not to superimpose and confuse flavors, but rather to isolate and throw them into relief (Mennell: 148).

Despite his own success in creating "simple" and distinctive flavors, in general Carême's approach encouraged ostentation and, with it, the sacrifice of savor for grand visual effects. Master cooks had yielded to this temptation since at least Roman times: thus Petronius described a feast in which a hare was tricked out with wings to look like a Pegasus, and roast pork carved into models of fish, songbirds, and a goose. For millennia, then, chefs in the West have often "played with food," treating edibles as materials for sculpture and architecture, as though the creation of alluring flavors could not in itself win for them high standing.

Closer to our time, Georges Auguste Escoffier rivaled Carême in celebrity and influence. Like his predecessor, Escoffier was capable of architectural grandeur, but his reputation rested even more on achieving a perfect balance between a few superb ingredients—sometimes such rare items as truffle and crayfish, but also quite ordinary ingredients that even the most common middle-class kitchen could afford. One of Escoffier's best-known creations was Peach Melba: to a coupling of vanilla ice cream with peach, he gave a final touch of perfection by balancing the smooth sweetness of the cream and the textural resistance and flavor of the peach with the tartness of raspberries (Mennell: 160).

Food is basic, and people's taste for food tends to be traditional, conservative, associated with old family recipes and perhaps also regional ones. People tend to like what they have always had. The business of "inventing" new flavors seems a questionable venture. Yet cooking and the tastes developed for it have a long history of innovation and change. In post-Revolutionary France, chefs who established their own businesses after the departure or demise of their aristocratic patrons competed with one another for a growing, gastronomically sophisticated clientele. They were driven to offer fresh gustatory pleasures. In the nineteenth century, this demand for originality became ever more insistent. Escoffier, to maintain his reputation, was compelled to devise new dishes all the time. He writes: "I have ceased counting the nights spent in the attempt to discover new combinations, when, completely broken with the fatigue of the heavy day, my body ought to have been at rest" (quoted in Mennell: 161).

The greatest challenge lay not in the profusion of expensive ingredients and strong flavors, but (as Escoffier had seen) in obtaining a deeply satisfying gastronomic experience with a few choice ingredients. In the history of Western cooking, the virtues of simplicity and subtlety were periodically recognized and elevated to serve as criteria of excellence. The latest rejection of rich sauces and complicated foods in general occurred in the 1960s, giving rise to a style known as *nouvelle cuisine*. Chefs insisted on buying the freshest vegetables and meats available in the market each day. The elevation of freshness—the desire to bring out the qualities inherent in the material—called for reduced cooking time for most seafoods, game birds, and veal, but especially for green vegetables. Steaming as a method of cooking also found favor in *nouvelle cuisine*. Both the emphasis on reduced time and on steaming reflect Chinese influence.

Food and Manners in China

Perhaps no other civilization has put as much emphasis on the art of cooking or taken so much pleasure in food as the Chinese. Since the earliest times, cooking in China has carried a prestige unmatched and perhaps somewhat incomprehensible to people in other cultures. The *Li Chi*, a Confucian classic with materials dating back to the fifth century BC and earlier, treats the evolution of culture as though it were a matter of the evolution of cooking skills.

> Formerly the ancient kings knew not yet the transforming power of fire, but ate the fruits of plants and trees, and the flesh of birds and beasts, drinking

> their blood and swallowing the hair and feathers. The later sages then arose, and men learned to take advantage of fire. They toasted, grilled, boiled, and roasted. They produced must and sauces… They were thus able to nourish the living, and to make offerings to the dead; to serve the spirits of the departed and God.
>
> (*Li Chi*: 369–70)

Ritual disciplines attention and encourages people to develop their powers of discernment and discrimination. "In putting down a boiled fish to be eaten," the *Li Chi* asseverates, "the tail was laid in front. In winter it was placed with the fat belly on the right; in summer with the back… All condiments were taken up with the right hand, and were therefore placed on the left…." (quoted in Chang 1977: 37–8). Everything in ritual, not least food, must be done correctly. Confucius reportedly "did not eat meat which was not cut properly, nor what was served without its proper sauce" (*The Four Books*: 130). Clearly, the sage was a fastidious ritualist, but this fact does not exclude the likelihood that he also had a sophisticated palate and a well-developed aesthetic sensibility.

Food is also medicine, and no doubt the understanding of foods—not only their texture and taste but their nutritive and curative powers—has gained enormously by the association. In China, the exceptionally varied kinds of food eaten reflect in part the poverty of the people, who could not afford to disdain anything that assuaged hunger, and in part the unending search for *materia medica*—the healing qualities of plants, animals, and their minutely differentiated parts. That health depends on dietary regulation is a belief that the Chinese have shared with Westerners through the millennia. What distinguishes the Chinese is the way they have subsumed food and medicine under the overarching, universal principles of *yin* and *yang*. Most foods can be classified as having either *yin* or *yang* properties, and the wise eater is one whose diet exhibits a proper balance. Harmony in food is the desideratum, as it is in all other areas of Chinese life. Extremes and excess are to be avoided.

Nevertheless, excesses have occurred. Ordinary people tended to overeat because they had no assurance that food would always be available to them. The rich offered mountains of food on social occasions and overindulged from the desire to impress. An eighteenth-century poet and hedonist, Yuan Mei, wrote in his book *Recipes from Sui Garden*: "I always say that chicken, pork, fish, and duck are the original geniuses of the board, each with a flavor of its own, each with its distinctive style; whereas sea-slug and swallows-nest (despite their costliness) are commonplace fellows, with no character—in fact, mere hangers-on." But swallows-nest carried prestige, whereas mere chicken and pork did not. When a provincial governor offered Yuan Mei "plain boiled swallows-nest, served in enormous vases, like flowerpots," the poet was unimpressed and declared that "it had no taste at all" (Waley 1957: 196).

The other extreme is abstinence. In the Western world, hermits and other aspirants to spiritual elevation have restricted themselves to stale bread and water. The Chinese have seldom carried abstinence so far. Buddhists, required to abstain from meat, ingeniously concocted "imitation meats" of the most mouthwatering texture and flavor. A scholar-official, disaffected with the luxuries of city and court, might sing of rural simplicity, but it was a simplicity that—at least in matters of food—did not necessarily sacrifice taste. Thus a thirteenth-century dramatist envisaged, no doubt somewhat ideally, a simple harvest meal under the gourd trellis, where workers could "drink wine from earthen bowls and porcelain pots, swallow the tender eggplants with their skins, and gulp down the little melons, seeds and all" (Mote in Chang 1977: 238).

The Chinese love of food—their search for pleasures of the palate—is reflected, first, in the sheer variety of what they eat. The Chinese are true omnivores, with few taboos, and these local. Frederick Mote writes of the animal fare alone: "Beyond such relatively ordinary items (in the West) as hares, quails, squabs, and pheasants, a Ming dynasty (1368–1644) source also mentions as standard foods: cormorants, owls, storks and donkeys, mules, tigers, deer of several varieties, wild boars, camels, bears, wild goats, foxes and wolves, several kinds of rodents, and mollusks and shellfish of many kinds" (Mote 1977: 201).

A second indicator of this love of food is the number and popularity of specialized restaurants. In Hang-chou, at about the time Marco Polo visited it, a resident could go to a place where only iced food was served; other specialized shops and their offerings included:

> The sweet soya soup at the Mixed-Wares Market, a pig cooked in ashes in front of the Longevity-and-Compassion Palace, the fish soup of Mother Sung… , boiled pork from Wei-the-Big-Knife at the Cat Bridge, and honey fritters from Chou-number-five in front of the Five-span Pavilion. Among the more exotic dishes were scented shellfish cooked in rice wine, goose with apricots, lotus seed soup, pimento soup with mussels, fish cooked with plums; and among the most common, fritters and thinly-sliced soufflés, ravioli and pies.
>
> (Gernet 1962: 137)

A third indicator is the exceptionally rich vocabulary of taste and texture. The words used are not limited to cooks and gourmets but are a part of ordinary speech in daily use. *Ts'ui* describes a highly desired texture closely tied to freshness and the critical importance of not overcooking. *Ts'ui* offers resistance to the teeth followed by, as E. N. Anderson puts it, "a burst of succulence," as exemplified in newly picked bamboo shoots, fruit ripe enough to eat but not soft, fresh vegetables quickly stir-fried, and chicken boiled a very short time so that it is just done. Anderson goes on to list other evaluative words:

> *Shuang* (resilient, springy, somewhere between crunchy and rubbery, like some seaweeds), and *kan* (translated "sweet," but including anything with a sapid, alluring taste). Fried foods should be *su*—oily but light and not soggy—rather than *ni* (greasy). Above all, foods should taste *hsien,* which means not just fresh but *au point* in general... In south and east China particularly, foods are often praised by being described as *ch'ing,* "clear" or "pure." This means that they have a delicate, subtle, exquisite flavor—not obtrusive, heavy, or harsh.
>
> (Anderson 1988: 158)

The final reflection of the Chinese love of food is the detailed knowledge of its geography, possessed by the literati simply as part of the baggage of being cultured. A special food is often named after its locality—for example, Peking duck. The way to offer an irresistible invitation to dine is to say that a delicacy—be it only a vinegar—has been obtained from a locality famed for that particular product. Connoisseurship of tea and spring water can be carried to great heights. A scholar of the early seventeenth century, Chang Tai, was such a connoisseur. One day he called on a fellow scholar and expert on tea, Min Wenshui, who lived in another town. As soon as he entered Min Wenshui's residence, his nostrils were assailed by a wonderful fragrance.

> "What is this tea?" I asked. "Langwan," Wenshui replied. I tasted it again and said, "Now don't deceive me. The method of preparation is Langwan, but the tea leaves are not Langwan." "What is it then?" asked Wenshui smiling. I tasted it again and said, "Why is it so much like Lochieh tea?" Wenshui was quite struck by my answer and said, "Marvelous! Marvelous!" "What water is it?" I asked. "Huich'uan," he said. "Don't make fun of me," I said. "How can Huich'uan water be carried here over a long distance, and after the shaking on the way, still retain its keenness?" So Wenshui said, "When I take Huich'uan water I dig a well, and wait at night until the new current comes, and then take it up. I put a lot of mountain rocks at the bottom of the jar, and during the voyage I permit only sailing with the wind, but no rowing. Hence the water keeps its edge."
>
> (Lin Yutang 1939: 342–44)

To the modern Western reader, this exchange between two Chinese friends on the quality and provenance of tea and water may seem excessive—an exercise in connoisseurship better suited to the high arts of music and painting. The exchange does show, however, the extraordinary importance the Chinese have traditionally given to the palate. To be cultured is, first, to know the rites and the classics; second, to have a certain flair for poetry and painting; third, to be an aesthete of food—to appreciate its precise flavor and texture. But although good professional cooks are respected, cooking, with its unavoidable violence of chopping and cutting, boiling and frying, and its intimate association with blood and death, tends to arouse unease.

Tasting itself should be suspect, since it ends in destruction, but somehow the Chinese (like people in the West) have managed to repress this knowledge. Tasting now seems almost wholly an aesthetic activity.

References

Anderson, E. N. (1988), *The Food of China*, New Haven: Yale University Press.

Burton, Elizabeth (1976), *The Early Tudors at Home, 1485–1558*, London: Allen Lane.

Chang, K. C. (ed.) (1977), *Food in Chinese Culture: Anthropological and Historical Perspectives*, New Haven: Yale University Press.

Escoffier, Georges Auguste (1957/1903), *A Guide to Modern Cookery*, London: Hutchinson.

The Four Books (1966), trans. James Legge, New York: Penguin.

Gernet, Jacques (1962), *Daily Life in China on the Eve of the Mongol Invasion: 1250–1276*, London: George Allen and Unwin.

Henisch, Bridget Ann (1976), *Fast and Feast: Food in Medieval Society*, University Park, PA: Pennsylvania State University Press.

Lewis, W. H. (1978), *The Splendid Century: Life in the France of Louis XIV*, New York: Morrow Quill Paperbacks.

Li Chi (1967/1885), trans. James Legge, Hong Kong: Hong Kong University Press, Vol. I.

Lin Yutang (1939), *My Country and My People*, New York: John Day.

Mandrou, Robert (1977), *Introduction to Modern France, 1500–1640*, New York: Harper Torchbooks.

Mennell, Stephen (1985), *All Manners of Food: Eating and Taste in England and France from the Middle Ages to the Present*, Oxford: Blackwell.

Mote, Frederick W. (1977), "Yuan and Ming," in Chang (ed.) *Food in Chinese Culture*, New Haven: Yale University Press.

Thubron, Colin (1987), *Behind the Wall: A Journey through China*, London: Heinemann.

Waley, Arthur (1957), *Yuan Mei: Eighteenth-Century Chinese Poet*, New York: Grove Press.

Part VI

Fine Discernments and the Cultivation of Taste

Preface

The early modern theories of aesthetic taste presented in the last section were historically accompanied by movements designed to improve the taste of the general populace. In the world of gastronomy, this took the form of a literature on eating and tasting, which was eventually followed by guides to a newly burgeoning restaurant culture. The first entry of this section by Stephen Mennell discusses the origins of this literature—one of its founders was Brillat-Savarin, whose work opened this volume—and its development into contemporary food-writing. Mennell queries the standards that gastronomic writings assume, speculating that they create as much as uncover the standards of taste for the food that they evaluate. At the same time that gastronomic guides disseminate the eating preferences of an elite, they serve to democratize taste by the fact that they reach a large public. Thus some of the social relations embedded in eating and taste preferences that were discussed in Part II can also be regarded from the perspective of the differences between "elite" and "democratic" eating that Mennell presents.

Soviet Russia offered virtually unique circumstances for oversight of the development of taste. Jukka Gronow describes how Stalin sought to bring about conditions in which the Soviet people would develop "good taste" in all areas of life, including food. Hence the remarkable production of caviar, champagne, and chocolate even in times of economic stringency when other goods were hard to find. Gronow refers to these foods as "Soviet kitsch" and opens another window on the notion of the cultivation of taste.

The French, who so often consider cuisine their special territory (see Peterson's conclusion in Section IV), have developed their own special category of taste: *terroir*, or the local taste of the earth—the very soil in which a food is grown or raised. Amy Trubek analyzes how the French came to valorize the *goût du terroir*, and she suggests that what is often regarded as nature's contribution to flavor must equally be considered a cultural phenomenon.

Trubek ends with a personal anecdote, and the last two entries of this section also give expression to first-person narratives, in contrast to the social accounts of taste that have constituted the dominant fare of this volume. These final contributions are concerned not only with the circumstances when taste affords fine discernment, but also when it fails to remark distinctions. Carrying on the theme of Hume's wine tasters from the previous section, Emile Peynaud comments on the conditions under which even the wine connoisseur will make mistakes, arousing the suspicion that imagination provides its own contribution to taste sensation. Part VI is capped off by Richard Watson, who recounts a sabbatical stay in Holland tracing the footsteps of Descartes, where he discovered his inability to taste the differences among the local cheeses, cookies, porridges and licorices—though he never doubts that there are such differences. His chapter reminds us of the many ways that small distinctions affect our lives, whether in the intimate realm of tastes or the terrain of public life.

23
Of Gastronomes and Guides

Stephen Mennell

The gastronome as a distinct and recognizable figure, and gastronomic writing as a distinct genre, emerged after the French Revolution. From then onwards there has been a continuous line of development linking Grimod de la Reynière's *Almanach des Gourmands* (1803–12) to the restaurant guides of today. Gastronomy has generally been seen as the preserve of an elite, laying down canons of 'correct' taste for those who were wealthy enough to meet them. I shall argue that gastronomes have, whether they intended to do so or not, also performed a democratizing function in the shaping of taste. Gastronomic writings, in common with all manners books, perform this function because the moment they are printed they disseminate knowledge of elite standards beyond the elite – and, of course, authors and publishers seek the financial rewards of sales outside the most exclusive circles. Both functions – of articulating elite standards and of democratizing taste – always coexist in gastronomy, though the balance between the two has tilted gradually during the last two centuries.

The word 'gastronomy', learnedly derived from Greek, seems to have been invented by Joseph Berchoux in 1801, who used it as the title of a poem. The term was rapidly adopted both in France and England to designate 'the art and science of delicate eating'. 'Gastronome' was a back-formation from 'gastronomy' – 'gastronomer' and 'gastronomist' were also sometimes used in English in the nineteenth century – to designate 'a judge of good eating'. The connotations of 'gastronome' partly overlap with those of the older words 'epicure' and 'gourmand', and the newer one 'gourmet'. Both 'epicure' and 'gourmand' had formerly had pejorative meanings close to 'glutton' – that is, they were applied to people who ate greedily and to excess. 'Epicure' had by the beginning of the nineteenth century, particularly in English, acquired a more favourable sense of 'one who cultivates a refined taste for the pleasures of the table; one who is choice and dainty in eating and drinking'. In France, the word *gourmand* had acquired the same favourable sense, and it was in that sense that Grimod used it in the title of the *Almanach des Gourmands*. The *Oxford English Dictionary* also records 'gourmand' as acquiring that favourable sense in English in the early nineteenth century, although to the present day English writers commonly make a distinction between a 'gourmand' with the pejorative sense of glutton, and 'gourmet' in the favourable sense of a person with a refined palate – a distinction not made in French. The word 'gastronome' differs from all these other words in one key respect: a gastronome is generally understood to be a person who not only cultivates his own 'refined taste for the pleasures of the table' but also, by *writing* about it, helps to cultivate other people's too. The gastronome is more than a gourmet – he is also a theorist and propagandist about culinary taste...

The Founding Fathers: Grimod and Brillat-Savarin

Between them, two writers effectively founded the whole genre of the gastronomic essay. They were Alexandre-Balthazar-Laurent Grimod de la Reynière (1758–1838) and Jean-Anthelme Brillat-Savarin (1755–1826). Virtually everything of the sort written since quotes or harks back to these two authors one way or another.

Grimod de la Reynière was the son of a rich farmer-general, and already noted before the Revolution for his eccentric hospitality – such as the black-edged invitations to what purported to be his own funeral supper. In reduced circumstances after the Revolution, his genius for publicity led him to found the Jury des Dégustateurs, whose members met weekly at the Rocher des Cancales restaurant (later the similar Société des Mercredis met at Legaque's establishment) to pass judgement on the dishes before them. The ingenuity of the scheme lay in its revealing how eager were restaurateurs and food merchants of all kinds to supply their products for public evaluation by the Jury. The *Almanach des Gourmands*, published annually (except in 1809 and 1811) from 1803 to 1812, was a development of the same idea. Grimod apparently expected to be adequately and regularly rewarded for the praise he bestowed on restaurants and food shops. It was not until more than a hundred years later that the leading restaurant guides in France and England managed to establish a reputation for impartial and 'objective' evaluations uninfluenced by backhanders from the evaluated...

Unlike Grimod's writings, which have been little reprinted and thus remained rather inaccessible, *La Physiologie du Goût* (1826) by Brillat-Savarin has been in print ever since its first publication, and is much the most famous of all gastronomic essays. Brillat-Savarin was a lawyer from Belley in the French Alps, and a bachelor who spent most of his life in Paris eating at the best tables. His tastes were shaped by both rural and metropolitan traditions of eating, and further diversified by a brief period as an emigré which took him as far as the USA and shooting wild turkeys in New England. His book was many years in preparation and published in the last few weeks of his life. It opens with a series of aphorisms, the most quoted of which is 'Tell me what you eat: I will tell you what you are.' These are followed by the 148 'Gastronomic Meditations' in thirty chapters which form the bulk of the book. Brillat-Savarin sets out the physiological knowledge of the day, on the sense of taste, appetite, and the nutritional qualities of foodstuffs, but in a light and witty way enlivened by many anecdotes ... and concluding with a highly speculative 'Philosophical History of Cooking' from the origins of mankind to his own day...

Gastronomy as a Literary Genre

Gastronomic literature as developed mainly in France and much copied in England possesses certain characteristic themes. One frequent component is the disquisition on what constitutes 'correct' practice at the time on such questions as the composition of menus, sequences of courses, and techniques of service; the archetype of this is Grimod's *Manuel des Amphitryons*, though eighteenth-century cookery books usually had a section on such matters (*Les Dons de Comus* was chiefly concerned with them), and the manuals on carving and the ceremonial of the table date from the Middle Ages.

A second component is dietetic, setting out what foods and what forms of cookery are good for one according to the prevailing knowledge of the day. This was, as we have noted, a theme in Brillat-Savarin, and it has been especially prominent in the work of the not inconsiderable number of medical men – such Edouard de Pomiane and Alfred Gottschalk – who have written on food and gastronomy. Even so thoroughly unhealthy a cookery book as Ali-Bab's *Gastronomie Pratique* contained a section – an afterthought might be more accurate – on the treatment of obesity.

A third component, and one probably more central to the gastronomic literary tradition, is a brew of history, myth, and history serving as myth. The more solid kernel of this can be found in frequent potted biographies of historically famous eaters and, from the nineteenth century, cooks... Closely similar are the stories, most of them again lacking any solid foundation in history, about the origins of particular dishes, techniques, and their names. Favourites include mayonnaise (said by some to have been `invented' by the Duc de Richelieu's cook and named in honour of his military exploits at Mahon – but there are alternative speculations), and chaudfroid sauce. A typical story to explain the latter name tells how a famous host and minister of the crown in eighteenth-century France was called away to see the king just as dinner was served, and how when he and his guests finally sat down to eat on his return hours later, the sauce was found to be as good cold as hot. That story includes two traits common in gastronomic mythology: the involvement of the famous personage, and the element of accident. The supposed involvement of the great, either as passive witnesses of or active collaborators in the discoveries of cooks, well expresses the balance of power between cooks and their patrons or publics, which in the first great period of gastronomic writing in the nineteenth century was gradually shifting in the cooks' favour, though it was still unequal. The role of accident in gastronomic mythology is also interesting: just as mankind's conquest of fire, a process which almost certainly spread over hundreds of millennia, is represented in the mythologies of many cultures as a sudden event caused by the exploit of a Promethean hero, so advances in cookery are usually represented in gastronomic literature as unique individual inspirations rather than as gradual processes (see Goudsblom 1984).

A fourth and final component of gastronomic literature is the nostalgic evocation of memorable meals. Notable menus, lovingly amplified by discussions of why such and such a dish was so remarkable, are often a staple ingredient of gastronomic writing. This is one of several respects in which the literature of gastronomy resembles that of cricket: meals in place of memorable matches, cooks and gourmets of the past in place of the batsmen and bowlers of a bygone age – 'we shall not see their like again' – and so on.

Of course, not everything which can be counted as gastronomic literature contains all of these four basic components, and the relative prominence of each varies a good deal. Within the genre, some writing is mainly historical in slant, some mainly concerned to define what is correct and in good taste, some more practically concerned to provide a critical assessment of the eating-places of the day. Moreover, there is an ill-defined margin at which the gastronomic essay gradually shades into the cookery book. The more learned sort of cookery book, such as those of Dumas and Ali-Bab, or more recently of Elizabeth David or Jane Grigson, might be considered gastronomic literature as much as cookery books. In either case, they seem intended to be read as literature. Significantly, the charge (if it is a charge) has been levelled both at the gastronomic essay and the 'learned' cookery book that they have an affinity with pornography. Certainly, both gastronomy and pornography dwell on the pleasures of the flesh, and in gastronomic literature as in pornography there is vicarious enjoyment to be had. In gastronomy, however, vicarious enjoyment is more definitely intended to be a prelude to, not a substitute for, direct and actual enjoyment.

Whatever the problems of defining its boundaries, the core characteristics of gastronomy as a literary genre since the early nineteenth century are easily recognizable. So what role has it played in the shaping of culinary taste, and in society more widely?...

At first, what we have called the elite-defining function is more evident than the democratizing one. It is apparent in the display of expertise. The gastronomes encouraged talk about food; without talk, critical appreciation of the cooks' achievements would be impossible, and only critical appreciation would give the cooks an incentive to compete with each other for the patronage of an informed public...

Gastronomes and gastronomy had, in any case, also played a democratizing role from the earliest stages. It has to be remembered that as a distinct figure, the gastronome appeared on the scene in the course of a general widening of the market for sophisticated cooking. When appearing to be at their most elitist, effete and exclusive, gastronomes and gastronomy were also helping to widen the circle for good eating. In a more egalitarian period, their activities in making known the pleasures of the table, and encouraging more cooks and diners to share their own interest in them, have become more evident; and in the process the gastronomic tradition has itself evolved.

Gastronomy and Democratization

In France, the activities of Curnonsky and his circle marked an important development in the gastronomic tradition. Curnonsky ('Why-not-ski') was the pseudonym of Maurice-Edmond Sailland (1872–1956), who described himself as the 'Prince of Gastronomes' and in 1928 founded the Académie des Gastronomes modelled on the Académie Française, with forty seats, each named after one of the famous gastronomes of the past. He was thus at first glance an unlikely figure to play an important part in the democratizing of fine food. But Curnonsky's princely title had in fact been conferred by democratic means – in a popular referendum organised in 1927 by the magazine *Le Bon Gîte et la Bonne Table* (Arbellot 1965: 75). (The runner-up in the poll was Maurice des Ombiaux, and also-rans included Ali-Bab and Edouard de Pomiane.) Moreover, Curnonsky himself was not a Parisian but an Angevin, who speaks of having learned the pleasures of the table from his old family cook, whose cooking owed nothing to schools or books and everything to twenty generations of her peasant ancestors (Curnonsky 1958: 177–8).

The significance of Curnonsky and his friends was that they seized the opportunity of linking gastronomy and tourism, and thus initiated a great interest in and vogue for French regional cookery. Curnonsky himself tells the story with characteristically moderate modesty:

> After the 1914–18 war, Louis Forest, Austin de Croze, Marcel Rouff, Maurice des Ombiaux and myself created the gastronomic press and, particularly in *Comoedia*, consecrated the holy alliance between tourism and gastronomy. This pioneering work benefited from two novelties: the 'democratized' motor-car and the taste for good fare which, after some years of anguish and privation, developed in France from 1919 onwards... The motor-car allowed the French to discover the cuisine of each province, and created the breed of what I have called 'gastro-nomads'.
>
> (Curnonsky 1958: 53)

The alliance of tourism and gastronomy was particularly to the advantage of tyre companies like Michelin and Kléber-Colombes, who began to publish their celebrated guides to the restaurants and hotels of France. Curnonsky and his friends had links with them, but also wrote their own guides. In the 1920s, with Marcel Rouff, Curnonsky planned a 32-volume series on the provinces of France entitled *La France Gastronomique*. Of these, 28 were complete when Rouff died, so in 1933 Curnonsky produced with de Croze a one-volume synopsis, *Le Trésor Gastronomique de France*. A by-product of their activities was the richest crop of gastronomic anecdotes since the days of Grimod and Brillat-Savarin. A typical example was the story of the perfect cassoulet they ate at Castelnaudary. The point of the tale was that good cooking takes time. Curnonsky's friends had to wait from noon one day till noon the next to eat the cassoulet prepared by Mme Adolphine (semi-retired and rather selective about whom she chose to feed). 'A cassoulet for this evening!', she greeted them. 'Where do you think you are? In Paris, where all the dishes are always ready?' (Curnonsky 1958: 191–8). Cassoulet – a dish of beans, pork, sausages, and other meats to hand – is an archetypical peasant dish of a sort which certainly would not have appealed to fashionable Parisian diners a generation earlier…

Guides to Eating

Tourist guides to hotels and restaurants are an old-established institution, and the idea of grading establishments in terms of comfort, facilities, service and cuisine was familiar long before the Second World War. Guides like Michelin, however, made – and still make – their judgements without publicly discussing the grounds for reaching them in particular cases. Even the greatest eating-places simply receive their two- or three-star listings, with at most a laconic line or so mentioning a few of the *specialités de la maison*. The more 'talkative' kind of guidebook, which describes each restaurant and comments critically on its strengths and weaknesses, its particular style and the personality of its chef, is a post-war development in both England and France. In England the *Good Food Guide* and Egon Ronay's annual guides, and in France the Gault-Millau guide, have all appeared on the scene since the Second World War. Gault-Millau and Ronay are rather similar, in having been initially the work of campaigning individuals, but gradually growing into large organizations with trained and paid inspectors to visit and judge hotels and restaurants. The *Good Food Guide* is rather different in that it involves many hundreds of the dining public in making reports on their own experiences…

The editors of the *Good Food Guide,* and Egon Ronay too, sought to promote intelligent appreciation and criticism of eating places. But on what standards is such criticism based? By what criterion is cooking judged to be better or worse? There seems generally to have been more unspoken consensus about this in France than in England... The annual award of rosettes by the *Guide Michelin* has long been awaited with excitement, and while there may be disputes about whether a particular restaurant has been accurately rated, the general idea of a scale from better to worse appears unproblematic to the French. Even though Michelin is vague about its criteria – two stars 'worth a detour', three stars 'worth the journey' – a unilinear scale is understood and accepted. Gault-Millau introduced a refinement of red tocques for distinction in *nouvelle cuisine* and black tocques for outstanding *cuisine classique*, but this was not a major breach of the principle.

In contrast, the British guides took many years even to move towards a simple better/worse rating, and there were many greater problems in deciding what exactly this should mean. It was not just that there were fewer eating-places whose outstanding excellence could be taken for granted whatever the criterion used; there was also apparent a greater diversity of taste and less consensus about what constituted excellent cooking. For many years both Raymond Postgate [in the *Good Food Guide*] and Ronay claimed only that each eating place they listed was 'good of its kind', which left scope for enormous confusion. By around 1970, however, things had changed sufficiently for the guides to have more confidence in rating restaurants in linear, better and worse fashion. Partly it seems to have been a matter of changes in the restaurants themselves, but also partly a matter of greater consensus about critical standards – a consensus which the guides themselves appear to have done much to create...

Conclusion

These issues are by no means peculiar to matters of eating. They have wide ramifications. The same questions arise time and time again in discussions of cultural policy, when people at large seem not to like the forms of culture that the minority of 'experts' consider they ought to. The same questions arise in the problem of what is good behaviour: as Elias has shown, the definition of good manners provided at any given time by an 'expert' minority never coincides with how the majority of people then actually behaves. Gastronomes and food guide activists are comparable with such minorities. What effect overall have they had in shaping conceptions of good food and making it available to those who want it? And what is the basis – and extent – of their power?

The power of the campaigning guides today – and this includes Gault-Millau in France as much as Egon Ronay and the *Good Food Guide* in Britain – springs in principle from the same source as Grimod's at the beginning of the nineteenth century. It derives from their influence on the readers, and through them on public opinion more widely. Today that also involves organization on a larger scale than the Jury des Dégustateurs. The guides' teams of anonymous inspectors, paid or unpaid, and still more vast numbers of people who buy and consult the publications each year, make them a force which caterers can ignore only at some cost. To the independent, upmarket restaurateur, a recommendation in one of the guides whether in England or in France is worth money. Raymond Postgate, writing in the *Good Food Guide* in 1954, foresaw with his usual acumen the effects of the 'mass-observation' of eating-places he had organized. With Club members travelling around and 20,000–30,000 eyes watching them, restaurateurs newly entering a trade could become widely known for their good food much more quickly than before. Perhaps more important, 'an hotelier whose service and cooking is going down can never be at his ease. He can never be sure which quiet customer is watching him on behalf of the Club.' For if securing an entry is worth money, the loss of it can be costly. Thus the guides engender in the restaurateur a certain watchfulness and exert a constraint towards striving always to maintain high standards.

Grimod, with only a few associates, was able to influence the relatively small number of leading independent restaurateurs in post-Revolutionary Paris. It is scarcely surprising that many more independent restaurateurs today should pay heed to the larger-scale organizations which produce the guides. The targets of the guides' most interesting campaigns nowadays, however, are themselves vast organizations. They are far more formidable adversaries, and the balance of power between the mass caterers and the self-appointed upholders of catering standards is much more complex and indeterminate. The guides have hesitated to take on neither the giant private-sector conglomerates nor the great public-sector organizations. Egon Ronay's critique of the mass-produced hospital scrambled eggs or motorway steak-and-kidney pie poses recognizably the same sort of questions as gastronomes have always asked (if usually at a more esoteric level): What constitutes a *good* pie or *true* scrambled egg? But why should mass caterers pay any attention to their complaints?... Yet even the chains and public sector catering organizations like hospitals seem to have made some response to criticism: the gastronomic guides may have little financial power there, but they still have the power to cause public embarrassment and they do actively encourage their readers to complain. In short, they provide what Galbraith (1952) called 'countervailing power' on behalf of customers confronted with public or private conglomerations of power in the catering trades. It was highly appropriate that the *Good Food Guide* was taken under the wing of the Consumers' Association, publishers of *Which?* For today's gastronomic guides are part of the more general consumer movement found in most Western countries, whose successes include Ralph Nader's famous campaigns against motor manufacturers in the USA, to the highly successful Campaign for Real Ale in Britain, and campaigns against mass-produced bread in several countries. One of the general characteristics of consumer movements is that they are concerned to reverse, or mitigate the effects of, mass production.

In order to have any chance of success in their trials of strength with the mass producers, the leaders of any consumer movement have to ensure that they are seen as the delegates or spokesman for substantial numbers of followers. Thus, like the leaders of political parties, the editors of the guides have to pay as much attention to persuading their followers as persuading the caterers that their tastes are right. For Gault and Millau or Egon Ronay, who began as campaigning individuals, that raises no ideological problems. For the editors of the *Good Food Guide*, which at least pretends to be the democratic expression of its readers' taste, it causes some qualms. Christopher Driver reflected on the problem in the 1980 edition. Given that many, probably most, people were perfectly content with mass-produced food, by what right did the *Guide* rate more highly the preferences of those who were not so content?

Looking at the whole spectrum of more-or-less-edibles from *haute cuisine* to teenage junk food, what do you dismiss because you happen not to like it, and what are you prepared to call a bad idea, badly executed and unscrupulously priced?

The *Guide* itself, he admitted, had done at least its share in persuading the British bourgeoisie into eating more garlic per capita than the northern French did, and into eating its lamb and duck as pink as its sirloin. Most of those who made reports for the *Guide* liked their food that way – in part because the *Guide* had told them they should – but was it *objectively* better? Grimod de la Reynière would not have been troubled by such self-doubt. One reason for the doubt is that no matter what large numbers of the 'bourgeoisie' have come to share such tastes, they are manifestly a small minority of the people at large and of the market. In consequence, the outcome of trials of strength on the upper level between self-appointed leaders of culinary public opinion and the mass producers of food depends not only on the leaders carrying their followers with them, but also on the balances of power on the lower level between groups bringing to the market very different likes and dislikes. In the circumstances, the guides' successes in their battles are perhaps surprisingly numerous.

References

Ali-Bab (Henri Babinski) (1907), *Gastronomic Pratique: Etudes Culinaire Suivies du Traitement de L'Obésité des Gourmands*, Paris: Flammarion.

Arbellot de Vacqueur, Simon (1965), *Curnonsky: Prince des Gastronomes*, Paris: Production de Paris.

Brillat-Savarin, Jean-Anthelme (1826), *La Physiologie du Goût*, Paris: A. Sautelet.

Curnonsky (pseud. of Maurice-Edmund Sailland) (1958), *Souvenirs*, Paris: A. Michel.

Curnonsky and de Croze, Austin (1933), *Le Trésor Gastronomique de France*, Paris: Librairie Delagrave.

Curnonsky and Rouff, Marcel (1921–), *La France Gastronomique: Guide des Merveilleuses Culinaires et des Bonnes Auberges Françaises*, Paris: F. Rouff.

Elias, Norbert (1978), [1939], *The Civilizing Process* Vol. 1: *The History of Manners*, Oxford: Basil Blackwell.
Galbraith, John Kenneth (1952), *American Capitalism*, London: Hamish Hamilton.
Goudsblom, Johan (1984), 'The domestication of fire as a civilizing process', conference paper: *Civilization and Theories of Civilizing Processes*, Bielefeld, June 1984.
Grimod de la Reyniére, A.-B.-L. (1803–12), *Almanach des Gourmands*, Paris.
——. (1808), *Le Manuel des Amphitryons*, Paris: Capelle and Reynaud.

24

Champagne and Caviar

Soviet Kitsch

Jukka Gronow

In the Soviet Union there was not the drive to invent new products and promote them to consumers as found in capitalist societies. Under socialism, unlike under capitalism, customers were not meant to be manipulated for the sake of profit – to buy all kinds of products they did not really want or need. Nevertheless, in the 1930s the quest for new consumer goods became a preoccupation for the authorities, producers and traders. They were convinced that there was, among the Soviet population, an increasing demand for such things and that it was their urgent task to respond to such a demand. By the early 1930s, the government and the Party no longer felt that their role was simply to satisfy the basic needs of the population, to keep people nourished, warm and clothed. As they saw it, they had succeeded at the basic level, and it was time to raise the standard of living both quantitatively and qualitatively. They wanted to develop the Soviet taste, establish more cultivated manners and enjoy refined goods. Individual taste was also encouraged.

The development of the new material culture took place roughly in two stages closely following one another. The years 1933–35 are preserved in people's memories as the best years before the outbreak of the war. Food rationing was officially abandoned in 1935. The Soviet Union started, for the first time, to produce sausages, canned fish, canned vegetables, cheese, chocolate and other goods industrially and on a mass scale. The history of the rebirth of the Soviet chocolate industry is particularly revealing: within a couple of years its product variety jumped from just a dozen to several hundred. The main slogan for this period was 'for higher quality'. The progress of a factory and the merits of its director were measured by the amount of novelties it could turn out each year.

The second leap in the consumer goods industry was more complicated. In 1936–37 the country was again on the verge of an economic crisis. Many regions were suffering from a serious shortage of food. Yet, at the same time, the Soviet government and the Party started to worry about mass production of champagne. According to the new plan, by 1942 the country was to produce 20 million bottles of champagne per year compared with only a few hundreds of thousands in 1937. Stalin's aim to produce champagne proved to be long-lasting. It is one of the few consumer goods still available in every Russian kiosk and still proudly bearing the title Sovetskoe on its label. Champagne was, however, not the only luxury product 'invented' then. Vintage wines and cognacs were put into production also. The food industry, and in particular confectionaries, increased the production of many seasonal, celebratory products of its own...

The Soviet Union of the 1930s was a unique historical case: almost all its material culture was invented and created from nothing. Every decision to start the production of any single item was made at the highest levels of administration. The Minister of Food Industry, Anastas Mikoyan, personally signed, among others, recipes for the production of sausages and perfume. The rapidly increasing assortment of consumer goods was thus created in a highly conscious and reflective manner. Ministers, their deputies, assistants and factory directors took an active part in the planning of even the smallest details of production and distribution. Officials vigorously debated new product ideas and compared the merits of different varieties. The problems of packaging, paper wrapping or, say, new tops to perfume bottles, were all decided at the highest level. This situation offers a unique chance to follow from the very beginning the emergence of a particular culture of consumption.

The story is full of tragic and tragicomic features. It is, however, interesting from a more theoretical viewpoint too. The historical experience accumulated in the Soviet Union offers an interesting opportunity to reflect upon alternative ways of organizing and developing modem mass consumption. In the Soviet Union almost everything was consciously created and taken into production. The authorities had to present the reasons why something was being produced: for whom, what and why did the Soviet food and 'light' industries produce and the Soviet trade organizations sell or distribute? Once the shortage of very basic foodstuffs, such as potatoes, bread, cabbage, and vodka had been overcome, or at least thought to be overcome, bare necessity was not enough to legitimize the choices made.

In the beginning, there was no overall plan. The authorities probed their way forward by trial and error. The planned economy was in fact quite chaotic, subject to the whims of its leaders and vulnerable to popular reactions. For example, the idea of suddenly producing millions and millions of bottles of champagne – a plan that would demand huge investments and new infrastructure, from the opening of new training schools to the printing of new labels – came from Stalin himself. Likewise, Mikoyan brought back from America five huge production units for hamburgers because he personally felt they were a good idea. Who knows whether, if the war had not broken out, we might have witnessed the emergence of a MacMikoyan chain of hamburgers instead of McDonald's?

Such decisions reflect more than just the personal whims of Soviet leaders. They might have chosen different items to focus on, but the symbolic meaning of these goods and the message that they carried to the Soviet people were much more important than the actual products themselves. The Party optimistically promised every Soviet citizen the best that both the old and the new world had to offer, and at a moderate price...

The Invention of Soviet Champagne

The invention of Soviet champagne is sometimes dated back to the seventeenth Party Congress in February 1934. In a 1939 article, one Comrad Karpatsenko from the central administration of the wine industry notes that 'For the first time in the history of the congress of the Communist Party a special resolution was made about the growth of Soviet wine production...' According to Karpatsenko, wine and champagne had become ordinary objects of consumption among the working masses in the homeland of socialism (Karpatsenko 1939).

In reality, there is no evidence that the Party Congress of 1934 specifically mentioned champagne and wine in its resolutions. Both Molotov, then Minister of Light Industry, and Mikoyan, then Minister of Food Industry, paid special attention to the food industry, but they did not discuss champagne. Both emphasized the importance, not only of rapidly increasing the quantity of food production, but also of improving the quality and variety of food products available to the Soviet workers and peasants... The quality of meat and fish worried Molotov in particular. Mikoyan meanwhile was concerned with the problems of the chocolate and candy industry.

It appears that the birth of Soviet champagne really occurred in 1936 thanks to Stalin's personal initiative and intervention. This coincides with the time when Professor Frolov-Bagraev entered the public scene. He started enthusiastically propagating a new industrial method of champagne production, which was well suited to the purpose of mass production... The summer of 1936 was a busy time in the central and local governmental organs responsible for the measures taken during this time, but as usual the Council of Ministers and the Central Committee of the Party made the vital decisions. On 28 July 1936, Resolution no. 1366, concerning the production of Soviet champagne, dessert and table wines, was adopted and signed by a Deputy Chairman of the Council of Ministers, Chubar, and by Stalin himself... This bustling activity continued throughout the following year. Champagne remained a top priority, and at the beginning of 1937, the Council of Ministers and the Central Committee of the Party adopted another resolution about the growth of the raw material resources of champagne and dessert wines in the *kolkhozes* of the Russian federation...

The drive to mass-produce champagne was not forgotten or neglected even during the hard years of the Second World War. The always industrious Frolov-Bagraev reported in 1943 on the important task of organizing champagne production in central Asia – an area with no tradition of wine cultivation at all – since the old vineyards in the Crimea and in Georgia had fallen under enemy occupation. And shortly after the war, at the end of 1945, an expert in viticulture, Comrad Pronin, was encouraging his readers towards further successes in increasing champagne production. In the Fourth Five-Year Plan, the new target for the year 1950 was – again optimistically – 16 million bottles! [1]

[Thus] just a few years after a famine in which millions of people had died of malnutrition and in the midst of a time marked by a serious shortage of basic supplies, the government and the Party suddenly started to worry about the production of champagne. The authorities did not just dream up a beautiful picture of the coming happiness of humankind but undertook massive and expensive measures in order to realize the dream. Whether or not it could feasibly be put into practice is another question. Ultimately the war years made the realization of this dream impossible...

The Refinement of Soviet Taste: Cognac, Liquor and Vintage Wines

Champagne was not the only high-quality alcohol on the minds of the Party. During discussions on the Second Five-Year Plan, wine was included in a Ministry of Agriculture decree on 3 May 1934. All the wine-producing economic units were obliged to preserve no less than 25 decalitres of bottled high-quality wines of every type cultivated in their warehouses. Until that point, there had been no system of storing or preserving vintage wines in the Soviet Union. Regular wine tastings were also organized with the adjoining system of quality contro1. In 1937 the plan of the Moscow Wine and Cognac Plant was adjusted to include more expensive wines.

As Mikoyan later wrote in his memoirs, he had several wine-tasting experiences in the first-class diner on board the Atlantic liner going to the United States. The price of his dinner included two bottles of wine. Mikoyan decided to make use of the opportunity to get acquainted with good wines. Therefore, he asked the waiter to serve him different wines of good quality. After a while he noticed that he was not served the most expensive wines on the list. When asked why, the waiter explained that those wines were only on the list to satisfy rich Americans. He had not served them to Mikoyan because they were not actually among the best ones at all (Mikoyan 1971: 70).

In addition to changes in the production lines and tastes of table wines and champagne, similar transformations were taking place in the whole alcohol-producing industry. Vodka had been available even during the hard years of the First Five-Year Plan and forced collectivization – selling and producing vodka were declared a monopoly of the state in 1925. During the Second Five-Year Plan, even those factories that produced strong spirits were encouraged to develop their output of more processed drinks. The Moscow Vodka Factory, for instance, changed its production line from a very strong vodka (56 per cent proof) to 'milder' (less alcoholic) vodkas and other 'finer' alcoholic drinks in 1933 and 1934. The year 1934 saw the widening of product variety in this factory from fifteen to fifty-two, the new products generally being of a higher quality, and as a rule milder. In 1936, for instance, Soviet-made Dutch gin was advertised in *Pravda,* the central Party newspaper. Liqueur, generally regarded in the Soviet Union of the 1930s as a finer drink even suitable for ladies, appeared in the Moscow factory's product list for the first time. The factory also developed new, specially designed bottles. So-called export and special orders appeared in its plans for 1934. Export wines, like other export products, were at least partly sold on the home market (first at Torgsin and later at Gastronom shops). As with other industries, 1934 was a watershed moment in the policy of producing better and more refined alcoholic drinks.

In 1935 another ten new products were introduced at the Moscow factory. In 1936 a whole new plant specializing in the production of liqueur was developed. In 1934, the factory had produced only 10,000 hectolitres of liqueurs, but in 1936 the amount was five times greater. At the same time, the share of strong vodkas with very high proofs diminished, with the approval of the higher planning authorities. In 1938 the first 'vintage' liqueurs, liqueurs that had been kept in store for several years, appeared in the factory's product lists. This category had not even been included in the original plan. In 1939, 27,300 hectolitres of vintage liqueurs were delivered.

Cognac produced by the Armenian wine trust and also known under its own trademark Ararat experienced a similar, rapid rise in status a couple of years later. The 'invention' or rediscovery of the importance of cognac coincided with that of champagne; it took place mainly between 1936–37. In a memorandum about the state and future of wine growing and the wine industry in the Armenian Republic delivered to Mikoyan, the head of the Ararat trust, Comrade Balaian, detailed the tasks of cognac production. It is not clear whether the initiative had come from above or whether the director of Ararat was simply promoting his own cause. The document is not precisely dated, but it probably goes back to July 1937. While the recent Third Five-Year Plan had included directives for Armenian wine production, Balaian claimed that both the conditions of wine growing and the further refinement of wine lagged far behind adequate standards. The older preserves of vintage wines and cognacs had been totally destroyed and only young and low-quality wines had been released on the market...

A quantitative growth was promised not only in cognac but also in strong sweet wines, another speciality of the Armenian wine trust, as well as in table wines. This quantitative growth was, however, greatly limited by other priorities, in particular the large increase in the amount of wines and cognacs of longer preservation times. Whereas the amount of stored cognacs in 1937 was 400,000 litres and that of strong sweet wines 230,000 litres, the figures forecast for the year 1942 looked quite different: 2,150,000 and 1,360,000 litres respectively. In the case of the Ararat trust, the emphasis on higher quality in terms of longer preservation was thus quite explicit. In 1943, according to this plan, the trust should not release any cognac which had not been stored for a minimum of three to four years. Balaian also suggested the adoption of an international (French) quality classification of different wines (Port, Madeira, Malaga, Muskat and others) and cognacs based on the period of their maturation before release.

This programme demanded huge investment (the estimated minimum was 41 million roubles), opening of new vineyards, the construction of new factories and storehouses and the reconstruction of old ones. Mikoyan once again supervised the whole operation down to the smallest detail. This is evident in his communications with the directors of Ararat in the summer of 1937. For example, on 16 July Balaian reported to Mikoyan that he had with the latter's permission made a deal with Comrade Temkin, the head of the department of building materials, about the release of cement, iron, copper pipes and copper sheets. He reported that what was further needed, among other things, were electric machines and pieces of equipment as well as motor cars. In particular, Balaian mentioned that the factory needed 1.5 million velvet bottle tops to be put on high-quality cognac and wine bottles...

It is interesting to compare the development of the wine and cognac industry with that of beer production. Even though some initiatives were taken in beer production and new larger breweries were planned, the attention paid to beer was by no means comparable with that paid to the 'finer' drinks. Beer was clearly an everyday concern as opposed to a special treat or a sign of the good life. Its propagandistic effect was also evaluated as being of lesser value... In the minds of the Soviet leaders it did not enjoy the same aura of luxury and belonged, together with vodka, rather to the ordinary necessities of daily life.

Soviet Caviar

In 1935, the newly founded Gastronom food stores boasted a supply of 100 tons of black caviar as well as significant quantities of red (salmon) caviar. In addition, the shops sold other highly valued fish, such as different types of sturgeon, both fresh and smoked. A memorandum from the period called for regulations to improve not just the quality of caviar, but also its packaging and selling. The Ministry of Food Industry insisted that portions of caviar sold in Gastronom shops be packaged in small cans (of 100, 250 and 500 grams), better suited for retail sale. Furthermore, the cans were to be provided with hermetic caps with rubber rings, which could be opened and closed without any damage to whole caviar grains. A 1935 inspections report criticized the Moscow Gastronom food shops for failing to stock black caviar, which should have been regularly available. The report also noted that canned fish should be labelled in Russian and that shop assistants should be able to distinguish between different types of sturgeon.

Caviar was regarded as a necessity, at least for major public holidays or formal banquets. When there was no caviar available in Moscow before the celebration of 1 May 1935, it caused a scandal among local Party officials. Their anxiety was, however, alleviated by the fact that a large shipment was on its way to the capital. When publicly on sale, black caviar was certainly an expensive delicacy in the Soviet Union, which makes one wonder why it was so important to guarantee its wide availability. In 1934 in Leningrad, for example, the price of the most expensive caviar was 60 roubles per kilogram, or approximately one third of the monthly wages of a young industrial worker. In 1936 the trade journal *Sovetskaia Torgovlia* proudly reported that the price of caviar had decreased from 50 to 36 roubles per kilogram. Caviar was still, however, twice the price of high-quality ham or butter. While mostly limited to more privileged members of society, caviar was available to the average citizen in urban areas. A surgical nurse recounted living in 1930s Leningrad in her twenties and being able to purchase, along with her colleagues, a sandwich of black caviar at the Soloviev food store.[2]

Although caviar became a highly valued Soviet delicacy, often associated with the more memorable moments in life, in official policy it never attained the elevated status of champagne. As a result, it has left fewer traces in Soviet archives. It is unlikely that the production of caviar was suited to the ideal of highly centralized units of mass production. Caviar was after all a natural resource whose value was, at least to some extent even within the socialism of the Soviet Union, determined by its scarcity. Its cultivation could certainly be intensified but only to a certain limit. This was one of the reasons why the Soviet Union exported only a minor share of its annual production of caviar despite the fact that it could have been sold for a high price on the international market to get badly needed foreign currency (Saffron 2002: 115). Nevertheless in many other respects caviar shared with champagne and cognac a common characteristic. They could all be called ideal examples of Soviet *kitsch*.

Soviet Kitsch and the Birth of the Soviet Material Culture

Soviet *kitsch*, as I am using the term, can be defined as mass-produced, cheaper copies of finer, expensive goods which had the aura of luxury because they had been consumed – or the Bolsheviks believed they had been consumed – by the former Russian nobility (see also Gronow 1997: 51–3). The message that these goods carried was clear: now the ordinary Soviet worker had access to a standard of living that was earlier restricted to members of the nobility or rich bourgeoisie. The new luxuries were symbolic of a lifestyle lived by the Russian elite of the nineteenth century, or rather a life which the Bolsheviks had read about in Tolstoy, Chekhov and Gogol. Some modifications were necessary of course. Instead of horse carriages, for instance, big cars with chauffeurs were available to the new Soviet elite. Common luxuries – or one might even speak of plebeian luxuries – were meant to be an essential part of the everyday life of the Soviet people. Such luxuries played a part in numerous public and personal feasts and celebrations that were typical of Soviet life.

Champagne, cognac, caviar, chocolate and perfume were all part of this new luxury culture. All these goods have a certain sensual pleasure, meant to be enjoyed by drinking, eating or smelling. They were also feminine goods in the sense that they were mainly targeted towards female consumers, towards the new Soviet women, and were considered to be suitable gifts for women of all ages. In the mid-1930s such products were produced in great quantities. Later, other goods such as crystal glasses and vases, amber necklaces, scarves and fur hats were also found in special state shops in urban areas. This limited group of products preserved its extraordinary status throughout the history of the Soviet Union. These – in many ways rather modest – luxury goods were by no means all that was regarded as luxuries in the sense of transcending basic needs or exceeding the regular shared standard of life. Almost anything – other than very basic goods such as plain bread, cabbage, potatoes, or vodka – was a luxury in the eyes of Soviet citizens and the authorities.

Foreign products also held a special cachet in the luxury goods economy of the Soviet Union. In the late 1920s many special hard currency shops called Torgsin opened to serve a privileged Soviet clientele – first foreign workers and specialists who had foreign currency, later even Soviet citizens who had valuables, antiques, art, gold or silver to sell. These shops sold many products of foreign origin. In a country which imported few consumer goods almost any foreign goods became a rare luxury, difficult to obtain and prestigious to own. For instance, in 1939 only 1 per cent of the total sales of the Central Department Store in Moscow consisted of foreign, imported goods. If practically everything that this flagship of Soviet trade sold before the war was domestic, one can easily imagine what the situation was in other more provincial department stores, not to mention ordinary shops. This was a consequence of socialism, which called for a strong reliance on one's own resources and raw materials. Hard-to-earn foreign currency was used to buy machines and raw materials for heavy industry. This is one of the reasons why black markets have flourished throughout Soviet history even during relatively prosperous times. The black market trade in jeans and nylon stockings or Abba records in the post-war decades is probably the best-known example of this phenomenon, while, in the 1930s, Parker pens and imported cigarettes were typical black market commodities.

Other perks and privileges were also developing in the 1930s. Directors of factories and leaders of various organizations had cars with chauffeurs, private homes, large flats in city centres, summer villas, free vacations in health spas on the Crimea, and so on. The truly privileged could even take trips abroad and have access to foreign currency, which could buy almost anything... Historian Sheila Fitzpatrick describes a private car as an example of utmost Soviet luxury in the 1930s since it is unlikely that private individuals could buy cars (Fitzpatrick 1999: 102). On rare occasions they could be received as presents from the state.

From the mid-1930s some of the genuine luxury goods and services gradually became accessible not only to the rather narrow political elite, but also to a rapidly growing group of privileged people. This group consisted of educated specialists, or Stalin's intelligentsia (the name given to this group by Stalin in 1936); and top workers, *udarniki* and Stakhanovites. Real luxuries such as cars, large apartments or *dachas* mostly belonged to one's 'office' or were presented as rewards for exceptional work. In principle, they could not be bought with money but were regarded as rewards to be earned through hard work or exceptional talent.

A culture of material goods unique to the Soviet Union was created in the 1930s. What defined the 'good life' is often illuminating. A standard Soviet history of economy published in 1978, for example, proudly summarizes the achievements of the Second Five-Year Plan in the development of consumption: 'Many food items which in pre-Revolutionary Russia were only available to the representatives of the ruling classes were strongly anchored into the everyday life of Soviet people'.[3] If the above catalogue of luxury goods is representative at all, this characterization by a Soviet historian was indeed true to a degree.

Naturally, it would have been difficult to combine some elements of the 'good life' with the ideals of socialism. But it was still possible, in principle, for a Soviet worker in the 1930s to dine *à la Parisienne* under a crystal chandelier and enjoy the services of a butler in a tailcoat, say in Metropol', Natsional' or Praga restaurants. Or drink a cocktail on the terrace in the new Soviet showpiece, the Moskva Hotel next to the Kremlin Wall, built at the end of the 1930s. The price of a formal dinner was most likely too expensive for the most common workers, but even they could, at least occasionally, afford a box of chocolates, a bottle of champagne or a trip to an ice cream bar. Many ordinary workers and *kolkhoz* peasants could also enjoy these privileges at the state's expense as invited guests to the capital as members of Party delegations or representatives of labour collectives.

The irony is that many wageearners living in highly developed capitalist societies of the 1930s could ill afford the treats that their Soviet counterparts could. The price of champagne was likely to be prohibitively expensive. In addition, the capitalist worker had other modern consumer goods to strive for, rather than luxury knock-offs of the rich. The luxury goods offered by Stalin were a form of *kitsch* in that they imitated models and artefacts that were thought to be valued by or belonging to the world of 'high society'. Their propagandistic message was that every Soviet worker lived like an aristocrat. Yet, at the same time, the country was in a perpetual state of deficit, lacking basic necessities such as bread. Such inconsistencies have been rife throughout Soviet history. To buy a bottle of champagne was certainly beyond the reach of millions of *kolkhoz* peasants. On the other hand there were hundreds of thousands of workers and technical specialists who were more prosperous now…

The greater availability of consumer goods, which came to mark the major public holidays, also helped make these holidays an integral part of the life of most ordinary Soviet citizens. One could even argue that the consumption of particular foods and drinks, such as champagne and chocolate, and other consumer goods, such as gramophones and musical instruments, at certain political rituals was an effective way of inculcating loyalty among the citizens of the state. Rather than relying on previous methods of straightforward political agitation, this new mode of using consumer goods as incentives helped unify the public around the Soviet state. When political punishments became both more severe and more arbitrary with Stalin's repressions, the system of rewards likewise became more varied. In a sense, Stalin's 'engineering of human souls' was less straightforward and allowed for more individual gratification and variation than the earlier political manipulations…

However, even in this society there were factors that promoted the emergence of a monetary economy and a commodity culture that allowed gradually more room for the development of individual taste and fashion. To improve taste and to create a new socialist way of life, alternatives and mutually competing objects of choice were required. Soviet leaders were convinced that a totally new and more advanced human civilization was on its way. It was only natural that the majority of commodities of material culture had to be created anew as well…

Even in the Soviet Union, however, elements of an individualistic culture of consumption gradually emerged despite the existence of strong countertendencies. The emerging culture was still, at the same time, characterized by a great degree of conformity. It was also constantly centrally monitored and regulated. As we have seen, Stalin and other leaders took a strong personal interest in developing the taste and etiquette of the common people. As a consequence, Soviet material culture offered many – smaller and bigger – delights and pleasures to its consumers – but only in strictly controlled ways. As such it was reminiscent of a culture of estates with strictly determined and separate lifestyles and tastes. In this sense, the government liked to compare the situation of the Soviet worker to an aristocrat living under the tsarist times – even though the luxuries available in the socialist society were certainly far less luxurious or even simply cheap imitations and kitsch.

Notes

1. Production figures in this essay and quotations from memos and correspondence were obtained from archival materials in Russia. For details of these and other Russian sources, see Gronow 2003: 155–7.

2. Interviews with old inhabitants of Leningrad about their lives in the 1930s conducted as part of Timo Vihavainen's project financed by the Academy of Finland, 'Norms, values, and deviation in the Soviet society and culture in the 1920s–1950s'.

3. *Istoriia Sotsialisticheskoi Ekonomiki SSSR,* T. 4 Moskva, 1978: 475.

References

Fitzpatrick, Sheila (1979), *Education and Social Mobility in the Soviet Union 1921–1934,* Cambridge: Cambridge University Press.

Gronow, Jukka (1997), *The Sociology of Taste*, London: Routledge.

——. (2003), *Caviar with Champagne: Common Luxury and the Ideals of the Good Life in Stalin's Russia*, Oxford: Berg.

Karpatsenko, P. K. (1939), 'Zadachi sovetskogo vinodeliia i vinogradarstva', *Vinodelenie i Vinogradarstvo SSSR*, No. 1: 4–7.

Mikoyan, A. (1971), 'Dva mesiatsa v SShA', Part 2. SshA, *Ekonomika, Politica, Ideologiia.* No. 10.

Saffron, Inga (2002), *Caviar: The Strange History and Uncertain Future of the World's Most Loved Delicacy*, New York: Broadway Books.

25
Place Matters

Amy B. Trubek

In the act of tasting, when the bite or sip moves through the mouth and into the body, culture and nature become one. Universally, eating (and drinking) is a process of bringing the natural world into the human domain, leading many cultures and religions to focus on the moment of ingestion, for example Kosher dietary rules and Hindu notions of purity and pollution. Unusual to France is the attention put on the role of the natural world in the *taste* of food and drink. When the French take a bite of cheese or a sip of wine, they taste the earth: rock, grass, hillside, valley, plateau. They combine gustatory sensation and the evocative possibilities of taste in their fidelity to the taste of place, or *goût du terroir*.

Place, however, is a poor substitute for *terroir*, a word that merits many definitions in French. *The Concise Oxford Dictionary* defines it as soil, ground, locality, place, or part of the country. The nineteenth-century version of Larousse's *Grand Dictionnaire Universel* defines *terroir* as "the earth considered from the point of view of agriculture." These definitions rely on the natural world, but others focus on the human element. A contemporary French dictionary says *terroir* is either when something has a particular flavor that can be *attributed* to the soil, or the typical tastes and habits that come from a region or a rural area. This approach is longstanding; the nineteenth-century Larousse clarifies the definition of *terroir* with a discussion of *goût du terroir*. This is the "flavor or odor of certain locales that are given to its products, particularly with wine." For example, "Ce vin a un goût du terroir; Je n'y trouve pas le parfum de terroir." [This wine has a local (or site-pecific) taste; I don't smell "place."] Food and drink from a certain place have a unique *flavor*.

These problems of definition do not lie solely with the dictionary compilers. These are difficult words to define because they signify so much to the French.

More than words, they are *categories* that frame perceptions and practices—a worldview, or should we say here, a foodview? The agrarian roots of *terroir* best explain the origins and persistence of this foodview. *Terroir* and *goût du terroir* are categories for framing and explaining people's relationship to the land, be it sensual, practical, or habitual.

France is intensely cultivated. Usable agricultural land still covers the majority of France, 77,803,000 acres in 1985 (Fremont 1996: 3). The nation's geography is described as a combination of urban and rural, and little attention is spent exploring France's "wilderness." The agrarian view dominates. Contemporary French geographer Armand Fremont says: "No other major civilization in Europe or elsewhere has ever valued the soil more than the French or associated it more intimately with the good." Fremont feels that "soil is a focus of all France's thoughts and emotions" (34). A foodview associating taste, soil, and the bounty of the earth thus makes sense.

Describing *Terroir* and Creating *Goût du Terroir*

In France, *terroir* is often associated with *racines*, or roots, a person's history with a certain place. This connection is considered essential, as timeless as the earth itself. Agriculturalist Olivier de Serres, in his seventeenth-century treatise, *Le Théâtre d'Agriculture et des Mesnages des Champs* states: "the fundamental task in agriculture is to understand the nature of the *terroir*, whether it is the land of your ancestors or land recently acquired." Soil and roots create the basis of French cuisine as well. Le Grand d'Aussy, in his 1789 work *History of Private Life* discussed French cuisine as the natural fruition of provincial agriculture, tracing back at least two centuries the connection between the cuisine and what "nature has seen fit to allow each of our provinces to produce" (Csergo 1999: 502).

Examining discussions of *terroir* and *goût du terroir* from the eighteenth-century through today, the approach of all the authors, be they journalists, farmers, vintners, chefs, or citizens, is remarkably consistent. Their discourse does not adopt a *point of view*; rather it is considered to *reflect reality*. This fundamentalist view always begins with a defined place, tracing the taste of place back from the mouth to the plants and animals and ultimately back into the soil, creating a very Gallic twist to the oft-used American adage of "location, location, location."

In this discourse, places make unique tastes, and in turn such flavor characteristics and combinations give those places gastronomic renown. *Le Cours Gastronomique*, first published in 1809, includes a map of France that merely outlines the nation's borders and then charts the inner territory solely with agricultural products. Included are the wines of regions such as Bordeaux and the Rhône; Roquefort and Brie are named, with drawings of cheeses, and many charcuterie items are shown as well, such as sausages and cured hams. During the same period, Madame Adanson, in her influential and widely published book *La Cuisinière de la Compagne et de La Ville* lists cheeses by place name: Neufchâtel, Brie, Marolles, Cantal, and specifies the flavor characteristics and methods of proper storage of each. The flavor of the fromage des Vosges, Adanson writes, "is unique among all cheeses; the method of fabrication is a secret of the locality" (1827: 56).

Almost 200 years later, the esteemed *Oxford Companion to Wine* explains *terroir* as the "much-discussed term for the total natural environment for any viticultural site," where the primary components are soil, topography, and climate (Robinson 1999: 700). Although the Bordeaux, Napa Valley, and South Australia regions all use merlot and cabernet sauvignon grape varietals in their wine, and often similar production methods, their wines taste markedly different. In France, such variations are understood to have everything to do with where the grapevines are planted, hillside or valley, clay or calcareous soil, mild or harsh climate. With *goût du terroir*, location is destiny.

Hugh Johnson, leading wine expert and journalist, embraces this (seemingly) inevitable destiny (as do many other oenophiles). In *A World Atlas of Wine* he explains the varying flavor profiles of French wines with complex descriptions of the geography, climate, and geology: "[Bordeaux's] position near the sea and threaded with rivers gives it a more moderate and stable climate. Forests on the ocean side protect it from strong salt winds and rainfall" (Johnson 2003: 50). Within the region, "the distinctions between different soils and situations produce remarkable difference of flavor and keeping qualities" (Johnson 1983: 45), and finally, at one of the premier châteaus, Château Lafite-Rothschild, "Quality starts with the soil: deep gravel dunes over limestone. It [also] depends on the age of the vines: at Lafite an average of forty years" (1983: 60).

For French cheeses, the *goût du terroir* emerges in the type of grasses and wild plants the sheep or goats or cows eat when they are grazing, which depend on the geography of the pasturelands and thus influencing the flavor of the milk. In the pamphlet "Le Goût des Fromages; Le Goût de la France" (The Taste of Cheese; The Taste of France), part of an ongoing series put out by the French Ministry of Agriculture, the very taste of France is said to consist of a "mosaic of regional tastes which derive their flavors from geographical, historical, and cultural roots." The pamphlet goes on to discuss the various products and distinctive dishes of each region in France, providing recipes using local cheeses to show how "the nature of the soil, the climate, and the topography shape the cuisine and flavor." In these analyses, the physical environment (soil, weather, topography), not the tiller of the soil, or the shepherd, or the vintner, are the primary sources in creating the distinctive tastes of French wine and cheese.

Creating Their Own Destiny

A closer examination of historical events tells a different story. The natural environment *influences* the flavors of food and beverages, but ultimately the cultural domain, the foodview, creates the *goût du terroir*. The taste of place does not originate with the Mesozoic period collision of the African and European continental plates that defined France's geography and geology. Rather, beginning in the early 1900s, a group of *people* began to organize around this naturalized connection of taste and place, for they saw the potential benefits of a foodview celebrating the agrarian and rural way of life. French *taste-makers*—journalists, cookbook writers, chefs—and *taste producers*—cheese-makers, wine-makers, bakers, cooks—have long been allied in an effort to shape taste perceptions. Taste producers and taste makers intervened in an everyday occurrence, eating and drinking, and these advocates guided the French toward a certain relationship between soil and taste, *le goût du terroir*.

They worked hard to shape French judgments of the morsels and liquids that they put in their mouths. These artisans, critics, and commentators elaborated a new language of taste. This language was never purely aesthetic, however, solely an interaction of taste receptors in the mouth and the brain. These new translations of taste were part of a dialogue with nature. In France, this took place on the edge of their civilized world, the agrarian countryside. They created arguments linking place, taste, types of agriculture and quality that helped protect certain forms of agricultural production, and ultimately, helped to define French national cuisine. These discussions helped shape taste perceptions beyond France as well, for their claims about the taste of place now play an important role in twenty-first-century discussions of food and beverages.

Gastronomic writings of the period expressed these ideas. Madame Pampille says in her charming book, *Les Bons Plats de France: Cuisine Régionale*, first published in 1919, "Il n'est bon gibier que de France" (The only good game is to be found in France), and goes on to assert, "And don't talk to me about the German and Hungarian hares that have infested the markets over the past few years: these are large hares, stupid and without flavor" (1925: 23–24). Found in the "National dishes" chapter, her dictums on quality when it comes to game—that it needs to come from France and be raised in certain environments—disclose an emerging vocabulary and grammar of taste in twentieth-century France. She describes the taste of partridges grown in confined in spaces and fed rapeseed as being faded and dim, whereas the wild (or free) partridges roaming the plains and feeling hunger and thirst, have another taste entirely (1925: 24).

This book is full of recipes certainly, but perhaps it should also be considered a gastronomical treatise, a new physiology of taste in the manner of Brillat-Savarin. Here quality of flavor is linked to location and production style.

And speaking just of the glory and splendor of France and French cuisine is not sufficient for Pampille; distinct geographic regions provide specific taste experiences. The Savoie and Dauphine are lauded for their river trout, whose delicate flesh can only be appreciated when you eat it there. She has even stronger views about bouillabaisse, "the triumph of Marseille, it is only good when eaten in Marseille. Don't try to eat it in Paris" (1925: 143). Place matters.

Rural agricultural practices—a reliance on certain crops or livestock because they responded to the local climate and geography, harvesting the bounty of nearby rivers and seas—became the building blocks of what were named *regional cuisines*. A new connection emerged between agricultural practices, rural life, and food and drink, very much a reaction to the increased urbanization and industrialization of society. This may have been particularly strong in France since agriculture remained a large sector of the economy well into the twentieth-century. Cookbooks, food journalism and regional food guides were instrumental in developing this regional gastronomy and celebrating the taste of place.

At the turn of the century, Jean Fulbert Dumonteil, journalist and native of the Perigord region wrote: "The Alps and the Pyrenees, the Landes, Cevennes, Auvergne and the Jura send us small goat cheeses which have a marvelous flavor. The Limousin, Poitou, Bourbonnais, and Berry create sheep cheeses with a fine *saveur*" (1996: 40–41). Using *goût du terroir* to analyze not just individual ingredients or products like cheese and wine, but also dishes, emerges in the same period, a result of a new leisure activity: traveling in the countryside.

Curnonsky was an instrumental figure in the development of regional gastronomy, publishing inventories of regional dishes and guidebooks of stores and restaurants highlighting regional cuisine. The "Prince of Gastronomes," Curnonsky, born Maurice-Edmond Sailland, was the author of numerous books on food and gastronomy in France, publishing in every decade of the twentieth-century until he died in 1956. Included in over fifty works are *La France Gastronomique* (with Marcel Rouff) published in the 1920s, *Le Trésor Gastronomique* (an inventory of regional dishes written with Austin de Croze) in 1933, *Eloge de Brillat-Savarin* in 1931 and *Bon Plats, Bons Vins* in 1950. His life and career spanned a period that witnessed great changes in French cuisine and gastronomy, and he helped make them.

Curnonsky linked the physiology of taste to the particularity of place, taking the everyday practices of locals in various regions of France and creating encyclopedias, guides, and atlases dedicated to advertising and codifying their knowledge. His books are notable for their breadth, with listings of hundreds of recipes, or regional dishes, or restaurants. Depth, on the other hand, is another matter. You never hear the experiences and stories of the people responsible for these recipes, restaurants, or dishes, nor their histories. In his writings the taste of place is made timeless. In *Recettes de Provinces de*

France he says, "this work celebrates, in a very artistic fashion, the alliance between tourism and gastronomy I have promoted for fifty years and which is only possible in France, because this is a land of tremendous diversity" (1953:27).

Curnonsky lived during a period when many in France, from small *chambres de commerce* to corporations, became very interested in the development of rural tourism, linked to the rise in railway and car travel and the growth of urban areas. A gastronomic literature emerges that glorifies the various regions of France during 1910–1930, declaring it part of the glory of the French nation. Some of these efforts were initially part of a larger set of marketing initiatives by Michelin, the tire company, interested in developing various ways of getting people to use their cars to journey into the countryside for purposes of leisure (Harp: 2001). These are the earliest versions of what became the green Michelin guides, references on dining and lodging for all the regions of France, which became powerful arbiters of taste for tourists, French or from abroad. Curnonsky, along with his colleagues Austin de Croze and Marcel Rouff, helped develop regional gastronomy in part to support car and rail travel to the French countryside.

If people were going to leave the cafés and bistros of Paris, Lyon, and Marseille, they needed to have a destination and a celebration in mind—what could be better than wonderful food and wine? Another gastronome of the period, Edmond Richardin, in his book *L'Art du Bien Manger* devotes his introduction to a "gourmet geography of the regions of France." Essentially a prose poem that starts in Flanders and ends in Bearn, Richardin lists the gastronomic wonders of France, region by region: "the andouillettes of Cambrais, the trout of Dunkirk, the triumphant asparagus of Argenteuil." And "onwards to Brittany . . . with its Cancale oysters, lobsters and langoustines of Roscoff." In Bresse, Bugey, and the land of Gex: "Poulardes de Bresse, Belley sausages, Feillens apples, the cheese of Passin, a rival to the best Gruyère, and the blue cheese of Gex" (1913). He ends by exhorting gourmets to open their minds to the vast gastronomic possibilities of the French provinces.

These ingredients and dishes, now immortalized and codified, came to represent their regions and ultimately guaranteed their permanence, for they came to signify more than a dish using the locally available ingredients (bouillabaisse in and around Marseille, cassoulet in and around Carcasonne), but also to represent the taste of that place, wherever the dish may be consumed. Pampille's admonition to eat bouillabaisse only in Marseille notwithstanding, bouillabaisse became the iconic dish of the French Mediterranean the world over. In the spirit of Proust's madeleine, these ingredients and dishes became iconographic, the *lieux de mémoire* of certain places, their tastes of a France defined as a rich and diverse geography.

Grapes for wine have historically been one of France's largest agricultural products, and apparently *vignerons* were the earliest group of taste producers to realize the possibilities in promoting the link between place and quality;

they were the first to take this foodview and use it to their economic advantage. The 1855 Bordeaux wine classifications are generally considered the first attempt by those involved in wine production and sales to promote the quality of wines by their place of origin. These were developed internally by those involved in the Bordeaux wine industry, particularly wine brokers, to be used at the 1855 Exposition Universelle in Paris. These classifications were not monitored by the French state however. The movement to use ideas about place to make arguments about quality became increasingly important in the late nineteenth-century and became part of a serious sociopolitical movement to protect French agricultural products in the early twentieth-century, culminating with the founding of L'Institut National des Appellations d'Origine in the 1930s.

As the link between taste and place evolved in the early twentieth-century, taste producers, particularly the *vignerons*, involved the French state, arguing that legal and political means were needed to protect unique French products from international competition. They succeeded. The *vignerons* of the Champagne region were the first to use the legal system to create delimitations on production related to locale. The elevated status of champagne amongst the international bourgeoisie in the late nineteenth-century did little to contribute to the livelihoods of the laborers in the fields and much to threaten their identity. Their response was to turn to *terroir*, to fight for champagne as a product of the soil rather than as a placeless pretty label. The *vignerons* wanted to retain some proprietary rights to the name "champagne," now used all over the globe, so they turned to the soil. A series of events, especially the phylloxera epidemic of the 1890s, which threatened *vignerons* and *negotiants* alike, helped legitimize the idea that Champagne as a defined region was fundamental to the identity of champagne as a beverage, nationally or internationally. By 1908 Champagne was granted "the first recognized regional delimitation" (Guy 2003:150). *Certain* areas were judged to be in the Champagne region and only wines produced in that area could be sold with the label "Champagne." This came to be the model for protection of wine, cheese, and other products throughout France.

Taste, *Terroir*, and Quality

The Institut National des Appellations d'Origine (INAO) has been part of the French Ministry of Agriculture since 1935. Despite the activist legacy behind its creation, the direct result of the organizational efforts of vintners and others, the Institute's philosophy, enumerated in the official literature, is to "protect terroir." As the official literature of 1999 states:

> It has been known from ancient times that certain lands are made more suitable to the creation of products that retain, and in fact, draw out the specific flavors of that place.

> Due to this phenomenon, at the beginning of the century, the idea was born to create the notion of appellation d'origine, to acknowledge and protect it under the rubric of *Appellations d'Origines Contrôlées.*

As stated later on, the INAO was created in part to police the link between taste and place: "The INAO was initially charged to *identify* Wines and Eaux de Vie, to *codify* their usage for protection in France and abroad against all encroachments" (emphasis mine). Awarding a wine or cheese or any other food product the status of *Appellation d'Origine Contrôlée* put the official stamp on the connection between taste, locale, and quality.

In an explanation of *Appellations d'Origines Contrôlées* (AOC) and the management of terroir, the INAO states that the AOC system provides the "instruments" growing regions can use to fully take advantage of their resources: "With the extraction of the specifics (or characteristics) of their *terroir*, and the search to value and protect the agricultural possibilities in a geographic zone, AOC products can be genuine instruments for managing and supporting territory." But the consumer also needs to be involved in order for the system to work. Thus, though "standardization leads to delocalization ... [and so] supposes that the consumer takes the initiative, recognizes the superiority of a strongly identified product and agrees to pay the price." Therefore, the INAO oversees the local production process but also encourages the consumer to find and appreciate those items. The award of AOC status provides producers in the growing region with the economic, political, technical, and marketing support of a government agency. From the point of view of the INAO, places create distinct tastes. A phenomenon of nature, the mission of the Institute is to be a steward of the relationship between locale and flavor, and to encourage producers and consumers to embrace that concept.

The French foodview linking taste and place possesses a tremendous consistency over the past century, in effect preserving agrarian values and practices now often considered quaint and old-fashioned. Today, the INAO's mission could be seen to preserve a philosophy of production from an earlier era, before the advent of large-scale production, national and international distribution systems, and global consumption patterns. In France, though, the AOC system, and the artisan methods and locale-specific production it champions represent the best of France's agricultural riches. The other possibilities—large-scale industrialized farming, export commodity production of food and wines—is considered anomalous and problematic.

The state plays an important part in the continued possibility of a *goût du terroir* that remains powerful in an era of agriculture characterized by industrialization of practice and globalization of supply. This is a time when McDonald's is not found just on the St.Germain des Près but near Cavaillon in southwest France, and the European Union wants to regulate the size of duck cages used for holding ducks raised for foie gras (or liver) to appease animal rights activists in Britain. French farmers, historically well-organized and culturally powerful, protest regularly against the encroachment of regional and global market forces and regulations on their territory. In a 1999 trade dispute between the US and the EU, the US decided to create a 100 percent tariff for imported European luxury goods, including Roquefort cheese and foie gras. In protest, French farmers attacked a number of McDonald's restaurants in southwest France (the region where foie gras and Roquefort are produced) with rotten apples, tomatoes, and manure. A French farmer was quoted in the *New York Times* as saying: "My struggle remains the same ... the battle against globalization and for the right of people to feed themselves as they choose" (Cohen 1999).

How do the French keep fidelity to the *goût du terroir* in the face of all these changes? There are many strategies, and most revolve around the persistent commitment to traditional production methods, thus preserving what is now considered the *historical* quality of local flavors. Thus, there exists but one way to make a true cassoulet or bouillabaisse, only one place to find the real Roquefort cheese, only one type of red wine that truly speaks of "Bordeaux." Authenticity dominates the discourse when French food and wine producers talk about their wines, cheeses, foie gras, and more. In this case, authenticity is primarily determined by the production locale, though the "authentic identity" of the person making the cheese or wine comes under discussion as well.

Looking for Home

If you look at the link between taste and place made today, this association clearly contains a dimension of nostalgia. And such nostalgia extends beyond a taste memory for certain foods and drinks of a region, but also for a certain way of life. Barbara Kirschenblatt-Gimblett's definition of "heritage" can help make sense of why *goût du terroir* continues to be embraced in France: "Heritage is a 'value added industry'; heritage produces the local for export; heritage is a new mode of cultural production in the present that has recourse to the past" (1998: 149–53). The foodview based on *terroir* and *goût du terroir* initially elaborated a century ago as a means of protecting, preserving, and promoting artisan practices and regional identities allows the French, now primarily living in cities and towns, to flirt with a lifestyle more representative of the past than the present.

Local taste, or *goût du terroir,* is now evoked when an individual wants to remember an experience, explain a memory, or express a sense of identity. People themselves can possess the taste of their birthplace, or "*sentir le terroir.*" Despite their often very modern, urban lifestyles, the French retain a powerful connection to the land of their ancestors. *Gourmet* magazine explains to its American audience: "Even the most urbane boulevardier can become near-maudlin about his *terroir,* acknowledging roots reaching back to a province, a village, a family vegetable patch … his allegiance to the land of his fathers remains intact." In this form, "taste" in France mediates between the body and culture: the gustatory moment incorporates people's belief that the very soil, plants, climactic conditions, and animals make France a unique piece of the Earth, rather than a nation among many others. And for the French, the moment when the Earth travels to the mouth is a time of reckoning with their local memory and identity.

In an interview with the operators of a small press that prints books related to the Dordogne region, including cookbooks, they argued that the emphasis on "*terroir* has increased in the past thirty years, and it is primarily a form of nostalgia; people are searching for their *racines* or roots as an anecdote to their increasingly fast-paced, urban lives." Only in the last ten years, they argued, have urban sophisticates begun to embrace *cuisine du terroir*. Earlier it was considered uncomplicated peasant food, heavy and often bland and not of interest for cosmopolitan French people. The twenty-first-century understanding of the taste of place adopts the long-held view that places within France create unique flavors, only now celebrating these flavors increasingly involves rejecting the trappings of modernity and returning to earlier ways.[1]

In France, taste thus is a form of local knowledge. The success of the taste producers lies in their ability to create an association between place and quality. They appropriated the link between taste and place, and helped create legal and governmental mechanisms to champion location-based food and beverages. Thus today, local tastes define superior quality, which means the French are willing to pay a higher price. Burgundy wines are known to have different taste profiles than wines from Bordeaux and Languedoc, though all may be red wines. In contrast, Americans do not associate specific locales with flavor profiles in wine, rather they buy and taste according to grape varietal: Pinot Noir, Merlot, etc. The French also perceive that goods produced locally using a smaller scale of production are superior. An AOC wine produced from a single vineyard in Bordeaux is considered better than a blended wine from vineyards all over the Languedoc. Wine producers and consumers use *terroir* as an ordering and evaluative concept when it comes to quality of flavor, to the point that now in France *terroir* is used as a major means of marketing wines and asserting their quality. The main marketing slogan for the AOC region Coûteaux du Languedoc, located outside of Montpellier, is "L'art de faire parler le terroir" (The art of expressing the soil). Local taste is worth the price.

Goût du Terroir: Nature or Culture?

People's investments—cultural and economic—made the French word for soil signify so much: a sensibility, a mode of discernment, a philosophy of practice and an analytic category. *Terroir* and *goût du terroir* represent the gastronomic glory of France. What they *say* may embrace the timeless and essential notion of mother Earth, but what they have *done* is create a vision of agrarian rural France and convincingly put it in people's mouths.

The more I think about taste and place, however, the more I wonder if *goût du terroir* transcends France. The historical particulars of the "production of locality" are certainly unique to France, along with the tremendous cultural commitment to the notion. But when it comes to the idea that quality of flavor is linked to locally based, small-scale production that pays attention to natural conditions, I wonder if the French have captured and bottled, so to speak, a powerful dimension of taste more broadly defined. Along those lines, I would like to tell a story. Several years ago I was asked to speak to a group of professionals who run the food service at a leading Ivy League university. I discussed the importance of thinking about food from a cultural and historical perspective. As an introduction to the next event, a port tasting led by the school's sommelier, I spoke briefly about my research on *goût du terroir* in France and the AOC system. The director of the university food service, savvy to the importance of marketing in America to create elite market niches for certain products, looked at me skeptically, and said, "They are just trying to sell the sizzle and not the steak."

I stayed for the tasting and sat next to the director. The sommelier led us through a tasting of four different ports. (Though produced in Portugal, ports are subject to a control system similar to the French *Appellations d'Origine Contrôlées*, in fact some consider the system for port to be the historical precursor of that in France.) He began with two fairly inexpensive blended ports produced in large quantities. The third port was a vintage port, which means it was created from an unusually good harvest. Every year could be labeled "vintage"; however not every year is declared a vintage year because conditions were not considered favorable for producing high-quality wines. All the grapes came from a single vineyard (most ports are made from grapes picked in a number of vineyards), and only 39,000 bottles were produced, a very small quantity. The sommelier gave us this information, and we tasted the port.[2] After tasting two blended non-vintage ports, you could truly taste a difference. There was greater clarity and depth to the flavor. The Director looked at me, laughed, and said, "OK it's not just the sizzle. This port simply tastes better." Thousands of miles away, part of a culture with a very different foodview, we tasted place and understood quality.[3]

Notes

1. It could be argued that *goût du terroir* has come to define an aspect of French identity that is locally defined, but is ultimately part of the national project to preserve

and promote "Frenchness" in all its forms. In Arjun Appadurai's terms, the "production of locality" through taste helps constitute the meaning of "France."

2. It was a 1990 Quinta do Vesuvio Vintage Porto, stamped bottle number 14,295.

3. Thanks to Priscilla Parkhurst Ferguson and Kyri Claflin for their thoughtful readings of an earlier draft of this chapter.

References

Adanson, Aglae (L. E. Audot) (1827), *La Cuisinière de la Campagne et de la Ville*, Paris: Audot.

Appadurai, Arjun (1996) *Modernity at Large*, Minneapolis: University of Minnesota Press.

Cadet de Gassicon, Charles-Louis (1808), *Cours Gastronomique, ou les Diners de Manant-Ville*, Paris: Capelle et Renand.

Csergo, Julia (1999), "The regionalization of cuisines," in *Food: A Culinary History*, (ed.) J. L. Flandrin and M. Montanari, New York: Columbia University Press 502.

Cohen, Roger (1999), "Fearful over the future, Europe seized on food," *New York Times*, August 29, (4), 1.

Curnonsky (1950), *Bon Plats, Bon Vins*, Paris: M. Ponsot.

Curnonsky and Rouff, Marcel (1921). *La France Gastronomique*, Paris: F. Rouff.

Curnonsky and de Croze, Austin (1933), *Le Trésor Gastronomique*. Paris: Librairie Delagrave.

Curnonsky (1953), *Recettes de Provinces de France*, Paris: Les Productions de Paris.

Dumonteil, Jean Fulbert (1996), *Le Perigord Gourmand*, Castelnaud: L'Hydre.

Ferguson, Priscilla Parkhurst (1998), "A cultural field in the making: gastronomy in nineteenth-century France," *American Journal of Sociology*, 104: 3 (November).

Fremont, Armand (1996–98), "The land," *Realms of Memory: Rethinking the French Past*, (ed.) by Pierre Nora, New York: Columbia University Press, 2–36.

Guy, Kolleen (2003), *When Champagne Became French*, Baltimore: Johns Hopkins University Press.

Harp, Stephen (2001) *Marketing Michelin: Advertising and Cultural Identity in France*, Baltimore: Johns Hopkins University Press.

Institut National des Appellations d'Origine (1999), Official literature.

Johnson, Hugh (1983), *Modern Encyclopedia of Wine*, New York, Simon and Schuster.

——. (2003), *World Atlas of Wine*, London: Mitchell Beazley.

Kirschenblatt-Gimblett, Barbara (1998), *Destination Culture: Tourism, Museums, Heritage*, Berkeley: University of California Press.

Le Cours Gastronomique ou Les Divers de Menant-Ville (1809), Paris: Capelle et Renand.

Pampille, Mme. (1925), *Les Bons Plats de France: Cuisine Régionale*, Paris: Fayard.

Richardin, Edmond (1913), *La Cuisine Française du XIVe au XXe Siècle*, Paris: Editions de l'Art et Littérature.

Robinson, Jancis (ed.) (1999), *The Oxford Companion to Wine*, Oxford: Oxford University Press.

Serra, Sylvie (2000), Interview, Dordogne, March.

Serres, Olivier de (1600/1805), *Le Théâtre d'Agriculture et des Mesnages des Champs*, Paris: Societé d'Agriculture de la Seine.

26

Tasting Problems and Errors of Perception

Emile Peynaud

Tasting is a Difficult Art

The wine taster encounters difficulties at every stage of tasting, above all when learning to taste. The first of these is the problem of considering taste sensations at a given moment, in particular conditions, and of being able to focus one's attention at will on a specific characteristic. There is also the problem of freeing oneself from the influence of external factors and the various forms of suggestion which might alter one's perceptions. No less significant are the difficulties encountered when trying to describe sensations which are always difficult to put into words. The requisite effort of memory is also demanding, as are interpreting and evaluating the sensations one perceives. And these in turn presuppose a quick, accessible memory for wines and a wide tasting experience to provide the necessary comparative yardsticks.

The primary difficulty arises from the subjective nature of wine tasting, for it is based on personal impressions where the key factor is the taster's own personality. Unlike wine tasting, an objective phenomenon lends itself to measurements which can be expressed in figures; it exists independently of the observer. When weighing or measuring, for example, the result is always the same, whoever is doing it and whatever the time, technique, or equipment. It is not possible, however, to measure a taste or a smell, and attempts to do so have not met with much success.

We [can see] how arbitrary measuring individual primary tastes can be, how much more so, then, when measuring a combination of flavors. And sweetness, acidity, saltiness, and bitterness counteract and modify each other; they are not simply cumulative. Numerous olfactometers have also been tried, but none of them can dispense with the human nose. In one method, a given concentration of an odorous substance is placed at one end of a long tube, and at the other end the nose notes when the smell is first detected, measurement is made of the time it takes to become deodorized. Here again, the length of time for which the air retains aromatic elements is a measure of volatility rather than intensity. In another method, a measured amount of an odorous substance is released into a room with a controlled, odorless atmosphere; the apparatus serves to determine precisely the olfactory thresholds of the substance being tested per liter of air, but it is useless for measuring the odor intensity of a complex solution. In other experiments, air impregnated with wine odors is passed through a column of substances such as charcoal, silica, and alumina, and a measurement is made of the time it takes to become deodorized. Here again, the length of time for which the air retains aromatic elements is a measure of their nature and concentration, not necessarily of their odor intensity.

It is only possible to define the intensity of a taste or an odor by comparing it to an equivalent or alternative stimulus, an exercise which only makes any sense when the taste or smell involved is the same. And while we can state with certainty that one is stronger than the other, it is impossible to say by how much.

In other words, there is no simple proportional relationship between the concentration of any sapid or odorous substance and the sensation it provokes. It has been found that the relationship between the variation in concentration of stimulus required to produce a perceptible change in sensation and the total concentration is a constant. Put more plainly, this means that there is a perceptible change when a given amount of stimulus is added to a small initial quantity, but when the same amount is added to a large initial quantity the difference is no longer perceptible. Sensations are proportional to the logarithms of the concentrations of the stimuli. Without being an absolutely precise description, what this law expresses is that sensations increase in an arithmetic progression as the substance concentration increases in a geometric progression, which is also why they are difficult to evaluate. To double the intensity of a sensation requires four times the dose.

Tasting results depend on the overall competence of the professional taster; on his tasting ability, vocabulary, and the exact meaning he attributes to individual words, as well as on the importance he attaches to various qualities and faults... [I must] emphasize the importance of the taster's personality, for the value of any tasting judgment will depend on the quality of the taster. Every time he takes a glass in hand, the taster calls on all his expertise and professional experience. As the training of tasters varies, one can appreciate why judgments can vary, especially where borderline or unusual wines are concerned.

If one compares the notes and marks given to a series of wines by a group of tasters, one generally finds there is broad agreement for, say, eight out of ten wines. The two on which opinions differ are often enough either very fine wines or those that are technically faulty in some way. Some tasters disagree categorically and no amount of discussion will alter their opinion. Such disagreements used to irritate me until I realized that the aim of group tasting was precisely to highlight such differences in opinion. Tasters generally disagree less about what they perceive than how they interpret these perceptions, for each individual will have a personal image of the quality norms for a particular type of wine, and will consider this or that fault as more or less serious depending on his or her training. If wine tasters were unanimous in their judgments, then tasting as a group would be pointless; one opinion would suffice. By appealing to several people one gains a wide range of views, a sort of protective umbrella against error.

Some Tasting Pitfalls

Tasting and tasters are not infallible, and it must be said that the opinion of the same taster can vary with the conditions in which he is working.

When a taster has become accustomed to certain conditions, a regular tasting room, a particular shape of glass or *tastevin,* for example, then he may well be put off in different circumstances. For this reason tasting conditions should be as systematically organized as possible. [There are] numerous external factors which influence one's perceptions. Professional tasters try to avoid such errors by always tasting in the same environment, and by a consistent use of the same terms of reference for their comparisons.

The worst type of tasting takes place when visiting wine cellars, where the proprietor or cellar master wants to show his wine. Poupon and many others share this view: "There is such an abundance of vinous odors in a cellar and such an optimistic atmosphere that you find yourself in an olfactory context where impressions are easily distorted. In spite of habit, and whatever one thinks, the cellar is the place where one tastes least well."

The cellar master fills your glass from a vat, using a spigot or a pipette. He wipes the foot of the glass with his thumb and passes it to you. Even assuming the wine has been cleanly and correctly drawn, your tasting is very likely to be valueless. In the vinous atmosphere of the cellar it is impossible to judge the wine's own nose; all wines appear good because one cannot perceive their defects, and because there are no independent points of reference. It comes as a surprise when retasting the wine in a tasting room the following morning, to find oneself judging it much more severely.

Our daily physiological rhythm has a considerable influence on the sensitivity of our senses, and one should not be surprised if notes on the same wine vary, especially if they have been made at different times before, during, or after a meal, for example. One's appetite for wine varies according to the time of day, as does the sharpness of one's senses, which are at their keenest on an empty stomach. Thus the best time for tasting is at the end of the morning, before lunch, between say 11 a.m. and 1 p.m. Tastings very early in the morning are an unattractive proposition, but those which take place in the early afternoon, coinciding with digestion, are the most arduous and least effective of all. If need be, another possible time is around 6 p.m., even though one's tasting performance will not be so good.

When interpreting what one tastes there are other factors which need to be taken into account: palate fatigue and the phenomena of saturation with and habituation to certain characteristics, or what the specialists call the effects of convergence, when one's response to differences in stimulation is diminished. And the nature of the sensations themselves may change. The sense of smell especially is rapidly dulled; it cannot continue to perceive the same odor, even a strong one, for a prolonged period. Indeed, the stronger the odor and the longer one continues to smell it, the longer one's sense of smell will be inhibited. One gets accustomed to the smell of the apartment where one lives, the locality or laboratory where one works, precisely because one can no longer smell it. Similarly, people become so used to the smell of their own perfumes or the lingering smell of tobacco smoke that they no longer notice it themselves; but it can offend the people around them.

A similar mechanism accounts for the way in which the consumer gets used to the taste of a certain wine and then will not accept, or at any rate will be less appreciative of, other wines even if they are a better quality. How many people, having regularly drunk a faulty wine, find they can no longer recognize its defects?!

It is sometimes said that certain characteristics change rapidly during the course of tasting and that bouquets fade; but having disappeared they may also return. This is said to be the case with the moldy, vegetal smell called *rambergue* (garden mercury) in Bordeaux. On tasting a wine with this character, the first impression is very unpleasant, but it gradually becomes less obtrusive, and at the third or fourth sip the fault becomes acceptable; finally, by dint of continued tasting, one no longer notices the fault. It is not that the characteristic increases or diminishes, as is said to be the case, but that one is more or less sensitive to it according to the mood of the moment and, above all, because habituation has blunted perception. After a few minutes' rest the same unpleasant smell will be found again in the same glass.

For me the following incident is the best illustration of the temporary inhibition of the sense of smell. A Médoc vineyard owner heard from his clients that his wine had an unpleasant and unacceptable taste, one which he could not detect himself. He asked for my advice as an independent judge. The wine was lodged in barrels in a new cellar which had been treated against woodworm. Immediately upon opening the door, the moldy smell of the product used was suffocating, but after a few minutes in the building it became imperceptible, as though it had disappeared. Tasting the wine on the spot, I found it attractively fruity and showing its class—not a trace of the nasty odor. However, half an hour later, in the car on the way back,

I suddenly found I could smell the insecticide again very strongly. In the tasting room the next day, I found the wine overwhelmed by this chemical stink. The wine had acquired the defect in the cellar atmosphere, saturated with the vapors of the insecticide, but one could not notice it in the building itself. This example demonstrates how background smells can influence one's judgment. Inside the cellar my sense of smell, selectively saturated by the odor of the product in the air, had become insensitive to the same smell in the wine while remaining capable of detecting all the other odors. When the inhibitory effect had passed, the incriminating smell became quite clear again and then obliterated the rest.

In a different category, certain unpleasant tastes such as acidity, bitterness, and astringency are said to tire the palate rapidly. During the course of repeated tasting, they reinforce each other so that, when comparing two tannic wines, for example, the impression of hardness becomes more pronounced at each successive taste and the wines appear increasingly harsh. In the case of acid wines they become sharper and sharper. Long tastings can also irritate the mucous membranes and make them unduly sensitive to acidity and astringency.

The passage of alcohol across the mucous membranes of the mouth and nose also results in a certain fatigue during extended tasting; even spitting all the wine out will not avoid this effect. The taster should not wait until he is tired before breaking off.

Finally, the effects of contrast can also alter one's judgment: A dry white tastes more acid after a sweet one; a tannic red seems harder when tasted after a supple red. To avoid these misleading results, the wines should be grouped in a logical order before being tasted. Where professional tastings are concerned in Bordeaux, red wines are generally tasted first, starting with the lightest, followed by dry whites, and finishing with medium-dry and sweet whites in order of increasing sweetness. Rosés can be tasted before the reds or the whites. In regions making predominantly dry white wines, these are usually tasted before red wines.

The aim of this chapter has been to point out some of the many pitfalls which the taster should know how to avoid. What singles out a taster as a professional is precisely the fact that he is well aware of these problems and takes them into account when tasting.

The Wine Taster is Easily Influenced

Suggestion is the insinuated thought, the idea planted in someone's mind. When a wine taster has a tasting problem to solve, he is wide open to suggestion, very susceptible to the impressions of other people. He is easily influenced and easily led astray, at least when the perceptual differences involved are small. He may be pointed in one direction or another quite discreetly, simply by the way a question is framed, by the wording of a label, or by the way samples are presented. Thus he may be put on the right path or deliberately misled.

The taster is subject to autosuggestion as well. When short of information he tends to imagine, extrapolating from the slenderest of details glimpsed and interpreted. Suggestion and autosuggestion can both induce tasting errors, and the taster must be able to resist them. He needs to be wary; a taste imagined or anticipated is already half perceived.

Some cases of suggestion have already been mentioned, in particular, the effect that color and appearance have on the perceived tasting qualities of rosé wines, and there are numerous other examples.

Let us look first at the evidence presented by Pasteur, and quoted by Got. He describes a revealing episode which he observed during a series of tastings by a group of expert tasters, where wines which had been subjected to heat treatment were compared with the identical wines which had not.

> The group had just got used to telling the differences, large and small, between the two samples that I gave simultaneously to each member. From then on it was easy to predict that if, without their knowing it, I were to ask them to compare two identical samples, which they still thought were different and in which they had hitherto found differences, their imaginations would lead them to find further real differences.
>
> So, without having said or done anything which might arouse suspicion, I gave each person two glasses containing the same wine from the same bottle. Each of them, convinced that one glass contained a wine which had been heat-treated and the other glass an untreated wine, noticed differences between the two samples.
>
> (Got 1955)

In the same way, if a taster is asked to compare a filtered wine with the same wine unfiltered, and he already has the preconceived idea that filtering tires and thins a wine, he will indeed find that the clearer wine is leaner and less rich than the other.

What passes through the mind of a taster when, confronted with two glasses of wine to compare, he is asked to describe the differences? He tastes the first glass attentively and methodically, carefully noting its appearance and nose, and then, on the palate, its attack, evolution, finish, and length. Moving on to the second glass, he compares the same sequence of impressions to his memory of those in the first wine. Having been told there is a difference to be found, he will always find one; or, more precisely, he will perceive one, real or imaginary. Suppose the taster has judged the second glass to be more supple and thus more attractive than the first, he does not stop there. He will go back to the first wine and make the same comparison in reverse. If he finds it less supple than the second, his initial conclusion is confirmed and he has good ground for saying that there is a real difference. If, on the other hand, his first impression is not confirmed, or if he judges the wine differently on this occasion, he has to say that he can find no perceptible difference between the two glasses. However he will not say "It's the same wine," rather "There is no appreciable difference." It is difficult for a taster to admit that he can find no difference between two wines and few are capable of such a frank admission.

The following incident which I experienced made me think about the powerful influence of autosuggestion. In a grand restaurant in the Etoile quarter of Paris, we were having oysters, and to go with them we ordered a bottle of 1970 Château Carbonnieux, a classed growth Graves from Léognan. The wine waiter, his official *tastevin* hanging around his neck, questioned our choice: "But that's a Bordeaux, and you don't drink a sweet wine with oysters..." "But Carbonnieux is a dry wine..." (I knew it was dry, I have analyzed it, it has but a trace of fermentable sugar in it: 1.5 grams.) "Gentlemen, everybody knows that all white Bordeaux are sweet." We insisted on our choice of course and enjoyed the vigor and aromatic concentration in this fine wine. Afterwards we suggested to the wine waiter that he might like to try the wine to confirm that it was actually quite dry. He tasted it and declared triumphantly: "Just as I said, it isn't dry, it's sweet!" He had the deep-seated and erroneous conviction that all white Bordeaux are sweet, and thus, in good faith, he found the Carbonnieux to be sweet.

Just for the pleasure of it I will round off the discussion of this subject with an extract from Rabelais. The content is perhaps a bit exaggerated but it is, after all, allegorical and must be one of the clearest ever descriptions of autosuggestion. His point is that where worship of the divine bottle is concerned, even fountain water will taste like wine if the drinker's imagination so wishes.

> Bacbuc said to us: "A long time ago a wise and chivalrous Jewish captain, leading his people through the desert in a state of famine, obtained manna from heaven which their hunger led them to imagine tasted like the meat they used to eat. The same applies here. As you sip this wonderful water you will taste whatever wine you care to call to mind. Now, use your imaginations and drink!" Which we did. Then Panurge exclaimed:
>
> "By Jove, this is Beaune, and better than any I ever drank before."
>
> "Well, I'll be... ," cried brother Jean, "this is a fine and lively Graves..."
>
> "To me it's a Minervois," said Pantagruel, "because that's what I thought of before drinking."
>
> "Drink, drink," urged Bacbuc, "once, twice, thrice; and by changing your minds you will taste whichever flavor or liquor you have thought of."

References

Got, N. (1955), *La Dégustation des Vins*, Perpignan.

——. (1958), *Les Livres de l'amateur de Vins*, Perpignan.

Poupon, P. (1957), *Pensées d'un Dégusteur*, (1975), *Nouvelle Pensées d'un Dégusteur*, Nuits-Saint-Georges: Confrérie des Chevaliers du Tastevin.

——. (1973), *Plaisirs de la Dégustation*, Paris: Presses Universitaires de France.

27
On the Zeedijk

Richard Watson

In late December 1628, or early January 1629, René Descartes arrived in Franeker in Friesland. Just a few weeks earlier, he had had a private interview with Cardinal Bérulle, founder of the Oratorian teaching order in France, rival of the Jesuits, who was in the process of forming the Compagnie du Saint-Sacrement, a militant secret society of laymen to fight for the Catholic cause by eliminating Protestantism in France. The cardinal was a strange mixture of astute politician, courtier, and mystic. He talked familiarly with God, angels, and the Queen Mother every day. He had convinced the First Minister Richelieu to crush the last stronghold of Protestantism in France, La Rochelle, which fell in late October with Cardinal Bérulle marching triumphantly among the victors.

No one knows what Cardinal Bérulle, flushed with triumph, said to Descartes, but the result was that within weeks Descartes was about as far away from militant Catholicism as you could get in Europe in the seventeenth century, standing on the steps of a Protestant university founded in 1585 and known as a haven for persecuted Protestants from all over Europe. He did not return to France for sixteen years, well after Cardinal Bérulle was dead.

In Franeker—literally God's Acre—Descartes lived in a castle nearly as large as the Reformed church it faced down the wide main street. It was owned by the Sjerdemas, a prominent Catholic family. In this castle Descartes wrote the first draft of his famous *Meditations on First Philosophy* in which he bases certainty on the phrase "I think, therefore I am" and which earned him the title of The Father of Modern Philosophy. But in the winter of 1629, at the age of thirty-two, although he had a high reputation as a mathematician and philosopher, he had published nothing. He sat in his room, looking north out over the flat *polder* to the *zeedijk,* the low dike that held back the sea.

I sit now in an old fisherman's cottage under that zeedijk and look across the flat polder south toward Franeker just six miles away, visible only as points of orange light at night. I wonder why Descartes came here. I am writing a book titled *The Death of Descartes*. After it is finished I am going to write *The Birth of Descartes*. Yes, I know. But for most great men—perhaps for anybody—you have to understand their deaths before you can comprehend their births.

The Netherlands is a land of low relief but of infinite variation. When I was being shown around the grounds of Endegeest Castle near Leiden (a small but very elegant château that Descartes later rented for several years—servants, livery, and moat), my guide, Baron Schimmelpenninck, publisher of Martinus Nijhoff books, said, "See that large drop-off over there? We're on higher ground here. That's what protects the castle during floods."

I strained to see.

"There, at the line of trees."

Then I saw it. Eighteen inches. Actually, my guide said, it was slightly over three feet because it slanted down gently after the drop-off.

"You'll begin to see the differences after you've been here awhile," he said.

But I lived under the zeedijk for several months before I saw what someone pointed out to me, that inland was a parallel road that was in fact a lower dike, and beyond that another lower ridge, barely discernible at all. Three lines of defense are common against the sea. They are known as the waking dike, the sleeping dike, and the dreaming dike. Like Descartes, I thought, who was known to sleep late, to lie in bed of a morning meditating, and who found his profession as a philosopher in a dream.

Soon after we arrived in the Netherlands, my wife Pat and I went into a large cheese shop. "What shall we get?" she said.

On the shelves were perhaps a hundred large rolls of hard yellow cheese, six inches thick and nearly three feet in diameter. We had just spent seven months in Paris, eating cheese. I looked at the array and smiled. "It doesn't matter," I said. "They're all the same."

The proprietress heard me and was outraged. First, they differ as to the farms where they were made. Then they differ in being young, middle-aged, and old. Middle age is actually *belegen* cheese, that is, cheese lying there, aging, between youth and old age, and this middle-aged cheese is also divided into young, middle-aged, and old. But more than that, in a fine shop like hers, we need not be restricted only to five ages. She could give us cheese of any age, month by month, from one to twenty-four. So what did I want?

"The oldest," I said.

She grumbled quietly as she cut a piece. It was the right choice, and the most expensive. This is plain cheese. It also comes, all ages, spiced with cumin or cloves or various herbs. Very old clove-spiced cheese is most Frisian, the finest product. The whole cloves have become soft, there are many of them, and you chew them up. Descartes must have eaten such cheese—he remarked on the pungent smell of spice in the Netherlands—and he must have been as bemused as we were.

Descartes said nothing about Dutch cheese in his letters, nothing about food at all except that he recommended that one should eat lightly—not easy in the Netherlands. And he once said that if the Netherlands did not have as much honey as God promised the Israelites, it was within the bounds of probability that it had more milk. He was said to be a virtual vegetarian, and like any Frenchman who has a piece of ground at least two feet square, he kept a garden. Here in Friesland in winter he would eat carrots and cabbage, potatoes and parsnips, leeks and lentils, of which you can be sure there are many varieties.

The wind is almost always blowing in Friesland. In the dead of winter it reaches gale force for days at a time and will knock you flat if you are not prepared for it. We sleep in a loft under the eaves. The wind howls around our ears and the roof tiles clack and clatter. Like being on a ship in a storm on the North Sea, Pat says, without the inconvenience of a heaving deck. When we sit around the stove reading at night, outside the wind rages with such fury that you imagine you are on the Russian steppes. But if you step out the door, although the wind may take your breath away, it isn't cold. All winter the temperature has ranged between 33 and 45 degrees Fahrenheit. It has rarely been below freezing, with ice on the pond in mid-December for only three or four days, and then not strong enough for skating. They say it has been an unusually mild winter—no doubt like the one Descartes complained of in 1633–34 when he was writing his *Meteorology,* during which he managed to study only one snowflake. When Samuel Sorbièrre visited Descartes in 1642, he characterized the Netherlands as four months of winter and eight months of cold. A neighbor says the prediction for this year is that it will warm up in July. He tells of the year you could eat outside from mid-April to mid-October. This mid-April the temperature continues the same, but the length of the day has increased from pitch-black at 4 p.m. in December to dusk now at 9 p.m. The birds are nesting and the jonquils are in bloom.

There is not a lot of sun here. Pat marks time by referring to the day the sun shone all day. When the sun does shine on a warm day—which means no wind—everyone moves dinner tables outside to eat. In the towns where the houses are continuous and face right onto the sidewalks, at noontime you have to walk in the street because everyone is sitting at a table on the sidewalk in front of their houses eating dinner.

The weather changes a dozen times a day. Fog, overcast, light rain, heavy showers (squalls, actually, for we are in fact in the middle of the sea, held back by the zeedijk, our house a stationary boat planted on the sea bottom, nothing but the zeedijk keeping us from casting adrift in our bed), snow flurries, sleet and hail, and sun. The sky is enormous as are the clouds, and huge rainbows reach almost to the zenith. Sun and moon through clouds, spectacular sunrises and sunsets in tulip colors, rays of sun and shadow on the sky. All that billows and blows…

But on the ground all is straight lines. The green line of the grass-covered zeedijk, the brown reeds along the long blue pond, the green-and-brown fields beyond extending into blue haze on the horizon. Farmhouses, small villages, steeples rise tiny out of the flat polder in the distance. All colors shade into pastels. Out every window are Dutch landscape and skyscape paintings, always the same, always different.

Why did Descartes come here? He said he preferred living in a desert, where there are few people, where there is silence and solitude so one can think. In Paris, the bustle and busyness of the city ran away with his thoughts. His friends importuned him. In Friesland he could escape.

"In what other land," he wrote in 1630 to his friend the poet Guez de Balzac, "can one enjoy freedom so entire?" He was living in Amsterdam then, but for him it was another desert. "In this great city," he said, "where everyone but me is engaged in commerce, each is so concerned for his own profit that I could stay here all my life without ever being noticed. I walk every day among the confusion of the crowds with as much freedom and repose as you would have in a park, and I pay no more attention to the people I see than I would to the trees and animals I might encounter in a forest." This is perhaps the first statement, not of alienation, but of the joyful anonymity one can have in a great city and nowhere else.

But most of Descartes' years in the Netherlands were spent outside small towns like Franeker, in isolated houses like our fisherman's cottage. He tended his garden, he dissected animals for his treatise on anatomy, he lay abed thinking and writing. In his leisure—but this was all his leisure—he rode, hunted, fenced, listened to music, and talked with friends. He claimed that he did not read books, but he did. He was enthusiastic about the use of the organ in the Reformed church. He complained that country neighbors can sometimes be more bothersome than city friends. Did visitors then, as now, just drop in and think nothing of staying for four or five hours? Probably. Descartes apologized for his Dutch, although he wrote and spoke it fluently, and also knew Frisian. We know neither, but Frisian and English make up a subgroup of the Germanic family of languages, and since it is the closest relative of English, we often halfway understand.

Our closest neighbors are a retired zeedijk worker and his sister, about a hundred yards down the road. They loaned us a book on dikes. The land is sinking and the sea is rising and "a day will come when nothing more can be done. Then the time will have come for the Netherlands, like children's sandcastles when the tide comes in, to disappear from the scene." The first zeedijk here was built in 1570 and was 2.01 meters high. It was raised to 2.81 meters in 1571 and was at that height when Descartes was here. In 1930, it was raised to 5.25 meters, and then after disastrous storms and floods to 9.4 meters in 1975. It cannot be raised higher because additional weight would just make it sink into the soft sea bottom on which it rests. Our house is a meter below mean sea level, the fields out there a bit lower. At night we can hear waves rolling onto the zeedijk.

We are from St. Louis, the home of Switzer's licorice, a favorite since childhood, so we were naturally attracted to the open bins of licorice in the stores here. Licorice is called *drop.* Drop ranges in color from light brown to dark black, and in hardness from very soft to crystal, but on first view they differ most obviously in shape. There is a bin of small cats, one of farmers and farmhouses, another of money—fat disks with a number impressed on one side and a dollar sign on the other—and many, many more. I picked up a licorice drop and popped it into my mouth and promptly spat it out. It was licorice, but...

Licorice drops come in mild, medium, and severe strength; these in plain, or in low sweet, medium sweet, and double sweet, and in low salt, medium salt, and double salt. I had made my first test on a double salt. Unbelievable. They differ also, of course, in brand name. My classification is the result of empirical tests, but I thought I might be exaggerating the number of kinds, so I asked a native Frisian. He was aghast.

"There are forty or fifty varieties, *at least,*" he said. And this merely in taste alone. He warned me against getting an inferior brand of his favorite small cats. He also recommended laurel leaf licorice—not only in the shape of laurel leaves but wrapped around laurel leaves—that he particularly liked. Licorice also comes wrapped around mint leaves and with sal ammoniac. He also told me that I had missed a distinction in the cheese. All varieties come in either 48 percent, 40 percent, or 28 percent fat.

Two miles from our house in the village of Tzummarum there is an excellent bakery, Striksmas. (All Frisian surnames end in *-ma,* meaning "of.") The bread comes with hard or soft crust in white, whole wheat, and rye; fine, medium, and coarse grained; and plain or sprinkled on top with oatmeal, poppy seeds, or sesame seeds. They bake all of these every day and all are delicious. When I remarked on this to our landlords who live in The Hague, they commiserated with us and brought us samples from their neighborhood bakery that produces a dozen different kinds of white bread alone, and varieties of another dozen different kinds of dark bread.

Sixteen years is a long time to stay away from your native land when it is virtually just across the border. In a few days Descartes could have been in Paris. He had spent over a year in the Netherlands when he was twenty-two, studying mathematics and architecture in the military school run by Maurice, prince of Nassau, the most brilliant military strategist of his time. Maurice is an excellent patron saint for Descartes. The prince loved mathematics. On his deathbed in 1625, a minister asked him to state his beliefs. "I believe," Maurice said, "that 2 + 2 = 4 and that 4 + 4 = 8. This gentleman here," he said, referring to a mathematician at his side, "will inform you of the details of the rest of our beliefs."

For nine years between 1619 and 1628, Descartes had traveled in Denmark, Germany, Poland, Hungary, Austria, Moravia, Bavaria, Bohemia, Switzerland, Venice, Italy, and France. He had been in Paris much of the two years before his interview with Cardinal Bérulle, and had talked about locating in the country. The Descartes family owned houses and farms in Poitou, Touraine, and Brittany. He had wide choice and obviously enjoyed his stays in the French countryside. He apparently had said nothing about going to the Netherlands, although he had visited the Frisian Islands from northern Germany during his travels. But soon after seeing Cardinal Bérulle he packed up and left. These flat polders and this cool, even climate are an immense change from the hilly, wooded land where he grew up. I feel the difference because the landscape in southwestern Iowa where I was born is much like that in Touraine where Descartes was born. Did he miss the lack of mystery and hidden things, the continual change of prospect, that the flat, treeless polder rules out?

Descartes left his financial affairs in the hands of his closest friend in Paris, Claude Picot, later known as the Atheist Priest. This is probably because of the notorious story of Picot's deathbed benefice. Picot was traveling in rural France—this was long after Descartes' own death—when he was taken violently ill. Perhaps he had a stroke. They knew he was dying at the inn where he lay, so summoned the village priest. Picot said to this priest that he would bestow a very handsome benefice on the local parish, on one condition. No mumbo jumbo. No chanting, no last rites, no Latin. He was himself a priest. His conscience was clear. Just let him die in peace. The local priest was not happy with this, but agreed. Then when Picot seemed very near the end, in a coma apparently, the priest could restrain himself no longer. He began the incantation. Picot opened one eye and said, "I can still take back the money." So the priest fell silent and Picot died in peace.

Koek translates as "gingerbread." It comes spiced mild, medium, and strong; fine, medium, or coarse textured; dry, medium, and moist; in loaves, long slices (called calves' legs), and cupcake. It also comes in the form of cake, brownies, cookies, and puff pastry. Also plain, with raisins, or with frosting. In fact, I am told that this is all wrong. Just because all these items are basically what I perceive as brown gingerbread, they do not at all belong to only one category. Mine is an outsider's empirical categorization that the Dutch do not recognize. But could an outsider ever get it right? Once I held up two packages of very dark, moist German rye bread and asked the grocery-van driver (he comes by our house once a week) if they were the same. He was scandalized.

"*Very* different," he said, but without enough English to be precise.

I bought them both. Indistinguishable.

Catholic commentators say Descartes would have been perfectly safe living and publishing in France. But Descartes opposed Aristotle, and the Parliament of Paris did pass a decree in 1624 forbidding attacks on Aristotle on pain of death. Vanini had been burned alive in 1619 for giving natural explanations of miracles—one of the advantages Descartes claimed for his physics—and more than a dozen heretics were burned alive in France during Descartes' lifetime. What is more, Descartes was making fun of astrology right at the time Richelieu was having horoscopes cast for making decisions of state.

In 1623, there was a Rosicrucian scare in Paris—placards appeared saying the Brethren were moving, invisible among the populace. Descartes was accused of being a Rosicrucian, and with mock indignation he defended himself by pointing out that everyone could see that he was not invisible. He rejected the magical and mystical beliefs of the Rosicrucians, but he took their motto as his own: *He who lives well hidden, lives well.* Like them, he practiced medicine without charge, tried to increase human longevity, was optimistic about the usefulness of science in improving the human lot, did not marry, and changed residences often. During twenty-two years in the Netherlands he lived in at least eighteen different places. Having lived here awhile myself now, I suspect he was simply looking for a change. In any event, if it were not for the Saint Descartes Protective Association, Descartes might be known now as The Greatest Rosicrucian (just as Sir Isaac Newton might be classified as The Greatest Alchemist). We are so in need of squeaky-clean heroes that we present our great thinkers as Paradigms of Truth and Virtue rather than as the cranks they really were. Of course great men have to get only one or two major things right for people to forget the hundreds of things they got wrong.

Descartes' happiest time in the Netherlands was when he lived with Helena Jans from 1634 to 1640. He prepared his greatest works for publication during these years. He and Helena had a child, Francine, who died at the age of five of scarlet fever; she couldn't breathe, she turned purple, and she died. Descartes said her death was the greatest sorrow of his life, and that he was not among those philosophers who thought one must refrain from tears to prove himself a man.

A number of Descartes' biographers don't even mention his daughter. Or they speak of the deplorable incident of his illegitimate child. But Francine was baptized and is listed in the register of legitimate births in the Reformed church at Deventer. What this might mean about Descartes' religious beliefs is more horrifying to good Catholic Cartesian scholars than illegitimacy.

The Dutch are precise. Our house is rented by the week, in seven-day measures, not by the imprecise month. That means that in twelve months there are thirteen four-week rent periods. (The Dutch have been the world's most astute capitalists for four centuries. Even the French still rent by the month.) It is a weekend house but it has everything we could want. First, no telephone. A grand piano. Good beds and chairs. It is the only house we've ever been in except our own where there is good light for reading everywhere and even a good light for the piano. We love it here.

Dutch houses have huge picture windows, and it is considered peculiar to pull the drapes or shades, day or night. In the seventeenth century when Descartes was here, foreigners commented on how beautiful Dutch interiors were, how elegant the furniture, how clean. The old paintings show it. You can still look in the windows to see. I run four or five miles every morning and cannot help but look into farmhouse windows as I pass by. Anyone inside looks back and waves. The window is not a barrier. I sit writing far back in a comer from the big windows facing onto the road, but everyone who walks by peers in, sees me, and waves. It is still surprising to me, but I wave back. The best views into houses are at night. We leave bare the windows facing the pond, but when we sit around the stove reading at night we pull the drapes across the windows facing the road. There really is no one out there, but it makes us feel more easy. We hope our neighbors will just think us foreign.

Is this openness a heritage of Calvinism? Nothing to hide in here? No one knocks when they come to the door, they just walk in. Neighbors, meter readers, postmen, repairmen, a schoolteacher from Franeker who heard we were here, and a newspaper reporter from Leeuwarden who learned from the schoolteacher that I was writing a book on Descartes. The schoolteacher stayed five hours. He was my informant about licorice drops. When the reporter left after two hours he asked if he could return to interview me.

"I thought that was what you were doing," I said.

"Oh no," he replied. "I wasn't taking notes."

Some days later he came and stayed the afternoon. The reporter warned me that after his story appeared, other reporters would come and disturb my solitude. I said I'd chance it. That was six weeks ago. The story has not appeared yet. He said when it did he would bring me a copy. Things are slow out here on the polder below the zeedijk. That's probably one good reason why Descartes came here.

The reporter had been a philosophy assistant at Groningen University, so he knew all about Descartes. There is very little hope of finding a permanent place in the Dutch university system these days, so he became a reporter. They are eliminating 250 teaching positions throughout the Netherlands just this year. The university business is shrinking all over Europe, but jobs of all sorts are scarce in the Netherlands. Government propaganda promotes the view that you have performed a national service if you are willing to go on unemployment, or to take early retirement, to allow someone else the opportunity to have a job. The retired dike worker down the way looks to be about fifty. He did not want to retire. He takes long walks along the dike half a dozen times a day.

"It is very difficult," the reporter said. "The Dutch like to work."

Storm warning! All out for the zeedijk! It is in their blood. The Netherlands is the grandest sandcastle ever made on a beach. Who would not cry at being drawn away from such colossal play?

Someone sent me a clipping from Ripley's "Believe It or Not": "René Descartes (1596–1650), the French philosopher and mathematician, learning that he would have to arise at 5 a.m. in a lucrative teaching position, warned that the cold morning air would be fatal to him—and died within four months."

Descartes had been invited to the court of Queen Christina of Sweden. Why did he go? He had turned down very handsome pensions from several French noblemen. He said he did not want to be anyone's servant. He did not need the money. He went probably because Sweden had been a big winner at the end of the Thirty Years' War in 1648, and that made Queen Christina the most powerful and important (is there a difference?) monarch in Europe. She was accumulating great scholars and writers, so why not add Descartes to her collection? Descartes was like the professor in the sticks who waits all his life for the fabled call from Harvard. And lo, one day it actually comes. But it is too late, he is past his prime, he is an extinct volcano, recognition is as much a burden as a joy to him now. But he has to go anyway.

Descartes was fifty-three. Christina was twenty-two. She had a reputation for disconcerting the composure of dignified men. Once she taught her maids—who purportedly did not know French—to sing some dirty French songs, and then had them perform in front of the very old and distinguished French ambassador. She knew perfectly well Descartes' reputation for lying in bed until eleven o'clock in the morning, meditating, but she perversely had the great philosopher rise early enough to get dressed and ride in an open carriage across town—he was staying with the French ambassador—to give philosophy lessons to her at 5 a.m. She had Descartes write the lyrics to a light ballet in which she herself danced the role of Pallas Athena. She had him write a five-act comedy.

More reasonably, she had him write the statutes for a Swedish Academy of Arts and Sciences. Descartes had already got the message. In the statutes he specified that foreigners could not be members of the academy. He wanted out.

It was while delivering these statutes, at five o'clock in the morning on February 1, 1650, that Descartes caught a chill. Ten days later, in a land where (he said) in winter men's thoughts freeze like the water, he died. This denouement is sometimes spoken of as Sweden's only contribution to Modern Philosophy. Descartes had often said that he expected to live to be a hundred. Christina quipped that the great mathematician miscalculated by nearly fifty years.

Queen Christina also said, "I love storm, and dread it when the wind drops."

On a rare day here when the wind does drop, the silence is deafening. Once I awoke in the middle of the night and it was the same sensation that I had years ago waking up in port with the engines turned off after having crossed the Atlantic on an ocean liner. The same thing—waking up in the middle of the night because it is suddenly quiet—happened to me a few times also in Paris. But there, after a few moments, the noise starts up again with the roar of cars and trucks. One is bombarded with noise in a city: construction, people, radio and television, the telephone, sirens, and bells—all jarring and startling, not like the wind. City noise, in itself and for what it draws your distracted attention to, is destructive of meditative thought. It can, perhaps, whirl you along in even higher flights of virtuosity. But city thoughts seldom come to rest.

The sugar cookies here are excellent—plain, or with peanuts, almond slices, raisins, or frosting on top. Yellow cake varies from bakery to bakery according to the amount of butter, sugar, and eggs. Pudding is called *vla* and is sold in wide-topped milk bottles. It comes in plain, vanilla, lemon, chocolate, and strawberry. A pretty combination is half-and-half strawberry and chocolate, lengthwise in the bottle. Again, our city landlords scoff at this paucity of country flavors of *vla*. We should see the selection in The Hague.

I had the most difficulty working out the differences in *pap*, which is porridge that also comes in wide-mouthed milk bottles. Whole or skimmed milk or buttermilk, made with barley, wheat, corn, or rice flour, with or without whole grains mixed in. Sweet or sour, plain or caramel flavored. Before I knew it was porridge that you were supposed to eat hot, I was testing it cold. The grocery-van driver set me straight. The next week I complained that when heated it is almost as runny as plain milk, not like porridge at all. He led me to understand, using a combination of English and Frisian, that any respectable family makes its own porridge at home, as thick as you like.

The days pass...

We may all of us, like Descartes, be overestimating the amount of time we have left to live.

"I am out of my element here," Descartes said in the depth of the Swedish winter in the glacial atmosphere of a snow queen and a court filled with intrigue.

"But it doesn't make any difference that he had to be up at five in the morning," a Swede remonstrated with me. "It is dark all the time in Sweden in winter, so people don't pay much attention to the hour. It doesn't matter."

The wind blows, the light changes continuously, and the urgent clouds fly over the patient polder.

In Franeker, just over there on the horizon, Descartes wondered about the possibility that he might be deceived in thinking the world existed. There might be nothing but his own mind and a demon making him think he was experiencing a world. The town is built on a low, pancake-shaped mound a few meters higher than the surrounding ground. You hope you can reach the church built on the highest part of the mound if the zeedijk breaks. One day it will. There are limits to all things. Descartes invented analytic geometry, the essential foundation of the infinitesimal calculus that operates on the principle that between any two points there are an infinite number of divisions. I sit here at dusk looking at the ever-changing sky. We all live between two points. Separated by infinite variations.

Part VII

Taste, Emotion, and Memory

Preface

Most readers will already know about Proust's celebrated account of sense memory from *The Remembrance of Things Past,* which has served as a reference point for so many discussions of taste recollection. But probably few can call the exact passage to mind. Therefore Part VII begins with several pages from Volume I of that work, *Swann's Way,* where the narrator experiences again a childhood moment from long ago after tasting a madeleine cake dipped into lime tea.

This is followed by a chapter by anthropologist Nadia Seremetakis about her childhood recollections of eating peaches (that are no longer grown) in Greece. Because the peach of her memory is now gone, the taste she refers to exists only in memory and discourse, for "peach" flavor, like so many others, is diminishing in range to a single type (a topic also discussed in the final part of this volume). This obliquely raises questions about the ontology of tastes that no longer have a referent, and also sadly reminds us that tastes, sensations that are by nature fleeting but usually repeatable, easily disappear and may become irretrievable, existing only in memory—itself fleeting.

Greece is also the focus for David Sutton's speculations about why taste and smell have their singular ability to evoke memory. Sutton analyzes the vivid tenacity of nostalgia and other emotions recalled by tastes and smells. His chapter investigates the convergence of the senses in "synesthesia"; he argues for the union of sense experience against the separation and hierarchy regarding the senses that we saw with Kant's treatment. Sutton offers some explanations for the peculiar power of the bodily senses to evoke memories, a phenomenon widely acknowledged but still rather mysterious.

Deborah Lupton continues the investigation of taste and memory by discussing the role of eating in the formation of subjectivity and social identity. Her analysis particularly brings out the "feminine" connotations of eating and the emotions it summons. Not only do pleasant memories supply the emotional valences of eating; that which revolts is equally part of taste subjectivity. Lupton directs our attention to the many ways in which tastes are—literally—"embodied," and the degree to which what appear to be biological processes are socially framed. (As she vividly puts it, "Appetite is emotionally-flavoured hunger.")

This section opens with a literary selection, and it closes with another: a short essay by the distinguished food writer M. F. K. Fisher. Fisher recounts four special memories of taste, displaying her characteristic wit and slightly scathing sensitivity to the feelings of others. No doubt readers will be able to supply many more examples from their own store of emotionally laden taste memories.

28
The Madeleine

Marcel Proust

And so it was that, for a long time afterwards, when I lay awake at night and revived old memories of Combray, I saw no more of it than this sort of luminous panel, sharply defined against a vague and shadowy background, like the panels which a Bengal fire or some electric sign will illuminate and dissect from the front of a building the other parts of which remain plunged in darkness: broad enough at its base, the little parlour, the dining-room, the alluring shadows of the path along which would come M. Swann, the unconscious author of my sufferings, the hall through which I would journey to the first step of that staircase, so hard to climb, which constituted, all by itself, the tapering 'elevation' of an irregular pyramid; and, at the summit, my bedroom, with the little passage through whose glazed door Mamma would enter; in a word, seen always at the same evening hour, isolated from all its possible surroundings, detached and solitary against its shadowy background, the bare minimum of scenery necessary (like the setting one sees printed at the head of an old play, for its performance in the provinces) to the drama of my undressing, as though all Combray had consisted of but two floors joined by a slender staircase, and as though there had been no time there but seven o'clock at night. I must own that I could have assured any questioner that Combray did include other scenes and did exist at other hours than these. But since the facts which I should then have recalled would have been prompted only by an exercise of the will, by my intellectual memory, and since the pictures which that kind of memory shows us of the past preserve nothing of the past itself, I should never have had any wish to ponder over this residue of Combray. To me it was in reality all dead.

Permanently dead? Very possibly.

There is a large element of hazard in these matters, and a second hazard, that of our own death, often prevents us from awaiting for any length of time the favours of the first. I feel that there is much to be said for the Celtic belief that the souls of those whom we have lost are held captive in some inferior being, in an animal, in a plant, in some inanimate object, and so effectively lost to us until the day (which to many never comes) when we happen to pass by the tree or to obtain possession of the object which forms their prison. Then they start and tremble, they call us by our name, and as soon as we have recognized their voice the spell is broken. We have delivered them: they have overcome death and return to share our life.

And so it is with our own past. It is a labour in vain to attempt to recapture it: all the efforts of our intellect must prove futile. The past is hidden somewhere outside the realm, beyond the reach of intellect, in some material object (in the sensation which that material object will give us) which we do not suspect. And as for that object, it depends on chance whether we come upon it or not before we ourselves must die.

Many years had elapsed during which nothing of Combray, save what was comprised in the theatre and the drama of my going to bed there, had any existence for me, when one day in winter, as I came home, my mother, seeing that I was cold, offered me some tea, a thing I did not ordinarily take. I declined at first, and then, for no particular reason, changed my mind. She sent out for one of those short, plump little cakes called 'petites madeleines', which look as though they had been moulded in the fluted scallop of a pilgrim's shell. And soon, mechanically, weary after a dull day with the prospect of a depressing morrow, I raised to my lips a spoonful of the tea in which I had soaked a morsel of the cake. No sooner had the warm liquid, and the crumbs with it, touched my palate than a shudder ran through my whole body, and I stopped, intent upon the extraordinary changes that were taking place. An exquisite pleasure had invaded my senses, but individual, detached, with no suggestion of its origin. And at once the vicissitudes of life had become indifferent to me, its disasters innocuous, its brevity illusory – this new sensation having had on me the effect which love has of filling me with a precious essence; or rather this essence was not in me, it was myself. I had ceased now to feel mediocre, accidental, mortal. Whence could it have come to me, this all-powerful joy? I was conscious that it was connected with the taste of tea and cake, but that it infinitely transcended those savours, could not, indeed, be of the same nature as theirs. Whence did it come? What did it signify? How could I seize upon and define it?

I drink a second mouthful, in which I find nothing more than in the first, a third, which gives me rather less than the second. It is time to stop; the potion is losing its magic. It is plain that the object of my quest, the truth, lies not in the cup but in myself. The tea has called up in me, but does not itself understand, and can only repeat indefinitely with a gradual loss of strength, the same testimony; which I, too, cannot interpret, though I hope at least to be able to call upon the tea for it again and to find it there presently, intact and at my disposal, for my final enlightenment. I put down my cup and examine my own mind. It is for it to discover the truth. But how?

What an abyss of uncertainty whenever the mind feels that some part of it has strayed beyond its own borders; when it, the seeker, is at once the dark region through which it must go seeking, where all its equipment will avail it nothing. Seek? More than that: create. It is face to face with something which does not so far exist, to which it alone can give reality and substance, which it alone can bring into the light of day.

And I begin again to ask myself what it could have been, this unremembered state which brought with it no logical proof of its existence, but only the sense that it was a happy, that it was a real state in whose presence other states of consciousness melted and vanished. I decide to attempt to make it reappear. I retrace my thoughts to the moment at which I drank the first spoonful of tea. I find again the same state, illumined by no fresh light. I compel my mind to make one further effort, to follow and recapture once again the fleeting sensation. And that nothing may interrupt it in its course I shut out every obstacle, every extraneous idea, I stop my ears and inhibit all attention to the sounds which come from the next room. And then, feeling that my mind is growing fatigued without having any success to report, I compel it for a change to enjoy that distraction which I have just denied it, to think of other things, to rest and refresh itself before the supreme attempt. And then for the second time I clear an empty space in front of it. I place in position before my mind's eye the still recent taste of that first mouthful, and I feel something start within me, something that leaves its resting-place and attempts to rise, something that has been embedded like an anchor at a great depth; I do not know yet what it is, but I can feel it mounting slowly; I can measure the resistance, I can hear the echo of great spaces traversed.

Undoubtedly what is thus palpitating in the depths of my being must be the image, the visual memory which, being linked to that taste, has tried to follow it into my conscious mind. But its struggles are too far off, too much confused; scarcely can I perceive the colourless reflection in which are blended the uncapturable whirling medley of radiant hues, and I cannot distinguish its form, cannot invite it, as the one possible interpreter, to translate to me the evidence of its contemporary, its inseparable paramour, the taste of cake soaked in tea; cannot ask it to inform me what special circumstance is in question, of what period in my past life.

Will it ultimately reach the clear surface of my consciousness, this memory, this old, dead moment which the magnetism of an identical moment has travelled so far to importune, to disturb, to raise up out of the very depths of my being? I cannot tell. Now that I feel nothing, it has stopped, has perhaps gone down again into its darkness, from which who can say whether it will ever rise? Ten times over I must essay the task, must lean down over the abyss. And each time the natural laziness which deters us from every difficult enterprise, every work of importance, has urged me to leave the thing alone, to drink my tea and to think merely of the worries of today and of my hopes for tomorrow, which let themselves be pondered over without effort or distress of mind.

And suddenly the memory returns. The taste was that of the little crumb of madeleine which on Sunday mornings at Combray (because on those mornings I did not go out before church-time), when I went to say good day to her in her bedroom, my aunt Léonie used to give me, dipping it first in her own cup of real or of lime-flower tea. The sight of the little madeleine had recalled nothing to my mind before I tasted it; perhaps because I had so often seen such things in the interval, without tasting them, on the trays in pastry-cooks' windows, that their image had dissociated itself from those Combray days to take its place among others more recent; perhaps because of those memories, so long abandoned and put out of mind, nothing now survived, everything was scattered; the forms of things, including that of the little scallop-shell of pastry, so richly sensual under its severe, religious folds, were either obliterated or had been so long dormant as to have lost the power of expansion which would have allowed them to resume their place in my consciousness. But when from a long-distant past nothing subsists, after the people are dead, after the things are broken and scattered, still, alone, more fragile, but with more vitality, more unsubstantial, more persistent, more faithful, the smell and taste of things remain poised a long time, like souls, ready to remind us, waiting and hoping for their moment, amid the ruins of all the rest; and bear unfaltering, in the tiny and almost impalpable drop of their essence, the vast structure of recollection.

And once I had recognized the taste of the crumb of madeleine soaked in her decoction of lime-flowers which my aunt used to give me (although I did not yet know and must long postpone the discovery of why this memory made me so happy) immediately the old grey house upon the street, where her room was, rose up like the scenery of a theatre to attach itself to the little pavilion, opening on to the garden, which had been built out behind it for my parents (the isolated panel which until that moment had been all that I could see); and with the house the town, from morning to night and in all weathers, the Square where I was sent before luncheon, the streets along which I used to run errands, the country roads we took when it was fine. And just as the Japanese amuse themselves by filling a porcelain bowl with water and steeping in it little crumbs of paper which until then are without character or form, but, the moment they become wet, stretch themselves and bend, take on colour and distinctive shape, become flowers or houses or people, permanent and recognizable, so in that moment all the flowers in our garden and in M. Swann's park, and the water-lilies on the Vivonne and the good folk of the village and their little dwellings and the parish church and the whole of Combray and of its surroundings, taking their proper shapes and growing solid, sprang into being, town and gardens alike, from my cup of tea.

29

The Breast of Aphrodite

C. Nadia Seremetakis

I grew up with the peach. It had a thin skin touched with fuzz, and a soft matte off-white color alternating with rosy hues. *Rodhákino* was its name (*ródho* means "rose"). It was well rounded and smooth like a small clay vase, fitting perfectly into your palm. Its interior was firm yet moist, offering a soft resistance to the teeth. A bit sweet and a bit sour, it exuded a distinct fragrance. This peach was known as "the breast of Aphrodite" (*o mastós tis Afrodhítis*).

A relation of this peach appeared eventually in the markets, which was called *yermás*. It was a much softer, watery fruit with a yolkish yellow color and reddish patches. Its silky thin skin would slide off at a touch revealing its slippery, shiny, deep yellow interior that melted with no resistance in the mouth. Both fruits were very sensitive, easy to bruise. I learned to like them both but my heart was set for the *rodhákino*.

In the United States, all fruits resembling either the *rodhákino* or *yermás* are named "peach." Throughout my years in the States, the memory of my peach was in its difference.

Every journey back was marked by its taste. Summer was its permanent referent, yet its gradual disappearance from the summer markets passed almost unnoticed. A few years ago, I realized that the peach was nowhere to be found in the markets, in or outside of Athens. When I mentioned it in casual conversations to friends and relatives, they responded as if the peach was always out there although they had not happened to eat it lately. What they were mainly buying, they explained, was a kind of *yermadho-rodhákino* (a blend *of yermás* and *rodhákino*). People only alluded to the disappearance of the older peach by remarking on the tastelessness of new varieties, a comment that was often extended to all food: "Nothing tastes as good as the past."

As my search for the peach became more persistent, my disappointment matched their surprise in the realization that the peach was gone forever.

I asked my father to plant it in our fields in the country to rescue it, but he has yet to find it. My older friends began to bring me tokens from their neighborhood markets, as well as from the country whenever they traveled out of the city. We all agreed that there were varieties that carried one or two of the characteristics of "our peach" but they were far from it. The part had taken the name of the whole.

In the presence of all those "peaches," the absent peach became narrative. It was as if when something leaves, it only goes externally, for its body persists within persons. The peach was its memory, and as if both had gone underground, they waited to be named. My naming of its absence resurrected observations, commentaries, stories, some of which encapsulated whole epochs marked by their own sensibilities. "Ah, that peach, what an aroma! and taste! The breast of Aphrodite we called it. These (peaches and other food) today have no taste (*á-nosta*)."

The younger generation, whenever present, heard these stories as if listening to a captivating fairy tale. For me the peach had been both eaten and remembered, but for the younger generation it was now digested through memory and language. At the same time, we are all experiencing the introduction from foreign markets of new fruits with no Greek precedents, such as the kiwi. For the younger generation, the remembered first peach exists on the same exotic plane as the kiwi. For the generation that follows, the kiwi, no longer exotic, may evoke a different sensibility.

The disappearance of Aphrodite's peach is a double absence; it reveals the extent to which the senses are entangled with history, memory, forgetfulness, narrative and silence. That first peach of my childhood carried with it allusions to distant epochs where the relation between food and the erotic was perhaps more explicit, named, and sacrilized; a relation that although fragmented and gone underground, was carried over through the centuries by the *rodhákino,* a fruit bearing myth in its form.

The new fruits displaced the *rodhákino* and together with it, a mosaic of enmeshed memories, tastes, aromas. The surrogate remains as a simulation with no model, emptied of specific cultural content and actively producing forgetfulness. A shift has been accomplished from sedimented depth to surface with no past. Aphrodite's peach in its presence and later absence materialized experiences of time which are searched for fruitlessly in the peach of today. This complicity of history and the senses also refers to the relation between *Eros* and *Thanatos* where the latter is not mere absence or void but rather material closure, a cordoning off of the capacity for certain perceptual experiences in such a manner that their very disappearance goes unnoticed.

How are the transformations of the senses experienced and conceptualized? This is also to ask, how is history experienced and thought of, on the level of the everyday? What elements in a culture enable the sensory experience of history? Where can historicity be found? In what sensory forms and practices? And to what extent is the experience of and the capacity to narrate history tied to the senses? Is memory stored in specific everyday items that form the historicity of a culture, items that create and sustain our relationship to the historical as a sensory dimension?

Is the disappearance of Aphrodite's peach an idiosyncratic event? Or does the disappearance of the "particular" peach as micro-history materialize on the everyday sweeping, macro-historical, sociocultural changes? The vanishing of tastes, aromas, and textures is being writ large in contemporary European margins with the joint expansion and centralization of EEC market rationalities. The erasure of one Greek peach poses the question: At what experiential levels are the economic and social transformations of the EEC being felt? Under the rationale of transnational uniformity the EEC may have initiated a massive intervention in the commensal cultures of its membership by determining what regional varieties of basic food staples can be grown, marketed, and exported. Certain types of Irish potatoes, German beer, and French cheese are no longer admissible into the public market, no longer eligible for subsidies because they look, appear, and taste different, and in some cases violate new health regulations.

In Greece, as regional products gradually disappear, they are replaced by foreign foods, foreign tastes; the universal and rationalized is now imported into the European periphery as the exotic. Here a regional diversity is substituted by a surplus over-production. This EEC project implicitly constitutes a massive resocialization of existing consumer cultures and sensibilities, as well as a reorganization of public memory. A French cheese is excluded because it is produced through a specific fermentation process, one that market regulations deem a health risk. What is fermentation if not history? If not a maturation that occurs through the articulation of time and substance? Sensory premises, memories and histories are being pulled out from under entire regional cultures and the capacity to reproduce social identities may be altered as a result. Such economic processes reveal the extent to which the ability to replicate cultural identity is a material practice embedded in the reciprocities, aesthetics, and sensory strata of material objects. Sensory displacement does not only relate to cultures of consumption but to those local material cultures of production where the latter is still symbolically mediated and not yet reduced to a purely instrumental practice. Sensory changes occur microscopically through everyday accretion; so, that which shifts the material culture of perception is itself imperceptible and only reappears after the fact in fairy tales, myths, and memories that hover at the margins of speech.

The imperceptible is not only the consequence of sensory transformation but also the means by which it takes place. Thus the problematic of the senses in modernity resurrects the old theme ignored in recent anthropological theory, that of the historical unconscious.

The Impeachment of Nostalgia

The memory of Aphrodite's peach is nostalgic. What is the relation of nostalgia to the senses and history? In English the word "nostalgia" (in Greek *nostalghía*) implies trivializing romantic sentimentality. In Greek the verb *nostalghó is* a composite of *nostó* and *alghó. Nostó* means "I return," "I travel" (back to homeland); the noun *nóstos* means "the return," "the journey," while *á-nostos* means "without taste," as the new peaches are described (*ánosta,* in plural). The opposite of *ánostos is nóstimos* and characterizes someone or something that has journeyed and arrived, has matured, ripened and is thus tasty (and useful). *Alghó* means "I feel pain," "I ache for," and the noun *álghos* characterizes one's pain in soul and body, burning pain (*kaimós*). Thus *nostalghía* is the desire or longing with burning pain to journey. It also evokes the sensory dimension of memory in exile and estrangement; it mixes bodily and emotional pain and ties painful experiences of spiritual and somatic exile to the notion of maturation and ripening. In this sense, *nostalghía* is linked to the personal consequences of historicizing sensory experience which is conceived as a painful bodily and emotional journey.

Nostalghía thus is far from trivializing romantic sentimentality. This reduction of the term confines the past and removes it from any transactional and material relation to the present; the past becomes an isolatable and consumable unit of time. Nostalgia, in the American sense, freezes the past in such a manner as to preclude it from any capacity for social transformation in the present, preventing the present from establishing a dynamic perceptual relationship to its history. Whereas the Greek etymology evokes the transformative impact of the past as unreconciled historical experience.[1] Does the difference between nostalgia and *nostalghía* speak of different cultural experiences of the senses and memory? Could a dialogical encounter of the terms offer insights for an anthropology of the senses?

Sensory Exchange and Performance

Nostalghía speaks to the sensory reception of history. In Greek there is a semantic circuit that weds the sensorial to agency, memory, finitude, and therefore history—all of which are contained within the etymological strata of the senses. The word for senses *is aesthísis*; emotion-feeling and aesthetics are respectively *aésthima* and *aesthitikí.* They all derive from the verb *aestháname or aesthísome* meaning I feel or sense, I understand, grasp, learn, or receive news or information, and I have an accurate sense of good and evil, that is I judge correctly. *Aesthísis is* defined as action or power through the medium of the senses, and the media or the *semía* (points, tracks, marks) by which one senses. *Aésthima,* emotion-feeling, is also an ailment of the soul, an event that happens, that impacts on one viscerally through the senses; it also refers to romance, or love affair. A strong *aésthima* is called *páthos* (passion). This includes the sense of suffering, illness, but also the English sense of passion, as in he has a passion for music. The stem verb *pathéno* means I provoke passion in both its meanings; I am acting, moving by an internal forceful *aésthima,* passion; I get inspired, excited; I suffer. Among Greek youth the word *pathéno* as in "When I hear this song *pathéno,"* is common. The gestures accompanying it, such as hitting and holding the forehead, and the matching sounds, express both (sudden) suffering and extreme enjoyment.

A synonym of *pathéno* in this case *is pethéno,* I die. *Páthos* (passion) is the meeting point of *éros* and *thánatos;* where the latter is an internal death, the death of the self because of and for the other; the moment that the self is both the self and a memory in the other. Death is a journey; a sensorial journey into the other. So is *éros.* The common expression during lovemaking *is Me péthanes* (You made me die, I died because of, for you and through you). Éros is desire. It also means appetite. The expression often used in vernacular Greek, e.g. from mother to child, to show extreme desire is: "I'll eat you." The same expression is used for someone causing suffering, e.g. child to parent, "You ate me." In the journey of death, to the other world, the earth "eats" the body.

In these semantic currents we find no clear-cut boundaries between the senses and emotions, the mind and body, pleasure and pain, the voluntary and the involuntary, and affective and aesthetic experience. Such culturally specific perspectives on sensory experience are not sheer comparative curiosities. They are crucial for opening up a self-reflexive, culturally and historically informed consideration of the senses. Sensory semantics in Greek culture, among others, contain regional epistemologies, inbuilt theories, that provoke important cross-cultural methodological consequences...

Sour Grapes

Not only have some foreign fruits arrived in Greek markets—it is no coincidence that in colloquial Greek a strange or weird person is referred to as "a strange fruit" or "a new fruit"—but also familiar fruits have made their timid appearance in fancy supermarkets at the "wrong season." For instance grapes, emblematic of the summer for Greeks, have appeared in the winter under the sign "imported from EEC." Observing local women shopping, touching, picking, and choosing, one notices that they pass them over as if they never notice them, or comment on how sour they look. Sour implies not yet ripened, thus not in season, and so tasteless (*ánosta*). And while the EEC in this case becomes identified with sour grapes, a whole epoch, the present, is characterized as *ánosto.*

When and how does an epoch, a slice of history, become something *ánosto?* To say that aspects of daily life have become tasteless, to make parts substitute for the whole, implies that the capacity to synthesize perceptual experience is only accessible through dispersed fragments. The movement from real or imagined wholes to parts and fragments is a metaphorical slide that captures the movement of history through a shifting perceptual focus. The capacity to replicate a sensorial culture resides in a dynamic interaction between perception, memory, and a landscape of artifacts, organic and inorganic. This capacity can atrophy when that landscape, as a repository and horizon of historical experience, emotions, embedded sensibilities, and hence social identities, dissolves into disconnected pieces. At the same time, what replaces it?

When new forms and items of an emerging material culture step in between a society's present perceptual existence and its residual socio-cultural identity, they can be tasteless because people may no longer have the perceptual means for seeking identity and experience in new material forms. Because the cultural instruments for creating meaning out of material experience have been dispersed with the now discarded past sensory landscape. The latter was didactic as much as it was an object of perception and utility. The characterization *ánosto* (tasteless) then deals with the cultural incapacity to codify past, present, and anticipatory experiences at the level of sensory existence. This is so because such codifying practices are never purely mentalist but embedded in and borne by a material world of talking objects.

This is why the enthusiastic reception of the "new" is imported, culturally prepared, and programmed with the simultaneous fabrication or promise of new sensory powers—the latter are automatically bonded with the items of the penetrating culture. Thus each commodity form is introduced through the creation of its own self-generating experience and memory. The latter are themselves promised as substitutions, replacements, and improvements of prior sensory experience.

In cultures that undergo colonial and post-colonial experiences of transformation, the experience of tastlessness can be self-imposed, for they have internalized "the eye of the Other" (Seremetakis 1984) and see their own culture and residual experience from a position of defamiliarization and estrangement. This can result in a newly constructed archaicization of recent and unreconcilable experiences, practices, and narratives. Particular and now idiosyncratic cultural experiences are described as having long disappeared, as lost, when in fact they are quite recent and their memory sharp. As one moves deeper into conversation with people, their intimacy with these distant practices comes out as fairy tales, anecdotes, folklore, and myth. The historical repression of memory that the cultural periphery can impose on itself is as rapid, shallow, profound, and experientially painful as any other disorienting penetration of metropolitan modernity. The discourse on loss is an element of public culture, an official ideological stance taken toward the past that aligns the speaker with the normative view of the present, i.e. modern times. Yet as the discourse of loss congeals into an element of public culture, that which has never been lost, but which can no longer be said, shared, and exchanged, becomes the content of unreconciled personal and privatized experience...

Mnemonic sensory experience implies that the artifact bears within it layered commensal meanings (shared substance and material reciprocities) and histories. It can also be an instrument for mobilizing the perceptual penetration of historical matter. As a sensory form in itself, the artifact can provoke the emergence, the awakening of the layered memories, and thus the senses contained within it. The object invested with sensory memory speaks; it provokes recall as a missing, detached yet antiphonic element of the perceiver. The sensory connection between perceiver and artifact completes the latter in an unexpected and nonprescribed fashion because the perceiver is also the recipient of the unintended historical aftereffects of the artifact's presence or absence.

Note

1. To conduct an etymological analysis of a term or concept is not to assume that all the sediments of meaning are operant at all times and with a uniform prevalence. However, etymological analysis is complementary to the uneven historical development of European peripheries which is characterized by the incomplete and disjunctive articulation of the pre-modern, different phases within modernity, and the postmodern. Etymology captures the uneven shifts of semantic history that may be present at any given moment in a society.

Reference

Seremetakis, C. Nadia (1984), "The eye of the other; watching death in rural Greece," *Journal of Modern Hellenism* Vol. 1 (1): 63–77.

30

Synesthesia, Memory, and the Taste of Home

David E. Sutton

A flowerpot of basil can symbolize the soul of a people better than a drama of Aeschylus.

Ion Dragoumis

The reference to basil by Greek folklorist Ion Dragoumis provides a point of entry into my subject, the power of tangible everyday experiences to evoke the memories on which identities are formed. Dragoumis' aphorism was given substance by a comment passed on to me by Eleana Yalouri, a PhD student in anthropology living in London, who was visited by a recent migrant from Greece. Smelling a pot of basil on her windowsill, he told her with evident longing, "It really smells like Greece!" She noted that the ubiquitous leavening used for making bread contains and smells strongly of basil. That this is not an uncommon experience is further confirmed by Helen Zeese Papanikolas, in her account of Greek immigrants in the American West in the early years of the twentieth century. Papanikolas writes, "Basil plants grew in dusty cans on the window ledges of the restaurants and coffeehouses; men broke off sprigs to put in their lapels and from time to time brought them to their noses and breathed in the piquant scent. 'Ach, patridha, patridha,' [homeland, homeland] they said" (Papanikolas 1987: 156).

This chapter looks at food memory from the perspective of the senses. That is, it addresses issues of how and why food is memorable as a sensory as well as a social experience. It does this through a consideration of cross-cultural, cognitive aspects of sensory memory, but without neglecting how such cognitive potentials can be culturally elaborated or downplayed in specific ways. I begin with transnational food exchange, which has, I argue, interesting aspects as part of a process of revitalization or "returning to the whole," through multisensory or synesthetic food experiences. I then describe certain synesthetic qualities that are elaborated in Kalymnian and Greek experiences of food. (The Greek island of Kalymnos is in the eastern Aegaen Sea.) Synesthesia is defined as "the union of the senses," or the way that sensory experiences cannot be compartmentalized, but seem, rather, to feed off each other. Finally I consider more general questions regarding synesthesia, memory, and categorization that lead back to the social quality of food memories...

That food frequently accompanies people in their travels across national borders may be obvious to customs officers worldwide, but its significance has only begun to be explored by anthropologists. While there has been some interest in the way migrant food has transformed eating in the US and other migrant destinations (Raspa 1984), less attention is given to the implications for identity of the food that migrants might bring with them, or have sent from home; indeed its importance is explicitly dismissed by Hannerz in his theorizing concerning "cosmopolitans" and "locals" (1996:103). Yet Fog Olwig and Hastrup (1997) argue for the importance of "cultural sites," localized cultural wholes that become points of identification for people displaced by migrations caused by larger global processes. Here I suggest that food might be analyzed as just such a cultural site, and is especially useful in understanding Kalymnian and Greek experiences of displacement, fragmentation, and the reconstruction of wholeness.

The experience of displacement is culturally elaborated in Greece under the concept *xenitia*, or absence from home. *Xenitia* is described as a condition of estrangement, absence, death, or of loss of social relatedness, loss of the ethic of care seen to characterize relations at home (Danforth 1982: 93ff.; Seremetakis 1991: 85, 175–6). It provokes a longing for home that is seen as a physical and spiritual pain, as Frantzis describes for the Dodecanese migrants to Tarpon Springs, Florida: "The sun-drenched shores of Florida [are] verdant with pine trees, orange trees, palms, beautiful tropical trees, and multicolored fragrant flowers. All of them resemble and remind them of their islands. Nevertheless, and in spite of it all, their heart withers, and the longing for the wild beauty of these chunks of rocks where they were born is alive in them" (Frantzis 1962: 105). Here the sensual landscape of Florida serves as a painful reminder of the home they have left. More usually, however, migrants are moving to an urban environment where there is a more striking sense of disjunction. Hence the need to have some physical object as a tangible site for memory which can facilitate a "return to the whole."

In using the concept of "wholeness" I am drawing on the ongoing work of Fernandez on the process of "returning to the whole," which he first discusses in the context of religious revitalization movements in West Africa. Bwiti, the revitalization movement among the Fang of Gabon where Fernandez worked, is seen as a response to the alienation and fragmentation brought on by "the agents of the colonial world and simply modern times" (1982: 562). In the face of these radical changes in their society, the Fang use Bwiti to reintegrate the past and the present, to "recapture the totality of the old way of life" (1982: 9). Thus, as against the celebration of fragmentation in postmodern analysis, Fernandez provides an analysis of some of the ways that those whose worlds are being rent asunder attempt creatively to reconstruct them. Fernandez's approach is potentially applicable to many sorts of alienation, from that of victims of war, to that of refugees, migrants, downsized workers, those caught in major political shifts such as the fall of Soviet socialism, and all those who in the midst of change "are looking for firm ground under their feet" (Thomassen 1996: 44).

The originality in Fernandez's work comes in his focus on the symbolic processes by which the "return to the whole" is attempted. Fernandez describes the "whole" as a "state of relatedness—a kind of conviviality in experience" (1986: 191). He suggests some of the difficulties of imagining or experiencing the whole given the atomization and fragmentation of present-day Fang society. It is the sense that there is a "lack of fit" or coherence between different domains of experience that leads to attempts to return to the whole. Returning to the whole requires a "mutual tuning-in" based on shared sensory experiences that are explicitly synesthetic (crossing sensory domains). "Hearing, seeing, touching, tasting—in primary groups, families, ethnic groups, fraternal or sororal associations, etc. If we don't have these things to begin with we have to somehow recreate them by an argument of images of some kind in which primary perceptions are evoked" (193). This is where revitalization comes in, the process by which a domain of experience that is experienced as fragmented or deprived is revalued by simply marking it for ritual participation: "The performance of a sequence of images revitalizes, in effect, and by simple iteration, a universe of domains, an acceptable cosmology of participation, a compelling whole" (203).

In speaking with Greek students studying in Oxford, I found that the food they received from home (either through the mail or brought by friends or family members on visits) fell into three categories: (1) olives, olive oil, meat (in one case, two whole goats for Easter), eggs and other products produced by family members on family land; (2) baked goods associated with Easter and other festive times, either prepared by family members or store-bought; (3) mass-produced Greek products such as feta cheese. The first type of item produced immediate local knowledge: one woman, who had lived in London for ten years working in various jobs while taking courses in art and design (with hopes to become an icon painter), told me about the olive oil that her father made from family trees in Crete, and that the olives were especially good for oil because they weren't watered, but raised only on rainwater. She said it had zero percent acidity; that it sometimes became more acidic if you let the olives fall off the tree, but her father used a stick to knock them off the tree, and you had to knock in a certain direction, otherwise the olives would not grow again.

Aside from such local knowledge, sensory aspects of food sent from Greece were also stressed. Another woman, studying environmental planning, who had been in England for five years, spoke of the eggs sent from her father's farm, which she contrasted with "plastic" eggs in England, which had a particularly unpleasant smell, while eggs from Greece had a deep orange color to the yolks and an "intense" flavor. The second category had an obvious connection to Greek traditions as well as to the family, usually mothers, who had baked some of these items. But it was certainly not only mothers who put together such packages. Fathers, grandmothers, and grandfathers might send separate packages of foodstuffs, items that they had actually produced or that they had shared in the past with the receiving child...

The third category of mass-produced Greek products was less common in the late 1990s. One man noted that now (in 1998) it was possible to get these same products at British supermarkets, so that the only connection they had to Greece for him was the thought of his mother sending them. But others spoke of the importance of feta at earlier periods of migration, when Greek feta was not widely available. Dimitris Theodossopoulos, an anthropologist at the University of Lampeter in Wales, noted that new students who came from Greece wouldn't realize how much they were going to miss feta. "When they would return to Greece for Christmas, they would really stock up, fill their suitcases and bags with feta in all different kinds of containers. One trip I came back from Greece with a 10-kilo tin of feta cheese, which I preserved in brine... I would cut a little piece with my meal every night. It was like 'white gold' to me (laughing)."

What is the actual experience of such food events? They are often experienced in terms of a "burning desire" that is satiated through a sensory experience evoking local knowledge, at the same time that a domain of experience that has fallen into disuse, in Fernandez's terms, is revalued. They often explicitly evoke a wholeness, or fullness in experience, as in the following report by Kapella of a letter from a woman living in Germany upon receiving a package of Kalymnian honey and other local propducts: "My joy was indescribable, I laughed and cried at the same time. I took the package, left the post office, and in the street I felt like I was holding the whole world in my arms" (Kapella 1981: 36). The woman noted that she used the honey to make doughnuts and she "soothed her insides." She contrasts this feeling to her experience of the sensory deprivation of work in Germany in a few descriptive images: "We've made money, but we've moldered in the factories. We don't see outside and we're dying of cold..." (1981: 36).

This gives a clear sense of one strategy for returning to the whole: through what Fernandez calls the shock of "recognition of a wider integrity of things" captured in the metaphor of the "whole world," but specifically triggered by *memory* of taste and smell. It is this memory that leads to the emotional affect described in the passage: simultaneous laughing and crying, and then a sense of soothing fullness, suggesting the evocation of other memories. The expression "laughing and crying" implies that such moments of wholeness are bittersweet and temporary, a reminder of a homeland the return to which is deferred. Yet the soothing fullness also suggests that such moments give the migrants the strength to carry on with their *xenitia*. This sense of emotional/ embodied plenitude evoked above is echoed in the following passage from Papanikolas (1987: 217), describing several Greek immigrant men, cousins who were working in Idaho in an endless task of clearing sagebrush to homestead:

> One night, working nervously, swearing obscenely, Louis made a *pita*. He could have waited for Sunday, gone the six miles to Pocatello... and had one of the Greek women who ran boarding houses make it for him, but he wanted it right then. Louis rolled out the pastry leaves, layered each sheet with butter and eggs mixed with crumbled feta. The helper gazed with tearful eyes, Yoryis avidly. That night they fell on their cots, satisfied.

Once again, the terrible emotional overload of *xenitia*—living in a foreign land—is temporarily relieved in the experience, which demands and receives immediate satisfaction.

And once again it is the iteration of a neglected domain, metonymically described ("Louis rolled out the pastry leaves...") that revitalizes it for the participants. Implicitly, the revitalization of one domain brings others with it, a point made by recent theorists of refugee displacement. For example, Nordstrom (1995) describes the everyday and ritual practices of resistance to the destruction wrought on people's lives by war in Mozambique. She concludes: "Worlds are destroyed in a war; they must be recreated. Not just worlds of home, family, community, and economy but worlds of definition, both personal and cultural" (1995: 147)... As Fernandez describes, integrity is restored through a remembered coherence, or structural repetition between domains. This occurs because the food event evokes a whole world of family, agricultural associations, place names and other "local knowledge." Even memories of water have this characteristic, partly owing to the fact that different qualities of water are said to produce different qualities of food (for example, water used for olive trees or water used to soak beans before cooking them). Papanikolas recounts migrants' memories of water sources from home (1987: 167), illustrating the almost sacred power of invocation:

> The men talked constantly of the water in their part of Greece, which often had to be carried a long distance over rocky trails, how cold it was, a special taste, its curative qualities, how its fame was known throughout the province and people came from afar to drink it. They spoke the names of waters with reverence: Kefalovrissi—Head Springs, Palaios Platanos—Old Plane Tree, Mahi Topos—Slaughtering Place, Nifi Peplos—Bride's Veil, Nerolithi—Water Rock.

It is this same sense of the part that holds the key to revivifying a whole structure of associations that animates Marcel Proust's project of exploring involuntary sensory memory. Here is Proust describing the memory of the senses evoked by food, in his famous *madeleine* description:

> But when from a long-distant past nothing subsists, after the people are dead, after the things are broken and scattered, taste and smell alone, more fragile but more enduring, more unsubstantial, more persistent, more faithful, remain poised a long time, like souls, remembering, waiting, hoping, amid the ruins of all the rest; and bear unflinchingly, in the tiny and almost impalpable drop of their essence, *the vast structure of recollection.*
>
> (Proust 1982: 50–1; italics mine)

Of course Proust was not speaking of migration, as I have been. But if the past "is a foreign country," then similar processes can be at work in temporal as in spatial or spatiotemporal displacement. And indeed Proust directs us once again to the power of sensory parts to return us to the whole, of the unsubstantial fragment to reveal the vast structure. Like the memories discussed above, Proust also points us to the emotional charge of the moment of consumption for keying, involuntarily, these associative memories. But why taste and smell?...

Evocative Senses

Note that in his *madeleine* description, Proust does not single out taste, but rather taste and smell, as the senses that hold the promise of the return of the memorable whole. Taste and smell, it is generally noted, are interrelated senses. The chewing of food forces air up through the mouth to the nose, and a blocked nose can cause considerable reduction in the ability to taste (Vroon 1997: 24). In his 1975 work *Rethinking Symbolism,* Dan Sperber directly addresses the Proustian phenomenon in a consideration of the evocative power of smells. I believe his discussion could equally well be applied to taste, as will become clear from what follows. Sperber begins by contrasting smells with colors. While colors have a fairly elaborate classificatory terminology, hierarchically arranged so that we recognize shades of the same color, smells are organized much more simply along an axis of good–bad, and in terms of their causes and sometimes their effects: "the smell of coffee brewing," "a nauseating smell" (see also Engen 1991: 86). Attempts at scientific classification of smells in something equivalent to classes have led to little consensus concerning what might constitute clusters of smells and "primary smells," and attempted taxonomies seem forced and vague, such as Linnaeus' division of smells (on a gradient of best to worst) into (1) Aromatic, (2) Scented or perfumed, (3) Ambrosia or musk-like, (4) Sharp or garlic-like, (5) Stinking or goat-like, sweaty, (6) Repulsive and (7) Disgusting.

Sperber continues his contrast by noting that it is fairly easy to recall colors to mind, even when not in the presence of the actual stimulus. In other words, if asked to imagine the color of a Granny Smith apple, most people experience little difficulty seeing the color in their mind, or the apple itself. The same is not true for smells, or, I might add, for tastes. As Sperber notes, if one does want to recall a scent, one often employs an image: the church where one smelled a certain type of incense: "And I will almost have the impression that I sense that scent—a misleading impression, however, which will fade as soon as, relinquishing the recollection of the object it emanated from, I try mentally to reconstitute the scent itself" (1975: 117).

The failure to recall scents is related for Sperber to the way they are categorized, or rather, not categorized; in other words, there is no "semantic field of smells." By contrast, in the presence of a stimulus, smells can be recognized over a distance of many years. Recognized, but not analyzed and described in the fashion one might do for a color. Or for the face of someone one has seen before whom one runs into at the supermarket: once recognized, one can access or invoke prior information one has about the person to whom the face belongs, and add the fact that you shop at the same supermarket. With smells, however, because of the difficulty of analysis and invocation, one attempts evocation: "In the case of smells, the evocational field comprises all recollections likely to corroborate the feeling of recognition, and it is these recollections that evocation passes in review" (1975: 121). In other words, smells evoke what surrounds them in memory, what has been metonymically associated with the smell in question. Smells are prototypical symbols, in Sperber's terms "by virtue of the accepted definitions according to which the symbol is the part for the whole, or the object that gives rise to something other than itself, or the motivated sign, etc." (1975: 118).

Recent research has borne out Sperber's view of the relation between smell and memory. First, the idea that memory often works by synchronous convergence, i.e. the association of diverse things occurring at the same time, is "well documented" (Fuster 1997: 451). "If, for example, you are reading Dante's *Divine Comedy* about Beatrice while watching scenes on the television of refugees, then images of Beatrice and the suffering of refugees are likely to be associated in your memory" (Reyna 2002: 112; see also Engen 1991: 3ff.). But this property is more true of smells, as Vroon notes, because smells more easily connect with "episodic" than "semantic" memories (i.e. life-history memories as opposed to "recognition of a phenomenon" memories), and also because of the tendency for smell memories to be emotionally charged (Vroon 1997: 95, 104). This emotional charge is touched on by Sperber in noting that in trying to place a smell that one is re-experiencing "one may revive memories that are more captivating than the smell itself, more insistent than the original desire one had to identify it" (1975: 122). Or to quote a food author discussing the phenomenon of taste memory: "the hunger is in the memory, not in the biscuit, berries and cream…" (Lust 1998: 175).

Once again, if we extend this view to taste, which shares limbic system location, and low semantic/high episodic recall, then we have a confirmation that, on both counts, Proust was right!...

Sperber speculates on the absence of other analyses of smell in anthropological discussions of symbolism, given that they are for him "*symbols par excellence*," and places the blame on their seemingly individual and idiosyncratic nature which "bypass[es] all forms of coded communication" (1975: 118). In other words, apricots evoke the Second World War for Yiannis, but they just give me hives. But say the words "Chinese Pressed Duck" and I am sent into reveries of early college years and love in bloom. However, Sperber goes on to argue that culture does in fact play a role in these types of phenomena. Through repetition in ritual and other forms, cultural symbolism "focuses the attention of the members of a single society in the same directions, determines parallel evocational fields that are structured in the same way, but leaves the individual free to effect an evocation in them as he likes" (1975: 137).

These ideas form a bridge to our consideration of the sensory worlds within which Kalymnian evocative fields are shaped, if not determined. And it is a bridge that, while hopefully leading us forward, also returns us to Fernandez's conception of the whole, since, as I will argue, it is the notion of synesthesia that best sums up the sensory experiences with which I will be concerned.

"Listen to That Smell!": The Cultivation of Synesthesia

In studying phenomena in comparative, cross-cultural perspective—from concepts of personhood, gifts and commodities, to embodiment—recent anthropological work has stressed that we are dealing not, for the most part, with radical cultural difference, but with shifting emphases, with cultural elaborations on a continuum of experience. Thus ideas of the "individual" vs. the socially embedded "dividual" do not characterize entire cultures, but rather may represent dominant understandings without precluding the coexistence of subordinate understandings opposed to these within the same culture. Such a view is applicable to the attempt to describe different, "non-Western" sensory worlds: we are not dealing with phenomena of radically different perceptions, but rather with the cultural elaboration of certain sensory registers and the relative dormancy of others. The study of smell and taste in one society might lead one to look at the realm of myth and the afterlife (Bubant 1998), in another to issues of healing (Rasmussen 1999), and to the domain of advertising in a third (Classen, Howes, and Synnott 1994: Ch. 6). In trying to give a sense of Kalymnian smell- and taste-scapes, I will focus on the domains of religious experience and cooking, stressing the cultural elaboration of the synesthetic nature of these domains that leads to their prominence in memory processes. By synesthesia I refer to the way that the different senses elaborate on each other, rather than being considered separate domains of experience. Thus in the case of taste, we must also consider not only smell, but vision, touch, and even hearing (see below). Cultural elaboration of these sensory properties is reflected, but not completely comprised, in linguistic elaboration. Thus, while I will focus on Kalymnian discussions of taste and smell, which of course provide the easiest access for the ethnographer, I will also describe ways in which these senses may be elaborated non-linguistically.

"Orthodox ritual stimulates the senses—sight, sound, touch, taste and smell" (Hirschon 1998: 21). Indeed, it is difficult to enter a church on Kalymnos and not feel overpowered by sensory stimulation, from the smells of myrrh and frankincense that are spread by the priests swinging censers rhythmically back and forth, to the flicker of the candles that each person lights and places in front of the icon when entering the church. One experiences the kinesthetics of making the cross and kissing the icon, the press of bodies in the often confined space of many of the small chapels on Kalymnos, and the reverberating nasal pitch of the liturgy being sung by the cantors. And, of course, there is the multicolored sight of the icons, illustrating key stories from the Bible, and the taste of the communion bread and wine mixed to the consistency of gruel and presented by the priest on a spoon…

Another key sensory aspect associated with Orthodoxy is the question of the smell of decay associated with sin and death. Although the body and other matter is not inherently sinful, matter is corruptible as well as redeemable, a distinction made by Ware between "body" and "flesh" (1979: 79; see discussion 59ff.). On Kalymnos this distinction tends to play out in the realm of smell, with sinful flesh smelling putrid, while redeemed flesh smells "wonderful," perhaps an association with the incense that envelops priests and the church (cf. Classen, Howes, and Synnott 1994: 52). The corpse of a bad person is said to putrefy quickly, and to stink very soon after death. One man told me a story about someone on his deathbed who feared he might have such a fate. He instructed his wife to place a small vial of perfume in his funeral jacket when he was buried, so that later people would smell it and say, "Mmm (making a gesture of smelling) this must be a saint, he smells of frankincense"; and thus gravediggers checked the pockets of the people they were burying against such frauds. Similarly, the proof adduced by many people that a Kalymnian man who had died in the 1960s was indeed a saint was the fact that his remains, on display at one of the island monasteries, had not putrefied after all those years. A considerable part of this was seen as related to a rejection of food and animal flesh in particular, the food most directly associated with religiously required abstinence from certain foods (see Sutton 1997 for a full discussion). One man told me of the decayed smell of meat that remained caught between his teeth overnight, as compared to vegetables, which he claimed did not have such a smell.

Discourse surrounding food focuses on sensory qualities as well, smell in particular. One particularly striking one is the expression "Listen to that smell" which is used approvingly to refer to the odor of food cooking, and is often accompanied by a noisy intake of breath through the nose. The opposite, to indicate the failure to taste a dish, is "It is not hearable," a seemingly direct appreciation of the process of synesthesia, even if coded in everyday metaphor. One way to refer to a tasteless food is "water-boiled," in one case used by a woman to describe the noodle casserole made by her cousin on the neighboring island of Kos without nutmeg to give it its proper aroma. Metaphor is also prominent in Kalymnian discourse on food. A particularly delicious batch of bean stew is called Turkish Delight… A man tells his friend that he ate prickly pears the other day and they were tasteless, but today "they were honey!" A woman refers to fresh-caught tuna as "souvlaki!" and a man describes a batch of oranges he bought as "banana!" In these cases it seems that a superordinate category of "sweet foods" is used to relate prickly pears and honey, or oranges and bananas. What is interesting is the vividness of the metaphors, so that in the latter two examples, any conjugation of the verb "to be" is dropped entirely: "I ate one of those oranges … banana!" The Kalymnian practice of using multisensory terms and metaphor is not in itself unusual. In his study of restaurant workers, Fine (1996: 207ff.) discusses the imprecision of discourse surrounding food taste, even among chefs. The tendency is either to use superlatives ("it tastes wonderful"; "It tastes like shit") or to rely on similes and metaphors, although interestingly all the examples he provides are of similes rather than metaphors, while in my Kalymnian examples the seemingly more direct and vivid metaphor is employed: "The prickly pear today, it was honey."

These materials have a number of suggestive implications. First, memory theorists note the importance of "encoding specificity" for later recall: "What is stored is determined by what is perceived and how it is encoded, and what is stored determines what retrieval cues are effective in providing access to what is stored" (Tulving and Thompson, cited in McGlone 1996: 557). Second, as Tilley notes: "A vivid metaphorical image, such as saying 'they cooked the land,' is likely to be remembered far longer than a statement such as 'they burnt down the forest.' In so far as metaphors can evoke vivid mental images, they facilitate memory" (Tilley 1999: 8). This suggests some basis for the Proustian phenomenon of remembering through evocation of a powerful sensory image: the sweetness of a banana hardly seems similar to that of an orange, and yet, as an image of a food with a strikingly sweet flavor, "banana" does have a certain evocative power. It should be pointed out here that, as noted in my discussion of Sperber, the significant quality of smell and taste is that *it is possible to recognize them, but much more difficult to recall them.* As Engen (1991: 80) notes, in cases in which people do claim to be able to recall odors, as with perfumers working on creating a new scent, it is more likely that a visual image is what is evoked. Through metaphor,

Kalymnians seem to be providing the powerful images that might facilitate recall.

One other aspect of odor memory stressed by Engen (1991: 81ff.) is that time seems to have no effect on dissipating recognition ability. Indeed, a powerful (positive or negative) first experience of the smell of a certain food may color all subsequent sensory experiences of that food (or other odor). In the cases discussed above, the food referred to had been consumed recently. However, in one case I recorded, a man discussed the meats and cheeses that the Italians brought to Kalymnos during the Occupation (sixty or more years previously) first by a metonymical listing: "Mortadella, prosciutto, provolone," and ending with the declaration: "Aroma!," here citing the sensory experience directly through invocation rather than metaphor. He did follow this, however, with a striking metaphor, phrased in the infinitive: "To eat and to have your insides open up from joy." Through use of metaphor, as well as through invocation, the sensory intensity of the experience is either stressed for the interlocutor or recalled to mind by the person himself or herself…

While the relationship of synesthesia and memory seems to be an open question from the point of view of experimental psychologists (see for example Jones 1976; but cf. Cytowic 1993: 129 fn. 2), intuitively it seems to be the case that synesthesia is an aid to memory. This relationship has been particularly described by Luria, in his classic study *The Mind of a Mnemonist*. According to Luria, S. used synesthetic associations to code words and other objects for future remembrance. This additional information acted both as a prompt to recollection, and as a screen for false memories, i.e. if a word was altered by the experimenters, it would not produce the same taste, sense of weight, or emotions (Luria 1968: 28). S. was, of course, synesthetic in a clinical sense, rather than having been culturally encouraged toward synesthesia, so his case must be used with caution. But his subjective perception that synesthesia aided his memory is what is of interest to me here. For my purposes it is these subjective associations that are crucial, rather than experimental assessments of synesthesia and memory, since I am looking at *claims* to remember food, the accuracy of which I have little way of testing.

Conclusion

> Perfume is symbolic, not linguistic, because it does what language could not do—express an ideal, an archetypal wholeness, which surpasses language.
>
> (Gell 1977: 30)

The experience of synesthetic memory brings us back to where we began this chapter: the return to the whole. In this chapter I have argued that we can understand the evocative power of food by examining some of the properties of taste and smell, which are universal but which can be culturally elaborated to different degrees and in different ways. The fact that taste and smell have a much greater association with episodic rather than semantic memory, with the symbolic rather than the linguistic, and with recognition rather than recall, helps to explain why taste and smell are so useful for encoding the random, yet no less powerful, memories of contexts past than, say, vision or words. But at another level there is no need to counterpoise the senses in this way, since I have argued that the experience of food in Greece is cultivated synesthetically and emotionally, so that eating food from home becomes a particularly marked cultural site for the reimagining of "worlds" displaced in space and/or time... The union of the senses is not only a metaphor for social wholeness; it is an embodied aspect of creating the experience of the whole. Food is not a random part that recalls the whole to memory. Its synesthetic qualities, when culturally elaborated as they are in Greece, are an essential ingredient in ritual and everyday experiences of totality. Food does not simply symbolize social bonds and divisions; it participates in their creation and recreation.

References

Bubant, Nils (1998), "The odour of things: smell and the cultural elaboration of disgust in Eastern Indonesia," *Ethnos* 63: 48–80.

Classen, Constance, Howes, David, and Synnott, Anthony (1994), *Aroma: The Cultural History of Smell*, London: Routledge.

Cytowic, Richard (1973), *The Man Who Tasted Shapes*, London: Abacus.

Danforth, Loring (1982), *The Death Rituals of Rural Greece*, Princeton: Princeton University Press.

Engen, Trygg (1991), *Odor, Sensation and Memory*, New York: Praeger.

Fernandez, James (1982), *Bwiti: An Ethnography of the Religious Imagination in Africa*, Princeton: Princeton University Press.

——. (1986), *Persuasions and Performances*, Bloomington, IN: Indiana University Press.

Fine, Gary Alan (1996), *Kitchens: The Culture of Restaurant Work*, Berkeley, CA: University of California Press.

Fog Olwig, Karen and Hastrup, Kirsten (eds.) (1997), *Siting Culture: The Shifting Anthropological Object*, London: Routledge.

Frantzis, George (1962), *Strangers at Ithaca: The Story of the Spongers of Tarpon Springs*, St Petersburg, FL: Great Outdoors Publishing Co.

Fuster, Joaquin (1997), *The Prefrontal Cortex: Anatomy, Physiology and Neuropsychology of the Frontal Lobe*, Philadelphia: Lippincott-Raven.

Gell, Alfred (1977), "Magic, perfume, dream," ... *Symbols and Sentiments: Cross-Cultural Studies in Symbolism*, (ed.) Ioan Lewis, London: Academic Press: 25–38.

Hannerz, Ulf (1996), *Transnational Connections*, London: Routledge.

Hirschon, Renée (1998), *Heirs of the Greek Catastrophe*, Oxford: Berghan Press.

Jones, Harriet (1976), "Synesthesia and its role in memory," PhD dissertation, Department of Psychology, University of Texas, Austin.

Kahn, Miriam (1994), *Always Hungry, Never Greedy: Food and the Expression of Gender in a Melanesian Society*, Prospect Heights, IL: Waveland Press.

Kapella, Themelina (1981), *Kalymnian Echoes*, Athens. (In Greek.)

Luria, A. R. (1968), *The Mind of a Mnemonist*, London: Avon.

Lust, Theresa (1998), *Pass the Polenta and Other Writings From the Kitchen, With Recipes*, South Royalton, VT: Steerforth Press.

McGlone, Matthew (1996), "Conceptual metaphors and figurative language interpretation: food for thought?," *Journal of Memory and Language* 35: 544–65.

Nordstrom, Carolyn (1995), "War on the front lines," *Fieldwork Under Fire*, (ed.) C. Nordstrom and A. Robben, Berkeley: University of California Press: 129–53.

Papanikolas, Helen (1987), *Amalia-Yeiorgos*, Salt Lake City: University of Utah Press.

Proust, Marcel (1982), *Remembrance of Things Past*, Vol. 1, trans. C. K. Scott Moncrieff and Terence Kilmartin, New York: Vintage.

Rasmussen, Susan (1999), "Making better 'scents' in anthropology: Aroma in Thareg sociocultural systems and the shaping of ethnography," *Anthropological Quarterly* 72: 55–73.

Raspa, Richard (1984), "Exotic foods among Italian-Americans in Mormon Utah," *Ethnic and Regional Foodways in the United States*, (ed.) Linda Brown and Kay Mussell, Knoxville: University of Tennessee Press: 184–95.

Reyna, Stephen (2002), *Connections: Brain, Mind and Culture in Social Anthropology*, London: Routledge.

Seremetakis, C. N. (1991), *The Last Word: Women, Death and Divination in Inner Maui*, Chicago: University of Chicago Press.

Sperber, Dan (1975), *Rethinking Symbolism*, Cambridge: Cambridge University Press.

Sulton, Nancy (1999), *Exile and the Poetics of Loss in the Greek Tradition*, Lanham, MD: Rowman and Littlefield.

Sutton, David (1997), "The vegetarian anthropologist," *Anthropology Today* 13: 5–8.

Theodossopoulos, Dimitrios (1999), "The pace of the work and the logic of the harvest," *Journal of the Royal Anthropological Institute* (NS) 5: 611–26.

Thomassen, Bjørn (1996), "Border studies in Europe: symbolic and political boundaries, anthropological perspectives," *Europaea* 2: 37–48.

Tilley, Christopher (1999), *Metaphor and Material Culture*, Oxford: Basil Blackwell.

Vroon, Piet (1997), *Smell, The Secret Seducer*, trans. Paul Vincent, New York: Farrar, Straus and Giroux.

Ware, Fr. Kallistos (1979), *The Orthodox Way*, Crestwood, NY: St. Vladimir's Seminary Press.

31 Food and Emotion

Deborah Lupton

Food and eating habits are banal practices of everyday life; we all, as living beings, must eat to survive. This apparent banality, however, is deceptive. Food and eating habits and preferences are not simply matters of 'fuelling' ourselves, alleviating hunger pangs, or taking enjoyment in gustatory sensations. Food and eating are central to our subjectivity, or sense of self, and our experience of embodiment, or the ways that we live in and through our bodies, which itself is inextricably linked with subjectivity. As such, the meanings, discourses and practices around food and eating are worthy of detailed cultural analysis and interpretation...

It is now rarely asserted within sociology that a bodily process – be it a disease, a sexual longing, an emotional response or a craving for a certain food – is purely a product of biology. The social constructionist perspective is commonly articulated, an approach which I have adopted in my own analysis of the sociocultural meanings of food and eating. While I accept that there is, to some degree, a physiological component to the meanings and experiences around food – for it cannot be denied that without some form of nourishment, human bodies simply cannot exist – I argue that phenomena which are often understood to be largely biological, such as hunger, taste and food preferences, are also products of the sociocultural environment into which we are born. Thus, while humans enter the world with the need to eat to survive, from the moment of birth the ways in which individuals interact with other people and with cultural artefacts shape their responses to food.

There are manifold cultural meanings and discourses surrounding food practices and preferences in all human societies. Indeed, food is 'the symbolic medium par excellence' (Morse 1994: 95). Food consumption habits are not simply tied to biological needs but serve to mark boundaries between social classes, geographic regions, nations, cultures, genders, lifecycle stages, religions and occupations, to distinguish rituals, traditions, festivals, seasons and times of day. Food 'structures what counts as a person in our culture' (Curtin 1992: 4). Dietary habits are used to establish and symbolize control over one's body. Food may be classified into a number of binary categories: good or bad, masculine or feminine, powerful or weak, alive or dead, healthy or non-healthy, a comfort or a punishment, sophisticated or gauche, a sin or a virtue, animal or vegetable, raw or cooked, self or other. Each of these binary oppositions contains the power to shape food preferences and beliefs in everyday life, to support some food choices and militate against others, and to contribute to the construction of subjectivity and embodied experiences...

Laura Esquivel's best-selling magical realist novel, *Like Water for Chocolate* (1993), also made into a popular film, centres its action around the interaction of food preparation and eating with the protagonists' emotional states. In the novel there is a symbiotic relationship between food and emotion: food becomes a form of the communication of the emotions of Tita, the Mexican heroine, to the members of her family. The exotic dishes prepared by Tita absorb her emotional state at the time of preparation, and induce similar emotions in those who eat the dish. Thus the wedding cake prepared in great sorrow by Tita for her sister's wedding to Pedro, Tita's true love, causes the wedding guests to be overcome with great longing and tears at their first bite, followed by feelings of pain and frustration strong enough to induce nausea and vomiting. The quail in rose petal sauce Tita makes when her passion for Pedro is first ignited serves to incite a powerful lust in another of her sisters and communicates feelings of passion between Tita and Pedro as they eat the meal. Even the novel's title denotes the passions described in the book in the metaphor of boiling water to make hot chocolate.

As is so vividly demonstrated in the events in *Like Water for Chocolate*, there is a strong relationship between food, emotion and subjectivity. While this link has often been made in elite and popular culture, the emotional dimension of food has rarely been discussed in sociological writing. Yet there are clear associations between the sociocultural dimensions of the emotions and those of food and eating... The histories of the management of the emotions and the regulation of food practices and development of table manners in Western societies developed in parallel in relation to understandings of the 'civilized' body. Both emotional states and food and eating practices threaten self-containment and the transcendence of the mind by forcibly reminding individuals of their embodiment. Emotions, like food and eating, are commonly regarded as the preserve of the embodied self rather than the disembodied, philosophizing mind. Like food and eating practices, the emotions are traditionally linked with the feminine, with the disempowered and marginalized. The term 'emotion' is associated with disorder, with being non-systematic. The state of being 'emotional' is often contrasted with that of being 'rational'. The concept of 'giving in' to either the emotions or to gluttony, of 'losing control', is redolent with moralism. Such loss of control is positioned as 'uncivilized', for it reveals the base animality of 'drives' or 'instincts' that appear purely natural.

Food stirs the emotions, both because of its sensual properties and its social meanings. For many, the pleasures to be gained from food are the high points of their everyday sensual experiences. There is a particularly strong link between the senses of taste and smell and the emotional dimensions of human experience. Clearly the physical nature of food is an integral factor in the emotional responses it evokes. The actions of touching it, smelling it, preparing, it, taking it into the mouth, chewing and swallowing it are all sensual experiences that may evoke particular emotions on both the conscious and unconscious levels. The 'mouth feel' of foods is considered by food manufacturers to be integral to the popularity of foodstuffs quite apart from their actual taste. Hence the addition of gums to soft drinks sweetened with sugar substitutes to make the fluid feel as heavy in the mouth as if it were flavoured with sugar (Mintz 1986: 209). An important part of the popularity of chocolate as a food substance, it has been argued, is the pleasure aroused by its tactility: chocolate, unlike most other foods, literally melts in the mouth (Hamilton 1992: 26). Chillies excite the senses: they sting the hands when cut, and burn the mouth; the aroma of freshly baked bread inspires both hunger and a feeling of security. The sensation of consuming a food may inspire revulsion if a food is too soft, slippery, chewy or gritty, while the sensation of an overly full or empty stomach may inspire discomfort or pain.

However, like alcohol (which occupies a liminal category as a 'food') the feelings inspired by and associated with the consumption of food cannot easily be separated from its symbolic nature. Alcohol, taken in enough quantities, is assumed to have a directly physiological effect upon the body, inspiring exhilaration, relaxation, dulled senses. Yet these effects are inextricably interlinked with the cultural expectations around alcohol consumption. Alcohol is deeply connected with mood-setting, as a substance that divides the everyday working world from times of enjoyment and festiveness (Gusfield 1987: 79). Its consumption signals escape from the 'civilized' body into self-indulgence and physical and emotional release. We expect that alcohol will raise our spirits, and more often than not, it does. As a symbolic marker of relaxation and gaiety, alcohol prepares the body for release before it is even imbibed. So too, the symbolic meanings around food serve to prepare the body for either pleasure or revulsion. These meanings are constructed via acculturation into a culture, by learning the rules around which types of food are considered pleasurable and which revolting, but also through personal experience, including the unconscious.

There is a strong relationship between memory and the emotional dimension of food. Given that food is an element of the material world which embodies and organizes our relationship with the past in socially significant ways, the relationship between food preferences and memory may be regarded as symbiotic. Memory is embodied, often recalled via the sensations of taste and smell. The effects of memory are inscribed upon the body, in terms of such factors as posture, styles of walking, gesture and appetite for certain foods. The taste, smell and texture of food can therefore serve to trigger memories of previous food events and experiences around food, while memory can serve to delimit food preferences and choices based on experience. Preparing a meal may evoke memories of past events when that meal was prepared and eaten, conjuring up the emotions felt at that time, or the experience may cause one to look forward to the sharing of the meal with another, anticipating an emotional outcome.

There is a well-known and oft-quoted scene in Marcel Proust's work *Remembrance of Things Past*, in which the protagonist tastes a crumb of madeleine biscuit and finds himself transported back to the world of his childhood through its taste and odour. A more recent paean to the virtues of soup, published in a gourmet food magazine argued that soup, above all meals, is redolent with the feelings of belonging, well-being, consolation, reassurance and a sense of warmth, a means of self-fortification and restoration. The writer argues that:

> The food memories that haunt me most are carried on the drifting curls of steam from a soup bowl ... the soup I remember most vividly is a simple chicken broth strewn with giblets and egg noodles, that tasted of love, smelled of friendship and settled a gnawing, uneasy, restless feeling somewhere deep inside me.
>
> (Durack 1994: 13)

For some people, the smell of boiled cabbage is all that it takes to immediately transport them back to their years at school, evoking memories not only of the institutional food they received then but also the relationships and emotions of the whole schooling experience. The relationship works both ways: a certain memory may in turn generate a desire for a particular food to relive the emotions of that memory (or indeed, should the eating experience have been negative, a desire to avoid a certain food). Hence, bumping into an old schoolfriend may evoke nostalgic memories of meals eaten at school, producing a longing for such food to evoke the feelings of childhood (perhaps this would explain the recent phenomenon of the popularity of 'nursery' food such as cottage pie and steamed puddings at expensive and sophisticated restaurants!).

The power of the food/memory/emotion link is such that fragrances have been especially created to encapsulate our emotional responses to food tastes and smells. Vanilla is currently popular in perfumes, because it is soothing and comforting, evoking memories of childhood and simple pleasures like home-cooked cakes, and emotions of reassurance, familiarity and security. Other perfumes incorporate the smell of candyfloss and chocolate to achieve the same effect. By contrast, peppermint is believed to have an uplifting, invigorating effect. It has also been claimed by researchers that the smell of chocolate chip cookies reduces aggression. Indeed, one fragrance expert has claimed that the 'taste notes' of successful perfumes are 'all evocations of holidays and childhood'. He points to the close association between culinary culture and perfumery, pointing out that perfumes with aldehyde notes have been particularly successful in Asia because the key ingredients of Asian cooking – coriander, citrus flavours, coconut and ginger – are rich in aldehydes (Goldstein, 1994). For similar reasons, the smell of baking bread and biscuits is routinely channelled to shoppers in malls to attract them to purchase food, and people trying to sell their house are counselled to brew fresh coffee or put some biscuits in the oven before potential buyers arrive, to invoke positive emotions. This linkage may take place at a subconscious or unconscious level, at which certain tastes and smells of food may evoke emotional responses derived from previous experiences without that connection being consciously recognized.

Hunger is not often regarded as an emotion, as it is viewed more as a drive or instinct unmediated by social states. Yet, it would be difficult to argue that hunger is purely a biological phenomenon, given the web of cultural significations that surround and govern the ways and amounts and times that we eat. The physiological relationship between the body's recognition of the need for food and the emotional state is clearly complex. There are different kinds of hunger, related to the concept of appetite. An appetite is an emotionally flavoured hunger: the appetite experienced when a favourite food is being cooked and is almost ready to be served differs from that of the simple hunger felt when the stomach is empty and requires food. So too, lack of appetite is often an emotional response, an interaction between a feeling of anxiety, nervousness, grief or even joy or elation (the emotion of being 'in love' is often associated with a loss of appetite). In such an emotional state involving loss of appetite, hunger may still be experienced as a gnawing feeling, an awareness of an empty stomach, but the desire to eat is stifled; food may even appear nauseating. On the other hand, the experience of hunger, if strong enough, and if not satisfied, may inspire the emotions of anxiety, irritability or anger. An appetite, or desire, for a certain food may exist independently of a feeling for hunger, and hunger may exist without having much of an appetite.

Humans' relationships with food and eating are subject to the most powerful emotions experienced in any context. Halligan notes that the terms used in cooking are typically violent and cruel, associated with rage:

> Look at this list of verbs associated with the preparation of food: pound, beat, strip, whip, boil, sear, grind, tear, crack, mince, mash, crush, stuff, chop. Images of torture occur: *sauter* is to make jump in the pan while applying heat, there is skinning and peeling and bleeding and hanging and binding, not to mention skewering and spitting, topping and tailing. Medieval cookbooks say 'smite them in pieces', 'hew them in gobbets'. The process of turning raw materials into stuff fit to eat is a series of bloody battles and underhand tricks.
>
> (Halligan 1990: 118–19)

Food/non-food is a potent opposition that may be manipulated to serve the emotions of vengeance, anger and hatred. One of the worst retaliations a person can inflict upon an enemy (short of killing or physically attacking that person) is to contaminate their food; to trick them or force them into eating a substance that is poisonous, disgusting or defiling. In illustrating this point, an Australian magazine article entitled 'Cooking with a vengeance: food for people you hate' discussed the ways in which 'Food and revenge have gone together as naturally as wine and cheese from the beginning of time' (Littlewood 1994: 113). The writer went on humorously to describe the 'perfect' meal for guests 'we loathe or need to get even with'. Such a meal is a Sunday lunch barbecue, in which the guests are given disgusting food... Peter Greenaway's film *The Cook, the Thief, His Wife, and Her Lover* is filled with vivid images connecting food, violence and anger. The thief makes a man eat faeces, the wife's lover is killed by being stuffed with the leaves of his books, the wife retaliates by having the cook prepare the corpse of the lover and serve it to her husband, who is forced to eat the roasted flesh as an act of humiliation and contamination.

One source of negative emotions such as revulsion, disgust, anger and hate is the disjuncture between individuals' understandings of 'appropriate' foods and that of others. Revulsion for the food eaten by another is a common expression of discrimination and xenophobia, a means of distinguishing between social groups: 'As Montaigne long ago pointed out, everyone is attached to the food habits of his [sic] childhood and finds himself inclined to consider foreign foods and ways of preparing them absurd and even disgusting' (Revel 1992: 244). Pierre Bourdieu has commented on the ways in which a distaste for another group's food serves to distance oneself from that group, as a means of distinction: 'Tastes are perhaps first and foremost distastes, disgust provoked by horror or visceral intolerance ("sick-making") of the tastes of others... Aesthetic intolerance can be terribly violent. Aversion to different lifestyles is perhaps one of the strongest barriers between the classes; class endogamy is evidence of this' (1984: 56). While Bourdieu is referring to differences between social classes, perhaps an even more potent source of disgust is that felt for foods prepared and eaten by people of another ethnicity or race. Those who eat strikingly different foods or similar foods in different ways may sometimes even be thought to be less human. People from Western countries routinely depict the dishes eaten in countries such as China as disgusting, as in the following excerpt from an Australian magazine:

> The Chinese are renowned for their pragmatic approach to food. The basic tenet appears to be if it's not poisonous, eat it. Depending on the province you're in, the slippery morsels atop the flinty rice could be fish lips or eyeballs, the meat may be *chat du jour* or chopped owl, while those bony little things which look like a baby's hands are likely to be chicken or duck feet... In Hong Kong, snake restaurants abound, while at streetside stalls, little rice sparrows are roasted whole (yes, beaks, startled eyes, the lot) and threaded on to skewers. Sweet and sour snake or sparrow on a stick, anyone? The concept is decidedly Monty Pythonesque.
>
> (Kurosawa, 1994: 8)

Asian people have been equally appalled by some of the food eaten by Europeans. Driver (1983: 73) quotes a Chinese description of strong cheese as the 'putrefied mucous discharge of an animal's guts'.

Food, of course, is not only associated with negative emotions, but is surrounded with the strongest pleasurable feelings that may be experienced with any phenomena. In Mintz's study of the history of sugar he remarks that 'Sugar represents power – the good life, the rich life, the full life' (1986: 8). In ancient British and classical Greek and Latin literature, sweet substances such as honey and sugar were associated with happiness and well-being, the elevation of mood and erotic feelings (1986: 154–5). It has become a stereotype that chocolate is a sign of romance, also symbolizing luxury, decadence, indulgence, reward, sensuousness and femininity (Barthel 1989). When it was first introduced into Europe, chocolate was a luxury item, becoming a status symbol as a drink of the French aristocracy in the seventeenth century (Schivelbusch 1993: 91). While coffee at that time was represented as a stimulant, preparing individuals for the day ahead, chocolate denoted the meanings of indolence, leisure and erotic languor. Well into the nineteenth century, chocolate was believed by Europeans to be an aphrodisiac (Schivelbusch, 1993: 91–2). These meanings remain strongly evident today. Advertisements for chocolates routinely depict them as part of a scenario of young heterosexual love, as in the advertisement for Baci (Italian for 'kisses') chocolates using the slogan, 'One kiss and you'll fall in love'. Similarly, chocolate boxes themselves depict other commodities coded as romantic such as roses, satin or champagne. Boxes of chocolates are sold to men to give to women as 'an essential step in seduction... Women are supposed to give in to men as they give in to sweets, with chocolates symbolizing the impending breakdown of sexual resistance' (Barthel 1989: 433). There is a conflation in such representations of the emotional experiences of being 'in love' and of eating chocolate. Just as romantic love is believed to 'sweep you away', to immerse individuals in an intense experience of heightened feeling and euphoria (Jackson 1993), so too, chocolate is culturally understood as a highly emotionally coded food that inspires feelings of self-indulgence and hedonistic ecstasy. Both experiences are transitory and relatively fleeting, but intense in their emotionality; both are highly sensual and embodied. Both experiences remove the individual from the everyday, mundane world.

Food and eating, then, are intensely emotional experiences that are intertwined with embodied sensations and strong feelings ranging the spectrum from disgust, hate, fear and anger to pleasure, satisfaction and desire. They are central to individuals' subjectivity and their sense of distinction from others.

References

Barthel, D. (1989), 'Modernism and marketing: the chocolate box revisited', *Theory, Culture and Society* 6: 429–38.

Bourdieu, P. (1984), *Distinction: A Social Critique of the Judgement of Taste*, London: Routledge and Kegan Paul.

Curtin, D. (1992), 'Food/body/person', *Cooking, Eating, Thinking*, (eds), D. Curtin and L. Heldke, Bloomington, IN: Indiana University Press: 123–44.

Driver, C. (1983), *The British at Table, 1940–1980*, London: Chatto and Windus/ Hogarth Press.

Durack, T. (1994), 'The meaning of soup', *Australian Gourmet Traveller*, June: 10–13.

Goldstein, N. (1994), 'Edible scents', *Vogue Entertaining*, December/January: 36.

Gusfield, J. (1987), 'Passage to play: rituals of drinking time in American society', *Constructive Drinking*, (ed.) M. Douglas, Cambridge: Cambridge University Press: 73–90.

Halligan, M. (1990), *Eat My Words*, Sydney: Angus and Robertson.

Hamilton, S. (1992), 'Why the lady loves $C_6H_5(CH_2)$ NH_2', *New Scientist* 19/26 December: 26–8.

Jackson, S. (1993), 'Even sociologists fall in love: an exploration in the sociology of emotions', *Sociology* 27(2): 201–20.

Littlewood, F. (1994), 'Cooking with a vengeance: food for people you hate', *Good Weekend*, 3 December: 112–18.

Mintz, S. (1986), *Sweetness and Power: The Place of Sugar in Modern History*, New York: Penguin.

Morse, M. (1994), 'What do cyborgs eat? Oral logic in an information society', *Discourse* 16 (3): 86–123.

Revel, J-F. (1992), from *Culture and Cuisine*, in Curtin and Heldke, *Cooking, Eating, Thinking*, Bloomington: Indiana University Press: 244–50.

Schivelbusch, W. (1993), *Tastes of Paradise*, New York: Vintage.

32

The Pale Yellow Glove

M. F. K. Fisher

Once at least in the life of every human, whether he be brute or trembling daffodil, comes a moment of complete gastronomic satisfaction.

It is, I am sure, as much a matter of spirit as of body. Everything is right; nothing jars. There is a kind of harmony, with every sensation and emotion melted into one chord of well-being.

Oddly enough, it is hard for people to describe these moments. They have sunk beatifically into the past, or have been ignored or forgotten in the harsh rush of the present. Sometimes they are too keen to be bandied in conversation, too delicate to be pinioned by our insufficient mouthings.

Occasionally, in a moment of wide-flung inebriation or the taut introspection of search for things past, a person hits upon his peak of gastronomic emotion. He remembers it with shock, almost, and with a nostalgic clarity that calls tears to his inward-looking eyes.

If you can surprise him at such quick times, and make him talk, you are more than fortunate. It is as tricky a business as to watch a bird of paradise at play.

Two or three times I have been successful. Of course there were a few other times when I have almost felt so, but then I had asked. And if you ask people, they search their memories, and occasionally produce a sad shadow of the spontaneity you desire, a pale image of the vivid shaking recollection that should have sprung forth unaware.

I remember once I asked a beautiful flat-faced actress with golden hair and skin. She spoke vaguely and with a kind of embarrassment of two steaks that she had stolen from a rich woman's dog, and broiled over a driftwood fire, and shared on the Cape Cod beach with a hungry stonecutter.

Two or three people, when I've prodded them, have mumbled of apples: biting into them, feeling the cold juice flow into the mouth corners, hearing the snap of skin and pulp.

But the spontaneous revelations are rare. They must, from what I have discovered, be inspired by wine or high emotional pressure. They are thus doubly poignant.

I

Miss Lyse was an English teacher in a middle-sized town in Bavaria. She had been one ever since her militantly British mother had brought her there, some sixty years before. She would be one until she died, helped always and in spite of her dwindling powers of instruction by the impatiently thoughtful families whose parents and grandparents had recited the verb TO BE at her virginal knee.

It was easy to see that she had once been very lovely. Even now her small dark-eyed head rose above its lumpy old body like the dream of a swan, or a piece of Chinese crystal.

It was hard to see why she had not long since married some member of the aristocratic families with whom she lived; hard, that is, until you heard her describe—so lovingly, too—her genteel Tartar of a mother, who on her deathbed had made Lyse swear never, *never* to forget her English accent. And now, with this old maid who for more than half a century had spent all her days with the fine flower of Germany, her soft flat voice was as British as a currant bun; her intonation so carefully preserved marked her anywhere as a "Miss," never *a Fräulein,* and her German was half English, her English very German.

She was garrulous, with the embarrassingly naive language of an aged person who has spent all her life explaining things simply to children who might have listened better had the explanations been complex.

She talked with a vivacity which had long since ceased to be affected, and was now as much a part of her as her jet brooch of the young Queen Victoria, or her lace fichu that had been admired (on another's shoulder) by Franz Josef.

"Once, my dears," she told us on a chill October afternoon when even shawls laid along the window ledges could not keep cold drafts from shushing into her high attic room, "once I stood so close to the great Sadi Carnot that to touch him I would have been able! Yes, then I was that near!

"That was the summer after we went to Garmisch, to the *Schloss* of my little pupils—you remember?"

She peered merrily at us, and we nodded recognition to a season dead some forty years before we were conceived. We poured another glass of sherry for her, the sherry we had brought to warm her bones while we were far from her and Bavaria.

(And here it is perhaps significant to say that all old pupils treated Miss Lyse thus, feeling a kind of guilty neglect if they did not often go to her stuffy pleasant garret with wine, a cold chicken, even a pat of sweet butter. I am sure that we kept her alive for years in this compulsive, desultory way—)

"Yes, that was *such* a nice summer! The trees in full bloom early were, and everybody said that *never* had there been so many forest flowers. I remember the *Graf* himself said that to me, one morning on the stairs!"

She colored delicately, and raised her young dark eyes above the rim of her glass. "I used to wear flowers in my hair—it was black then—except at dinner, of course, when I was invited down to dine with the family if they needed an extra one at table.

"But there was one thing about that summer—when was it, in 'sixty-eight?" She looked sharply at our blank faces, as if she had a good mind to rap our knuckles for inattention, and then laughed. "What does it matter? It was several years ago, yes? A beautiful summer.

"My dear blessed mother was with me, in the village near the *Schloss*—I had not been long away from England, and she watched over me—and one day, one day we had a picnic, a real English tea in the forest! It was lovely!

"My mother, a sweet young Russian girl who taught also at the *Schloss*, and—"

Suddenly she put down her glass, giggled, and peeked naughtily at us between her knobby, loose-skinned fingers.

"Now you must never tell, never!" She looked stern for a second, and then giggled again. "It was very daring, but my dear mother was there and Tanya, and – three – young – gentlemen – from—the *Schloss*!

"*Yes,* my dears ! We all went on the picnic, Tanya and the three young gentlemen (so handsome were they), and myself, and of course my dear good mamma to see that everything was proper.

"*Well,*" and she settled herself back in her chair as we filled her glass again, "we went far into the woods, with a servant to carry the tea-basket. We came to a stream, such a small sweet brooklet was it, with flowers and watercress on its borders.

"My mother sat down, and whilst the servant built a little blaze yet, she got out her silver teapot, which had gone to India twelve times with her. It was a pretty teapot.

"We gathered watercress. One of the young gentlemen—what *was* his name, now?—got his gloves quite wet. They were pale yellow gloves, of the thinnest kid, and from München, too.

"Then my dear mamma boiled water from the little brook, the most sparkling water I have ever seen, and when it just began to bubble she poured it over the tea, and then we drank. And, my dears, I never, *never* have such tea tasted!"

Miss Lyse looked at us almost sombrely. We felt very young and serious as we watched her raise her glass slowly to her lips and then set it down again.

"No, it was tea like no tea before—or since. I have often boiled the water from brooklets, and poured it over the same brand of tea, *and* in my dear mother's silver teapot that to India twelve times went. But that tea, that summer afternoon near Garmisch, with dear mamma and Tanya and the three young gentlemen—and the little flowers, and I remember the poor yellow gloves—"

Miss Lyse was silent. She sipped slowly, and her eyes looked far back, like the picture of Albrecht Dürer's mother.

"Thank God in heaven," she concluded, emphatically, "that my poor departed mother watched over me, or I should not be where I am! That tea, so clear, so piquant like fine *Liebfraumilch*—"

II

Occasionally I hear from Al a dreamy, half-coherent reference to one day when he went to a small restaurant in Paris, and sat alone before an iced silver bowl of wood strawberries, spooning them up all coated with the fine effervescence of a bottle of champagne.

That must have been a good day, like the far September Wednesday in 1819 when John Keats wrote to his friend:

> Talking of Pleasure, this moment I was writing with one hand, and with the other holding to my Mouth a Nectarine—good God how fine. It went down soft pulpy, slushy, oozy—all its delicious embonpoint melted down my throat like a large beatified Strawberry. I shall certainly breed.

III

Sometimes it is hard to say, even from remembrance, just what magic chord has sounded for you with the right blending of time, space, and the physical sensation of eating. On a hot day it is easiest to think back to such things as silver-green mint juleps, or the smooth golden taste of cold papaya on a freighter near Guatemala, or crisp lettuce anywhere.

On a cold day such things as hot baked potatoes, all sprinkled over with fresh-ground pepper and sweet butter, or creamy tomato soup with a faint smell of cinnamon to it, or rare steaming beef, pink and succulent: these are the things that flow first into our remembrance on cold days.

There is one time, though, one souvenir of eating, that I can keep with impunity throughout all seasonal changes. Perhaps I remember it oftener in winter, but that does not affect its poignancy.

When I belonged to the Alpine Club of the Cote d'Or, I felt rather lost. The robust elderly members were more than courteous to me; the walks were energetic but agreeable; the carefully planned feasts at little village inns were masterpieces, even though each day's march was so routed that the most difficult part of it came after the many courses and as many wines of the dinner.

Still, I felt rather lonesome, "foreign," until one bitter February Sunday when we stood panting on a hill near Les Laumes-Alésia. The earth was hard as granite beneath me, and air drawn into my tired lungs felt like heavy fire before it thawed. I broke a twig clumsily between my mittened fingers.

"Here!" a voice said, roughly. I looked with surprise at the old general, who stood, shaggy and immense, beside me. He had never done more than bow to me, and listen now and then with a face of stony suffering to my accent, which always grew ten times as thick when he was near. What did he want now?

"Here! Try some of this, young lady!" And he held out a piece of chocolate, pale brown with cold. I smiled and took it, resolving to say as little as possible.

He cleared his throat grumpily and shifted his eyes to the far thunderous horizon.

In my mouth the chocolate broke at first like gravel into many separate, disagreeable bits. I began to wonder if I could swallow them. Then they grew soft, and melted voluptuously into a warm stream down my throat.

The little doctor came bustling up, his proudly displayed alpenstock tucked under one short arm.

"Here! Wait, wait!" he cried. "Never eat chocolate without bread, young lady! Very bad for the interior, very bad. My General, you are remiss!"

The soldier peered down at him like a horse looking at a cheeky little dog, and then rumbled, "Give us some, then, old fellow. Trade two pieces (and big ones, mind) for some of our chocolate?"

And in two minutes my mouth was full of fresh bread, and melting chocolate, and as we sat gingerly, the three of us, on the frozen hill, looking down into the valley where Vercingetorix had fought so splendidly, we peered shyly and silently at each other and smiled and chewed at one of the most satisfying things I have ever eaten. I thought vaguely of the metamorphosis of wine and bread—

32a
Christmas Cake

Take five pounds of flour, mix with it a dessertspoonful of salt, rub in three-quarters of a pound of butter and one pound of lard. Put in half a pint of good fresh brewers' yeast, and knead as for common bread. If there is any difficulty about the yeast, baking powder may be used, allowing a heaped teaspoonful of ordinary baking powder for every pound of material. If yeast is used, let the dough rise before adding the other ingredients. Mix in three pounds of currants, one and one-half pounds of moist sugar, a whole nutmeg, a quarter of a pound of candied lemon peel finely minced, a tablespoonful of brandy, and four eggs, well-beaten. Butter the mold and bake in a moderate oven for about two hours.

Our Home Cyclopedia, 1889

32b
Sunshine Cake

Whites of seven eggs, yolks of five. One cup fine granulated sugar. One scant cup of flour measured after sifting five times. One-fourth teaspoonful of cream of tartar, one teaspoonful orange extract. Beat yolks till thick and set aside. Now add a pinch of salt and the cream of tartar to the whites and beat till very stiff, add sugar, beat thoroughly. Then add flavoring and beaten yolks, beat lightly and carefully stir in the flour. Bake in tube pan in moderate oven forty to fifty minutes. Invert pan to cool.

Recipe handwritten on flyleaf of *Our Home Cyclopedia*, 1889

Part VIII

Artifice and Authenticity

Preface

Several of the chapters that have gone before address taste and food in terms of group and individual identity. Part VII concerns memories of tastes so vivid that they can be revived with the smallest hint of an old, familiar flavor. The identification of a taste as "of" a region or society or as conjuring up the very essence of a moment from the past, presume that there is a way to detect that a taste is *genuine*. But by what gauge is such genuineness measured? This is the subject that unites the final essays of this volume.

The first two contributions concern the chemical manufacture of flavors, recalling some of the issues addressed in Part I regarding the science of taste and the triggers of sensation. As Constance Classen, David Howes, and Anthony Synnott observe, the generation of "artificial tastes" is widely practiced with current food production. Even natural flavors are "enhanced," leaving the unsuspecting consumer with a heightened expectation for taste that nature itself may not produce. Similar themes are explored by Roger Haden's study of the tastes that issue from cooking practices designed for speed and convenience, such as frozen foods readily heated and products from an entirely new technology for cooking, the microwave oven. Both these chapters confound the issue of "genuine" tastes, for many of the flavors of today's marketplace have no traditional standard for comparison. As all of these authors observe, artificial tastes are postmodern phenomena, and some of them—such as the cola flavor now popular in drinks—are simulacra with no genuine article to copy.

With expansive global migration has come an explosion of restaurants that provide exotic cuisines to their customers. As Allison James points out, the promise of most of these for an "authentic" eating experience is exceedingly complicated and indeed compromised. At the same time, no cuisine is static, and therefore there is no point at which an "ethnic" tradition of cooking can be frozen and exported. What is more, a good deal of global eating now occurs in chain and fast-food restaurants, where sameness rather than difference is valued. These eating options swing between the familiar and unfamiliar, the comforting and challenging, and questions of authenticity (and identity) require careful analysis in such circumstances.

Sometimes the search for authenticity invites reaching back into the past. In Part VI Jukka Gronow described the attempts in Stalinist Russia to cultivate the taste of Soviet citizens. Now Darra Goldstein considers dining in post-Soviet Russia and the Moscow restaurant scene, where various claims for authentic dining are as much the product of romantic imagination as of revived traditions of cooking. Performance, she points out, has a long tradition in Russian dining, a practice continued with extravagant surroundings of restaurants which impart the impression of eating in a time and place long gone.

In the end, if authenticity is to refer to tastes themselves, we return to the problematics of measuring experiences that are personal and fleeting. There are many meanings of "authentic," as Lisa Heldke argues, and while some are suspect not all of them are unattainable. This final chapter leaves us to reflect upon the possibilities for encountering expanded and generous worlds of taste.

33

Artificial Flavours

Constance Classen, David Howes, and Anthony Synnott

'I think it's the best blueberry flavor that's ever been made. And there's not a scrap of blueberry in it', boasts the head flavourist at International Flavors and Fragrances Inc. in an article in the *Smithsonian* (Shell 1986: 79). This remark provides a fitting introduction to the subject of artificial flavours[1] and their role in modern food.

Artificial flavours were invented in the late nineteenth century, but didn't become prevalent until the 1960s. At first such flavours were used to add taste and aroma to a limited range of foods – candies and beverages, for example – and to provide inexpensive substitutes for certain spices. No one expected them to completely replace natural flavours. Flavour engineers were accordingly modest about their achievements. A flavour company bulletin from the 1950s reads: 'We are proud to announce our new improved cherry flavor, of course it is still no match for Mother Nature's' (Rosenbaum 1979: 87).

In the 1960s, however, flavourists set out to recreate virtually the whole spectrum of food flavours, from fruits and vegetables to meats. They have not been completely successful: some flavours, notably chocolate, coffee and bread, have eluded accurate simulation. None the less, the majority of the food on supermarket shelves today has at least some artificial flavouring. The only reason why synthetic versions of even more foods are not available is not because imitations of their flavours are lacking, but because their texture and appearance has thus far proved difficult to duplicate: 'If manufacturers manage to mold a chicken shape from vegetable protein, [flavorists] can dress it immediately with imitation chicken breast flavor, chicken fat flavor, chicken skin flavor and basic chicken flavor' (Rosenbaum 1979: 86).

Major advances in flavour simulation have been made possible by the invention of the gas liquid chromatographer, which can chart the individual constituents of a particular flavour. This enables flavourists to identify the components of a flavour and reproduce them using chemicals known as 'flavomatics'. Not all the components or 'notes' present in the natural flavour are reproduced, only those deemed to be essential to its characteristic savour – perhaps twenty-five out of hundreds. In fact, by emphasizing certain flavour notes and downplaying or eliminating others, flavourists can create flavours that taste fuller and more palatable – at least to modern tastes – than the original.

The world of flavomatics has its unsavoury side as well, made up of an array of unappetizing flavour notes. 'Sweaty notes', for instance, are essential to the composition of such flavours as imitation rum and butterscotch, while 'faecal notes' give a fullbodied edge to cheese and nut flavours. Processed fruit flavours include a burnt undertone to mimic the effects of cooking. Artificial canned tomato flavours, in turn, must include the tinny taste consumers have come to expect from canned foods (Rosenbaum 1979: 81, 83–4). It is such graphic touches that enable artificial flavours to create a virtual reality of smell and taste.

Flavourists, indeed, are no longer willing to take second place to Mother Nature. Ads for their products now boast such wonders as coconut flavour that 'tastes more like coconuts than coconuts' (Rosenbaum 1979: 81). In this enchanted garden of ideal synthetic savours, natural flavours intrude like a bad memory. Next to a well-made, sweet, full, artificial orange flavour, a real orange will likely taste sour and bland – a poor imitation. Furthermore, nature is unreliable and inconstant. Fruits and vegetables will only be in season during certain times of the year, and their quality will vary from crop to crop. Artificial fruit and vegetable flavours are available year-round and are always at their peak. Fruits and vegetables grow old and decay, they carry dirt, they often have unpalatable peels. Their synthetic essences, in contrast, are pristine and unchanging: 'pure' flavour (87).

Some artificial flavours have no counterpart in nature. The cola flavour found in soft drinks, for example, is the invention of an American pharmacist and tastes nothing like the cola nuts from which it takes its name (Shell 1986: 80). Such purely synthetic creations, called 'fantasy flavours', are rare, however, as most artificial flavours are based on natural products.

Working against the complete triumph of artificial flavours is the public's growing distrust of synthetic food additives, which they fear may be carcinogenic or otherwise harmful. Such concerns notwithstanding, however, modern consumers have come to prefer strong and straightforward synthetic savours to their more subtle and complex natural counterparts. The trend is towards 'larger-than-life' flavours, especially popular among the young (Shell 1986: 84).

At first, the flavour industry tried to counter concerns over the safety of its chemical creations by questioning the safety of consuming the products of Mother Nature. An industry report from the 1970s thus describes natural foods as 'a wild mixture of substances created by plants or organisms for completely different non-food purposes – their survival and reproduction', which 'came to be consumed by humans at their own risk' (Rosenbaum 1979: 88). Artificial flavours, on the other hand, the argument ran, have been tailor-made for human consumption.

Much as it desired to, however, the flavour industry has been unable to stem the 'back to nature' tide. In recent years researchers have accordingly been working to find alternatives to artificial flavours which will be able to satisfy both the public's demand for strong flavours and its desire for natural foods. One project involves engineering super-flavourful fruits and vegetables especially for use in the flavour industry (Shell 1986: 84–6).

Of course, there is no real risk of artificial flavours definitively losing favour in the West. For one thing, the health concerns which prompt consumers to fear food additives also make them avid for safe substitutes for such suspect natural substances as sugar, fat and salt. For another, while artificial flavours can be used to give appealing savours to foods which are low in nutritive value (but big in profits) – such as soft drinks – they can also do the same to highly nourishing, low-cost foods – such as soybean products – making artificial flavours a potentially valuable tool in the struggle for a more equitable food order. Perhaps most importantly, modern consumers have become too accustomed to having a wide range of flavours at their disposal to willingly give up a number of their favourites, simply because their availability in a natural form is limited and their artificial counterparts suspect (Shell 1986: 82, Rosenbaum 1979: 91–2).

Many flavours (such as vanilla and maple) are currently known to the general public only in their synthetic forms. This may increasingly be the case in the future, as artificially flavoured foods become more common worldwide. To quote a flavourist:

> In 20 years… I'll bet you that only 5 percent of the people will have tasted fresh strawberry, so whether we like it or not, we people in the flavor industry will really be defining what the next generation thinks is strawberry. And the same goes for a lot of other foods that will soon be out of the average consumer's reach.
>
> (Rosenbaum 1979: 92)

For all those born into this new world of designer flavours, the scents and savours of dinner will often likely originate not in nature, but in laboratory vials, numbered and stored in an industrial flavour bank…

Smell: The Postmodern Sense?

In our postmodern world smell is often a notable (or, increasingly, scarcely noticed) absence. Odours are suppressed in public places, there are no smells on television, the world of computers is odour-free, and so on. This olfactory 'silence' notwithstanding, smell would seem to share many of the traits commonly attributed to postmodernity. Let us make a comparison.

The postmodern era we live in is characterized by a loss of faith in universalist myths, such as Christianity or Progress, and a corresponding emphasis on the personal and local, on allegiance to one's own group. The breakdown of social structures, including language, encourages border-crossing (or simply lane-hopping) between such formerly rigid cultural categories as 'art' and 'life' or 'male' and 'female'. The past irrelevant, the future uncertain, postmodernity is a culture of 'now', a pastiche of styles and genres which exists in an eternal present. Postmodernity is also a culture of imitations and simulations, where copies predominate over originals and images over substance. The driving power of postmodernity is consumer capitalism, the endless production of goods and their investment with a quasi-religious aura of desirability.[2]

How does smell also exemplify these characteristics? First of all, odours are, by nature, personal and local. This enables olfactory values to be used to reinforce the tribal allegiances of postmodernity, in which the 'goodness' of one's own group is contrasted with the 'foulness' of others. At the same time, smells resist containment in discrete units, whether physical or linguistic; they cross borders, linking disparate categories and confusing boundary lines. Furthermore, smell, like taste, is a sensation of the moment, it cannot be preserved. We do not know what the past smelled like, and in the future our own odour will be lost. While odours cannot be preserved, however, they can be simulated. Commercially produced synthetic odours pervade the marketplace, enveloping consumer goods in ideal olfactory images.

This last point is best illustrated by an analysis of the industry of artificial flavours. The widespread replacement of natural flavours with artificial imitations which we find in the contemporary food industry exemplifies how, in Jean Baudrillard's words, the world has come to be 'completely catalogued and analyzed and then artificially revived as though real' (1983: 16). Artificial flavours are created by the synthetic reproduction of individual flavour notes present in the original natural flavours. The flavourist may thus be regarded as the arch-agent in the process of production outlined by Baudrillard where: 'The real is produced from miniaturized units ... and with these it can be reproduced an indefinite number of times' (3).

Ironically, in order to create 'larger-than-life' savours, flavourists actually reduce the number of components present in the natural flavour. By reproducing only those notes deemed essential to a flavour's characteristic taste and smell, they are able to produce a heightened sensation of that flavour. Artificial flavours are consequently at once much less than their originals and much more. Our contemporary craving for larger-than-life flavour is reminiscent of the medieval appetite for spices. While spices brought medievals a taste of Eden, however, artificial flavours are reminiscent rather of Disneyland, a synthetic paradise of consumer delights.[3]

The recession from and reinvention of reality occasioned by artificial flavours is aptly symbolized by the way Coca-Cola, with its undeniably artificial flavour, is paraded as 'the real thing'. Coke is not a real thing in that it is not natural. Coke is an artificial thing. Nonetheless, in that the reality of our world is increasingly defined and created for us by artifice (television, cinema, advertising), Coca-Cola is real. Put otherwise, having no basis in nature, Coca-Cola is able to represent the new, infinitely desirable, imagineered reality, with no tattered shreds of the shabby old reality clinging to it.

Smell . . . was considered an important force in the premodern West. This fact has not been lost on fragrance marketers, who make use of many of the ancient associations of smell – with magic, with sexual power, with healing – in order to promote their products. The very commercial process which ostensibly promotes traditional olfactory meanings, however, obviates the possibility of any real return to them, by transforming images of olfactory power into advertising copy.

In the past, essences were indicative of the intrinsic worth of the substances from which they emanated. Indeed, to encounter a scent was to encounter proof of a material presence, a trail of existence which could be traced to its source. Today's synthetic scents, however, are evocative of things which are not there, of presences which are absent: we have floral-scented perfumes which were never exhaled by a flower, fruit-flavoured drinks with not a drop of fruit juice in them, and so on. These artificial odours are a sign without a referent, smoke without fire, pure olfactory image.

This then is the manner in which smell, denied and ignored by scholars of modernity, can be called a 'postmodern' sense. Postmodernity, however, in no way allows for a full range of olfactory expression. Odours are rather eliminated from society and then reintroduced as packaged agents of fantasy, a means of recovering or recreating a body, an identity, a world, from which one has already been irrevocably alienated. The question is, will smell, seduced by an endless procession of olfactory simulacra, succumb to its postmodern fate, or will it – ever elusive – transcend its postmodern categorizations to remind us of our organic nature and even hint at a realm of the spirit.

Notes

1. In the flavour industry, flavour is defined as 'the perception of volatile flavoring substances by the nose before and during the consumption of food', hence primarily relating to the sense of smell (van Ejik 1992: 3–4).

2. On the condition of postmodernity, see Kearney 1988, Connor 1989, Bauman 1991.

3. On the magic consumer kingdom of Disneyland, see Eco, 1986: 43–8.

References

Baudrillard, J. (1983), *Simulations*, trans. P. Foss, P. Patton and P. Beitchman, New York: Semiotext(e).

Bauman, Z. (1991), *Intimations of Postmodernity*, London: Routledge.

Connor, S. (1989), *Postmodernist Culture: An Introduction to Theories of the Contemporary*, Oxford: Blackwell.

Eco, U. (1986), *Travels in Hyperreality*, trans. W. Weaver, San Diego, CA: Harcourt Brace Jovanovich.

Kearney, R. (1988), *The Wake of Imagination: Toward a Postmodern Culture*, Minneapolis: University of Minnesota Press.

Rosenbaum, R. (1979), 'Today the strawberry, tomorrow…' in N. Klein, (ed.) *Culture, Curers, and Contagion*, Novato, CA: Chandler and Sharp.

Shell, E. Ruppel (1986), 'Chemists whip up a tasty mess of artificial flavors', *Smithsonian*, vol. 17, no. 1.

van Ejik, T. (1992), 'The flavor of cocoa and chocolate and the flavoring of compound coatings', *Dragoco Report*, no. 1.

33a
Rainbow Delight Cake

1 package lemon-flavored cake mix
1 egg or low-cholesterol substitute
1 cup lemon soda—either diet or regular
Instant vanilla pudding
Assorted multicolored jelly beans

Spray the bottom and sides of a cake pan with nonstick cooking spray. Mix together in a large bowl the cake mix, egg or egg substitute, and soda. Bake in a moderate oven for 30 minutes or until the cake pulls away from the sides of the pan. While the cake is cooking, mix the instant pudding. Prick the cool cake all over with a fork. Spread the pudding over the cake. Top with jelly beans or colored sprinkles.

34

Taste in an Age of Convenience

From Frozen Food to Meals in 'the Matrix'

Roger Haden

The use, understanding and experience of the sense of taste has been and continues to be shaped within particular historical contexts by means of specific technologies: technoscientific and discursive, artefactual and conceptual. To situate taste in the contemporary Western context therefore requires consideration of the major forces (contingent upon such technologies) which on a number of levels have affected the experience of taste. Firstly, both modern and postmodern food cultures need to be conceived of in relation to radical changes to food production techniques and to modes of consumption. Secondly and due in part to the modern separation of food producers from food consumers, the ways in which meanings ascribed to foods have been constructed via the mediation of advertising, packaging and food-related discourses need to be assessed. These have contributed significantly to altering Western attitudes and responses to the experience and understanding of taste. It has often been stated that once nutritional needs are met, the capacity of food to take on a plethora of culturally specific meanings pushes it beyond its role as nutrient and into that of being a 'language'. In the pursuit of profit and through various media, commercial enterprise has exploited the fact that food is a mode of communication, one which continues to drive the sale of new food products. The sense of taste has been configured within such a context.

The Taste of Convenience

The main marketing plank of the twentieth-century marriage between the production of food and the consumption of food-related images was 'convenience', a hugely flexible term which could not merely be applied to foods, but to all goods and services supposed to 'make life easier'. Technologies, products and even flavours and images could embody or at least express a notional convenience. Sweet foods like soft drinks were construed as providing 'easy energy', along with being fun, for example.[1] More generally, so-called convenience foods became synonymous with saving effort, time and money and with ending the 'drudgery' of home cookery.

By the 1920s, American families were consuming significant quantities of tinned and frozen convenience foods, although the production techniques used proved to be of cost-saving convenience primarily to industry, rather than to consumers. Freezing could halt the deterioration of foods already 'going off', for example. Additionally, crude food processing succeeded in leaching out taste, colour and nutrients. Public awareness of such deficiencies hampered any hoped-for boom in sales. Therefore, stopping frozen foods from 'deteriorating into an ugly mess when the food thawed' would become a crucial public image issue for industry (Levenstein 1993: 106–107).

By 1929, Massachusetts-based inventor Clarence Birdseye 'had developed his plate freezer. The modern phase of food freezing with retail packaging and quick and deep cooling down to minus 18°C (0°F) begins from this date' (Borgstrom 1969: 41). Snap-freezing and colourfast printing helped greatly to redeem the image of frozen foods. Birdseye developed a moisture-proof cellophane wrapping which allowed foods to be frozen more quickly, while the waxed cardboard used for the outer packaging prevented thawing products from becoming misshapen. Birdseye chose to call his products 'frosted' rather than using the pejorative term 'frozen' and also designed display freezer cabinets that would be mass-produced for supermarkets. Filled with a range of meat, fish, fruit and vegetable products, supermarket freezers 'became the "miracle" that produced fresh foods out of season and changed eating habits so radically…' (Shephard 2000: 303).

During World War II, industrial freezing, dehydrating and canning were scaled to help provide food for the military, while the upward trend in post-war frozen food sales were in part the result of adopting such technologies to service a growing civilian populace. In terms of consumption, frozen convenience foods triumphed, facilitated by the use of the car and the spread of supermarkets and further encouraged by television advertising and by the return of individual earning power: 'By 1959 Americans were buying $2.7 billion worth of frozen foods a year … 2700 per cent more than in 1949' (Levenstein 1993: 108). A growing number of ready-to-heat meals were showcased, 'retouched' products that could attract shoppers with colourful promises and photographic images of foods: information they could 'consume' prior to actual consumption. Such products lined the supermarket aisles making possible the 'grazing' phenomenon of the 1970s. During the same decade the microwave oven (an unforeseen by-product of 1940s radar science) added a functional, networked link within a technological matrix of food processing, information, convenience and consumption. 'Freezer-to-table' microwave foods, in particular, would become a multi-billion dollar industry in the 1980s.

Today, still underpinning the empire of food-processing industries is the technological means to drive marketing and to make things look and taste to industry specifications. Indeed, 'convenience food' now depends on a specialized flavour industry:

> About 90 per cent of the money that Americans spend on food is used to buy processed food ... since the end of World War II, a vast industry has arisen in the United States to make processed food palatable. Without this flavour industry, the fast-food industry could not exist.
>
> (Schlosser 2001: 121)

This industry was engendered in the 1960s with the development of new technologies for commercial use (principally, mass spectroscopy and gas chromatography) which eventually enabled scientists to create thousands of artificially produced colourings and flavourings. So-called 'natural food flavours' could thereby be chemically copied. While product labels which boasted 'natural flavour' might have reassured consumers, this information could also be misleading, since the chemical reproduction of natural flavours capitalized on a loophole in labelling laws. With chemical solvents used to isolate a natural food's flavour compounds, that flavour could then be replicated. Sold under the appellation of 'natural flavour', any number of artificial tastes could, technically speaking, be added to any food (the latter being treated as merely a substrate). Furthermore, a base-product like milk could be flavoured, texturized, cooked, whipped, aerated or frozen, while other food items, like soy beans, could be used to create various 'milk' products – a process industry would call *interconversion* (Cantor and Cantor 1967: 445). Loath to rely on the inconsistency and quality variability of seasonal produce as a source of revenue and keen to extend the perishable life of food, industry has opted for the technoscience of preservation, product manipulation through the use of various forms of processing, artificial additives and chemical agents. As a result, the taste of a particular food product can bear little relationship to that of a 'real' (that is, unprocessed) product.

Of course, there is no question as to whether the industrialization and historical advance of the sciences involved in food production, processing, preservation, storage and transportation represent a positive advance. Indeed, a modern revolution of the food system underpins our present-day food habits and diet. Absolute availability, continuity, food quality and price have (at least in theory) seemingly banished the problem of absolute need, of nutritionally poor food and of the general scarcity of food commonplace in the premodern West.[2] Notwithstanding, the provision of better foods is in fact no guarantee of better health or well-being. Commerce and industry do not always act in the interests of health. Excessive 'consumption' has brought many diet-related ills.

In this context, legislation related to label misrepresentation, for example, always seems to lag behind the aggressive and 'strategic' connotative marketing adopted to continuously make products attractive to consumers. Today, a product's 'no-fat' guarantee may be disguising the nutritional deficiency of a food which is packed full of many unhealthy additives, including sugar. Moreover, a consumer's reception of product images is typically that related to a large range of similarly processed foods, like bread, with each bread 'type' being packaged merely to look different. Following Marx, we could say that commodity-appeal (and desire for convenience) overtakes our experience of the tangible qualities of smell and taste and touch. 'In the desert of modern life things take the place of affections and feelings and quantity has to compensate for quality', writes Piero Camporesi (Camporesi 1998: 186). In his bleak assessment of contemporary supermarket shopping, it is the 'superficial and distracted' senses of hearing and sight which have 'abolished touch' and 'eliminated smell ... the most delicate senses' (171).

If Seeing is Believing, Where does that Leave Taste?

Taste relations – that is, the sum of those factors affecting the experience of taste within the mediating world (or context) in which it operates – have entered a brave new world. At the same time, this can sometimes imply the reinscription of even centuries-old prejudices, like the ennobling of the ocular and auditory senses above the 'animal' senses of taste and smell, for example. As if reconfirming this historically philosophic understanding, Australia-based biscuit manufacturer Arnott's now advertises its cocktail crackers, 'Shapes', with the byline: 'Flavour you can see'. Starkly attesting to an ability to commodify food and flavour as 'image', such marketing reinforces cultural perceptions of what characterizes a particular sense modality (in this case, both taste and sight); what it can experience and how this occurs; and the nature of what that sense might contribute to knowledge. Exposure to the coded signs of advertising can thereby also serve to determine the experience of each of the sense modalities themselves. In this instance, sensory interdetermination is marked by a kind of gustatory 'mimesis', whereby taste's knowledge of its putative objects is eclipsed.

Additionally, a recent trend in advertising has been to give expression to the notion of 'no-frills' hedonism and guilt-free pleasure. By representing particular sensory *affects* which connote a kind of maximization of intense feelings, sensations and pleasures, one advertisement for Pioneer hi-fi, for example, celebrates such corporeal pleasures by configuring taste. It depicts, in close-up, parted red lips, before which slender feminine fingers poise a single red – presumably 'hot' – chilli pepper. The ad claims that 'Pioneer makes them hotter than this' and conflates sound, taste and sexual allure with a supposedly hip sense of the contemporary music scene. The ad promises a gamut of 'sensory' pleasures: 'Hotter Chilli Peppers. Juicier Cranberries. And the smashingest Pumpkins'.

The possibilities for multiplying both the material qualities and semiological connotations of edible objects are today virtually limitless and so bring about profound changes to diet, often by interrelated means. Conjured up in the space between the product-sign and consumer consciousness, 'tastes' themselves – like sweetness, creaminess or the 'crisp' – act as representations: predigested in the sense that they are already the products of conditioned consumer responses; popular tastes which act as 'interpreters' in the consumer's experience of taste (Barthes 1979: 69–70). Our cultural common sense of what gustation is and of what it can know, changes accordingly. Subject to the literal and semiotic manipulation of food as sign and as thing, various new and altered 'tastes' emerge, influenced by the mix'n'match production logic of industry.

Displacing any reasoned sensory engagement with food are the food-related discourses we willingly – but often unreflectively – enter into at the surface of things. In terms of taste, advertising mantras promise that products will deliver on pleasure, sensation and satisfaction, yet semiotically, they also trade on fears, phobias and anxieties linked to such issues as weight, health, beauty and social status. The ultimate cost of this mediation by advertising – between us, our food and our sense of taste – is that the total complement of possible gustatory experiences (which both nature and culinary craft provide) is circumscribed by contrived and prescriptive standards of taste set by media constructions of 'health' and 'beauty'. Routinely associated with food and eating, such ideals can cause the individual anxiety and even illness.[3] Whether we earnestly regulate our eating habits according to available dietary advice or are duped into an excessive food consumption pattern by the unrelenting commercialized command to 'Eat, enjoy!' or even knowingly indulge our appetite for food in an 'ignorance is bliss' fashion, the mediation of taste by applied technoscience, slogans, images and advice in effect trivializes taste as both flavour and as sensory faculty.

Typically, taste appears to have been recast as simply a sensory *effect*: that is, as a sensation cut off from the wider ambit of taste's functions as a mode of knowing. In both Ayurvedic medicine and traditional Chinese medicine, tastes themselves are understood to have specific medicinal values. The trivialization of taste in the West not only sets this knowledge of taste adrift from pharmacology, but inscribes the notion that in the everyday understanding and experience of an individual's sense of taste, 'sensation' is the *raison d'être* of *gustation*. KFC's 'Zinger' chicken-burger, for example, is described as 'the taste bud thumper', while its deep-fried 'popcorn chicken' is advertised as being 'mouth-poppin' fun for ya tongue'. Such a trivialization also points to the potentially dangerous affiliation of drug, food, sign and sensory effect, a 'cocktail' that already serves as the model for many so-called smart foods and drinks.

In a wider historical context, the culinary-cultural legacy of the knowledge gained through the sense of taste has been one related to all those practices, technologies and experiences that have affected taste; taken together, this represents our present-day 'archive of taste'.[4] The *'commodification of sensation'* is a phrase suggestive of how the fragile, 'chemical' history of taste is being usurped by simulations, as the focus is tightened on the immediacy of thrilling sensations. Chemical additives simulate the qualities of tastes, textures and other gustatory sensations, as the experience of tasting an actual food, of thinking about that food and of the way it tastes, becomes an impossibility.[5] Ultimately, such contrivance not only detracts from the appreciable diverse pleasures and healthful benefits gained through savouring flavours and foods; it also subtracts from the very possibility of knowing-through-taste. The senses require an 'aesthetic education' – as some European countries offer – rather than the shock tactics of industry. *Homo sapiens*, the *knowing* human, is simultaneously the *tasting* human; and we should think before we taste. However, the powers at work in the world of taste today encourage an everyday forgetting of the senses, which is now the behavioural norm.

As taken-for-granted 'media', the senses have themselves become *mediatized*. What we therefore now meet halfway, as it were, is a product's image, a powerfully motivating force in choice-making. As if by default, in relation to taste, we opt for the visual aesthetics of the big, bright and blemish-free. However, this overemphasis on the visual signs of quality has also misled consumers. The efforts of producers to make even natural foods like fruits and vegetables appear 'perfect', has in recent decades contributed to, as it has (perhaps ironically) obscured the fact that a marked decline in the nutritional value of these products has also been discovered. Having studied scientific records of plant analysis dating back to 1940, British researcher David Thomas discovered 'stunning declines' of trace elements in 'all fruits and vegetables'. Supposedly one of the vegetable kingdom's most nutritious members, broccoli, had lost seventy-five per cent of its calcium in the intervening years, for example (Engel 2001). Copper, sodium and magnesium were also shown to be in decline in many other vegetables and fruits. Modern agribusiness, artificial fertilizers and hydroponics are obviously geared for speedy growing and breeding (for looks, size and colour) while such processes adversely affect nutritional content. More importantly with regard to flavour, the taste complexity produced by natural processes of idiosyncratic growth and maturation, soil and climate is lost, constantly losing ground – or perhaps one might say *terroir* – to 'looks'. Our palates and tongues are 'dumbing down', no longer able to judge or enjoy the living vitality and potential flavour variance of foods produced outside the networks of the industrial-commercial matrix. Combined in so many processed foods, the obliterating power of sugar, salt and fat (a seemingly perennial taste triumvirate) are complemented by cheap 'filler' and artificial flavour. Such foods seem designed to replace gustatory sensitivity with a taste bud 'thumping'. With recourse to high-speed data-processing of consumer-sourced information and to lab statistics based on tests using bionic 'noses' and 'tongues', food product research, development, design and marketing strategies rapidly advance. Well synchronized, the invention, processing, packaging, transportation and retailing of food products takes place within a seamless web of operations which also *produces* taste.

If it is to be valued as a corporeal sense, we must be careful not to reduce taste in this way. Sensory effects and personal tastes, do not sufficiently account for taste as a mode of knowing. We must not trivialize, but seek to acknowledge the material history involved here. Taste is as much a product of taste-related cultural and technological forces as it is of ideas like 'convenience'; of philosophical prejudices (like that which ennobles sight, but not gustation); and of the related forms of *separation* (social, economic and political) which appear to be fundamental to capitalist economics. It is within this wider context that the potential uses and pleasures of sensory taste must be situated; indeed, recognized and explored.

Unfortunately and with regard to taste, the information age has compounded separations; perhaps most fundamentally, that between sign and substance. A new 'state' pervades, which both Jean Baudrillard and Umberto Eco have designated as 'hyperreality'. Baudrillard writes:

> The world of the pseudo-event, of pseudo-history and of pseudo-culture ... a world ... produced not from the fluctuating and contradictory nature of reality, but *produced as artefacts from the technical manipulation of the medium and its coded elements*. It is this and nothing else, which defines all signification whatsoever as *consumable*.
>
> (Baudrillard 1990: 92)

The media, but also Western culture (viewed as a communication system) functions according to this logic, whereby the multiplication and over-determination of signs, as much as their 'consumption', is simply a necessity. Media reality demands this 'nourishment', which typically takes the form of advertising and whereby the blurring of fact and fiction becomes absolute. Daniel Boorstin once described advertising as 'the characteristic rhetoric of democracy' (cited in Borgmann 1984: 53). The incessant production of thousands of 'new and exciting' food products and ideas (and of convenience meals in the guise of 'old favourites') also makes good the sociologist Niklas Luhmann's statement that '[A]fter truth comes advertising' (Luhmann 2000: 44). In effect, consumer understanding and appetites are continually exposed to recursive forms of mediation which undermine any real freedom (of choice); the momentary elation felt as an effect of attaining the 'free', the 'best value' or of experiencing a 'taste sensation', suggests an even greater need for the repetition of such feelings.

This promise of 'elation' has also often been linked to technology and, as a supposed by-product of the latter, to 'convenience'. When, in the 1970s, the 'futuristic' microwave oven became a popular icon of modern convenience (and a commercial success some twenty years after its invention), selling it required a heavy reliance on images of conventionally cooked foods (roasted or grilled, for example). This 'magic' was required because 'the microwave' could not actually cook like its electric or gas counterparts. It left foods flaccid and looking 'uncooked'. Even though 'the nuker' would in practice be used less for actual cookery than for the reheating of pre-packaged and processed convenience foods, it was hailed as 'the greatest cooking discovery since fire' (no author cited 1975: 9). In the US, 'microwaves' would outsell conventional ovens in 1975, thus turning a 'culinary' fiction into a social fact. The only 'cookery' worth noting here is that which combines advertising and industrial technoscience in an attempt to win over consumers.

Signs, Things and Foods of the Future

In the 1950s, Roland Barthes coined the word 'myth' to describe the modern overdetermination of 'things' by 'signs'. 'Myth is a *value*', Barthes wrote 'and truth is no guarantee for it; nothing prevents it from being a perpetual alibi' (Barthes 1972: 123). Barthes conceived the alibi as a representational form of truth which, signified by the product, lent the latter an appealing honesty by connoting some historical or cultural 'truth' or a functional attribute. Industrially produced pasta, for example, might carry with it a logo-alibi suggesting simple, peasant food. Barthes refers to the alibi as a 'constantly moving turnstile', in that nothing in the nature of myth stops the alibi's turning or figuratively speaking, troping (Barthes 1972: 123). 'Good home cooking' can thereby easily be 'turned' into parody. But perhaps this only infers that the experience of food and taste is always interpreted through images and texts; whereby, as fundamental aspects of the *psychological mediation* of eating, imagination builds or weakens appetite. Food may not have to be good to think before it is eaten, but arguably it must on some level be *thought*. However, in the age of convenience cookbooks would make a mockery of 'origins', exploiting representations of the exotic for commercial ends. After the Second World War, recipes designated *à la française*, for example, could use 'garlic' as an alibi. While only a hint of this culinary bulb might be specified in the recipe, the presence of the status-term 'garlic' was enough to connote French sophistication. 'Mexican chicken' with pineapple, avocado, bananas, grapes, chilli powder and cinnamon and Tahitian chicken with rum and currants were typical examples of a cruder form of semiotic seasoning (Mason 1955).

Commenting on the recipe form, Luce Giard explains that this kind of allocation of culinary-gustatory values 'is not strictly analytic and explanatory'. More importantly, '... it designates someplace other than here'; a kind of culinary *fort da*, establishing the play of desire within a symbolic geography of food (de Certeau et al. 1998: 222). Indeed, as Barthes noted in his discussion of myth, 'there never is any contradiction, conflict or split between the meaning and the form: they are never at the same place' (Barthes 1972: 123). 'Tahitian chicken' is the imaginary scene where meaning inscribes the form of food. Like the recursiveness of the media, this use of language equally implies how particular *tastes* can act metaphorically. Serving as advertising referents, *tastes* appear to have a sustaining semiotic power, while the substance of food itself can ebb away, as it were, into *taste-signs*. In the late 70s, microwave cookbook author, Ginger Scribner, took pains to endorse the purchase and use of specialist convenience foods like 'liquid smoke', 'instant tea' and 'dehydrated salad mix'. (Scribner 1978: 6–7).

More recently, of the 11,000 new food products introduced into the market in the US in 1998, over 'two-thirds were condiments, candy and snacks, baked goods, soft drinks and dairy products (cheese products and ice cream novelties)' (Nestlé 2002: 25). Even though some of these products are sold on the premise of being 'low-fat' or 'no-salt' or are claimed to be nutritionally enhanced with vitamins ('enhancement' now suggests so-called functional foods and nutroceuticals as well), Marion Nestlé argues it is the promotion of sales which drives the need to create such products. Both image and the delivery of gustatory thrills, combined, have become the 'new taste'. The detrimental outcomes of such a marriage are clearly evident: diet-related illnesses among children have climbed rapidly in recent years. While at least since the dawn of industrialization, the commercial imperative has spurred on those willing to adulterate foods for profit, in the era of bioengineering such products fall under a new appellation: 'franken-foods'. According to bioengineering gurus, genetic 'recipes' will make entirely new foods possible: 'Kid-friendly foods are on the way. Researchers will develop tastier vegetables, such as chocolate carrots and pizza-flavoured corn' (Toops 1998: 71).

Meals in 'the Matrix'

For the purposes of enlightenment and entertainment, science fiction film-makers have milked the ideological implications of so-called franken-food, which (at least in the science-fiction genre) has often been equated with a single food, 'scientifically designed' to answer all dietary needs. Ever since

French chemist, Marcellin Berthelot (1827–1907), looked forward to the day when modern chemistry would reduce the human diet to a 'little white pill', products like the green pap which constituted the diet in the film *Soylent Green* (dir. Richard Fleischer 1973) have been depicted in order to satirize such utopian bravado (Berthelot 1894). The pap in this case turns out to be made from processed human bodies. This type of story no doubt highlights the fear that if some 'superfood' were produced which could sustain us all, the 'law' of social inequality suggests that any such 'us all' (once called 'the masses') would soon be established as a readily exploitable majority. Yet, even the glamorous technological décor of Stanley Kubrick's *2001: A Space Odyssey* (1968) is belied by the sombre sucking of crewmen who eat through straws or scrape coloured pap from colourfully labelled dispenser trays. Closer to home, so to speak, liquefied spacefood with appetizing names like 'Chicken Salad Spread' now narrows the technological gap between the fantasy and reality of such 'superfoods' (see: http://spacelink.nasa.gov – accessed 20.10.00).

One recent film in the tradition mentioned, *The Matrix* (dirs. Andy and Larry Wachowski 1999) parodies current technologies, conventions and beliefs related to food, fantasy and reality. The so-called matrix is a 'neural interactive simulation' which has been imposed on Earth by 'the machines'. The matrix allows 'humans' to think themselves to be real, living as they do, vicariously, immersed in an artificial world. If one chooses, this includes eating a beautifully cooked steak and drinking good red wine in a classy restaurant. However, in reality, the machines are using the ecologically devastated Earth as the base for growing actual human babies in a 'battery': a vast womb-like incubator which in turn produces the vital homiothermic energy needed by the machines to power the matrix with electricity.

While planning to overcome the machines, a small band of would-be heroes eke out a precarious existence in a spacecraft, evading 'sentinels' in a netherworld outside the matrix. At breakfast, the crew dish themselves a mucous-like substance, pumped from a dispenser and described as 'everything the body needs':

> *Tank*: Here you go buddy. Breakfast of champions. If you close your eyes it almost feels like you're eating runny eggs.
>
> *Apoc*: (interrupts) Yeah or a bowl of snot.
>
> *Mouse*: You know what it really reminds me of? *Tasty Wheat*. Did you ever eat *Tasty Wheat*?
>
> *Switch*: No, but technically neither did you.
>
> *Mouse*: That's exactly my point, exactly! Because you have to wonder now, how did the machines really know what *Tasty Wheat* tasted like? Maybe they got it wrong. Maybe what I think *Tasty Wheat* tasted like actually tasted like oatmeal or, ah, tuna fish. That makes you wonder about a lot of things. You take chicken, for example. Maybe they couldn't figure out what to make chicken taste like which is why chicken tastes like everything.

As in the film, where simulation is the reality, *in reality* what we eat today, as I have suggested, can also largely be a simulation. Within our present-day matrix, the interconversion of foods by 'machines' – that is, our own technologies of food, flavour and image synthesis – makes of food a *substrate*: a base product to which is added not only taste, texture, vitamins or 'functions', but also added values: *the signs* of convenience, health or 'sexiness' – *everything our minds need*.

In a deeply ironic way, Lévi-Strauss's dictum that food must be good to think about before it is good to eat reasserts itself at the cutting edge of contemporary taste relations. That 'chicken' can (be the) taste of 'everything else' is but a reminder of how abstracted, statistical and synthesizable 'chicken' has become: battery chickens engineered to industry specifications; the manufacture of various synthetic *chickenized* products; even the adoption of 'chicken' as a signifier – word, image or artificial taste. Since for most, chicken *means* chicken (if it tastes like 'chicken' then it is chicken), the media-brokered equality between words, *taste* and things remains the undergirding support of our particular 'matrix'. 'Figur[ing] out what to make chicken taste like' is just one aspect of the technical information-gathering needed to produce a growing range of chickenized products.

Both the contemporary synthesizing of taste and the design and production of processed food, appear to be based on an accretive model of knowledge, one perhaps inadvertently satirized in *The Matrix*. Put simply, it is a model long held in contempt and recalls the warning explicit in Mary Shelley's *Frankenstein*: that (a scientific) understanding of the parts will not allow for a reproduction of the living whole. Such a model certainly sustains the technologies of taste which now thrive with the help of industry and commerce. Treating food as a substrate to which tastes, in this instance, can be added at will, accords with the notion that accretion (or accumulation) is constitutive of knowledge; as such, it lies at the root of the 'knowledge' which produced the microwave oven, the tasteless tomato and BSE.[6]

What we have witnessed but not thought deeply enough about is how informatic technologies 'instruct' nature. More specifically, perhaps cybernetic control (cybernetics: from the Greek, *kybernetes*, a helmsman) denotes the very form through which we have now come to 'know'. As Paul Virilio puts it in relation to cognition: 'We cannot but notice today the decline of ... *analogue* mental process, in favour of instrumental, *digital* procedures...' (Virilio 2000: 2). At the same time, if what we know is what we control, how can this ever be adequately representative of the complex world of organic nature or of tastes, which act as 'messages' passed between organism and environment, those which we have been 'interrupting' for decades? *In the image of control*, taste is yet the corporeal register of a complex communication of living, flavoursome things which have now been overdetermined by semiotic 'cookery' and industrial interconversion.

The flavourless foods of battery production and the processed industrial flavours of the laboratory, mark the absence of real taste. By comparison, living food and flavour and the sense of taste, represent a biologically established nexus of pathways from which such knowledge took form, but which now has been undermined. Given that living food is assimilated by all organisms, including humans, the under-utilization of taste as a corporeal mode of knowing, linked to the gustatory qualities of natural foods, is a serious matter. In part the result of our collective disrespect for traditional knowledge systems, the 'communicational' relation between organism and environment is eroded. One might add that in our favour, as a sense, taste has not lost any of its potential power, but it remains to be seen how interest and overdetermination can coexist.

When Virilio writes of the 'damage caused by the onset of the computerized dissuasion of perceptible reality, which is more and more closely tied to a veritable industrialization of simulation' he relates digitalization to the *visual* realm (Virilio, 1995: 141). 'Our vision is that of montage', he argues elsewhere, 'a montage of temporalities which are the product not only of the powers that be, but of the technologies that organize time' (Virilio 1989: 31). So when we dine out at a local 'Thai' restaurant, eat 'peasant cuisine' at an urban trattoria or consume a McDonald's burger of 'grilled' chicken that has had fake stripes added to the meat subsequent to cooking, are we not also consuming 'hyperreal' foods that occupy a space within a dissuaded reality?[7] Dissuasion may in fact be the new form of *persuasion*: a word derived from the Indo-European word, *swad*, meaning to sweeten and persuade. Yet, whether one is being persuaded by the actual sensual qualities of food or dissuaded within the technosphere, the question must be asked: is the 'space' of sensory experience not always that of a dissuaded reality, in so far as this is always-already one mediated and constituted by a montage of corporeal and cognitive effects – and by substances and signs? The common understanding that the visual-aesthetic appeal of food is directly linked to taste satisfaction appears to affirm a reality (rather than the hyperreality) of the visual-gustatory montage of flavours, signs and substances.

As mentioned, in *The Matrix* the eponymously named digitalized construct of reality allows humans to 'live, breathe, smell, see, hear, touch and taste', yet at the same time be no more than immersed digital entities. One scene in particular provides the occasion for an elementary cybernetics lesson on the separation of cognition from sense experience and so puts the question of whether we live in a 'dissuaded reality' or not nicely in perspective.

So that he can better carry out his dangerous mission against 'the machines' inside the matrix, the hero, Neo (played by Keanu Reaves), must first be convinced by his mentor, Morpheus (played by Laurence Fishburne), that what he has previously 'experienced' is not real.

> *Morpheus*: What is 'real'? How do you define 'real'? If you are talking about what you can feel, what you can smell, what you can taste and see then 'real' is simply electrical signals interpreted by your brain.

This logic is based on the cybernetic principle that nothing which happens in the brain is 'real' in the sense that our experience of something 'really happening' is not simultaneously the register of an event occurring in a world 'out there'. The real is always-already the result of cognitive processing. Put another way, sensory experiences are the product of the digital processing of analogue information received from sense receptors.[8] Therefore, the term 'reality' can only ever relate to the already processed information received from the environment, constituting an objective complement of material relations which remains unknown. In this context, 'the result of mental information processing is an artificial reality' whereby 'sensory modes only launch the construction of this artificial reality, the only reality we can know' (Kampis 1993: 142, 143).

Signs, representations and 'electrical impulses' appear to be the principal shaping forces of perceivable reality. In relation to food and taste, I would therefore reject the notion that some 'undissuaded reality' is an open possibility; that taste could be de-conditioned or, as such, lead us in search of some perfect diet. But gustatory experience in the contemporary world is doubly conditioned: by cognitive processing and by a hyperreal mediation whereby foods, flavours, conceptual understandings and attitudes are knowingly manipulated. Without engaging with taste *as a mode of knowing* in its own right, means experiencing sensory taste as gustatory effect; as taste sensations cut off from any real knowledge of the morsel which transports them. Taste has the power to create a sensory bridge to a living reality 'outside the matrix', one which implies an ecology of inclusion and relationship between culture and nature; one that promotes the activity of knowing as accessible, engaging and corporeal, rather than one pre-tuned for reception. Sea, sun, air, soil and water produce food and taste within interconnected living systems in which humans have evolved and often thrived; by our own efforts, we have learned how to enjoy the fruits of taste relations. The sensory mode we call taste is surely one 'flavoured' by culturally variable, yet corporeally robust, inter-sense relationships and linked perceptions, as much as by natural and culinary histories, cultural discourses, ideas and beliefs, and by food production and consumption practices. As Neo must learn he is a fake before he can be real, so too as tasters we must also learn how taste is, and has been, constructed before we might benefit from re-engagement with the chains of forces and processes which link taste to a living and organic reality. The cultural 'physiology' of taste is fragile and variable. Consequently, it has been overdetermined by forces like those outlined above. Taste has powers which nature's largesse has provided for our pleasure and as a source of knowledge, but that pleasure and knowledge also depend on whether we actively exercise our 'taste' rather than allow it to be adversely influenced in ways which we have not yet paid enough attention to.

Notes

1. See Roland Barthes (1979), 'Toward a psychosociology of contemporary food consumption', in Forster and Ranum (eds.), *Food and Drink in History: Selections from the Annales*, Vol 5, Baltimore: Johns Hopkins University Press, a seminal paper dealing in part with the versatile and at times contradictory cultural meaning of 'sweetness'.

2. See Rachel Laudan (2001), 'A plea for culinary modernism: why we should love new, fast, processed food', in *Gastronomica* 1:1, February: 36–44.

3. Of course, the present-day obesity crisis reveals that, particularly in relation to the links between advertising, television, and childhood behaviour patterns, there is evidence enough to support the notion that personal ideals can have little or nothing to do with what people choose to eat. Surely it is more their absence that brings disaster. Notwithstanding, the physical effects of semiological manipulation are also frighteningly apparent. The fact that television-viewing time has been linked to obesity provides us with a physiological explanation for 'fatness', and without even contemplating how the eating-related messages gleaned while watching also contribute to an individual's eating habits.

4. A phrase which echoes that of the Slow Food Movement's 'Ark of Taste'. 'The Ark of Taste aims to rediscover, catalogue, describe and publicize forgotten flavours. It is a metaphorical recipient of excellent gastronomic products that are threatened by industrial standardization, hygiene laws, the regulations of large-scale distribution and environmental damage'. http://www.slowfoodfoundation.com/eng/arca/lista.lasso. Accessed 15 July, 2004.

5. 'The snack food of the future could rely more on sensations in the mouth than flavour or texture. Food companies are experimenting with "sensates" ... to make your mouth tingle, warm, cool, salivate, or tighten ... the next step is to manipulate the sensates to change the length or intensity of the sensation'. Caitlin Fitzsimmons, 'Snacks to be a real sensation', *The Australian*, 20 August, 2003.

6. Bovine Spongiform Encephelopathy, or 'mad cow disease', devastated the UK beef trade from the mid-1980s to the mid-90s. It was caused in part by feeding cattle products to cattle. The deadly human equivalent is known as Creutzfeldt-Jacob Disease.

7. In Sydney, Australia, McDonald's ceased production of its 'grilled' McChicken burgers after authorities found McDonald's product-related advertising 'constituted misleading or deceptive conduct'. It was discovered that the 'grill' marks usually associated with barbecue-style cooking over a hot grill were in fact applied – after cooking – by 'a hot roller'. See article, 'Mac chick is plucked', *Sydney Morning Herald*, 18 June, 1999: 3.

8. For an information-theory description of sense-perception, see, Fred I. Dretske, *Knowledge and the Flow of Information*, Stanford: CSLI Publications, 1999 [MIT Press, 1981]: 135ff.

References

Barthes, R. (1972), *Mythologies*, St Albans: Paladin.

——. (1979), 'Toward a psychosociology of contemporary food consumption', in R. Forster and O. Ranum (eds), *Food and Drink in History: Selections From the Annales*, Vol. 5, Baltimore: Johns Hopkins University Press.

Baudrillard, J. (1990), 'The Pseudo-event and neo-reality', in *Revenge of the Crystal: Selected Writings on the Modern Object and its Destiny, 1968–1983*, Sydney: Power Institute/Pluto Press.

Berthelot, M. (1894), 'En l'an 2000', paper given at the banquet for the Chambre Syndicale des Produits Chimiques.

Borgmann, A. (1984), *Technology and the Character of Everyday Life*, Chicago: Chicago University Press.

Borgstrom, Georg (1969), *Principles of Food Science, Vol. 1: Food Technology*, London: MacMillan.

Camporesi, P. (1998), *The Magic Harvest: Food, Folklore and Society*, trans. J. K. Hall, Cambridge: Polity Press.

Cantor, S. M., and Cantor, M. B. (1967), 'Socioeconomic factors in fat and sugar consumption', in M. Kare and O. Maller (eds), *The Chemical Senses and Nutrition*, New York: Academic Press.

de Certeau, M., Giard L. and Mayol P. (eds) (1998), *The Practice of Everyday Life*, Vol. II, trans. T. J. Tomasik, Minneapolis: University of Minnesota Press.

Dretske, F. (1999), *Knowledge and the Flow of Information*, Stanford: CSLI Publications.

Engel, M. (2001), 'That green vegetable: who needs it?', *Sydney Morning Herald*, 25 February.

Fitzsimmons, C. (2003), 'Snacks to be a real sensation', *The Australian*, 20 August.

Kampis, G. (1993), 'On understanding how the mind is organised: cognitive maps and the "physics" of mental information processing', in Laszlo, Masulli, Artigiani and Csányi (eds), *The Evolution of Cognitive Maps: New Paradigms for the Twenty-First Century*, Amsterdam: Gordon and Breach.

Lauden, Rachel (2001), 'A plea for culinary modernism: why we should love new, fast, processed food', in *Gastronomica* 1 (1): February.

Levenstein, H. (1993), *Paradox of Plenty: A Social History of Eating in America*, New York: Oxford University Press.

Luhmann, N. (2000), *The Reality of the Mass Media*, trans. Kathleen Cross, Cambridge: Polity Press.

Mason, A. (1955), *Cook a Good Dinner with Anne Mason*, Melbourne: Whitcombe and Tombs.

No author cited (1975), *The Amana Guide to Great Cooking with a Microwave Oven*, New York: Popular Library.

Nestlé, M. (c.2002), *Food Politics: How the Food Industry Influences Nutrition and Health*. Berkeley: University of California Press.

Schlosser, Eric (2001), *Fast Food Nation: The Dark Side of the All-American Meal*, New York: Houghton Mifflin.

Scribner, G. (1978), *The Quick and Easy Microwave Oven Cookbook*, New York: Weathervane.

Shephard, S. (2000), *Pickled, Potted and Canned. The Story of Food Preserving*, London: Headline.

Toops, D. (1998), 'Forecasts for the millennium: advertising gurus predict meals on wheels, pizza-flavoured corn', in *Food Processing*, Nov, V. 59.

Virilio, P. (2000), *The Information Bomb*, trans. Chris Turner, London: Verso.

——. (1995), *The Art of the Motor*, trans. J. Rose, Minneapolis: University of Minnesota Press.

——. with Lotringer, S. (1989), *Pure War*, trans. M. Polizotti, New York: Semiotext(e).

35

The Play's the Thing

Dining Out in the New Russia

Darra Goldstein

During the Cold War years it seemed straightforward enough for American observers to understand the Russians' daily life, as long as you could understand their language. The Soviet Union was a society defined by ideology; the contrast between communist ideology and capitalist consumption presented a neat dichotomy that made for an easy explanation of the differences between the two countries. Doctrine determined everything from the political life of the people to the clothes they could wear and the foods they could eat. Russians lived "life as idea" (Efimova 1999); only through illicit channels could they know about the possibility of "life as material"—a life lived through the tangible consumption of goods that are meant to fulfill desire.

Contemporary reports of post-Soviet Russia underline the changes that the country has undergone in only a decade. A different reality now exists, one defined by consumer culture and a developing free market. Not surprisingly, many American journalists see this new Russia in terms of Western values and conclude that the country is on the right path to American-style capitalism (if not American-style democracy). But given the centuries-old struggles between Slavophiles and Westernizers—those who see Russia's strength as based in internal cultural values and those who see it as achievable only through borrowings from the West—this journalistic view, in which the more the Russians become like us the more they are praised, seems overly simplified. In fact, despite their initial enthusiastic embrace of Western goods and ideas, the Russians are creating a society not merely modeled on the West.

A case in point is Russia's dynamic new restaurant culture, which journalists eagerly partake of but rarely study. Indeed, enthusiastic observers describe Moscow's restaurants as a "taste of the future," a "hot *prospekt*" (von Bremzen

2002; Dryansky 2003). It's true that the Soviet style of dining is a thing of the past. The grim eateries have disappeared—the endless undifferentiated *zakusochnye, stolovye, pel'mennye, chainye*, and *kafeterii* [snack bars, dining halls, dumpling houses, tea houses, cafeterias], where the same brusque service, greasy soup, unidentifiable chunks of meat, and weak tea were dished out. Understandably, most Soviet citizens tried hard to avoid public eateries in favor of meals at home. So, a decade after the Soviet Union's collapse, the transformation is striking, particularly in Moscow, where most of the country's wealth is concentrated.[1] But beyond the obvious proliferation of restaurants offering a wide variety of cuisines, just how new is the current dining culture? Are there any aspects of the dining experience that express specifically Russian values? In June 2003 I traveled to Moscow to find out.

On 1905 Revolution Street, near a newly fashionable embankment of the Moscow River, stands the Russian World Trade Center. This hulking Soviet-era structure once housed the city's only Japanese restaurant, where sushi could be purchased with hard currency, though the kitchen was rumored to serve fish from the polluted river a few blocks away. Such was the state of fine dining (and popular belief) in Russia's capital in the late 1970s. Now, an entire row of restaurants with appealing names faces the Trade Center: Oblomov, Bochka [Barrel], Shinok [Tavern], Le Dyuk [Le Duc], each promising a different form of escape—a nineteenth-century mansion, a charming Russian cottage, a Ukrainian tavern, a Gothic cathedral.

Shinok is typical of the stylization of the new Russian restaurants. Located on the third floor, it can be reached only by ascending a rustic wooden staircase, in an atmosphere so dim that it is difficult to see. The dining rooms are laid out in a circle surrounding a brightly lit central area, which, were it on the first floor, would appear to be a courtyard. It is, in fact, disorienting to discover that this bright third-floor interior is a farmyard complete with a horse, a goat, a rooster, chickens, rabbits, and even a babushka who takes care of them all. The tables are placed next to windows that look out on this bucolic scene, causing the diner to feel that she has stepped right into a page out of Gogol by way of Alice in Wonderland. This impression persists on perusal of Shinok's eleven-page menu, where one dish is more fabulous than the next. Here are cockscomb salad with quail tongue, marinated onion, and chicken; fried rabbit liver; duck salad with prunes and spices; eggplant and peppers stuffed with vegetables; cutlets of sweet-fleshed river fish and mushrooms; and, of course, cherry *vareniki*, Nikolai Gogol's favorite dumplings. The owners of Shinok want patrons to feel transported to another world, one that is both familiar and idealized, thanks to Gogol's tales, but also exotic—where else in downtown Moscow can you find a barnyard with a babushka? (No, not even at the zoo.) To eat at Shinok means to suspend belief in temporal reality, to enter into a different realm that exists simultaneously behind closed doors.

Yet the experience at Shinok isn't an isolated one. Moscow now has over 4,000 restaurants, so you can pretty much pick your fancy—and your fantasy. If you want the deserts of Central Asia, go to Beloye Solntse Pustyni [White Sun of the Desert], decorated like a set from its namesake cult film. Tsarskaya Okhota [Royal Hunt] offers a macho escape into the world of the hunt. At Sirena [Siren], you enter a watery kingdom with a glass floor that reveals huge sturgeon swimming beneath your feet. At Ulei [Beehive] you can pretend you're in Los Angeles, or New York for that matter, especially if you hear Isaac Correa, the New York-raised chef, talk. If all this is too bourgeois for your taste, or if you're feeling nostalgic for the old Soviet Union, Petrovich is the place to visit. There, your menu is presented in a *papka* [a Soviet-era school folder] and you're surrounded by Soviet kitsch. The restaurant is even run like an exclusive club where the operative words are "*Myest nyet*" ["There are no seats"]. The point is that dining at all of these restaurants means more than just having a meal; it is a cultural event. The décor, the menu, the uniforms of the wait staff—all are part of a studied theatricality that enables the diner to enact a role in the larger performance of the play (the meal).

Moscow's new restaurant culture might best be epitomized by Café Pushkin. Like Shinok, Pushkin is the brainchild of the entrepreneur Andrei Dellos. It takes up an entire townhouse on Tsvetnoi Boulevard, and appears to be an elegant eighteenth-century mansion. In fact, the building was constructed only in 1999, but the attention to interior detail is so great that people are easily fooled. The original building housed a German pharmacy on the first floor, and Café Pushkin replicates its décor. Russian food is offered on a menu printed in pre-Revolutionary orthography on a broadsheet titled "Gastronomicheskii Vestnik" ["Gastronomic Herald"], which includes light articles and anecdotes in addition to the menu items, many of which appear in obsolete linguistic forms. The café is open round the clock and has become *the* place for Moscow power meals. The restaurant's second floor is designed as a private library and includes actual eighteenth- and nineteenth-century leather-bound volumes. This is the more deluxe dining room, which is frequented by expats and foreigners. The leather-bound menu—itself like a book—is presented in rather highfalutin Russian, with arcane culinary terms and convoluted syntax. The food itself reinforces the impression that dining at Pushkin is largely about image. The Olivier Salad, for instance, is breathtaking in its presentation, arriving at the table as it must have in Chef Olivier's original incarnation at his late nineteenth-century restaurant, Hermitage—an architecturally crafted salad of hearts of lettuce, endive, caviar, crayfish, veal tongue, and chicken breast. But the cornucopia that follows it—a literal horn of plenty shaped out of rye bread and filled with shrimp, scallops, and tuna and doused with a red pepper sauce—is all about appearance, not taste.

And that's precisely the point. Pushkin is not designed merely to express refinement or beauty, like most of the fine dining places of New York or Paris.

Instead, it aims to stage a meal, not to serve one. When you go to the new Moscow restaurants, you enter into a theme park, leaving reality behind. As Café Pushkin's promotional leaflet states (in English):

> It is nice to feel an aristocrat staying in a marvelous mansion and admire antique engravings, crystal chandeliers glimmering mysteriously in the fire-place room.
> Under the roof of a gorgeous building there is an antique library where books, telescopes and globes dispose to philosophic meditation. The atmosphere of "Café Pushkin" is amazing not only due to the interior specificity but also to the unique cuisine including Russian meals cooked according to old recipes as well as French cullinary [sic] chef d'oeuvres.

The word "specificity" is key to this description. Café Pushkin isn't the same as a Disney creation, which in the spirit of charm trivializes its subject without understanding its essence. Instead, the restaurant's interior bespeaks a genuine interest in and knowledge of eighteenth-century Russia, interpreted to appeal to contemporary sensibilities.

Here, among the power brokers and the beautiful people, you can announce yourself as someone to be taken seriously. You can arrive in style, leaving your car under the watchful eye of your bodyguard, who will park it right on the sidewalk in front of the restaurant without fear of towing, there for all to see. (In what other major city in the world can you do that?) In creating Café Pushkin, Andrei Dellos has recognized certain of Moscow's advantages, which have to do not only with the Russian propensity for lavish spending, but also with the fact that the consumer market is still in its chaotic formative stages, which means that it's still up for grabs. Where American and European diners generally follow the food in new high-end restaurants, going from one cuisine to another, one celebrity chef to the next, food is not yet the real draw in early twenty-first-century Moscow dining. True connoisseurship has yet to develop (though it is beginning). Instead, diners are drawn to the trendiest restaurants in order to live out a fantasy, if only for the duration of an evening's meal. Is this phenomenon simply a reaction to seventy years of grim cafeterias under Soviet rule, or does it have deeper roots in Russian culture?

In fact, Russians have long been preoccupied with performance and illusion, and restaurants are only one of the arenas in which these elements have been played out. Part of this need for escapism has to do with Russia's harsh physical environment, from which diversions provide welcome relief. But it goes deeper than that, beyond the varieties of Cockaygne myth that most European cultures share. Historically the Russians have also endured cruel leaders, and as a result they have developed a certain willingness to believe that which is patently false, not only to survive, but as a strategy for making their lives meaningful. In our time, for instance, the majority of

Soviet citizens lived under the spell of a workers' paradise in which "life is getting merrier all the time" and "things are better for us than for you."[2] No matter that the store shelves were empty, that restaurants had only a couple of menu items available at any time, that the wheat and potato harvests were too often left to rot in the fields for lack of tractor parts. The popular deceptions widely practiced during the Soviet era, which demanded a willing suspension of disbelief, were not merely the result of a successful propaganda machine. They can also be seen as a continuation of the escapist strategies that the Russians have engaged in for centuries (the widespread abuse of alcohol being another).

How have these deceptions played out at the table? As related by the *Primary Chronicle*, Russia's first written document dating from the eleventh century, a great commensal drama occurred in 945, when Princess Olga avenged the death of her husband, Igor, by inviting his killers, the fierce Derevlians, to a funeral feast in his memory. Olga plied the Derevlians with vast quantities of mead, and when they were thoroughly drunk, she had them massacred, 5,000 in all. Olga's combination of great acting and great savagery has earned her a secure place in Russian history, but her story also reveals an important site for the enactment of societal relations in Russia: the communal table.

For as long as there have been pleasure-seekers, hosts have sought publicly to prove their worth by projecting their desired image onto the metaphorical dining room stage. The performance of a meal serves as a vivid means of self-promotion and advertisement; the tables of the wealthy announce a host's power and prestige even as their surfeit expresses the host's personal fantasies and desire to manipulate societal standing. Whether a magnificent feast staged in the past by a nobleman to consolidate his political power, or a restaurant debauch of a contemporary oligarch, Russian dinners are consciously performative. We may recognize the American and Western European power meal as a form of drama, but for Russians the showmanship is more complicated and culturally rooted.

Over the course of the eighteenth century, food moved from the realm of sacrament (feasts held on Church holidays, weddings, funerals, baptisms, and so on) to that of daily life (Sipovskaia 2003). While the Russians historically had regaled with excess, the new mode allowed them to follow an inclination to live a life outside of prudence, even outside the bounds of reality, if only for a spell. Foreign travelers to Russia have frequently commented upon this immoderation. Yet the excess they perceive is not simply an expression of vulgar ostentation; it also comprises an expansive generosity and a fatalism about life. Russians have always celebrated the moment and aestheticized their otherwise deprived lives by dramatizing the ordinarily quotidian meal. For those of means, when it came to regalement, the attitude was quite distant from the "waste not, want not" mentality that has prevailed in much of Western culture. In addition, the rigid Russian Orthodox sequence of feast days and fast days, in which roughly two hundred days a year are designated for fasts, meant that the Russians were continually aware of imminent deprivation. Feasting represented a fleeting opportunity for celebration, an opportunity built into the Church calendar for rich and poor alike. The sanctioning of excess allowed for hope and offered individuals something to look forward to beyond the meagerness of a daily diet of not quite enough food rationed equally throughout the year. For Russians, a continual state of caution and parsimoniousness in one's approach to food held little sway.[3] Thus, when feasting was allowed, they went to extremes, with apparently total disregard for restraint, experiencing glee at their own wantonness.

A brief look at the history of the Russian banquet reveals the deliberate expansiveness and theatricality of the meal. In medieval Europe, the formal banquet offered guests a variety of entertainments. During "interludes" (brief plays performed during breaks between courses), carts carrying actors and musicians were wheeled in to distract guests from the clearing of dishes and the setting out of the next course. The Russian table, by contrast, *was* the performance, with attention focused on the groaning board and the actual service of the meal, rather than on any extrinsic entertainment. Although Russia had its share of dwarfs and jesters to entertain and mediate among guests, noble Russians did not develop the art of mealtime pageantry as diversion. Instead, the meal itself served as spectacle through the sumptuous presentation of a multitude of dishes.

Early travelers to Russia frequently found this abundance "excessive and vulgar," filling even "the most courageous stomachs ... with horror" (de Segur 1911). Overly ample portions of beef, wildfowl, fish, eggs, and pies were brought to table in seemingly random order, and seemingly without end. This distinctive Russian style of service contrasted markedly with the more restrained French style of service accepted at noble tables throughout Western Europe. The French banquet table entailed an exquisite set piece, intended primarily to delight the eye. On entering the banquet hall, diners found tables already set with an artful array of dishes, many of them in fanciful *trompe l'oeil*. However, although an entire course comprising dozens of dishes may have been beautiful to behold, eating it was likely another matter. The preset display meant that hot foods were no longer hot; fats were congealed. And as each course concluded, the table had to be fully rearranged, like scenery between acts in a play. Similar to a stage set, the French table provided a backdrop to the meal.

Russian service differed profoundly. On entering the hall, diners found the stage nearly bare: only salt and pepper cellars and vinegar cruets stood on the tables (although sideboards at the tsar's banquets did sag under the immense weight of the royal gold plate). But as soon as the guests were seated, the drama began, as each dish was brought individually to table and presented with great fanfare. Dining *à la russe* provided live performance as liveried waiters—often one for each guest—paraded repeatedly into the banquet hall with platters held high. Chroniclers tell of a single huge sturgeon brought to table by four dozen cooks struggling to hold the immense fish steady (Pyliaev 1897); or of great silver vats that required three hundred men to fill them with mead (Tereschenko 1848). Considering that banquets consisted of no less than four courses, with up to one hundred dishes in each course, royal feasts could be an ordeal, especially for foreign visitors used to the orderliness and self-containment of a French-style meal.

In the wake of Peter the Great's Westernizing reforms in the first quarter of the eighteenth century, the Russian nobility worked hard to be as sophisticated as their European counterparts, avidly imitating the latest European trends, in which the idea of illusion, so much a part of eighteenth-century French aesthetics, was prominent (faux fruits in bowls, *trompe l'oeil* paintings and table settings). The Russians particularly enjoyed creating magical, neoclassical settings that transported guests to distant places and times. For one famous party Prince Grigory Potemkin, Catherine the Great's favorite, transformed his dining room into a Caucasian grotto complete with a fully engineered stream spilling down an artificial mountainside. Roses and other fragrant flowers grew in profusion, while myrtle and laurel trees were resplendent with fruits crafted of gems. On Catherine's arrival, a chorus broke into song, limning her praises in ancient Greek (Lotman and Pogsian 1996). The empress's willingness to participate in her consort's famous illusions only enhanced everyone's enjoyment of the evening (certainly the dining grotto was more playful than the "Potemkin villages" the prince had constructed on the Volga).

Count Alexander Stroganov turned his dining room into a Roman triclinium replete with tables of marble and mosaic and mattresses stuffed with swan's down so that his guests could recline. Each guest was served by a beautiful young boy, who brought in one exquisite dish after another. The most extravagant appetizers were the herring cheeks, for which more than one thousand herrings were required to compose a single plate. Guests enjoyed salmon lips, boiled bears' paws, roast lynx, cuckoos roasted in honey and butter, cod milt and fresh turbot liver, oysters, wildfowl stuffed with nuts and fresh figs, salted peaches, and pickled pineapples (which were, of course, unknown in ancient Rome but were such a desirable novelty in eighteenth-century Russia that their authenticity was overlooked). When Stroganov's guests felt sated, he encouraged them, as the ancients had, to tickle their throat with a feather to vomit and make room for more (Pyliaev 1897).

As in other aspects of Russian life, the performance (in this case, the meal) served to push reality aside, even to eclipse it, in order to distract the players from more fundamental concerns. Such extravagance was both a display of wealth and an expression of boredom—too much leisure prompted the nobility and gentry to seek ever more novel diversion. Tolstoy, Turgenev, and Chekhov all created memorable portraits of the "superfluous man" so prevalent in nineteenth-century Russian society. During that century, mealtime escapades among the leisured class became common as hosts engaged in ever more outrageous behavior—behavior that asserted fantasy over reality, often to the point of deception, and constituted a supposedly national trait against which foreign visitors to Russia repeatedly warned.[4]

Yet immoderate as the behavior of the bored nobility may have been, it was actually exceeded by that of the merchants, who found themselves newly (and often fabulously) rich as the nineteenth century wore on; in many ways they may be seen as the precursors of today's New Russians. Like today's entrepreneurs, the merchants of yesteryear chose to entertain in taverns or restaurants, rather than at home. They frequently reserved private rooms for their entertainments and spent inordinate amounts of money on dishes like *ukha*, a soup of sterlet poached in imported champagne, which could cost up to 300 gold rubles (Ivanov 1982). But the food itself was generally secondary to the mealtime amusements, for which the maître d' might bring in a huge tray of food garnished with flowers and greens. On a bed of napkins lay the centerpiece, a naked woman, the exotic dish of the day. While an orchestra played, the merchants would shower the woman with rubles and pour wine and champagne over her, nibbling all the while on the surrounding food. At nearly 5,000 rubles, this entertainment did not come cheaply (Ivanov 1982).

Merchants were not the only carousers. The Russian literati also liked to gather in taverns or restaurants. In the late 1880s the writer Nikolai Leskov and his circle frequented a rather disreputable tavern by the name of Grigoriev's. Here, in a private room, they indulged in food and drink, then acted out "Golgotha," a sort of passion play. More often than not, the pale, bearded S. V. Maksimov played the part of Christ, with the actor I. F. Gorbunov in Pilate's role. After demanding Maksimov's crucifixion, the other players led him, hands tied with a napkin, to an adjoining room, where Gorbunov actually nailed him onto the wall. As a parting gesture, Maksimov was brought vinegar from a cruet to moisten his lips, and then his chest was "pierced" with a spear—Leskov's famous walking stick that sported a *memento mori* in place of a handle. Once Maksimov's head had dropped to his chest, he was removed from the cross and wrapped in a "shroud"—a tablecloth from one of the tables—then laid in a "grave" (an ottoman). As a chorus broke into song, a guard stood watch until Maksimov miraculously rose from the grave. The performance over, everyone repaired to the table to resume their interrupted feast and to drink away the sorrows of Christ's passion (Leskov 1984). This behavior—witty sophisticates making sport of the Resurrection—bears only superficial resemblance to that of the late nineteenth-century Decadent writers in England or France. Although Leskov and his friends acted in a spirit of irreverence, genuine religiosity underlay their play; even as they burlesqued Christ's passion they celebrated it, along with the transitory pleasures of a good meal.

This sort of carousing came to an abrupt end with the 1917 Revolution. In addition to food shortages, people had to contend with a new, puritanical attitude toward pleasure, which demanded that good Soviet citizens not indulge in excess or caprice. Personal gratification was frowned upon in favor of asceticism, and every action became morally fraught. Sex and overeating—both forms of indulgence—were officially looked down upon. Aleksandr Tarasov-Rodionov's classic socialist realist novel, *Shokolad* [*Chocolate*], chronicles the downfall of the stalwart functionary Zudin through the twin temptations of lust and chocolate. A moralistic discourse took root in which all desires, both sexual and gastronomic, were equated with bourgeois decadence, and young communists were encouraged to engage only in healthy, collective forms of pleasure, eschewing the consumption of rich or luxury foods (Naiman 1997).

A revolution in the kitchen never materialized. Although giant *fabriki-kukhni* [factory kitchens] were built to centralize meal production, the large communal dining halls envisaged as a way to liberate women from their labors did not succeed. In the culinary sphere, conformity took hold, and apart from forays into the ethnic cuisines of the "fraternal republics," the Soviet era was marked by a continual narrowing of the range of available ingredients, a reduction of dishes to their most prosaic interpretations, and a pervasive coarsening of the national palate. While the ideological purity of the 1920s was, by the 1930s, a thing of the past, for the most part public dining never really recovered, and restaurant culture was lost. By the late Soviet period the fine restaurants of Moscow could be counted on one hand (and even here the term "fine" is relative). Going out to a good restaurant was still a mark of prestige, but the terms had changed. The issue was not money, but whether you were deemed worthy of getting a table at all. Not everyone was allowed in, even when the place was virtually empty. Members of the Writers' Union could eat at the elite TsDL [Central House of Writers] dining room, where the food was excellent, even if less exquisite than it had been when so deliciously described in Mikhail Bulgakov's novel *Master and Margarita*. Soviet restaurants continued to serve up illusion, but it was illusion created by the exigencies of the Soviet State. The pretense of abundance and plenty went only as far as the printed menu, from which only one or two items were typically available. Nevertheless, the menu was duly presented by the wait staff; it was studied by the diners; and everyone pretended that the list of appetizers and entrées, wines and desserts, had some resemblance to the reality of the dishes that would come out from the kitchen.

Today, the thought of that single Japanese restaurant at the Russian World Trade Center seems laughable: landlocked Moscow arguably has more sushi restaurants than any comparable Western city. But just what is involved in Moscow's re-creation of itself as a world-class city for dining, as befits the capital of Russia's commercial and political life? The most obvious factor is the rise of a middle class, which, along with the New Russians, has created a thriving consumer market. Since consumer spending not only reflects but also shapes the culture of a place, it is one of the most revealing ways to understand any society, and the growth of restaurants in Moscow provides a prime example. After decades of Soviet life, people are hungry for pleasure, and willing to spend money for it. The sacramental Soviet-style restaurant meal as a ritual marking important occasions such as weddings has given way to a new style of eating out simply for pleasure, on ordinary days. This reversal has called for a new psychology, a new ideological framework, in which it is all right to indulge oneself, to engage in pleasurable activity for its own sake. Restaurants offer not only entertainment, they are also a vehicle for the public presentation of self, the twenty-first-century counterpart to the domestic dinners staged by Russians in the past to reflect both their wealth and their largesse.

Two savvy businessmen have tapped into this national longing for living a life that is, in a way, larger than life itself. In addition to Andrei Dellos, the mastermind behind Café Pushkin, the other major player in the Moscow restaurant scene is Arkady Novikov, who actually began his career as a chef under oil tycoon Roman Abramovich. Like his mentor, Novikov has set his sights beyond the city limits and is courting foreign investors, most notably the empire-building Alain Ducasse, who is planning to open a branch of his American-style "Spoon" restaurant. (Novikov also worked with Hédiard, the venerable Parisian food purveyor, to open a retail store in Moscow.) Both Dellos and Novikov have recognized the need to offer their patrons everything that was unattainable under Soviet rule. The fantasy restaurants they have created promise indulgence and pleasure by means of illusion—unique spaces, magical arenas that cater to every whim.

The fact that Russians have embraced the idea of restaurant-as-fantasy tells us much about Russian culture, particularly when we compare it to contemporary styles of dining in other major European and American cities. Elsewhere, for sophisticated diners food is the thing, and any suggestion that entertainment might be an important component of the dining experience is met with disdain. For instance, when the restaurant impresario Warner LeRoy sought to recreate New York's venerable Russian Tea Room in 1999, he was roundly criticized for his fantasy vision of Russia (it was, admittedly, over the top, with mirrored Firebird-like shards on the walls, a revolving crystal bear with fish in its belly, and an oversized tree hung with Murano glass apples). Notably, LeRoy had grown up on the film set of the *Wizard of Oz*, which his father, Mervyn LeRoy, produced, and so he spent much of his youth surrounded by illusion and understood the delight it can bring. But the New York press was quick to object to his penchant for theatrical effect. "Some said that his taste for rococo shimmer and dazzle was just noisy kitsch," pronounced LeRoy's *New York Times* obituary, "that his pursuit of the fantastic sometimes crossed the line from exuberance to wretched excess" (Asimov 2001). By contrast, hyperbole is what the most celebrated Russian restaurants in Moscow today are all about. In other words, the performance of the meal trumps the meal itself; such is the contemporary Russian restaurant culture. A decade after the collapse of the Soviet Union, high-end restaurants provide a stage upon which performance, so much a part of dining in Russia's storied past, is once again paramount.

The focus of Moscow's restaurants on the mythical and nostalgic rather than on the creation of a cutting-edge cuisine reveals a good deal about the nature of Russia's social transformation, as well as about cultural continuity and change. The presentation of "authentic" Russian food in an "authentic" atmosphere serves to affirm the idea of Russianness, which is tied up with closely held beliefs about national identity. As one review of Novikov's restaurant Tsarskaya Okhota [The Royal Hunt] states, "Finely tuned style isn't what's important here, but emotion" (Chernov 2002).

The impetus for a celebration of things Russian was, paradoxically, provided by the opening of Russia's first McDonald's in January 1990, for which 30,000 people showed up. Rather perversely, McDonald's set a new standard for service and quality in Moscow: Here was a restaurant where everything on the menu was always available, where quality was controlled, and where service was quick and friendly. In short order, Pizza Hut, Dunkin' Donuts, and Baskin Robbins all appeared (Pizza Hut and Dunkin' Donuts subsequently pulled out of the Russian market). Significantly, most of the early American fast-food chains gave way rather quickly to Russian chains, such as Russkoye Bistro [Russian Bistro], where the food was friendly and fast but obviously Russian. Other popular chains like Elki-Palki [Fiddlesticks] (another Novikov enterprise) and Mumu play on the idea of Russianness, too, with their cottage-like interiors and hearty comfort food. They reflect Russia's need to announce its identity through cuisine, but, notably, the symbolism is old rather than new. Even the high-end restaurants reveal an uncommon connection to Russia's cultural past. Think for a moment about restaurants in New York, London, or Paris. How many are named after literary, artistic, or historical figures? Yet among Moscow's top restaurants we find Godunov, Yermak, Pushkin, Oblomov, Vechera na khutore, Taras Bul'ba, Balaganchik, Petrov-Vodkin, Belyi kvadrat and Krasnyi bar (both in homage to Malevich), Beloye solntse pustyni and Kavkazskaya Plennitsa (named after the Soviet cult films), and Petrovich (named after the Soviet cartoon character).[5] Moscow's restaurants are reminders—if not keepers—of the country's cultural heritage.

As Ulrich Schmid has pointed out in regard to Switzerland, "Never has the nostalgia for cows and the homely sound of cowbells been as intense among the Swiss as in the age of e-mail and the Internet. The more modern and technically advanced the product, the more nostalgic its advertisements" (Schmid). A similar phenomenon is apparent in Russia. The greater the encroachment of the West, the more visible signs there are of a created Russianness, a commercial branding of authenticity that affirms Russia as

Russian. These restaurants may be seen as touchstones in the face of all that is new and unsettled in Russian society. The allure of such a commercially created Russian space should not be underestimated, nor should the appeal of Novikov's and Dellos's other fantasylands, for they allow citizens of the new Russia to experience entertainment devoid of political meaning. But will the focus on pure entertainment merely encourage philistines whose only interest in the dining experience is show, pretense, and ostentation?

For now, in the place of genuine connoisseurship we find the likes of Café Pushkin. It is here that culture and capital meet, as they once did in Moscow's famous Slavyansky Bazar, where Stanislavsky and Nemirovich-Danchenko met to create the Moscow Art Theater. Café Pushkin is the place to see and be seen. We witness today's wealthy New Russians actively constructing their public image, like the hyperbolic hosts of earlier eras. Largely unconcerned with the restaurant's edibles, they act out roles that befit their stations. Restaurants are complicit in the construction of identity, at both the individual and national levels, and Moscow, as Russia's commercial and political center, is home to a significant number of eating establishments where Russia's national character is in the process of being constructed. But whether Russia's national character is there for all to see is, in a way, beside the point. It is in these restaurants that we may glimpse Russia both posing and performing for herself.

Notes

1. Not even Russia's second city, St. Petersburg, matches Moscow in terms of disposable income. The situation in the provinces is often desperate; thus the information presented here is applicable only to the capital city.

2. These slogans were popularized under Stalin and Brezhnev, respectively.

3. Of course, the majority of Russians did not have the luxury to feast in style; more often than not, feast days meant simply the addition of a bit of lard to the cabbage soup, or a measure of vodka. These comments therefore apply to Russians of some means.

4. Visitors had warned about the deceptiveness of the Russians as early as the sixteenth century. See Sigismund von Herberstein, *Notes Upon Russia, Being a Translation of the Earliest Account of that Country, Entitled Rerum Moscoviticarum commentarii*. Translated and edited, with notes and an introduction, by R. H. Major (New York: B. Franklin [1963]); and Adam Olearius, *The Travels of Olearius in Seventeenth-Century Russia*. Translated and edited by Samuel H. Baron (Stanford: Stanford University Press, 1967). For the nineteenth century, see the Marquis de Custine, *Empire of the Czar: A Journey Through Eternal Russia*. (New York: Doubleday, 1989 a reprint of the original 1843 translation from the French).

5. The meanings of these names are as follows: Boris Godunov: sixteenth-century tsar, made familiar in Pushkin's verse play; Yermak: sixteenth-century Cossack conqueror of Siberia; Pushkin: Russia's great national poet; Oblomov: hero of Ivan Goncharov's 1859 novel of the same name; *Vechera na khutore* [Evenings on a Farm near Dikanka]: title of Nikolai Gogol's series of stories about a mythical Ukrainian village; Taras Bul'ba: Gogol story about the Zaporozh'e Cossacks; *Balanganchik* [Punch and Judy show]: title of a play by the Symbolist poet Alexander Blok; Petrov-Vodkin: important modernist painter and theorist; Belyi kvadrat: reference to Kazimir Malevich's famous 1918 painting *White on White*; Krasnyi bar: reference to Malevich's 1914 *Red Square*; *Beloye solntse pustyni*: [White Sun of the Desert]: 1970 film directed by Vladimir Motyl, whose hero is a Red Army soldier; *Kavkazskaya plennitsa*: 1966 film comedy directed by Leonid Gaidai; Petrovich: Soviet cartoon character.

References

Asimov, Eric (2001), Obituary of Warner LeRoy, *New York Times* February 26.

Chernov, Sergei (2002), *Chernovik 2003. Restorannyi reiting,* [M]: izd. PBOIuL: 114.

de Segur, Count Anatole (1865/1911), "Zapiski," in N. N. Rusov (ed.) *Pomeshchich'ia Rossiia*, Moscow: izd. mosk. knigoizd. T-va "Obrazovanie:" 41.

Dryansky, G. Y. (2003), "Hot *Prospekt*," *Condé Nast Traveler*: 189, May.

Efimova, Alla (1999), "Idea against materia: on the consumption of post-Soviet art." Retrieved August 3, 2004 from Artmargins. http://www.artmargins.com/content/feature/efimova1.html

Ivanov, Evgenii (1982), *Metkoe moskovskoe slovo*, Moscow: Moskovskii rabochii, 286: 287–8.

Leskov, Andrei (1984), *Zhizn' Nikolaia Leskova po ego lichnym, semeinym i nesemeinym zapisiam i pamiatiam*, Vol. 2, Moscow: Khudozhestvennaia literature: 236–7.

Lotman, Iu. M. and Pogosian, E. A. (1996), *Velikosvetskie obedy*, SPB: Pushkinskii fond: 28–30.

Naiman, Eric (1997), *Sex in Public: The Incarnation of Early Soviet Ideology*, Princeton: Princeton University Press: 210, 214.

Pyliaev, M. I. (1897), "Kak eli vstarinu," in *Staroe zhit'e: ocherki i razskazy*, SPB: tip. A. S. Suvorina: 8, 11.

Schmid, Ulrich, *Citizens, Not Subjects*, Zurich: Vontobel Foundation: 5.

Sipovskaia, Natal'ia (2003), "Vkus prazdnika," *4 chuvstva: Prazdnik vo Peterburge XVIII veka*, SPB: IPTs "Khudozhnik i kniga, n.p.

Tereshchenko, A. (1848), *Byt russkago naroda: narodnost', zhilishcha, domovodstvo, obraz zhizni, muzyka, svad'by, vremiachislenie, kreshchenie i pr.,* 7 Vols. SPB: Tip. Ministra vnutrennykh del: 249.

von Bremzen, Anya (2002), "Taste of the Future," *Travel + Leisure*, 76 (December).

36
Identity and the Global Stew

Allison James

At the side of the main road to Alnwick which runs through the lonely, windswept moorland of north Northumberland a sign catches the eye. Swinging forlornly from its white wooden post it advertises, in the silence of this landscape, the Carib-Northumbria restaurant. These words signify an intriguing pairing, heightened by the painted palm trees which adorn the sign set amongst that so English scene of fields where sheep safely graze. In Northampton, a Midlands town once thriving on the proceeds of the shoe industry, now displaced by warehousing and commuting, an Indian restaurant has been refurbished. Its Taj Mahal-like windows, fabricated from painted plywood placed over plate glass, strike a discordant note among a straggle of plain shop fronts, small businesses from video hire to home brew. Its claim, proudly advertised, is full air conditioning. It is as if the heat of an Indian summer can be, literally rather than just figuratively, experienced inside. Together with the Indian cuisine this contrives to simulate, for the customer, a momentary taste of India in central England. It is, however, short-lived. The meal's finale brings with it a swift and abrupt relocation: placed on the saucer, alongside the bill, lies a gold-wrapped sweet. Described on its wrapping as an After Curry Mint, it mimics – perhaps mocks – the seeming sophistication which the After Eight Mint, in its dark brown envelope, lent to the English suburban dinner party of an earlier era.

Such juxtapositions and mixing of cuisines, times, and locations are many and manifold in form, lending anecdotal support to the suggestion that we are all in the process of becoming creolized. Take a further example: the traveller on British Rail's first-class Pullman service is now offered a 'cosmopolitan dinner' from the Dishes of the World series, which features food 'from India, the Middle East, China, Greece, Italy, Scandinavia and France' (*Intercity*, November 1991). A suggested menu begins with dim sum with hoisin sauce from China, is followed by duck and mixed berry sauce from south-west France and ends with tiramisu from Italy for dessert. The food, described as 'sophisticated but fun', seems somehow a fitting twenty-first-century menu.

However, this observation leaves unquestioned the different ways in which particular individuals may embrace, or indeed reject, this culinary variety and the meanings with which they may imbue such postmodern menus through the act of food consumption. In exploring these issues, therefore, the relationship between food and cultural identity is central and raises a number of interconnected questions. Using England as a case study, I ask whether, in the context of an increasingly (global) international food production-consumption system and a seemingly 'creolized' world, food still acts as a marker of (local) cultural identity? If food is literally for thinking about identity – 'you are what you eat', 'one man's meat is another man's poison', and so on – then does the confusion of culinary signposts, exemplified above, signify the loss of the markers of distinctiveness which separate Others from ourselves? Or are contemporary food practices registering a modified English cultural identity? Is Hannerz correct in his assertion that:

> [An] openness to foreign cultural influences need not involve only an impoverishment of local and national culture. It may give people access to technological and symbolic resources for dealing with their own ideas, managing their own culture in new ways.
>
> (Hannerz 1987: 555)

If so, what kinds of cultural changes might be being marked (marketed) in Britain? What new forms of identity might we be confronting through the recent appearance of the Chinese pizza?

This chapter seeks tentative answers to some of these questions. Through an exploration of the ways in which English food is variously imaged in academic and popular writings about food, it will show that subtle distinctions in food practices shore up different, sometimes conflicting, statements about identity and how, through these discordant meanings, attention is drawn to the temporal flow through which identities come into being. Consumption practices are seen here therefore as precariously flexible, rather than fixed and constant, markers of Self and of identity.

Identity and Consumption

That food acts as a marker of cultural identity has long been noted within anthropological work on social classification, suggesting that food consumption practices are seemingly unequivocal indicators of cultural difference (Douglas 1966; Bulmer 1967; Lévi-Strauss 1962). It has been argued that acts of consumption register ideas of edibility through delimiting conceptual boundaries around that-which-can-conceivably-be-eaten within any particular culture, which is but a selection made from all-that-it-is-possible-to-eat. Through this, cultural differences of identity are mapped out: we eat horsemeat, they don't; they eat grasshoppers, we don't. Indeed, the very concept of 'foreign' food – which has become increasingly popular in Britain and about which I shall have a great deal more to say – derives from the marking-out of difference: 'foreign' food is food from abroad consumed at home, food of the Other, strange and unfamiliar. Shared patterns of consumption thus mark our difference from others. Mapping, as they often do, onto other signs of difference – from the organization of domestic space through to the division of labour and concepts of sexual intimacy – food consumption practices provide confirmation of wider differences between cultural orders (Tambiah 1969; Leach 1964; Douglas 1975: 249 ff.).

And yet, despite this confident mobilization of food as a stable and enduring marker of cultural identity, a certain fickleness characterizes the way in which food consumption practices shore up concepts of cultural identity. As recent work on food systems has shown, historically there has been a constant interchange between cultures in relation to food consumption (Mintz 1985; Goody 1982). Trade, travel, transport and technology have all played their part in facilitating a considerable exchange of consumption practices. This brings into question, therefore, the very notion of 'authentic' food traditions, raising doubts as to the validating role food might have with respect to cultural identity. For example, as Goody (1982) notes, it was not until the end of the nineteenth century that olive oil became an indispensable ingredient in Provençal cooking. Before then it had been but marginal to that particular food tradition. Similarly, pizza and pasta – now regarded as the most Italian of Italian foods (but fast becoming the most global of global foods) – were originally only to be found in Italy's southern regions. Likewise maize, now regarded as a staple, 'traditional' food in many regions of Africa, is not an indigenous plant. Introduced by the Portuguese in the sixteenth century, and originating in America, it became known as Turkish wheat in Britain, Spanish corn in France, Sicilian corn in Italy and 'foreign' corn in Turkey. As Tannahill observes:

> Among history's many ironies is the fact that a cheap food designed to feed African slaves on their way to America should have resulted, in Africa itself, in a population increase substantial enough to ensure that the slavers would not sail empty of human cargo.
>
> (Tannahill 1973: 205)

Such links, Goody notes, provide a salutary lesson for those attached either to the holistic or to the timeless view of culture (1982: 36). They also de-emphasize conceptions of society linked to the isolated and bounded nation-state (Featherstone 1990a: 2) and in so doing, re-emphasize the need for a reflexive concept of culture which takes account of its temporal and spatial minglings (Hannerz 1990: 239)...

A second cautionary note must be sounded. Although food clearly does mark out distinct local cultural identities, despite its globalizing tendencies, at the same time consumption practices work to fragment the idea of a unitary local culture. A plurality of intracultural identities are simultaneously registered in acts of food consumption. Again, this has been well documented. For instance, during rites of status passage, special kinds of food will be eaten, and commonly consumed foods may become temporarily taboo for the initiates undergoing transition to a new social identity (Richards [1956] 1982). Similarly, it has been noted that age and gender both shape consumption practices (Charles and Kerr 1988) and that the gift of food can cement social relations just as the withholding of food can negate them (Ortner 1978). And all of these processes of staking out diverse identities might take place within the confines of a single 'authentic' food tradition or cuisine.

Thus, the abundant referencing of identity through food consumption practices contains excluding, and often contradictory, statements about cultural identity. Mobilized in different social contexts and at different times through particular food items, fine lines of discrimination are revealed, markers of difference which are used to distinguish the self from other selves in everyday life: what you eat may tell me that you are a young/old/male/female/high-status/low-status/sick/well kind of person. At the same time, these identities may also testify to, or indeed become submerged by, a wider cultural referencing: that you are a Jew, a Muslim or a Hindu, or that you are also African, French or British. And on still other occasions, the food that you choose to eat might tell me that you would see yourself (and wish to be seen by others) as Scottish – haggis and mashed 'neeps' [turnips] on Burns Night – rather than British, as a city-dweller and sophisticate, or more specific still as a Londoner or Aberdonian or, indeed, through the regular consumption of jellied eels, a true East Ender.

Paradoxically, therefore, food provides a *flexible* symbolic vehicle for Self identity, precisely through the invocation of sets of '*inflexible* cultural stereotypes which link particular foodstuffs to particular localized identities' (J. James 1993). Given the present context of a global economic culture where, for the affluent West at least, the international food system ensures access to a spiralling diversity of foodstuffs, this chapter asks whether food can retain its role as a signifier of identity. If so, how are new foods and new identities made mutually reflective? If not, what cultural sense is being made of this potentially endless diversity of culinary markers within particular locales? What strategies of consumption (and production) are being brought into play and how are they being used to constitute the Self in society (Friedman 1990)?

Recent Changes in British Food Preferences

With respect to contemporary English society these issues are particularly pertinent, for since Elizabeth David first published her book about Mediterranean cooking in the 1950s, there has been a marked change in English food preferences (Mennell 1985). The cookery columns in women's magazines of the 1950s, which provided cooking hints and tips in recipes for traditional family food, were augmented, and later displaced, by a more sophisticated food journalism in the 1960s. This brought to the conservative English palate the tastes and textures of 'foreign food' and from the mid-1970s, radio and television programmes began to take food as a serious topic for discussion and reflection through the broadcasting of regular features on food and drink. In recent years these have been supplemented by more specialist series focusing on particular 'foreign' cuisines such as those of India, China, Spain and Provence. This reflects an interest in the consumption of foreign food which looks set to continue…

However, although these trends might seem to bear witness to an undeniable internationalization of English taste buds, the extent to which such shifts in consumption practices can be taken as a reliable index of a more global sense of identity remains unclear, for there are also signs of an opposite movement towards a more localized, even parochial, taste in food. Evidence for this is legion in the weekend pages of the quality British press with a relatively affluent readership. The consumption of food, increasingly positioned as a leisure activity rather than simply as a nutritional necessity, is now a mark of culture, rather than simply a cultural marker. This can be seen, for instance, in *The Guardian* newspaper's launch of the Big Cheese Club in 1993 to mark the renaissance of artisan cheese-making in Britain and in the foodie writers' celebration of quintessential English food: 'Baked goods encapsulate all the best qualities of traditional English cookery: simplicity, robustness, and forthright use of fine ingredients' (Ehrlich, *The Guardian*, 9 October 1993). Do such shifts in attitude suggest, therefore, that the consumption of 'foreign' food has been a mere stepping-out of role, a 'liminal' taste experience, which, through the contrast it presents, has reaffirmed a sense of what is truly English? Is there a reinvention of tradition occurring whereby English food is, ironically, becoming a mark of *British* cuisine? Or, instead, is a new form of English food emerging, a new authenticity represented by the Anglicized curry with chips?

To consider these questions I draw on Hannerz's (1990) discussion of cosmopolitanism. In this he emphasizes the importance of recognizing the subtle differences masked by concepts of world or global culture and suggests that these ideas be understood in terms of the 'organization of diversity rather than by a replication of uniformity' (Hannerz 1990: 237). Adapted for the food domain, Hannerz's discussion usefully distinguishes four contemporary food trends, described here in terms of overlapping discourses. In the first, the increasingly transnational character of food is emphasized. No longer limited to particular locales, foodstuffs are seen to have an international, increasingly homogeneous character. Diversity and difference in cuisines are consciously played down or understated. Second, and in seeming direct contrast, there is an urgent emphasizing of the heterogeneity of cuisines, of their cultural diversity, of the fine distinctiveness of particular local foodstuffs and of the peculiar and special experience of eating food within its own locale. A third trend vociferously defends the local, is truly anti-cosmopolitan, while the fourth acknowledges the gradual creolization of food, the mixing of cuisines as of cultures, redolent in the idea of curried pasta, lasagne with chips and vegetarian haggis. But, distinct though these different trends in cosmopolitan tastes are, they nonetheless share in a wider commonality: each refracts in different ways the motifs of authenticity and tradition and in so doing, the relationship between food and local forms of identity is constantly restated and reaffirmed in the face of more global claims.

Discourse 1: Global Food

The appearance of the big 'M' for McDonald's in the streets of Moscow as well as those of London bears witness to the globalization of fast food. During 1984–88 McDonald's increased its franchising by 34% and in 1988, its outlet in Belgrade, Yugoslavia was serving over 6,000 customers per day (Finkelstein 1989). Coca-Cola and other kinds of snack food have been similarly successful and for Sargent, show without doubt that:

> Food cultures are becoming more and more homogeneous as Western food conquers the world. Behind the standard-bearers of McDonald's and Coca-Cola, fast foods, snack foods, processed foods, food gimmicks and soft drinks are on the march. They have swept through North America and made inroads into Britain and parts of Europe.
>
> (Finkelstein 1989: 46)

But such food imperialism is not, I suggest, purely a matter of taste. It is also a matter of meanings: embedded within the hamburger or fizzy drink are images of identity waiting to be consumed, identities which are dependent on the form and presentation of the food itself.

In the majority of chain restaurants, for example, novelty and surprise are kept at a minimum. Worldwide, the decor and menus of chain restaurants will be familiar and recognizable, with only minor accommodations made to the local context, and even interactions with the consuming public will be routinized, domesticated and mundane:

> The training of restaurant personnel, as set out in the 600-page McDonald's staffing manual, includes suggestions for specific conversational exchanges.

> Greeting the customer is important: 'be pleasant, not mechanical' which means employ a convincing smile. Other suggested comments include 'Hi, I'm here to serve you', 'Come and visit us again'.
>
> (Finkelstein 1989: 11)

Through this standardization of consumption experiences the uniqueness of the Self is played down, making the identities on offer similarly safe and conventional. Traditionally cautious in their eating habits with a taste for plain food and with robust appetites (Mennell 1985), for the English the appeal of these fast-food outlets lies in their framing as family eating establishments. For the young they are places to go alone for informal, classless food consumption at any time of the day or night. The pleasures gained from eating a Big Mac derive, therefore, from its very uniformity, its lack of difference in a heterogeneous world culture. The global is made manageable, is rendered knowable: 'The diner knows exactly how to order the foods and what s/he will receive whether in Tulsa or Tokyo ... and the interest food can generate in different cultural practices and social styles is retarded' (Finkelstein 1989: 47). This global, homogenized identity imaged in such fast-food outlets is thus reassuringly *local* in feel, encompassing in a foreign land or urban cityscape a wide diversity of individual consumers. It is food from home at home and a place to locate or anchor the Self when abroad.

Elsewhere the ubiquitous burger may mean precisely the opposite. Embracing one particular local identity (American) in a global context this food may, for example, enable consumers to take on, momentarily, a more transnational, differentiated identity and lifestyle through taking in the authentic taste of America. A new convert to McDonald's in Beijing described this experience:

> I love it. I love the milk shake, I love the Big Mac, I love the apple pie, I love...
>
> (Gracie, *The Guardian*, 24 April 1992)

A few yards from Chairman Mao's mausoleum, McDonald's Beijing outlet does good business: 'Outside, the queues are shepherded through a maze of railings and gates, tripping over each other in their eagerness to taste "real American food"' (Gracie, *The Guardian*, 24 April 1992)...

The homogenizing of food across the globe, through the fast-food revolution, has not, however, produced a comparable set of homogenized identities. Indeed, as Chase (1992: 68) notes, in Istanbul the penetration of Western fast-food chains has led to an *increased*, rather than decreased, local culinary complexity through the revival of traditional Turkish snack foods which offer similar contemporary 'grazing' experience at half the price.

Global food has therefore yielded subtly different experiences and outcomes. It has simultaneously encouraged the expression of sameness *and* difference, universalism *and* particularism (Robertson 1992), re-authenticating local identities in a global context.

Discourse 2: Expatriate Food

Following Appadurai's suggestion that in the global cultural economy 'mediascapes ... help to constitute narratives of the "other" and proto-narratives of possible lives' (1990: 299), in this section I focus upon one contemporary and highly popular food narrative: the story and dramatic enactment of Peter Mayle's escape from the English climate and cuisine to that of Luberon mountains in the Provençal region of France, recorded in his book *A Year in Provence*...

The book traces one whole year in Provence, beginning and ending with a meal. New Year's Eve is described as taking place in a restaurant, and the following Christmas sees the Mayles dining in the kitchen. The intervening pages are no less concerned with food, constituting for the reader a seemingly complete menu for Provençal life and providing a taste of what it is to be French or, more specifically, to take on a Provençal identity. January sees 'foie gras, lobster mousse, beef *en croûte*, salads dressed in virgin oil, hand-picked cheeses, deserts of a miraculous lightness, *digestifs* ... a gastronomic aria' (Mayle 1990: 2). Feburary brings snow, 'lamb stuffed with herbs, *daube*, veal with truffles and an unexplained dish called the *fantaisie du chef*' (36). And so to March and on through the year, each month a new dish and a new taste of Provence, until November. Described by Mayle as 'good eating weather' we are introduced to:

> A crisp oily salad and slices of pink country sausage, an *aïoli* of snails and cod and hard-boiled eggs with garlic mayonnaise, creamy cheese from Fontvielle and a home-made tart ... the kind of meal that the French take for granted and tourists remember for years (181).

By this time Mayle sees himself as 'being somewhere between the two', that is between being a Frenchman and a tourist (180). And it would seem that this changed identity has been largely accomplished through ingesting Provençal food. He has quite literally been reconstituted by it: at Christmas, which in Mayle's Provence is dominated by food – by 'oysters and crayfish and pheasant and hare, pâtés and cheeses, hams and capons, gateaux and pink champagne' – the Mayles feel finally 'at home' (188–97)...

Ostensibly, of course, the book is not about food at all. It is about an Englishman abroad, hoping to divest his English identity. But as an expatriate/cosmopolitan figure who has eaten in Provence, Mayle can tell us 'what it is *really* like to live in Provence'. Described by the critics as 'bitingly funny about local rural mores' but none the less retaining a 'warm enthusiasm for local life and landscapes' Mayle's book is offered as 'advised reading for anyone planning to move to Provence'.[1]

What the book provides, therefore, is a claim to authenticity, and an authenticity authenticated through pages of gastronomic detail. Humble patrons and peasant-like café owners, ordinary people steeped in ordinary, everyday Provençal food, dish up a traditional Provençal life to a global-literate audience... Such claims to authenticity and tradition are common to much contemporary food writing and food journalism (cf. Levy 1986; Davidson 1988). As Mayle does, the foodie writers seek and find the marks of authenticity in diversity, in the small scale and in local, artisanal modes of production. Differentiation is celebrated through the quality and authenticity of local food traditions, worldwide...

This presents a stark contrast to the homogenization of food achieved within the globalized discourse and yet, curiously, shares part of its dominion through its celebration of locality. Here, then, is a resistance to both globalization and creolization as forms of cosmopolitanism. This is not a familiarity with a global, homogenized food culture but, rather, a global familiarity with the subtle distinctions of spice and herb which differentiate between regional specialities across the globe. Thus Davidson's discussion of Asian food begins with a description of the food traditions of Laos, which he insists are distinct from those served in neighbouring China, Vietnam, Cambodia, Thailand and Burma, and which make 'the cuisine of the Lao people truly distinctive' (1988: 198).

Discourse 3: Food Nostalgia

A variation of the celebration of locality in a global context is to be found in the food heritage/nostalgia industry, a sentiment expressed in a recent newspaper report. Referring to a prosecution brought by the trading standards department in Northumberland over a Stilton cheese, tradition and authenticity are marshalled to defend local interests in the face of global threats to standardize cheese production:

> A mature Stilton cheese, whose mites and maggots were such that Daniel Defoe said spoon was needed to eat them has won a legal battle over hygiene... The small residents were essential to genuine Stilton said Adrian Williams, solicitor for Safeways supermarket, rather than evidence of careless cheese-handling. He accused the trading standards officers of ignorance. 'Here is a product which has been English to the bone from the 1700s onwards', he said. 'It has had mites on it ever since'. The bench dismissed the case. Peter Pugson, chairman of the UK Cheese Guild called the decision 'a victory for English commonsense' and offered the standards department a place on the guild's diploma course.
>
> (Wainwright, *The Guardian*, 4 October 1991)

In 1993, *The Guardian* newspaper again made an appeal for authenticity and tradition in relation to food consumption:

> When was the last time a good piece of British cheese wrapped itself around your taste buds? Have you ever made the acquaintance of the spritely Cheshire made by the Appelby family; the majestic mature Lancashire of Mrs Kirkham; the Irish Cashel Blue; the beguiling Spenwood or the infinitely beguiling Wigmore; or the imperial Stilton from Colston Bassett?
>
> (Fort, *The Guardian*, 9 October 1993)

It was argued that the disappearance in the 1960s of such cheeses as the Blue Vinney of Dorset does 'not reflect well on the performance of the Dairy Council, and [speaks] much of the malign influence of large commercial concerns' (Fort, *The Guardian*, 9 October 1993). Like the newspaper's yearly endeavour to find a truly British sausage, often locally produced in small rural communities, the cheese club offers those who join the opportunity to sample traditional British cheese. Members can purchase rare artisan cheeses, dispatched with tasting notes to guide them in their consumption. Other foodie magazines provide similar services, putting their readers in touch with mail-order outlets for regional specialities...

Dishes such as steamed puddings, pies and pastries are also emerging out of their glorious domesticity. Gill, for example, notes that sticky toffee pudding is fast becoming the 'black forest gateau of the 1990s' (*Sunday Times*, 17 October 1993). Similarly, the appearance of bread and butter pudding and tripe on the menus of the more fashionable restaurants indicates a revival of English food in defiance of the trend towards more global food cultures. There is, then, within this discourse, a considerable resistance to heterogeneity in terms of food from across the globe, and an insistence on the distinctive homogeneity of local food traditions...

Discourse 4: Food Creolization

First published in 1989, Mayle's book has been heavily promoted ever since and, accompanying the TV serialization, the *Radio Times* magazine focused on 'Peter Mayle's Provence' for three consecutive weeks... With the help of Provençal cookery writer Mireille Johnston we were enabled to recreate this gastronomic Provence in our own homes (*Radio Times*, 6–12 March 1993). Week one saw recipes for appetizers, week two those for main courses, and week three the desserts.

As a symbolic mediator for the distrusting, fearful ordinary English – who dare not travel too far, who are as unadventurous in their diets as in their lives, whose stomachs recoil at drinking local milk (Mayle 1990: 105) – Mayle's cosmopolitan role was clear: he was to serve as a cultural guide, leading us carefully through the labyrinth of ways in which, if not becoming truly Provençal, we might at least take on a momentary French-like identity and 'become a cosmopolitan without going away at all' (Hannerz 1990: 249). For a meal, for a day, the reader could 'create the taste of Provence at home' (*Radio Times*, 6–12 March). Claims to authenticity and tradition abounded, as the step-by-step instructions revealed how to cook up a new and convincing Provençalness... Week 2 told us that 'the true flavours of Provence are found in the markets, from sun-ripened tomatoes to fresh, fragrant herbs. Many of the dishes are based on the local principle of "make something with nothing"' (*Radio Times*, 13–19 March 1993). Most dishes are served with a final drizzle of olive oil, that so traditional and indispensable ingredient which, as noted above, was only 'authenticated' at the turn of the century (Goody 1982).

But in Week 3 the pudding recipes signalled the end of this gastronomic adventure, the end of our dalliance with French ways and a return to a more puritanical, traditional English style. Of the desserts on offer only one smacked of French food; the other seemed to be more English in its appeal. Described as 'sinfully sweet', this pudding recalled the 'naughty but nice', puritanical Brit consumer for whom the eating of food is traditionally more a necessity than a pleasure (Mennell 1985; A. James 1990). In Mayle's Provençal world no food could be seen as sinful.

This subtle shift to an English-like Provençal cooking bears witness to a new culinary trend within British society: creolized food (Brown, *Sunday Times*, 9 May 1993). This rejects authenticity and through exploiting the heterogeneity of food is gradually giving shape to a new homogeneity. Creolized food appears in many guises, providing for the consumer a global experience of consumption often within a single meal if not on a single plate. One London café exemplifies this trend in consumption, describing its food as 'a sophisticated and mouthwatering mélange of the East with the West, illustrating the culinary style that has evolved in the UK over the past 30 years' (Brown, *Sunday Times*, 9 May 1993). Here the food is a cultural blending, reflecting the mixing of decor styles which envelop the diner: 'They cut down on ghee and chilli in Indian dishes, and ... they Indianize thoroughly Western dishes such as burgers, tuna and lamb chops' (*Sunday Times*, 9 May 1993).

Such mixing of tastes and cuisines might simply be seen as a response to local conditions where authentic ingredients may be lacking. For the exiled or labour migrant, whose personal circumstances may precipitate a journey across the globe, memories of home may linger, to be recreated in new localities through the medium of food. However, the proliferation of creolization of food traditions in England represents, I suggest, more than simple utility or an accident of history. It is a new mark of Englishness for, although decried by champions of the expatriate and nostalgia food discourses, creolized food represents in many ways an accommodation of the traditional English attitudes to food and consumption.

Conclusion: Discoursing on Food

In contemporary England, then, four discourses on food shape both local and global identities, with each laying claim to a particular kind of cosmopolitan identity through their different evocations of the motifs of tradition and authenticity. And yet, through their shared and overlapping themes, these discourses constitute an arena of choice for individual consumers. In embodying identities in a multiplex fashion, they offer ways of embracing Otherness, of confronting the global through localized, even personal, food styles and conversely, a way of living a local life with and through global imagery. Thus, the exotic fruit now routinely available on supermarket shelves may be used casually to enhance a traditional English fruit salad: a careless cosmopolitanism, invoked through ignorance or choice. Alternatively, these fruits may be carefully selected and deliberately employed, to recreate authentic 'local' tastes at home, by the food gourmet, the new immigrant, or the politically exiled.

The globalization of food is not, therefore, just a matter of the movement of foodstuffs between nations; nor is it simply the amalgamation or accommodation of cuisines. It is a complex interplay of meanings and intentions which individuals employ subjectively to make statements about who they are, and where and how their Selves are to be located in the world.

Note

1. These quotations are taken from the cover of the paperback volume.

References

Appadurai, A. (1990), 'Disjuncture and difference in the global cultural economy', *Theory, Culture and Society* 7, 2–3: 295–311.

Bulmer, R. (1967), 'Why the cassowary is not a bird. A problem of zoological taxonomy among the Karam of the New Guinea Highlands', *Man* (n.s.) 2 (1): 5–25.

Charles, N. and Kerr, M. (1988), *Women, Food and Families*, Manchester: Manchester University Press.

Chase, H. (1992), 'The *meyhane* or McDonald's: change in eating habits and the evolution of fast food in Istanbul', in S. Zubaida (ed.), *Culinary Cultures of the Middle East*, London: Centre of Near and Middle Eastern Studies.

Davidson, A. (1988), *A Kipper with My Tea*, London: MacMillan.

Douglas, M. (1966), *Purity and Danger: An Analysis of the Concepts of Pollution and Taboo*, London: Routledge and Kegan Paul.

——. (1975), *Implicit Meanings*, London: Routledge and Kegan Paul.
Featherstone, M. (1990a), *Consumer Culture and Postmodernism*, London: Sage.
——. (1990b), 'Global culture: an introduction', *Theory, Culture and Society* 7 (2–3): 1–15.
Finkelstein, J. (1989), *Dining Out*, Cambridge: Polity Press.
Friedman, J. (1990), 'Being in the world: globalization and localization', *Theory, Culture and Society* 7 (2–3): 311–29.
Goody, J. (1982), *Cooking, Cuisine and Class*, Cambridge: Cambridge University Press.
James, A. (1990), 'The good, the bad and the delicious: the role of confectionery in British society', *The Sociological Review* 38 (4): 666–88.
James, J. (1993), *Consumption and Development*, New York: St Martin's Press.
Hannerz, U. (1990), 'Cosmopolitans and locals in world culture', *Theory, Culture and Society* 7 (2–3): 237–51.
Leach, E. (1964), 'Anthropological aspects of language: animal categories and verbal abuse', in E. H. Lennenberg (ed.), *New Directions in the Study of Language*, Cambridge, MA: The MIT Press.
Lévi-Strauss, C. (1962), *Totemism*, trans. R. Needham, Harmondsworth: Penguin.
Levy, P. (1986), *Out to Lunch*, Harmondsworth: Penguin
Mayle, P. (1990), *A Year in Provence*, London: Pan.
Mennell, S. (1985), *All Manners of Food*, Oxford: Basil Blackwell.
Mintz, S. (1985), *Sweetness and Power: The Place of Sugar in Modern History*, New York: Viking.
Ortner, S. (1978), *Sherpas Through Their Rituals*, Cambridge: Cambridge University Press.
Richards, Audrey (1956), *Chisungu: A Girls' Initiation Ceremony Among the Bemba of Northern Rhodesia*, London: Faber and Faber.
Robertson, R. (1992), *Globalization: Social Theory and Global Culture*, London: Sage.
Tambiah, S. J. (1969), 'Animals are good to think and good to prohibit', *Ethnology* 8 (4): 424–59.
Tannahill, R. (1973), *Food in History*, Harmondsworth: Penguin.

37

But is it Authentic?

Culinary Travel and the Search for the "Genuine Article"

Lisa Heldke

Introduction

When Dorothy remarked to her little dog, "We're not in Kansas anymore, Toto," she uttered what has come to be the unofficial motto of those who travel outside of our cultural comfort zone.[1] Decoded, it means: "We have just encountered something that has reminded us that we are deep in unfamiliar territory and we're just not sure how to behave. Heck, we're not even entirely sure we want to *be* here anymore." The encounter with the unfamiliar might be as fleeting and as prosaic as attempting to use the telephone in a country to which one has never before traveled ("Is that the *ring,* or is that a *busy* signal I'm hearing?"), or something so profound and persistent that it challenges one's very identity—for example trying to participate in holiday traditions with the family into which one has just entered, and with whom one shares no ethnic ties. Whether one is a temporary traveler on holiday from one's own culture, or a long-term transplant away from one's cultural home for the foreseeable future, the experience is common to all travel. Indeed, such encounters are often taken to be the very reasons *to* travel.

According to a prevailing view in modern Western culture, we leave the familiar in order to encounter the unusual, unfamiliar, strange, exotic Other and to reflect on how this particular Other transforms our own identities. Understood in a context in which selves are set off sharply from each other and defined in terms of how we stand alone (not how we are connected), these encounters with Otherness have enormous power to "define our selves for ourselves." Given this understanding of how selves change, and given a traveler's yen to experience the greatest personal growth, it becomes imperative that one be able to verify the authenticity of the experiences that affect oneself. For maximum personal effect, we desire encounters with truly authentic Others, not mediated, hybridized Others who are already "influenced" by the likes of us.

Not infrequently, the "We're not in Kansas anymore" feeling hits strongly when one has put some unusual or unfamiliar food item into one's mouth. Though it would be hyperbolic and unverifiable to assert that gustatory encounters with the unfamiliar are *the* most profound perceptual experiences the traveler can have, anecdotal evidence suggests that the terrors and delights of the tongue affect so dramatically that their memories remain sharp even years later. Unusual flavors address us in those most intimate places—the insides of our noses and mouths. (How do you "step back" from the sensation of a just-died mussel on your tongue? From the odor of durian?) In doing so, tastes both remind us of who we are and point out to us who we are not.[2] Given an understanding of selves as discrete units defined in terms of our differences from each other, such encounters with the foods of the Other come freighted with heavy baggage indeed.

Consider "Anne," the proper Anglo-American who overcomes her revulsion, learns to love garlic and saves her marriage to Italian-American Joe. Her story was included in an Italian cookbook written for English speakers in 1936 as a response to northern European Americans' vigorously maintained racist and ethnocentric prejudice that garlic was a food for "dirty foreigners," used precisely in order to mask the foul, inferior foods such foreigners purportedly chose to eat. (Riello 1936: 59). Today it may be the "ketchup of the intellectual," but a century ago, even the smell of garlic evoked virulent disdain in those whose cultures did not use the seasoning—and marked as "foreign" all those who smelled of it. Consider this passage, from *Bohemian San Francisco: Its Restaurants and Their Most Famous Recipes*: "Garlic ... is a flavor and not a food, yet many of the lower-class foreigners eat it on bread, making a meal of dark bread, garlic, and red wine. It is offensive to sensitive nostrils and violates the taste when thus used..." (Edwards 1914: 108–9).

Flavors—be they unfamiliar or already "marked" as attaching to a particular ethnic culture—separate, with particular poignancy and power, the traveler from the culture in which she finds herself. For Anne, garlic was a pungent symbol of her outsiderhood, the gustatory emblem of who she was and wasn't. As an Anglo, her willingness to learn to cook with garlic stood as a genuine symbol of her love for her husband, for in embracing the flavor (as in embracing her husband), Anne was no doubt giving up some of her ethnic privilege. Her identity changed, in an important symbolic way, when she began adding garlic to her pasta sauce. Conversely, refusing to cook with, or even to ingest, such a symbolic savor serves to maintain one's ethnic and racial distinctness. Sometimes such refusal marks one's efforts to preserve membership in the privileged group (as exemplified by Edwards), but sometimes it constitutes an act of resistance, a refusal to be assimilated into the dominant culture (as when an Eastern European relocated to the United States refuses to develop a taste for ketchup).

No doubt the symbolic power of flavor to demarcate cultures derives in part from the strong connections linking taste and smell, on the one hand, and memory and nostalgia, on the other. If patriotism is the taste of the foods of our childhood, then unfamiliar tastes must stand as instances of global cosmopolitanism—or acts of treason.[3]

The power of flavor must also derive from the intimacy of the senses of smell and taste, and the concomitant feelings of vulnerability such intimacy inspires. As Carolyn Korsmeyer argues, eating, as a "mode of operation[,] requires that objects become part of oneself. Its exercise requires risk and trust" (1999: 101). It feels much more risky to taste the food of an unfamiliar culture than to listen to its music, look at its art, or read its literature, and indeed it is more risky. There is always, in principle, a danger involved in eating food. Tasting something just might kill you—something that can happen only in the most bizarre examples of listening or looking.

Whatever the reasons, flavors possess surprising power to remind us of our identities. Considered against a conception of selves as hermetically sealed units, new flavors threaten—or promise—to challenge our very boundaries as we either admit them onto our grocery lists, or refuse them access.

The Exotic-Authentic-Other Chain

Elsewhere, I have explored the relationships between ethnic food, identity and cultural interactions in some detail.[4] There, I suggest that, in tasting the foods of their Others, Euro-American culinary travelers often move along an implicit conceptual chain that begins with the recognition that one is in the presence of a flavor one has never before encountered, and ends with an "understanding" that this flavor stands as an authentic marker of the "true nature" of the ethnic Other—and, therefore, the thing that separates one most fully from this other.

Operating under the influence of this conceptual chain, the Euro-American food adventurer (the traveler for whom encounters with Otherness are not only welcome but sought after) sets out in search of authenticity—examples of the "genuine article" prepared "just the way they would do it," using the ingredients, cooking techniques, pans, even cooking fuel that would be used by a cook who is an insider to the culinary tradition. For the adventurer operating out of the particular understanding of the relation between self and Other I've identified, these encounters with the "truly" authentic cuisine of the Other serve the very purpose of travel. Here the traveler can make contact with the "not-me," and can hone the edges of her identity through the contact, either by absorbing the flavors of the Other into her own identity or by rejecting them as "what-I-am-not."

But the links in this conceptual chain won't hold. The first reason arises from the fact that, as culinary travelers, that which is new to us is taken to equal "exotic" and "exotic" to equal "authentic." "We mistake our interest in this [new food] for the discovery and appreciation of a truly authentic cuisine. What we identify as authentic in that culture is often simply what is new to us—which may or may not represent what insiders to that culture would identify as significant, traditional, or genuine elements of it" (Heldke 2003: 27). We paradoxically seek that which we are, by definition, least capable of identifying. Second, under scrutiny, the very notion of authenticity begins to break down; why, for instance, should "authentic" automatically and in principle mean that a dish was prepared exactly the way an insider cook would do it, in its "native habitat"? Such an understanding dismisses out of hand the possibility that an insider might regard it as "authentic" to *modify* a dish in order to respond to different local conditions and ingredients. Indeed, one might read the history of almost every cuisine on the globe as a history of just such modifications, made in response to new ingredients, new conditions, and new neighbors. There *is* no such thing as a cuisine untouched by "outside influences," and if what we really seek is a cuisine "untouched by the influences of people such as myself," then we ought to question the motives underlying our demand.

Tasting Authenticity

My earlier critique focused on problems of authenticity considered from the production side of things—the perspective of the cook. A separate but related set of problems arises if we analyze authenticity from the consumption side. Briefly stated, the idea that I can "really" taste the flavors of the Other is a simplistic reduction of the nature of taste, of what it means to experience a flavor. If, with Carolyn Korsmeyer, we understand taste as a cognitive activity involving memory, experience, emotion, etc., then we must necessarily be dissatisfied with any thin notion of authenticity that reduces it to a purely sensory *and replicable* quality *of* the food itself.[5]

These taste-related difficulties would arise for such a conception of authenticity even *if* we could somehow settle the matter of what constitutes authentic preparation. Even if we could agree, unambiguously, that a dish was *prepared* authentically, there is no guarantee whatsoever that the eater will be equipped to *experience* it as authentic (where authentic is taken to mean "the way it would taste for an insider to the cuisine"). A concept borrowed from John Dewey's aesthetics will help me to make this point—and will serve as the starting point from which to develop an alternative understanding of authenticity.

Writing in *Art as Experience*, John Dewey identifies a distinction between the art product, on the one hand, and the work of art on the other. He writes that "the actual work of art is what the product does with and in experience," and he emphasizes "the human conditions under which it was brought into being" as well as "the human consequences it engenders in actual life-experience" (1987:). The work of art "happens" as a result of the interaction of some product (a painting) with some perceivers (viewers).

Bracketing the matter of whether or not cuisine constitutes an art form, we can use Dewey's emphasis on the work of art as an *experiential* entity to develop a useful alternative notion of authenticity—one more effective than the view I've been describing thus far. (To guarantee that we bracket the question "But is it art?" I shall modify his terminology, referring to the work of cuisine for work of art, and the dish for product.)

Consider: The notion of authenticity I've been describing, a notion connected to the view of selves as independent, hermetically sealed packages, regards the *work* of cuisine as the *dish,* and understands that dish to possess stand-alone qualities that can be read from it by anyone trained to identify them (an insider to a cuisine, for example, or an outsider who has studied it). The meaning of the dish is inherent to it. One assesses authenticity, then, by determining whether or not the dish contains certain properties of taste, appearance, or preparation technique.

In contrast, an experiential conception of the work of cuisine understands that the work is (to paraphrase Dewey) what the dish is "in and with experience." On this view, the contributions made by the dish itself (via its creator) are just that—contributions to an experience, that are "met" by the contributions of the experiencer (the eater). Eating, on this model, is a kind of conversation (Dewey often speaks of "transaction"), in which each party contributes. Just as it would be inaccurate, in describing a work of cuisine, to ignore the contributions of the dish itself (and the cook who made it), so too would it be inaccurate to ignore the contributions of the eater, who comes to this experience with a history and a set of experiences of her own. These shape and flavor the work of cuisine—quite literally, as it turns out. The culinary traveler will *taste* the dish differently from the diner who has grown up eating it.

Thus, the work of cuisine is a different work for the cultural insider than it is for the cultural tourist. As Dewey puts it, "Every individual brings with him, when he exercises his individuality, a way of seeing and feeling that in its interaction with old material creates something new, something previously not existing in experience" (1987: 113). But this is not to say that "It's all relative," or that one cannot appeal to anything like criteria in assessing a work of cuisine. To adopt this view would be to suggest that the dish itself (its creator, its cultural context) makes no contribution to the work of cuisine; that the dish itself is infinitely malleable.[6]

If we adopt this experiential notion of the work of cuisine, we can develop a useful alternative conception of authenticity with identifiable roles for perceiver and context. Authenticity comes to be a property of the work of cuisine, which is itself a transaction between dish and eater (where the dish is understood to be a product of a particular cook operating out of an identifiable cultural context, and the eater is understood to be similarly culturally embedded).

When authenticity is understood to be a quality of this exchange, demands for authenticity end up being of a rather different sort. For instance, rather than identifying dishes prepared "just the way" they would be prepared "in their native context" as representing the "gold standard" of authenticity, we might valorize the gesture of a cook who recognizes the limited familiarity of her (non-native) diners, and cooks "to" them in a way that enables an interaction to develop. (She might do so by choosing flavors that introduce her diners to the most unusual features of her cuisine, or by choosing flavors that show the connections between her cuisine and that of her diners.)

Authenticity, conceived along these lines, differs from the view I'm rejecting in that it rejects the notion that properties of a dish inhere in the dish, independent of any perceivers, and instead conceives of taste or flavor as a property of the experiential work of cuisine. Authenticity is thus a property of the particular work of cuisine that is "happening"—a work that may involve cross-cultural elements, for instance. Rather than attempting to erase, minimize, or otherwise deny the "intrusion" represented by the non-native culinary traveler ("Just pretend you're cooking for your own family—don't do anything different for me"), this concept of authenticity begins with the understanding that *all* works of cuisine involve transactions between dish (cook) and eater—and calls us to *attend* to the particular kinds of transactions represented in the cross-cultural experience.

On the received view, the culinary traveler's own presence (in a restaurant, for example) always counts as evidence of the inauthenticity of the place; paradoxically, one's discovery of a "truly authentic" restaurant contains the very seed of the destruction of its authenticity. On the view I'm suggesting, the presence of an eater (with her own agenda) is always a given, in all contexts, cross-cultural or otherwise. While culinary travelers *may* "contaminate" a cuisine (by treating it as infinitely malleable, for example, and making endless demands upon it to change), they/we do not do so by definition, by our very presence.

It's important to note that all works of cuisine will involve this communication, and thus interpretation (and misinterpretation), on the part of the eater. It is not only works of culinary tourism in which there are gaps that must be traversed between cook and eater. Such gaps are part of the very nature of personhood and of interaction; we are always both comprehensible and opaque, both understood and misunderstood by others. In discussing culinary tourism, I simply draw our attention to one particular kind of gap that must be traversed. But the presence of eaters, of tasters (even ignorant ones) is necessary to the very existence of a work of cuisine. As such, our presence must be a part of any useful definition of authenticity.

To begin to imagine how this alternative view of authenticity might shape our desires and expectations (either as travelers or as the ones "traveled to") consider the following story.

Thai Ginger: Or, What Happens When Disparate Flavors Converge?

I vividly recall the first time I ate thom kha gai, a Thai chicken soup made with coconut milk and kha, or galangal, a knobby spice that also goes by the name Thai ginger. (Hold that fact for a moment.) The vividness of this sapid memory still brings me up short. This was not my mother's chicken soup—or the chicken soup of anyone's mother I knew. Today, this soup has achieved ubiquity in middle America; not only does it appear on the menus of *non*-Thai restaurants (a sure sign of its crossover status), but it also appears in powdered form on the shelves of ordinary mainstream supermarkets. In 1982, however, it was one hundred percent new, other, foreign, never before experienced—by me, anyway, and by most other Americans unaffiliated with a Southeast Asian community.

When I first encountered galangal, it appeared as dried, tough, woody chips floating in the hammered aluminum soup tureen. Though I was instructed not to eat them, I chewed on one and was rewarded with a flavor vaguely reminiscent of menthol. It was strange, exotic ... and *sui generis*. There was nothing in my universe like kha—or so I thought.

I continued to think that for years—and then I saw it referred to on an ingredient list as "Thai ginger." "That's straining for comparison," I commented. "There's no relation between galangal and ginger. Is there?" Indeed there is. "Regular" ginger and galangal are both members of the Zingiberaceae family. Once I learned of the relation, the similarities in appearance were so obvious it was unfathomable that I hadn't suspected their connection all along: knobby, tan, fibrous. Dry ginger and float it in soup and no doubt it would behave a great deal like that galangal behaved in my first bowl of thom kha gai.

But would it have tasted the same? If that first menu had offered "chicken soup with ginger and coconut milk," what would I have tasted? As a young graduate student, I was at least noddingly familiar with the taste of fresh ginger and would not have been utterly surprised to see it used in something other than cookies or sweet cakes. While the taste wouldn't have been routine, it would at least have counted as familiar, recognizable.

What would I have tasted, had the menu simply said "ginger," but presented me with Thai ginger? Would I still remember this experience with the vividness that I do? What combination of things left me feeling that I had tasted something the likes of which I'd never encountered before? (After all, I *had* encountered the likes of it before; I'd eaten chicken, drunk coconut milk, and used the cousin of galangal in my own cooking.)

Surely I would remember, no? After all, my experience of the flavor was not wholly shaped by the unfamiliarity of the word used to describe it—was it? Of course not—but such unfamiliarity definitely did play a part in the way I experienced that soup. So too did the unfamiliarity of my surroundings: the clothing of the servers, those hammered aluminum soup tureens, the elaborate, swirly appearance of the Thai written language on the menus. Perhaps even my mother's chicken soup would have tasted utterly unfamiliar to me, were it being ladled out of such a tureen in such surroundings. Indeed, experience tells me that, given an unfamiliar enough context, I will *not* recognize or identify even the flavors most familiar to me—ketchup, for instance. Turns out that ketchup is frequently used in pad thai, a noodle dish found in virtually every Thai restaurant in the United States. Take it away from the French fry and ketchup becomes an entirely different substance, unfamiliar, unidentifiable, even—yes—"exotic." What I taste *is* very much a function of what the context leads me to expect (or cannot lead me to expect, in the case of an utterly unfamiliar setting).

This experience solidifies for me the importance of experience and the need for our theories of culinary interaction, culinary travel, to draw meaning from the transaction—not the dish, in isolation. It suggests a view of selves (culinary travelers, cooks) as always already in relation, and of cultural markers (Thai ginger) as dialogic elements, not static, embedded symbols.

But what about the fact that food adventurers (eager to burnish our edges on the most Other dining experiences we can find) tend to be disappointed when we learn that "they" changed the food for "us?" Of course this practice disappoints (both culinary insider and traveler), if it always and only means a watering down and fast-foodifying of a regional cuisine. But if flavor is a kind of dialogic material—the medium of a conversation between two cultures—then I must take seriously the fact that you come from a particular location and so do I. On such a reading, the cook who considers her Euro-American diners' palates begins advisedly. We may go on to ask whether the resultant work of cuisine is an authentic one—but my point is that it is not rendered inauthentic in principle by the fact that the cook acknowledges the transactional nature of cooking-and-eating. Note that such an understanding challenges the notion that the culinary insider has some kind of obligation to preserve their culture "as is" and to present the traveler with the kind of experiences travelers take to be true to their culture, absent the tourist.

How might we use this transactional model of culinary travel to understand Anne's story? Anne has entered a new culinary conversation by marrying into an Italian-American family. She brings to that dialog her own prejudices and preferences—and finds them inadequate to accommodate the new experiences she's having. Frustrated by her inability to make pasta that tastes as delicious—even to her—as Joe's mother's sauce, Anne arranges a trip to her mother-in-law's house, in order to ask for her culinary secrets. When "Mother" asks Anne how she cooks her garlic, Anne replies, "I don't like garlic. It smells so." "Why, my dear, it doesn't smell any worse than an onion and I know you like those. It's just because you are so used to an onion and you are not used to garlic," replies her mother-in-law (Riello 1936: 59). Of course that's not the only reason—onions don't have nearly the "dirty foreigner" reputation that garlic carries. Anne has likely been warned off the stuff by her own mother. But she gamely gives it a try and by the end of the story she has wowed her husband with her "macaroni" and vowed to use garlic "in all my cooking hereafter" (59). Anne's embrace of garlic comes through literal and culinary conversation with her mother-in-law—conversation that acknowledges already-existent relations, new cultural connections and her responsibility to both.

Notes

1. For the purposes of this chapter, I count as travelers anyone who moves into a cultural location other than one's own, either temporarily or more long term. This includes travelers in the traditional sense, but also those whose travel does not require a passport or even a plane ticket. In this latter sense, you might be traveling if you move to a neighborhood with an ethnic/cultural identity unfamiliar to you; spend time with a new friend in a racial community not your own; or even attend a cultural event or visit a restaurant representing an unfamiliar racial or ethnic group.
2. I refrain here from discussing a related point—namely, the different places at which cultures mark the divide between edible and inedible. The differences in the location of this line have been used by both colonizing and colonized cultures as evidence of the non-human status of their Other. ("*They* are the sorts of people who eat dogs/pigs/carnivores/cattle.") While the point is related to the matter of taste, it is also separable. I confine myself to a discussion of the cultural meaning of differences of taste in those cases in which all parties involved agree that the tastes belong to undeniable *foods*.
3. "What is patriotism but the *love* of the good things we ate in our childhood?" Lin Yutang.
4. See my 2003.
5. See, especially, chapter four, "The Meaning of Taste and the Taste of Meaning."
6. In his introduction to Dewey's work, Abraham Kaplan makes a related note: "The respondent cannot simply project onto the work of art what is in his own mind, any more than the artist can create simply by saying 'Let there be... !' Artistic vision has an objective locus for both artist and respondent; only there does the work of art have a determinate content. Misreading what objectively is said is as much a possibility as is misstating an intention. Both artist and respondent can fail, each in his own way" (1987: xxix–xxx).

References

Dewey, J. (1987), *Art as Experience*, Vol. 10 of *John Dewey: The Later Works, 1925–1953*, Carbondale: Southern Illinois University Press.

Edwards, C. (1914), *Bohemian San Francisco: Its Restaurants and Their Most Famous Recipes*, San Francisco: Paul Elder.

Heldke, L. (2003), *Exotic Appetites: Ruminations of a Food Adventurer*, New York: Routledge.

Kaplan, Abraham (1987), "Introduction," in Dewey.

Kivy, P. (1995), *Authenticities: Philosophical Reflections on Musical Performance*, Ithaca: Cornell University Press.

Korsmeyer, C. (1999), *Making Sense of Taste*, Ithaca: Cornell University Press.

Riello, M. C. (1936), *Italian Cook Book Written in English*, New Haven.

Wertz, S. K. (2004), "Temporality and food: the duplication problem solved," paper presented at the Association for the Study of Food and Society/Agriculture, Food and Human Values conference.

Succulent Selection

A Select Bibliography of 50 Further Readings

Juneko Robinson

1. Achaya, A. F. (1994), *Indian Food: A Historical Companion*, Delhi: Oxford University Press.

2. Algar, Ayla (1991), *Classical Turkish Cooking*, New York: HarperCollins Publishers.

3. Algren, Nelson (1992), *America Eats*, Iowa City: University of Iowa Press.

4. Anderson, E. N. (1988), *The Food of China*, New Haven: Yale University Press.

5. Bell, David and Valentine, Gill (1997), *Consuming Geographies: We are Where We Eat*, London: Routledge.

6. Camporesi, Piero (1993), *The Magic Harvest: Food, Folklore and Society*, trans. Joan Krakover Hall, Cambridge, UK: Polity Press.

7. Camporesi, Piero (1994), *The Anatomy of the Senses: Natural Symbols in Medieval and Early Modern Italy*, trans. Allan Cameron, Cambridge, UK: Polity Press.

8. Capaldi, Elizabeth D. (1996), *Why We Eat What We Eat: The Psychology of Eating*, Washington, DC: American Psychological Association.

9. Chang, K.C. (ed.) (1977), *Food in Chinese Culture: Anthropological and Historical Perspectives*, New Haven: Yale University Press.

10. Chakravarti, Tapo Nath. (1959), *Food and Drink in Ancient Bengal*, Calcutta: K. L. Mukhopadhyay.

11. Coohihan, Carole M. (2002), *Food in the USA: A Reader*, New York: Routledge.

12. Diner, Hasia R. (2001), *Hungering for America: Italian, Irish, and Jewish Foodways in the Age of Migration*, Cambridge, MA: Harvard University Press.

13. Dobbing, John (ed.) (1987), *Sweetness*, Berlin: Springer-Verlag.

14. Edgerton, John (1993), *Southern Food: At Home, on the Road, in History*, Chapel Hill: University of North Carolina Press.

15. Esquivel, Laura (2000), *Between Two Fires: Intimate Writings on Life, Love, Food, and Flavor*, trans. Stephen Lytle, New York: Crown Publishers.

16. Falk, Pasi (1994), *The Consuming Body*, London: Sage Publications.

17. Farb, Peter and Armelagos, George (1980), *Consuming Passions: The Anthropology of Eating*, Boston: Houghton Mifflin.

18. Ferguson, Patricia Parkhurst (2004), *Accounting for Taste: The Triumph of French Cuisine*, Chicago: University of Chicago Press.

19. Fernández-Armesto, Filipe (2002), *Near a Thousand Tables: A History of Food*, New York: The Free Press.

20. Fisher, M. F. K. (1990), *The Art of Eating*, Hoboken, NJ: John Wiley.

21. Fukukita, Yasunoke (1932), *Cha-No-Yu: Tea Cult of Japan*, Tokyo: Maruzen Company.

22. Fürst, Elisabeth, Prättälä, Ritva, Ekström, Marianne, Holm, Lotte, Kjaernes, Unni, (eds) (1991), *Palatable Worlds: Sociocultural Food Studies*, Oslo: Solum Forlag.

23. Gabaccia, Donna R. (1998), *We Are What We Eat: Ethnic Food and the Making of America*, Cambridge, MA: Harvard University Press.

24. *Gastronomica: The Journal of Food and Culture*, 2001–. Darra Goldstein, (ed.), Berkeley and Los Angeles: University of California Press.

25. Glants, Musya and Toomre, Joyce (eds) (1997), *Food in Russian History and Culture*, Bloomington: Indiana University Press.

26. Harris, Jessica B. (1999), *Iron Pots and Wooden Spoons: Africa's Gifts to New World Cooking*, New York: Simon and Schuster.

27. Hess, Karen (1992), *The Carolina Rice Kitchen: The African Connection*, Columbia, SC: University of South Carolina Press.

28. Howes, David (ed.) (1991), *The Varieties of Sensory Experience: A Sourcebook in the Anthropology of the Senses*, Toronto: University of Toronto Press.

29. Khare, R. S. (1976), *The Hindu Hearth and Home*, Durham, NC: Carolina Academic Press.

30. Korsmeyer, Carolyn (1999), *Making Sense of Taste: Food and Philosophy*, Ithaca: Cornell University Press.

31. Kuper, Jessica (ed.) (1977), *The Anthropologists' Cookbook*, New York: Universe Books.

32. Laslo, Pierre (2001), *Salt: Grain of Life*, trans. Mary Beth Mader. New York: Columbia University Press.

33. Lentz, Carola (ed.) (1999), *Changing Food Habits: Case Studies from Africa, South America and Europe*, Amsterdam: Harwood Academic Publishers.

34. Logue, A. W. (1986), *The Psychology of Eating and Drinking*, New York: W. H. Freeman.

35. Macbeth, Helen (ed.) (1997), *Food Preferences and Taste: Continuity and Change*, Providence: Berghahn Books.

36. MacClancy, Jeremy (1992), *Consuming Culture: Why You Eat What You Eat,* New York: Henry Holt.

37. Mennell, Stephen, Murcott, Anne, and van Otterloo, Anneke H. (1992), *The Sociology of Food: Eating, Diet and Culture,* London: Sage Publications.

38. Okakura, Kakuzo (1964/1906), *The Book of Tea,* New York: Dover.

39. Om Prakash (1961), *Food and Drinks in Ancient India, from Earliest Times to c. 1200 AD,* Delhi: Munshi Ram Manohar Lal.

40. Richardson, Tim (2002), *Sweets,* New York: Bloomsbury.

41. Roden, Claudia (1994), *Coffee: a Connoisseur's Companion,* New York: Random House.

42. Roden, Claudia (2000), *The New Book of Middle Eastern Food,* New York: Alfred Knopf.

43. Rouby, Catherine, Schaal, Benoist, Dubois, Danièle, Gervais, Rémi, Holley, A. (eds) (2002), *Olfaction, Taste and Cognition,* Cambridge UK: Cambridge University Press.

44. Scapp, Ron and Seitz, Brian (eds) (1998), *Eating Culture,* Albany: State University of New York Press.

45. Sack, Daniel (2000), *Whitebread Protestants: Food and Religion in American Culture,* New York: Palgrave.

46. Toussaint-Samat, Maguelonne (1994), *History of Food,* trans. Anthea Bell, Malden, MA: Blackwell.

47. Turner, Jack (2004), *Spice: The History of a Temptation,* New York: Knopf.

48. Van der Post, Laurens (1978), *First Catch Your Eland,* New York: William Morrow and Company.

49. Varley, Paul and Isao, Kumakura (eds) (1989), *Tea in Japan: Essays on the History of Chanoyu,* Honolulu: University of Hawaii Press.

50. Weismantel, Mary J. (1988), *Food, Gender, and Poverty in the Ecuadorean Andes,* Philadelphia: University of Pennsylvania Press.

Notes on Contributors

Linda Bartoshuk is Professor in the Ear, Nose, and Throat section of the Surgery Department at Yale University School of Medicine. She has published widely in scientific journals on taste and the chemical senses, and the genetic and physiological determinants of taste sensations.

Pierre Bourdieu (1930–2002), French sociologist, held a chair at the Collège de France. He wrote more than twenty-five influential books, including *Distinction: A Social Critique of the Judgment of Taste* (1979), which was named one of the ten most important sociological works of the twentieth century by the International Sociological Association.

Jean-Anthelme Brillat-Savarin (1775–1826) was a French magistrate who wrote *The Physiology of Taste, or Meditations on Transcendental Gastronomy* (1825), a compilation of aphorisms, analyses, recipes, and reflections on eating. It is now recognized as one of the pioneering modern works on gastronomy and taste.

Marjo Buitelaar is Lecturer at the Centre for Religious Studies at the Rijksuniversiteit, Groningen, the Netherlands. She is the author of *Fasting and Feasting in Morocco: Women's Participation in Ramadan* (1993).

Elizabeth Carmichael is curator of the Latin American collections of the British Museum.

Constance Classen is an independent scholar based in Montreal. She is the author of *Inca Cosmology and the Human* Body (1993), *Worlds of Sense: Exploring the Senses in History and Across Cultures* (1993), and *The Color of Angels: Cosmology, Gender and the Aesthetic Imagination* (1998). She is also the editor of *The Book of Touch*, forthcoming from Berg.

Valerie Duffy is Associate Professor of Dietetics in the School of Allied Health at the University of Connecticut. Her research and publications concern chemosensory perception in humans and its influence on food preference, diet, and nutrition.

M.F.K. (Mary Frances Kennedy) Fisher (1908–92) was the author of many books on the art of eating, including *Serve It Forth* (1937), *The Gastronomical Me* (1943), and *How to Cook a Wolf* (1942).

Donna Gabaccia is the Mellon Professor of History at the University of Pittsburgh. Her research focuses on immigration, international migration, and culinary history.

Darra Goldstein is Professor of Russian at Williams College and founding editor of *Gastronomica: The Journal of Food and Culture*. She has published numerous books and articles on Russian literature, culture, art, and cuisine, and is also the author of three cookbooks: *A Taste of Russia* (nominated for a Tastemaker Award), *The Georgian Feast* (winner of the 1994 IACP Julia Child Award), and *The Winter Vegetarian*.

Jack Goody is Emeritus William Wyse Professor of Social Anthropology and a fellow of St John's College in Cambridge University, UK. He is the author of over thirty books.

B. N. Goswamy is an art historian and critic. He is Professor Emeritus of Art History, Punjab University, India. His books include *Painters at the Sikh Court* (1975) and *A Place Apart: Painting in Kutch 1720–1820* (1983).

Jukka Gronow is Professor of Sociology at the University of Uppsala, Sweden, and a docent at the University of Helsinki, Finland. His other works in the studies of consumption and taste include *The Sociology of Taste* (1997) and *Ordinary Consumption* (2001, edited with Alan Warde).

Roger Haden teaches in the Postgraduate Program in Gastronomy at the University of Adelaide, South Australia. His doctoral dissertation, *Technologies of Taste: Configuring the Oven as Cultural Text*, will be published in 2006.

Lisa Heldke teaches philosophy and women's studies at Gustavus Adolphus College, St. Peter, Minnesota. She is the author of *Exotic Appetites: Ruminations of a Food Adventurer* (2003) and the co-editor of *Cooking, Eating, Thinking: Transformative Philosophies of Food* (1992).

David Howes is Professor of Anthropology at Concordia University, Montreal. His recent works include *Sensual Relations* (2003) and the anthology *Empire of the Senses: The Sensual Culture Reader* (2004). He is general editor of the *Sensory Formations* series of books from Berg Publishers; and, with David Sutton, he is co-editor of Berg's series *Senses and Sensibilities*.

David Hume (1711–76), influential Scottish philosopher and historian, was a major contributor to the school of thought known as British empiricism.

Allison James is Professor of Sociology at the University of Sheffield. She is author of numerous books and articles; among her most recent publications is *Constructing Childhood: Theory, Policy and Social Practice* (2004).

Immanuel Kant (1724–1804), Enlightenment philosopher, was author of the influential *Critique of Pure Reason, Critique of Practical Reason* and *Critique of Judgment*, among many other works.

Ravindra S. Khare is Professor of Anthropology at the University of Virginia. He has published on social and cultural issues of India. His books include *Hindu Hearth and Home* (1976), *Cultural Diversity and Social Discontent* (1998), and *The Eternal Fire: Gastronomical Ideas and Experiences of Hindus and Buddhists* (1992).

Deborah Lupton is Professor of Sociology and Cultural Studies at Charles Sturt University, Australia. Her latest books are *Risk* (1999), *Risk and Sociocultural Theory* (1999), and *Risk and Everyday Life* (with J. Tulloch, 2003).

Stephen Mennell is Professor of Sociology at University College, Dublin. He is co-author of *The Sociology of Food: Eating, Diet, and Culture* (1992) and author of *All Manners of Food: Eating and Taste in England and France from the Middle Ages to the Present* (1985).

Sidney Mintz is Research Professor of Anthropology at Johns Hopkins University. His research has centered on the Caribbean, including its role in sugar production. His books include *Sweetness and Power: The Place of Sugar in Modern History* (1985) and *Tasting Food, Tasting Freedom: Excursions into Eating, Culture, and the Past* (1996).

Cheryl Olkes (1948–98) was Director of the Harmattan Gallery in Washington, DC, and co-author of *In Sorcery's Shadow: A Memoir of Apprenticeship among the Songhay of Niger* (1987).

Toby Sarah Peterson is an independent cultural historian living in Princeton, NJ. She is the author of *Acquired Taste: The French Origins of Modern Cooking* (1994).

Emile Peynaud (1912–2004) was an oenologist who pioneered wine-making techniques and wrote about the cultivation of the ability to discern the subtle tastes of wine.

Marcel Proust (1871–1922), French writer, is most famous for his eight-volume novel, *A la recherche du temps perdu* (*The Remembrance of Things Past*).

Jean-François Revel, a member of the Académie Française, is a former professor of philosophy and former editor of the political journal *L'Express*. He writes on contemporary social issues.

Elisabeth Rozin is the author of a number of cookbooks, among them *The Flavor Principle Cookbook* (1973), *Ethnic Cuisine* (1983), *Blue Corn and Chocolate* (1992), and *The Universal Kitchen* (1996).

Paul Rozin is Edmund J. and Louise W. Kahn Professor of Psychology at the University of Pennsylvania. His research concerns the operation of the sense of taste and of the emotion of disgust.

Chloe Sayer teaches at Central Saint Martin's College of Art and Design, London, and is the author of several works on Mexican art and culture.

Wolfgang Schivelbusch is an independent scholar and a historian of culture now based in New York. He is the author of books on war, railways, and politics, as well as the spice trade.

C. Nadia Seremetakis is a cultural anthropologist. She has served as advisor to the Minister of Public Health in Greece and visiting professor at the National School of Public Health in Athens. Her works include *The Last Word: Women, Death and Divination in Inner Mani* (1991).

Paul Stoller teaches anthropology at West Chester University and Temple University. His most recent books include *Money Has No Smell* (2002), which won the American Anthropological Association's Textor Prize, and *Stranger in the Village of the Sick* (2004). His new novel is entitled *Gallery Bundu: A Story of an African Past* (2005).

David Sutton is Associate Professor of Anthropology at Southern Illinois University, Carbondale. He is the author of *Memories Cast in Stone* (1998) and *Remembrance of Repasts*. With David Howes, he is co-editor of the Berg Press series *Senses and Sensibilities*, exploring the role of the senses in contemporary cultural practices.

Daisetz Teitaro Suzuki (1870–1966) was trained at the Zen monastery at Kamakura. He was the author of numerous works on Zen and Buddhism in Japanese and in English.

Anthony Synnott is Professor of Sociology at Concordia University, Montreal. With David Howes and Constance Classen, he has researched and written on the senses and the body in culture. His principal work is *The Body Social: Symbolism, Self, and the Body* (1993).

Amy B. Trubek is trained as an anthropologist and a chef. Her research covers the history of the culinary profession, cultural ideas about taste, and the contemporary food system. She is the author of *Haute Cuisine: How the French Invented the Culinary Profession* (2000).

Yi-Fu Tuan is emeritus Professor of Geography at the University of Wisconsin, Madison. He is the author of numerous books, including *Place, Art, and Self* (2004), *Escapism* (1998), and *Passing Strange and Wonderful: Aesthetics, Nature, and Culture* (1993).

Margaret Visser writes on the history, anthropology, and culture of food and manners. Her many books include the award-winning *Much Depends on Dinner* (1987) and *The Rituals of Dinner* (1991).

Richard Watson is the author of *The Philosopher's Diet* (1999), *The Philosopher's Joke,* (1990), *Niagara* (a novel) (1993), and *Cogito, Ergo, Sum: The Life of René Descartes* (2002).

Mary J. Weismantel is Professor of Anthropology at Northwestern University. Her books include *Food, Gender, and Poverty in the Ecuadorean Andes* (1998) and *Cholas and Pishtacos: Stories of Race and Sex in the Andes* (2001).

Permissions

I am grateful to the contributors and their respective publishers/copyright holders for permitting me to reprint their work here, and in some instances publish material for the first time. Spellings, notes, and references have been harmonized to accord with the Berg house style.

Chapter 1: Jean-Anthelme Brillat-Savarin. From *The Physiology of Taste*, chapters 1 and 2, the University of Adelaide e-text library of materials in the public domain. Translation 1854 by Fayette Robinson revised by the editor.

Chapter 2: Bartoshuk and Duffy. From "Chemical Senses," in *Comparative Psychology: A Handbook*, ©1998 by Gary Greenberg and Maury M. Haraway. Reproduced by permission of Routledge/Taylor and Francis Books, Inc. and by permission of the authors. Material abridged.

Chapter 3: Elisabeth Rozin and Paul Rozin, "Culinary Themes and Variations," *Natural History* February, 1981, pp. 6–14. ©*Natural History Magazine*, Inc. 1981, reprinted with permission.

Elisabeth Rozin's Flavor Principles appear in *Ethnic Cuisine: The Flavor Principle Cookbook*, The Stephen Greene Press, 1983. The recipes are found in *The Flavor Principle Cookbook*, Hawthorn Books, 1973. Printed here with the kind permission of Elisabeth Rozin.

Chapter 4: Jean-François Revel, "Retrieving Tastes: Two Sources of Cuisine," from *Culture and Cuisine*, ©1982 Doubleday, a division of Random House, Inc. Used by permission of Doubleday, a division of Random House, Inc.

Chapter 5: Jack Goody, "The High and the Low: Culinary Culture in Asia and Europe," from *Cooking, Cuisine and Class: A Study in Comparative Sociology*, © 1982 Cambridge University Press, reprinted with permission of the publisher and the author.

Chapter 6: Pierre Bourdieu, "Taste of Luxury, Taste of Necessity," reprinted by permission of the publisher from *Distinction: A Social Critique of the Judgment of Taste* by Pierre Bourdieu, translated by Richard Nice, pp. 176–78, 185–87, 190–93, 196–99, Cambridge, Mass: Harvard University Press, © 1984 by the President and Fellows of Harvard College and Routledge and Kegan Paul, Ltd.

Chapter 7: Donna R. Gabaccia, "Colonial Creoles: The Formation of Tastes in Early America," from *We are What We Eat: Ethnic Food and the Making of Americans*, © 1998 by the President and Fellows of Harvard College and Harvard University Press. Reproduced with permission of the publisher.

Chapter 8: M. J. Weismantel, "Tasty Meals and Bitter Gifts," condensed from "Tasty Meals and Bitter Gifts: Consumption and Production in the Ecuadorean Andes." © 1994 from *Food and Foodways* 5:1 by M. J. Weismantel. Reproduced by permission of the author and Taylor and Francis, Inc., http://www.taylorandfrancis.com .

Chapter 9: Margaret Visser, "Salt: The Edible Rock," from *Much Depends on Dinner* published by HarperCollins Publishers Ltd. ©1986 by Margaret Visser.

Chapter 10: Sidney Mintz, "Sweetness and Meaning," from *Sweetness and Power* by Sidney W. Mintz, © Sidney W. Mintz. Used by permission of Viking Penguin, a division of Penguin Group (USA) Inc.

Chapter 11: Wolfgang Schivelbusch, "Spices: Tastes of Paradise," from *Tastes of Paradise* by Wolfgang Schivelbusch, translated by David Jacobson, English translation © David Jacobson. Used by permission of Pantheon Books, a division of Random House, Inc.

Chapter 12: Paul Stoller and Cheryl Olkes, "Thick Sauce: Remarks on the Social Relations of the Songhay," translated and condensed from "La sauce épaisse: remarques sur les relations sociales songhaïs," *Anthropologie et Sociétés* Vol. 14: 2, 1990: 57–76. Translated by Kathryn Hunter. Reproduced with the permission of the journal and the author.

Chapter 13: T. Sarah Peterson, "Food as Divine Medicine," from Chapter 2, "Food as Divine Medicine," in *Acquired Taste: The French Origins of Modern Cooking*, © 1994 Cornell University. Used by permission of the publisher, Cornell University Press. Footnotes and references abridged.

Chapter 14: R. S. Khare, "Food with Saints," from "Food with Saints: Aspects of Hindu Gastrosemantics" from R. S. Khare, (ed.), *The Eternal Food: Gastronomic Ideas and Experiences of Hindus and Buddhists*, © SUNY Press 1992. Reproduced with permission of SUNY Press.

Chapter 15: D. T. Suzuki, "Zen and the Art of Tea" from Suzuki, Daisetz T., *Zen and Japanese Culture*. © 1959 Bollingen Foundation, Inc., New York, New York, renewed 1987 by Princeton University Press. Reprinted by permission of Princeton University Press.

Chapter 16: Marjo Buitelaar, "Living Ramadan: Fasting and Feasting in Morocco," from *Fasting and Feasting in Morocco: Women's Participation in Ramadan*. © Berg Publishers 1993. Reproduced by permission of the publisher.

Chapter 17: "Bitter Herbs and Unleavened Bread." Text adapted from several versions of the traditional Passover Haggadah. The portions of the text that quote from the Old Testament books of Exodus and Numbers conform to the Revised Standard Version of the Bible. Entry assembled by the Editor.

Chapter 18: Elizabeth Carmichael and Chloë Sayer, "Feasting with Dead Souls," from *The Skeleton at the Feast: the Day of the Dead in Mexico* by Elizabeth Carmichael and Chloë Sayer, © 1991. By permission of the University of Texas Press and the Trustees of the British Museum.

Chapter 19: David Hume, "Of the Standard of Taste," first published 1757. From materials in the public domain.

Chapter 20: Immanuel Kant, "Objective and Subjective Senses: The Sense of Taste," from *Anthropology from a Pragmatic Point of View* (1798). Reprinted from *Anthropology from a Pragmatic Point of View* translated by Victor Lyle Dowdell. © 1978 The Board of Trustees, Southern Illinois University, reprinted by permission of the publisher.

Chapter 21: B. N. Goswamy, "*Rasa*: Delight of the Reason," from B. N. Goswamy, *The Essence of Indian Art*, © 1986 The Asian Art Museum. Reprinted with permission of the publishers.

Chapter 22: Yi-Fu Tuan, "Pleasures of the Proximate Senses: Eating, Taste, and Culture," from *Passing Strange and Wonderful* by Yi-Fu Tuan, © 1993 Island Press. Reproduced with permission of Island Press, Washington, DC.

Chapter 23: Stephen Mennell, "Of Gastronomes and Guides," from *All Manners of Food: Eating and Taste in England and France from the Middle Ages to the Present*, © 1985, 1996 Stephen Mennell. Used with permission of the University of Illinois Press and the author.

Chapter 24: Jukka Gronow, "Champagne and Caviar: Soviet Kitsch," from *Caviar with Champagne: Common Luxury and the Ideals of the Good Life in Stalin's Russia*, by Jukka Gronow, © 2003 Berg Publishers. Reproduced with permission of the publishers and the author.

Chapter 25: Amy Trubek, "Place Matters," original material.

Chapter 26: Emile Peynaud, "Tasting Problems and Errors of Perception," from Chapter 6, "Tasting Problems and Errors of Perception" in *The Taste of Wine*, translated by Michael Shuster, © 1987, 1996 Michael Shuster. This material is used by permission of John Wiley and Sons, Inc.

Chapter 27: Richard Watson, "On the Zeedijk," first published in *The Georgia Review* XLIII: 1 (Spring, 1989). Reprinted with the permission of the author.

Chapter 28: Marcel Proust, "The Madeleine," from *Swann's Way*, Vol. 1 of *The Remembrance of Things Past*, from the University of Adelaide e-text of materials in the public domain. Translated by C. K. Scott Moncrieff.

Chapter 29: Nadia Seremetakis, "The Breast of Aphrodite," from *The Senses Still*, Nadia Seremetakis (ed.), © 1994 Westview Press, Inc. Reprinted by permission of Westview Press, a member of Perseus Books, L.L.C.

Chapter 30: David E. Sutton, "Synesthesia, Memory, and the Taste of Home," revised and abridged from "Sensory Memory and the Construction of 'Worlds'," *The Remembrance of Repasts*. © 2001 Berg Publishers. Reproduced with permission from the publisher and the author.

Chapter 31: Deborah Lupton, "Food and Emotion," from *Food, the Body and the Self* by Deborah Lupton, © Sage Publications Ltd. 1996. Reprinted by permission of the publisher and the author.

Chapter 32: M. F. K. Fisher, "The Pale Yellow Glove," from *The Art of Eating*. Reproduced with permission of Lescher and Lescher, and the publisher John Wiley.

Chapter 33: Classen, Howes, and Synnott, "Artificial Flavours," from *Aroma: The Cultural History of Smell*, Constance Classen, David Howes, and Anthony Synnott © 1994 Routledge. Reprinted with permission.

Chapter 34: Roger Haden, "Taste in an Age of Convenience: from Frozen Food to Meals in 'the Matrix'." Original material.

Chapter 35: Darra Goldstein, "The Play's the Thing: Dining Out in the New Russia." Original material.

Chapter 36: Allison James, "Identity and the Global Stew," condensed from "Cooking the Books: Global or Local Identities in Contemporary British Food Cultures?" in *Cross-Cultural Consumption*, David Howes (ed.). Reprinted with permission of the press and the author.

Chapter 37: Lisa Heldke, "But Is It Authentic? Culinary Travel and the Search for the 'Genuine Article'." Original material.

Index